Web Developer

Foundations

Using XHTML

Web Developer Foundations: Using XHTML
Terry A. Felke, William Rainey Harper College

ZYX 432   ISBN: 1-57676-100-2

Text and Cover Design: Mario Rodriguez
Copyediting: Carol Noble
Composition: Joshua Faigen

Proofreading: Kristin Furino, Holbrook Communications
Book Manufacturing: Corley Printing Company
Sponsoring Editor: Denise Simon

Scott/Jones Publishing Company
Editorial Group: Richard Jones, Mike Needham, Denise Simon, Leata Holloway, and Patricia Miyaki
Production Management: Audrey Anderson
Marketing and Sales: Victoria Judy, Page Mead, Hazel Dunlap, Hester Winn and Donna Cross
Business Operations: Michelle Robelet, Cathy Glenn, Natascha Hoffmeyer and Bill Overfelt

A Word About Trademarks

Additional Titles of Interest from Scott/Jones

Advanced Java™ Internet Applications, Second Edition
  by Art Gittleman

Developing Web Applications with Active Server Pages
  by Thom Luce

HTML for Web Developers
Server-Side Programming for Web Developers
  by John Avila

Preface

Web Developer Foundations: Using XHTML is intended for use in a first semester web development course. The text covers the basics that web developers need to develop their skills:

- Internet concepts
- Creating web pages with XHTML
- Formatting web pages with Cascading Style Sheets
- Recommended web design practices
- The web development process
- Using media and interactivity on web pages
- Web site promotion
- E-commerce and the Web

A special feature of this text is the *Web Developer's Handbook* at the back of the book, which includes a variety of resources such as an XHTML reference, a comparison of HTML and XHTML, and an introduction to FTP. In addition, brief introductions to two popular web authoring tools, Microsoft FrontPage and Macromedia Dreamweaver, are provided in two companion booklets available from Scott/Jones.

A companion web site located at http://www.webdev foundations.net contains additional material for each chapter, including links to web sites mentioned in the text and other useful information. Students are encouraged to visit this web site as they read each chapter.

Organization of the Text

The first six chapters provide an introduction to the Internet, HTML, and XHTML. These are the core of the text and should be completed in order. How the other topics are ordered is flexible. For example, Chapter 7 (Web Design), Chapter 8 (Web Development), and Chapter 10 (Web Site Promotion) could be presented at any time after Chapter 2. Certain topics, such as Chapter 13 (E-Commerce) or Chapter 12 (Web Page Interactivity) could be skipped in class and left for independent study, depending on the needs of the student. Sample syllabi are included on the Instructor's Resource CD and are posted in the Instructor area of the companion web site.

Brief Overview of Each Chapter

Chapter 1: The Internet and the World Wide Web This brief introduction covers the terms and concepts related to the Internet and the Web that web developers need to be familiar with. For many students, some of this will be a review. This chapter is included to provide the base of knowledge that the rest of the course is built on.

Chapter 2: XHTML Basics As HTML and XHTML are introduced, examples and exercises encourage students to create sample pages and get useful experience. Solution pages for the Hands-On Practice are on the student disk.

Chapter 3: XHTML Hyperlinks and Tables More XHTML tags are introduced, along with examples and exercises. Students are encouraged to create sample pages as they read through the text. Sample pages for the Hands-On Practice are on the student disk.

Chapter 4: XHTML Color and Visual Elements This chapter discusses the use of color and graphics on web pages. Students are encouraged to create pages as they read through the text. Sample pages for the Hands-On Practice are located on the student disk.

Chapter 5: XHTML Frames XHTML tags can be used to format frames, as a way of displaying multiple web pages in a browser window. This chapter provides examples and exercises that encourage students to create pages. Sample pages for the Hands-On Practice are located on the student disk.

Chapter 6: XHTML Forms The purpose of this chapter is to introduce XHTML tags used to format forms. It provides examples and exercises. Students are encouraged to create pages, and sample pages for the Hands-On Practice are located on the student disk.

Chapter 7: Web Site Design This chapter focuses on recommended web site design practices and accessibility. Some of this is reinforcement because hints about recommended web site design practices have also been incorporated in to the XHTML chapters.

Chapter 8: Web Site Development A focus on the process of web site development includes the job roles needed for a large-scale project, the web development process, and web hosting.

Chapter 9: Introduction to Cascading Style Sheets Cascading Style Sheets are a technology for separating the formatting, or style, of a web page from the content and XHTML tags. Students are encouraged to create sample pages as they read through the text. Sample pages for the Hands-On Practice are located on the student disk.

Chapter 10: Web Media As the use of audio and video on a web page is introduced, students are encouraged to create pages for themselves. Sample pages for the Hands-On Practice are located on the student disk.

Chapter 11: Promotion for Web Developers This chapter discusses site promotion, from the web developer's point of view, focusing on search engines and indexes.

Chapter 12: Introduction to Web Page Interactivity The methods of web page interactivity, such as JavaScript, Java applets, and Flash are discussed, and students are encouraged to create interactive pages for themselves. Sample pages for the Hands-On Practice are located on the student disk.

Chapter 13: E-Commerce Overview This chapter looks at e-commerce, security, and order processing on the Web.

Web Developer's Handbook The Handbook contains resources and tutorials useful to students, such as an XHTML reference, a list of special characters, a CSS property reference, an introduction to FTP, and a comparison of HTML and XHTML.

Features of the Text

- **Well-Rounded Selection of Topics.** This text includes both "hard" skills such as XHTML and CSS (Chapters 2, 3, 4, 5, 6, 9, and 10) and "soft" skills such as web design (Chapter 7), web site promotion (Chapter 11), and e-commerce (Chapter 13). This well-rounded foundation will help students in their careers as web developers. Both students and teachers will find classes more interesting because they can discuss, integrate, and apply both the hard and soft skills as students create web pages and web sites.

- **Hands-On Practice.** Web development is a skill and skills are best learned by hands-on practice. *Web Developer Foundations: Using XHTML* emphasizes hands-on practice through practice exercises within the chapters, end-of-chapter exercises, and the development of three different web sites as case study exercises throughout the text. The variety of exercises provides instructors with a choice of assignments for a particular course or semester.

- **Case Studies.** This text features not one, but three case studies that continue throughout most of the text (Chapters 2, 3, 4, 5, 6, 7, 9, 10, 12, and 13). These serve to reinforce skills discussed in each chapter. Instructors can cycle their assignments from semester to semester or allow their students to choose to do the case study that most interests them. The Instructor CD contains sample solutions to the case studies.

- **Web Research.** Each chapter offers Web research activities that encourage students to do further study on topics introduced in the chapter.

- **Focus on Accessibility.** Developing accessible web sites is more important than ever, and this text includes accessibility tips and hints throughout. A special accessibility logo makes this information easy to find.

- **Focus on Ethics.** Ethics issues as related to web development are highlighted throughout the text with a special ethics logo.

- **FAQs.** The author has taught web development courses for several years and is frequently asked similar questions by students. These have been included in the book and are marked with a special FAQs logo.

- **Web-Authoring Tools Tutorials.** These introductory tutorials are meant to help students become productive with the popular web-authoring tools Microsoft FrontPage and Macromedia Dreamweaver. Three introductory tutorials are provided for each web-authoring tool. The tutorials are in booklets provided separately from Scott/Jones.

- **Reference Materials.** A special *Web Developer's Handbook* offers reference material, including XHTML Reference, Special Characters, CSS Property Reference, Using FTP, and Comparison of XHTML and HTML.

- **Student Supplements.** A student disk included with each book contains sample Hands-On Practice exercises and any files students will need to complete the web page exercises and case study assignments. The companion web site at http://www.webdevfoundations.net contains links from each chapter and additional information on topics.

- **Instructor Supplements.** An Instructor Materials CD contains solutions for the end-of-chapter exercises and case study assignments, along with sample syllabi, test questions, PowerPoint presentations, and tutorial solutions. A special instructor area on the companion web site at http://www.webdevfoundations.net contains additional syllabi and a resource area for all instructors using this text. Contact Scott/Jones for the Instructor Materials CD and for the password to the instructor area on the course web site.

Acknowledgments

Many people contributed to this text. I'd like to thank Richard Jones, Denise Simon, and Audrey Anderson at Scott/Jones Publishing. I also appreciate the helpful ideas and opinions provided by the academic reviewers:

Kim Adams
Hillsborough Community College

Mark Barnard
Parkland College

Colleen Case
Schoolcraft College

Paul Chase
Becker College

R. Craig Collins
Texas State Technical College

Janet Conrey
Gavilan College

Charles Cowdrick
Kansas City Kansas Community College

Stephanie Cunnigham
Florida Atlantic University—Davie

Deanne Del Vecchio
Truckee Meadows Community College

William Dorin
Indiana University Northwest

Allan W. Futrell
University of Louisville

Charles Goodman
College of DuPage

Dorothy Harman
Tarrrant County Community College

Patricia Kelly
College of Charlston

Sally Kurz
Coastline College

Jennifer Lagier
Hartnell College

Leonard MacKey
Western Nevada Community College

Brian Martin
Pierce College

Keith Morneau
Northern Virginia Community College— Annandale

Ed Mulhern
Southwestern Community College and University of Phoenix

William Myers
Belmont Abbey College

David Oscarson
Brevard Community College

Angela Peace
Pulaski Technical College

Anita Philipp
Oklahoma City Community College

Hugh Poynor
University of Texas—Austin

Patricia Roy
Manatee Community College

David Salb
Kingsborough Community College

Everett Sandoval
Reedley College

Judy Scholl
Austin Community College

Tom Seymour
Minot State University

Cherie Stevens
South Florida Community College

Larry Trettin
Santa Rosa Junior College

Kenneth Wade
Champlain College

Kenneth Weeks
University of Wisconsin—Superior

Ed Weihrauch
Community College of Allegheny County—Boyce

Thanks are in order to full-time and adjunct faculty members at William Rainey Harper College for their support and encouragement, especially Sue Bajt, Ken Perkins, Geetha Murthy, and Savarra Anderson.

Most of all, I would like to thank my family for their patience and encouragement. My children, James and Karen, did not (usually) complain when their dinner was a little late because I was writing. My wonderful husband, Greg Morris, has been a constant source of understanding, support, and encouragement. I am very grateful for his assistance with proofreading during this project. Of course, this wouldn't be complete without mentioning my dog, Sparky, whose playful antics and quirky personality helped to brighten long hours spent at the computer.

About the Author

Terry Felke is an Assistant Professor at William Rainey Harper College in Palatine, Illinois. She holds a master of science degree in information systems and various certifications, including Microsoft Certified Professional, Master CIW Designer, and CIW Certified Instructor.

Ms. Felke published her first web site in 1996 and has been working with the Web ever since. She helped to develop the Web Development certificate and degree programs at Harper College and currently is the lead faculty member in that area.

Table of Contents

Chapter Six
XHTML Forms. **183**

Chapter Seven
Web Site Design **229**

Chapter Eight
Web Site Development. **263**

Color Chart on Inside Leaf of Back Cover

Chapter 1

Introduction to the Internet and World Wide Web

*T*he Internet and the Web are parts of our daily lives. How did they begin? What networking protocols and programming languages work behind the scenes to display a web page? This chapter provides an introduction to some of these topics and is a foundation for the information that web developers need to know. Some of this chapter may be review from your life experience or earlier studies.

Learning Outcomes

In this chapter, you will learn about

▶ The evolution of the Internet, Internet standards organizations, and the difference between the Internet, intranets, and extranets

▶ The beginning of the World Wide Web, ethical use of information on the Web, Web accessibility, and future Internet trends

▶ The client/server model, Internet protocols, networks, URLs and Domain names, and markup languages

The Evolution of the Internet

The Internet, the *inter*connected *net*work of computer networks, seems to be everywhere today. It has become part of our lives. You can't watch television or listen to the radio without being urged to visit a web site. Even newspapers have their place on the Net.

The Internet began as a network to connect computers at research facilities and universities. Messages in this network would travel to their destination by multiple routes or paths. This would allow the network to function even if parts of it were broken or destroyed. The message would be rerouted through a functioning portion of the network while traveling to its destination. This network was proposed to the Advanced Research Projects Agency (ARPA)—and the ARPAnet was born. Four computers (located at UCLA, Stanford Research Institute, University of California Santa Barbara, and the University of Utah) were connected by the end of 1969.

As time went on, other networks, such as the National Science Foundation's NSFnet, were created and connected with the ARPAnet. Use of this interconnected network, or Internet, was originally limited to government, research, and educational purposes. Even with this restriction, by 1989 there were over 100,000 hosts on the Internet. The ban on commercial use was lifted in 1991, and by end of 1992 there were over 1 million hosts connected. Hobbes' Internet Timeline reports that as of 2002, there were over 147 million host computers on the Internet. The communications protocol that enabled all this to happen is the Transmission Control Protocol/Internet Protocol (TCP/IP), proposed by Vinton Cerf and Robert Kahn.

If you are interested in the history of the Internet, visit any of the following links for more information.

- A brief history of the Internet written by the people who created it can be found at http://www.isoc.org/internet/history/brief.html.
- For a classic treatment of the Internet's history visit Hobbes' Internet Timeline at http://www.zakon.org/robert/internet/timeline/.
- PBS's *Life on the Internet* at http://www.pbs.org/internet/timeline/index.html provides an interactive look at the history of the Internet.

The Internet, Intranets, and Extranets

The Internet is an interconnected network of computer networks that is globally accessible. When an organization needs the communication capabilities of the Internet but doesn't want its information to be accessible to everyone, either an intranet or extranet would be appropriate.

An **intranet** is a private network that is contained within an organization or business. Its purpose is to share organizational information and resources among coworkers. When an intranet connects to the outside Internet usually a gateway or firewall protects the intranet from unauthorized access.

An **extranet** is a private network that securely shares part of an organization's information or operations with external partners such as suppliers, vendors, and customers. Extranets can be used to exchange data, share information exclusively with business partners, and collaborate with other organizations. Privacy and security are important issues in extranet use. Digital certificates, encryption of messages, and virtual private networks (VPNs) are some technologies used to provide privacy and security for an extranet. Digital certificates and encryption used in e-commerce are discussed in Chapter 13.

How can I tell whether a web page is a reliable source of information?

There are so many web sites—but which ones are good sources of information? Which sites are reliable? When visiting web sites to find information it is important not to take everything at face value.

First, evaluate the credibility of the web site itself. Does it have its own domain name, such as http://mywebsite.com, or is it a free web site consisting of just a folder of files hosted on a free web server? The URL of a site hosted on a free web server usually includes part of the free web server's name and might begin with something such as http://mysite.tripod.com or http://www.angelfire.com/foldername/mysite. Information obtained from a web site that has its own domain name will usually (but not always) be more reliable than information obtained from a free web site.

Also evaluate the type of domain name—is it a nonprofit organization (.org), a business (.com or .biz), an institution of higher learning (.edu)? Businesses may share information in a way that gives the business an advantage, so be careful. Nonprofit organizations or schools will sometimes provide a more objective treatment of a subject.

Another item to look at is the date the web page was created or last updated. While some information is timeless, very often a web page that has not been updated for several years is out of date and is not the best source of information.

The Evolution of the World Wide Web

Recall that the original Internet—the ARPAnet—began with four hosts. The number of host computers connected to the Internet grew each year. However, the communication was text-based and the information stored on computers connected to the Internet was not easy to obtain. Initially, the use of the Internet was limited to scholars, researchers, students, and government employees. Even with these restrictions there were over 300,000 hosts in 1990.

Why did the Internet grow from 300,000 hosts in 1990 to over 109 million in just over a decade? In the early 1990s, the convergence of three events occurred to cause explosive growth of the Internet.

In 1991, the NSFnet removed the restriction on commercial use of the Internet, setting the stage for future electronic commerce. Businesses were now welcome on the Internet. However, while businesses were no longer banned, the Internet was still text-based and not easy to use. The next developments solved this issue.

While working at CERN, a research facility in Switzerland, Tim Berners-Lee envisioned a means of communication for scientists where they could easily "hyperlink" to another research paper or article and immediately view it. He created **the World Wide Web** to fulfill this need and in 1991 posted the code in a newsgroup. This version of the World Wide Web used hypertext transfer protocol (HTTP) to communicate between the client computer and the web server, used hypertext markup language (HTML) to format the documents, and was text-based.

In 1993, the first graphics-based web browser, *Mosaic*, became available. Marc Andreesen and graduate students working at the National Center for Supercomputing Applications (NCSA) at the University of Illinois Urbana-Champaign developed Mosaic. Some individuals in this group later created another well-known web browser—Netscape Navigator.

The combination of commercial use, HTTP, and a graphical user interface made the information on the Internet much easier to access. The World Wide Web, the graphical user interface to the information stored on computers connected to the Internet, had arrived!

Internet Standards and Coordination

You are probably aware that no single person or group runs the entire Internet. Each separate network is managed individually. However, there are a number of groups that develop standards and guidelines. These groups have been a driving force in the growth and evolution of the Internet.

The **Internet Society**, http://www.isoc.org, is a professional organization that provides leadership in issues related to the future of the Internet. The Internet Society is the organizational home for the groups responsible for Internet infrastructure standards, including the Internet Engineering Task Force (IETF) and the Internet Architecture Board (IAB).

You can think of the IETF as the protocol engineering and development arm of the Internet. It is the principal body engaged in the development of new Internet standard specifications. The IETF is an open international community of network designers, operators, vendors, and researchers concerned with the evolution of Internet architecture and the smooth operation of the Internet. The actual technical work of the IETF is completed in its working groups. These working groups are organized into areas by topic, such as security and routing.

The IAB is responsible for defining the overall architecture of the Internet, providing guidance and broad direction to the IETF. As a function of this purpose, the IAB is responsible for the publication of the Request for Comments (RFC) document series.

An RFC is a formal document from the IETF that is drafted by a committee and subsequently reviewed by interested parties. RFCs are available for online review at http://www.ietf.org/rfc.html. Some RFCs are informational in nature, while others are meant to become Internet standards. In the latter case, the final version of the RFC becomes a new standard. Future changes to the standard must be made through subsequent RFCs.

The Internet Corporation for Assigned Numbers and Names (ICANN), http://www.icann.org, was created in 1998 and is a nonprofit organization. Its main function is to coordinate the assignment of Internet domain names, IP address numbers, protocol parameters, and protocol port numbers. Prior to 1998, the Internet Assigned Numbers Authority (IANA) coordinated these functions. IANA still performs certain functions under the guidance of ICANN and maintains a web site at http://www.iana.org.

Web Standards and the World Wide Web Consortium

As with the Internet in general, no one person or group runs the World Wide Web. However, the **World Wide Web Consortium (W3C)**, http://www.w3.org, takes a proactive role in developing recommendations and prototype technologies related to the Web. Four major areas that the W3C addresses are web architecture, user interface, technology and society, and the Web Accessibility Initiative (WAI). The W3C produces specifications, called recommendations, in an effort to standardize web technologies.

The W3C Recommendations are created in working groups with input from many major corporations involved in building web technologies. These recommendations are not rules but guidelines. Major software companies that build web browsers, such as Microsoft and Netscape, do not always follow the W3C Recommendations. This makes life difficult for web developers because not all browsers will display a web page in exactly the same way.

The good news is that there is a convergence toward the W3C Recommendations in new versions of major browsers. There are even organized groups such as *The Web Standards Project*, http://webstandards.org, whose mission is to promote W3C Recommendations (often called web standards) to not only the creators of browsers but also to web developers and designers.

 ## Web Accessibility

The Web Accessibility Initiative (WAI), http://www.w3.org/ WAI/, is a major area of work by the W3C. Since the Web has become an integral part of our everyday lives, there is a need for all individuals to be able to access it. According to Tim Berners-Lee at http://www.w3.org/WAI/, "The power of the Web is in its universality. Access by everyone regardless of disability is an essential aspect."

The Web can present barriers to individuals with visual, hearing, physical, and neurological disabilities. The WAI has developed recommendations for web content developers, web authoring tool developers, developers of web browsers, and developers of other user agents to facilitate use of the web by those with special needs.

Section 508 of the federal Rehabilitation Act was amended in 1998 to require that U.S. government agencies give individuals with disabilities access to information technology that is comparable to the access available to others. The Federal IT Accessibility Initiative, http://www.section508.gov, provides accessibility requirement resources for information technology developers.

The needs of individuals with visual disabilities also should be considered. As the Web has become more graphical, many web sites use images for navigation. A person with visual difficulties may not be able to use buttons and may be using a screen reader device to provide an audible description of the page. By making a few simple changes, such as providing text descriptions for the images and perhaps providing a text navigation area at the bottom of the page, web developers can make the web page accessible.

 ## Ethical Use of Information on the Web

This wonderful technology called the World Wide Web provides us with information, graphics, music—all virtually free (after you pay your Internet service provider, of course). Let's consider issues relating to the ethical use of this information.

- Is it all right to copy someone's graphic and use it on your own web site?
- Is it all right to copy someone else's web site design to use on your own site or on a client's site?
- Is it all right to copy an essay that appears on a web page and use all or parts of it as your own writing?
- Is it all right to insult someone on your web site or link to their site in a derogatory manner?

The answer to all these questions is no. Using another person's graphic without their permission is the same as stealing it. In fact, if you are linking to it you are actually using up some of their bandwidth and may be costing them money. Copying the web site design of another person or company is also a form of stealing. The web site http://pirated-sites.com presents a somewhat quirky look at this issue. Any text or graphic on a web site is automatically copyrighted in the United States whether or not a copyright symbol appears on the site. Insulting a person or company or linking to them in a derogatory manner on your web page could be considered a form of defamation.

Issues like these, related to intellectual property, copyright, and freedom of speech are regularly discussed and decided in courts of law. Good web etiquette requires that you ask permission before using others' work, give credit for what you use ("fair use" in the U.S. copyright law), and exercise your freedom of speech in a manner that is not harmful to others. **The World Intellectual Property Organization (WIPO)**, http://wipo.org, is dedicated to protecting intellectual property rights internationally.

Network Overview

A *network* consists of two or more computers connected together for the purpose of communicating and sharing resources. Common components of a network are shown in Figure 1.1 and include
- The server computer(s)
- The client workstation computer(s)
- Shared devices such as printers
- The media and devices that connect them

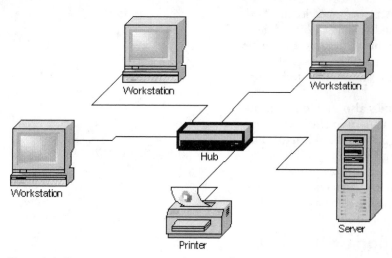

Figure 1.1 *Common components of a network*

The **clients** are the computers used by individuals, such as a PC on a desk. The **server** receives requests from client computers for resources such as files. Computers used as servers are usually kept in a protected, secure area and are only accessed by network administrators. The **media** connecting the clients, servers, and shared devices, or peripherals, may consist of cables and other devices, such as hubs and routers, that are needed to provide the network connections.

Networks vary in scale. A **local area network (LAN)** is usually confined to a single building or group of connected buildings. Your school computer lab may use a LAN. If you work in an office, you probably use a computer connected to a LAN. Recently, many people have begun to set up LANs in their homes to share resources between computers. A **metropolitan area network (MAN)** connects users with computer resources in a geographical area. It also can be used to connect two or more LANs. A **wide area network (WAN)** is geographically dispersed and usually uses some form of public or commercial communications network. For example, an organization with offices on both the East and West coasts of the United States probably uses a WAN to provide a link between the LANs at each of the offices. See Figure 1.2 for a diagram of this connectivity.

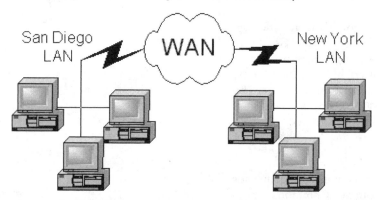

Figure 1.2 *WAN connecting two LANs*

A **backbone** is a high-capacity communication link that carries data gathered from smaller links that interconnect with it. On the Internet, a backbone is a set of paths that local or regional networks (MANs) connect to for long-distance interconnection. The Internet is a group of interconnected networks with very high-speed connectivity provided by the Internet backbones. An image of the AT&T IP Backbone Network map (from http://www.ipservices.att.com/backbone/index2.cfm) is shown in Figure 1.3.

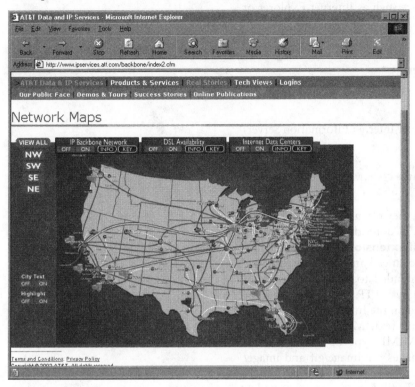

Figure 1.3 *Map of AT&T IP Backbone Network*

Access points or junctions to the Internet backbone in major cities are called **network access points (NAPs)**. Chicago, New York, and San Francisco are three key NAPs in the United States. Visit the Chicago NAP web site at http://www.aads.net/main.html to view photos of the actual hardware used and find out which Internet service providers are connected directly to the NAP.

The Client/Server Model

The term **client/server** dates from the last millennium (the 1980s) and refers to personal computers joined by a network. **Client/server** can also describe a relationship between two computer programs—the client and the server. The client requests some type of service (such as a file or database access) from the server. The server fulfills the request and transmits the results to the client over a network. While both the client and the server programs can reside on the same computer, typically they run on different computers. It is common for a server to handle requests from multiple clients.

The Internet is a great example of client/server architecture at work. Consider the following scenario: An individual is at a computer using a web browser client to access the Internet. The individual uses the web browser to visit a web site, let's say http://www.yahoo.com. The server is the web server program running on the computer with an IP address that corresponds to yahoo.com. It is contacted, locates the web page and related resources that were requested, and responds by sending them to the individual.

In short, here's how to distinguish between clients and servers:

Web Client
- Connected to the Internet when needed
- Usually runs web browser (client) software such as Internet Explorer or Netscape
- Uses HTTP
- Requests web pages from a server
- Receives web pages and files from a server

Web Server
- Continually connected to the Internet
- Runs web server software (such as Apache or Internet Information Server)
- Uses HTTP
- Receives a request for the web page
- Responds to the request and transmits status code, web page, and associated files

When clients and servers exchange files, they often need to indicate the type of file that is being transferred; this is done through the use of a MIME type. **Multi-purpose Internet mail extensions (MIME)** are rules that allow multimedia documents to be exchanged among many different computer systems. MIME was initially intended to extend the original Internet e-mail protocol, but it is also used by HTTP. MIME provides for the exchange of seven different media types on the Internet: audio, video, image, application, message, multipart, and text. MIME also uses subtypes to further describe the data. The MIME type of a web page is text/html. MIME types of gif and jpeg images are image/gif and image/jpeg respectively.

A web server determines the MIME type of a file before it is transmitted to the web browser. The MIME type is sent along with the document. The web browser uses the MIME type to determine how to display the document.

How does information get transferred from the web server to the web browser? Clients (such as web browsers) and servers (such as a web server) exchange information with each other through the use of communication protocols such as HTTP, TCP, and IP.

Internet Protocols

Protocols are rules that describe how clients and servers communicate with each other over a network. There is no single protocol that makes the Internet and Web work—a number of protocols with specific functions are needed.

File Transfer Protocol (FTP)

File Transfer Protocol (FTP) is a set of rules that allow files to be exchanged between computers on the Internet. Unlike HTTP, which is used by web browsers to request web pages and their associated files in order to display a web page, FTP is used simply to move files from one computer to another. Web developers commonly use FTP to transfer web page files from their computers to web servers. FTP is also commonly used to download programs and files from other servers to individual computers. See the section called "Using FTP to Publish Your Web Site" in the *Web Developer's Handbook* for more information on FTP.

E-mail Protocols

Most of us take e-mail for granted, but there are two servers involved in its smooth functioning—an incoming mail server and an outgoing mail server. When you send e-mail to others, **Simple Mail Transfer Protocol (SMTP)** is used. When you receive e-mail, **Post Office Protocol** (**POP**; currently **POP3**) and **Internet Message Access Protocol (IMAP)** can be used.

Hypertext Transfer Protocol (HTTP)

HTTP is a set of rules for exchanging files such as text, graphic images, sound, video, and other multimedia files on the Web. Web browsers and web servers usually use this protocol. When the user of a web browser requests a file either by typing a web site address or by clicking on a hyperlink, the browser builds an HTTP request and sends it to the server. The web server in the destination machine receives the request, does any necessary processing, and responds with the requested file and any associated media files.

Transmission Control Protocol / Internet Protocol (TCP/IP)

Transmission Control Protocol/Internet Protocol (TCP/IP), has been adopted as the official communication protocol of the Internet. TCP and IP have different functions that work together to ensure reliable communication over the Internet.

TCP. The purpose of TCP is to ensure the integrity of network communication. TCP starts by breaking files and messages into individual units called **packets**. These packets (see Figure 1.4) contain information such as the destination, source, sequence number, and checksum values used to verify the integrity of the data.

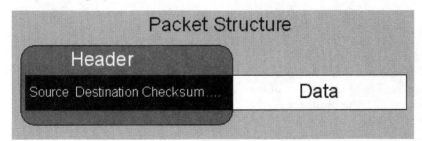

Figure 1.4 *TCP packet*

TCP is used together with IP to efficiently transmit files over the Internet. IP takes over after TCP creates the packets, using IP addressing to send each packet over the Internet using the best path at the particular time. When the destination address is reached, TCP verifies the integrity of each packet using the checksum, requests a resend if a packet is damaged, and reassembles the file or message from the multiple packets.

IP. Working in harmony with TCP, IP is a set of rules that controls how data is sent between computers on the Internet. IP routes a packet to the correct destination address. Once sent, the packet gets successively forwarded to the next closest router (a hardware device designed to move network traffic) until it reaches its destination.

Each device connected to the Internet has a unique numeric IP address. These addresses consist of a set of four groups of numbers, called *octets*. The current version of IP, IPv4, uses 32-bit (binary digit) addressing. This results in a decimal number in the format of xxx.xxx.xxx.xxx, where each xxx is a value from 0 to 255. The IP address may correspond to a domain name. The Domain Name System (DNS) associates these IP addresses with the text-based URLs and domain names you type into a web browser address box (more on this later). For example, at the time this was written the IP address of Yahoo! was 216.115.108.245.

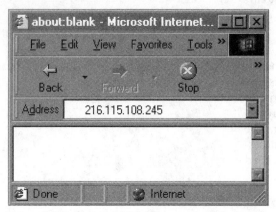

Figure 1.5 *Entering an IP address in a web browser*

You can enter this number in the address text box in a web browser (as shown in Figure 1.5), press Enter, and the Yahoo home page will display. Of course it's much easier to type "yahoo.com," which is why domain names such as yahoo.com were created in the first place!

Since long strings of numbers are difficult for humans to remember, the Domain Name System was introduced as a way to associate text-based names with numeric IP addresses.

URLs and Domain Names

URLs

The **Uniform Resource Locator (URL)** represents the address of a resource that is available on the Internet. This resource could be for example, a web page, a graphic file, or a Java applet. The URL consists of the protocol, the domain name, and the hierarchical location of the file on the web server.

The URL http://www.webdevfoundations.net, shown in Figure 1.6, denotes the use of HTTP protocol and the web server named www at the domain name of webdevfoundations.net. In this case the root file (usually index.html or index.htm) will be displayed.

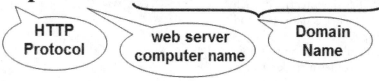

Figure 1.6 *Parts of a URL*

What is a Universal Resource Locator?

Although officially URL stands for Uniform Resource Locator, Tim Berners-Lee (the inventor of the Web) originally envisioned a *Universal* Resource Locator. That is why some texts or web pages refer to the URL in that manner. Read Tim Berners-Lee's book *Weaving the Web* for an interesting view of the creation of the Web.

If the URL was of the form http://www.webdevfoundations.net/chapter1/links.htm, as shown in Figure 1.7, it would denote the use of HTTP protocol and a web server named www at the domain name of webdevfoundations.net. The resource to be displayed is the web page named links.htm in the chapter1 folder.

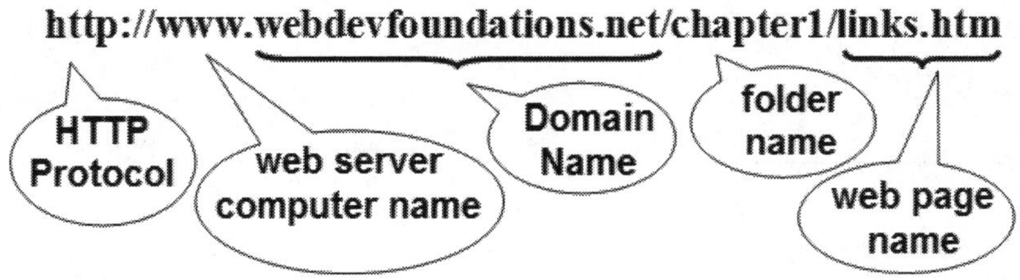

Figure 1.7 *URL describing a file within a folder*

Figure 1.8 depicts a URL used to display files available for FTP download in the format of ftp://ftp.microsoft.com. This denotes the use of the FTP protocol, the server named ftp, and the domain name of microsoft.com.

Figure 1.8 *URL using FTP*

Domain Names

A **domain name** locates an organization or other entity on the Internet. The purpose of the Domain Name System (DNS) is to divide the Internet into logical groups and understandable names by identifying the exact address and type of the organization. The DNS associates the text-based domain names with the unique numeric IP address assigned to a device.

Let's consider the domain name www.yahoo.com. The .com is the top-level domain name. The portion yahoo.com is the domain name that is registered to Yahoo! and is considered a second-level domain name. The www is the name of the web server (sometimes called **host server**) at the yahoo.com domain. Taken all together, www.yahoo.com is considered to be a fully-qualified domain name (FQDN).

Top-Level Domain Names (TLDs). A top-level domain (TLD) identifies the right-most part of the domain name. A TLD is either a generic top-level domain, such as com for commercial, or a country code top-level domain, such as fr for France. ICANN administers the generic top-level domains shown in Table 1.1

Table 1.1 *Top-Level Domains*

Generic TLD	Used by
.com	Commercial entities
.org	Nonprofit entities
.net	Entities associated with network support of the Internet, usually Internet service providers or telecommunication companies
.mil	Restricted to military use
.gov	Restricted to government use
.edu	Restricted to accredited degree-granting institutions of higher education
.int	International organization (This is rarely used.)
.aero	Air-transport industry
.name	Individuals
.biz	Businesses
.museum	Museums
.info	Unrestricted use
.coop	Cooperative
.pro	Accountants, physicians, and lawyers

The .com, .org, and .net TLD designations are currently used on the honor system. That means that an individual with a shoe store (not related to networking) could register shoes.net.

Country Code Top-Level Domain Names. Two character country codes have also been assigned as top-level domain names. These were originally intended to be meaningful and relate the domain name country code to the geographical location of the individual or organization that registered the name. In practice, it is fairly easy to obtain a domain name with a country code TLD that is not local to the registrant. See http://register.com and many other domain name registration companies for examples. Table 1.2 lists some popular country codes used on the Web.

Table 1.2 *Country Codes*

Country Code TLD	Country
.au	Australia
.de	Germany
.in	India
.jp	Japan
.nl	The Netherlands
.us	United States

The IANA web site at http://www.iana.org/cctld/cctld-whois.htm has a complete list. Domain names with country codes are often used for municipalities, schools, and community colleges in the United States. The domain name www.harper.cc.il.us denotes the United States, Illinois, community college, Harper, and the web server named www as the site for William Rainey Harper College in Illinois.

The DNS associates domain names with IP addresses. Here is what happens each time a new URL is typed into a web browser

1. The DNS is accessed
2. The corresponding IP address is obtained and returned to the web browser
3. The web browser sends an HTTP request to the destination computer with the corresponding IP address
4. The HTTP request is received by the web server
5. The necessary files are located and sent by HTTP responses to the web browser
6. The web browser renders and displays the web page and associated files.

The next time you wonder why it's taking so long to display a web page, think about all of the processing that goes on behind the scenes.

Markup Languages

Markup languages consist of sets of directions that tell the browser software (and other user agents such as mobile phones) how to display and manage a web document. These directions are usually called *tags* and perform functions such as displaying graphics, formatting text, and referencing hyperlinks.

Standard Generalized Markup Language (SGML)

SGML is a standard for specifying a markup language or tag set. SGML is not in itself a document language, but a description of how to specify one and create a document type definition (DTD). When Tim Berners-Lee created HTML, he used SGML to create the specification.

Hypertext Markup Language (HTML)

HTML is the set of markup symbols or codes placed in a file intended for display on a web browser. The web browser renders the code in the HTML file and displays the web page document and associated files. The W3C (http://www.w3.org) sets the standards for HTML. The most recent version of HTML is called XHTML 1.0. The previous version of HTML was HTML 4.0.

Extensible Markup Language (XML)

XML was developed by the W3C as a flexible method to create common information formats and share both the format *and* the information on the Web. It is a text-based syntax designed to describe, deliver, and exchange structured information. It is not intended to replace HTML but to extend the power of HTML by separating data from presentation. Using XML, developers can create whatever tags they need to describe their information.

Extensible Hypertext Markup Language (XHTML)

XHTML was developed by the W3C to reformulate HTML 4.0 as an application of XML. It combines the formatting strengths of HTML 4.0 and the data structure and extensibility strengths of XML. See Figure 1.9 for a diagram that depicts the relationship among XHTML, HTML, and XML.

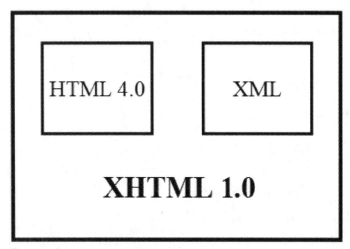

Figure 1.9 *The relationship among XHTML, HTML, and XML*

The primary advantages of XHTML include the ability to extend the language by creating new tags and the promise of increased platform interoperability as mobile devices are used more frequently to access the Web.

Future Internet and Web Trends

E-commerce, the buying and selling of goods on the Internet, is already an important part of the Web. A recent study found that over half of those who use the Web had made purchases online. With over 400 million people online worldwide, that's quite a few potential shoppers!

As wireless web access becomes more commonplace, e-commerce and Internet access will not only regularly be done from stationary computers but also from mobile devices—Palm Pilots, Pocket PCs, personal digital assistants (PDAs), cell phones, and Internet appliances we haven't even imagined yet.

As wireless access grows, so will the need for skilled technical workers. Expect to see a demand for network engineers familiar with wireless network technologies, such as Wireless Access Protocol (WAP), Bluetooth, and Ricochet. Web developers who are knowledgeable about markup languages such as WML, XML, and XHTML Basic will be sought as employees and consultants.

How do we keep track of all the devices (wireless and otherwise) that are connected to the Internet? You are already aware that each device on the Internet is assigned a unique number called an IP address. Currently, IPv4 is being used. This theoretically allows for at most 4 billion possible IP addresses (although many potential addresses are reserved for special uses). With the proliferation of mobile devices, even this many addresses may not be enough. **IP Version 6 (IPV6)** will provide a huge increase in the number of possible addresses and many technological advances.

The development of the Internet2 is another effort in advancing Internet technology. The Internet2 consortium is comprised of over a hundred U.S. universities in partnership with industry and government. Their mission is to develop and deploy advanced network applications and technologies, focusing on applications related to learning and research such as telemedicine, digital libraries, and virtual laboratories. Visit the Internet2 web site at http://www.internet2.edu for information on this initiative.

Another area to watch is that of web services. A **web service** is a self-describing, self-contained, application that provides some business functionality through an Internet connection. For example, an organization could create a web service to facilitate information exchange with its partners or vendors. The Universal Discovery, Description, and Integration (UDDI) standard, http://www.uddi.org, is backed by a number of technology companies, including IBM, Microsoft, and Sun Microsystems. UDDI essentially provides a method of describing a service, invoking a service, and locating available services. Microsoft's .NET platform supports web services. Microsoft and IBM jointly developed Web Services Description Language (WSDL) to facilitate the use of web services.

The single future trend that you can expect to remain the same is the **trend of constant change**. Internet- and Web-related technologies are in a constant state of development and improvement. If this constant change and the need to learn something new excite you, web development will be a fascinating field for you. The skills and knowledge you gain in this book should provide a solid foundation for your future learning.

What is an Internet appliance?

An Internet appliance is a device that is designed to access the Internet. It is different from PCs and Palm Pilots in that they are multipurpose devices, while an Internet appliance is a single-purpose device. As you read this, companies are working to develop new Internet-ready devices, ranging from digital cameras that instantly post photos on the Web, to Internet-connected wearable computers, Internet-enabled printers, and Internet-enabled point-of-sale (POS) terminals.

What is IPv6?

IPv6, Internet Protocol Version 6, is the most recent version of the Internet Protocol. IPv6 was designed as an evolutionary set of improvements to the current IPv4 and is backwardly compatible with it. Service providers and Internet users can update to IPv6 independently without having to coordinate with each other.

IPv6 provides for more Internet addresses because the IP address is lengthened from 32 bits to 128 bits. This means that there are potentially 2^{128} unique IP addresses possible, or 340,282,366,920,938,463,463,347,607,431,768,211,456. (Now there will be enough IP addresses for everyone's PC, notebook, cell phone, pager, PDA, automobile, toaster, etc.!).

Chapter 1 Review

Summary

This chapter provided a brief overview of Internet, Web, and introductory networking concepts. Much of this information may have been familiar to you. Visit the course web site at http://www.webdevfoundations.net for the links listed in this chapter and for updated information.

Review Questions

Multiple Choice

1. Choose the organization listed below whose purpose is to study technical problems of the Internet and propose solutions to those problems.
   a. Internet Assigned Numbers Authority (IANA)
   b. Internet Engineering Task Force (IETF)
   c. Internet Corporation for Assigned Numbers and Names (ICANN)
   d. World Wide Web Consortium (W3C)

2. A network that covers a small area such as a group of buildings or campus area is called a(n)
   a. LAN   c. Internet
   b. WAN   d. WWW

3. The World Wide Web was developed by individuals at
   a. CERN   c. NSF
   b. NCSA   d. ARPA

4. A unique text-based Internet address corresponding to a computer's unique numeric IP address is called a(n)
   a. IP address   c. URL
   b. domain name   d. user name

5. New top-level domains (TLDs) are coordinated by
   a. ICANN
   b. no one, because anyone can add a TLD to the DNS
   c. W3C
   d. TCP

True or False

6. ___ Markup languages contain sets of directions that tell the browser software (and other user-agents such as cell phones) how to display and manage a web document.

7. ___ The World Wide Web was developed to allow companies to advertise over the Internet.

8. ___ A numerical Internet address used to identify computers is called an IP address.

9. ___ A domain name that ends in .com indicates that it is a computer company.

Fill in the Blank

10. _____ combines the formatting strengths of HTML 4.0 and the data structure and extensibility strengths of XML.

11. A standard language used for specifying a markup language or tag set is _____.

12. _____ is the set of markup symbols or codes placed in a file intended for display on a web browser.

13. A language using a text-based syntax intended to extend the power of HTML by separating data from presentation is called _____.

14. Access points or junctions to the Internet backbone are called _____.

15. The purpose of _____ is to ensure the integrity of the communication.

Web Research

A. The World Wide Web Consortium is the organization that creates standards for the Web. Visit their site at http://www.w3c.org, then answer the following questions.

1. How did the W3C get started?

2. Who can join the W3C? What does it cost to join?

3. The W3C home page lists a number of technologies. Choose one that interests you, click on its link, and read the associated pages. List three facts or issues you discovered.

B. The Internet Society takes an active leadership role in issues related to the Internet. Visit its site at http://www.isoc.org and answer the following questions.

1. Why was the Internet Society created?

2. Determine the local chapter closest to you. Visit its web site. List the web site URL and an activity or service that the chapter provides.

3. How can you join the Internet Society? What does it cost to join? Would you recommend joining the Internet Society to a beginning web developer? Why or why not?

C. Visit any of the web sites referenced in this chapter that interested you. Print the home page or one other pertinent page from the site. Write a one-page summary and reaction to the web site. Address the following topics.

1. What is the purpose of the site?

2. Who is the intended audience?

3. Do you believe the site reaches the intended audience?

4. Was this site useful to you? Why or why not?

5. List one interesting fact or issue that this site addressed.

6. Would you encourage others to visit this site?

7. How could this site be improved?

Chapter Review Answers

1. b

2. a

3. a

4. b

5. a

6. True

7. False

8. True

9. False

10. XHTML

11. SGML

12. HTML

13. XML

14. network access points

15. TCP

Chapter 2

XHTML Basics

*T*his chapter introduces you to Hypertext Markup Language (HTML), the language used to create web pages, and to eXtensible Hypertext Markup Language (XHTML), the latest version of HTML. The chapter begins with an introduction to the syntax of XHTML, continues with the anatomy of a web page, and introduces text and block-level formatting as sample pages are created. You will learn more if you work along with the sample pages in the text. Coding XHTML is a skill and every skill improves with practice.

Learning Outcomes

In this chapter, you will learn about

▶ **The development of HTML**

▶ **The transition from HTML to XHTML**

▶ **XHTML syntax, tags, and document type definitions**

▶ **The anatomy of a web page**

▶ **Formatting the body of a web page**

▶ **Formatting the text on a web page**

▶ **Physical and logical style tags**

▶ **Special characters**

What Is HTML?

The World Wide Web is composed of files containing **Hypertext Markup Language (HTML)** and other markup languages that describe web pages. HTML was developed using Standard Generalized Markup Language (SGML). SGML prescribes a standard format for embedding descriptive markup within a document and for describing the structure of a document. SGML is not in itself a document language, but a description of how to specify one and create a document type definition (DTD).

The W3C, http://w3c.org, sets the standards for HTML and its related languages. HTML (like the Web itself) is in a constant state of change.

HTML is the set of markup symbols or codes placed in a file intended for display on a Web browser page. These markup symbols and codes identify structural elements such as paragraphs, headings, and lists. HTML can also be used to place media (such as graphics, video, and audio) on a web page and describe fill-in forms. The browser interprets the markup code and renders the page for you to see. HTML permits the platform-independent display of information across a network. That is, no matter what type of computer a web page was created on, any browser running on any operating system can display the page.

Each individual markup code is referred to as an **element** or **tag**. Each tag has a purpose. Tags are enclosed in angle brackets, the < and > symbols. Most tags come in pairs: an opening tag and a closing tag. These tags act as containers and are sometimes referred to as *container tags*. For example, the text that is in between the **<title>** and **</title>** tags on a web page would display in the title bar on the browser window.

Some tags are used alone and are not part of a pair. For example, a tag that displays a horizontal line on a web page, **<hr />**, is a stand-alone or self-contained tag and does not have a closing tag. You will become familiar with these as you use them. Most tags can be modified with attributes that further describe their purpose.

Why XHTML and Not HTML?

The newest version of HTML is actually **eXtensible HyperText Markup Language (XHTML)**. XHTML uses the tags and attributes of HTML along with the syntax of **eXtensible Markup Language (XML)**. While many web pages and web authoring tools still use HTML, as a web developer you need to learn about XHTML because you will be seeing a lot of it in the future.

Why is a new version needed? HTML was originally developed to provide access to electronic documents via a web browser. Web browsers that evolved along with HTML were written to forgive coding errors, ignore syntax errors, and allow "sloppy" HTML code. Web browsers contain a great deal of program instructions that are designed to ignore mistakes such as missing ending tags and to guess how the developer meant the page to display. This is not a problem for a personal computer, which has relatively large processing power. This could be an issue for electronic devices with fewer resources, such as a personal digital assistant (PDA) or mobile phone.

Also, as new versions of web browsers were developed and competed with each other for market share, they often created their own proprietary extensions to HTML—tags that were not part of the standard and only supported by one browser. This created a lot of nonstandard HTML pages, and browsers are coded to accept this and ignore tags they don't recognize. However, this extra processing is not efficient, especially for devices with limited resources.

Finally, HTML is a structural language—it was originally intended to mark up printed documents for online viewing. It describes the structure of the document instead of the contents or information contained in the document. The Web has changed from a medium used to display electronic versions of paper documents to a medium that provides diverse information for a variety of devices. HTML does not fit this need. How will a table 600 pixels wide be displayed on a mobile phone? With the expansion of the Web to include devices other than personal computers, the need for a descriptive rather than structural language became evident and XHTML was created.

XHTML was developed by the W3C to be the reformulation of HTML as an application of XML. Tim Berners-Lee, the W3C director and inventor of the Web, states in a press release (http://www.w3.org/2000/01/xhtmlpressrelease), "XHTML 1.0 connects the present Web to the future Web. It provides the bridge to page and site authors for entering the structured data, XML world, while still being able to maintain operability with user agents that support HTML 4." XHTML combines the formatting strengths of HTML and the data structure and extensibility strengths of XML. Since XHTML was designed using XML, let's take a quick look at XML.

XML is the W3C standard method for creating new markup languages that will support the display of nontraditional content such as mathematical notation, as well as support newer display devices such as PDAs or mobile phones. XML can fulfill these diverse needs because it is an extensible language—it is designed to allow the definition of new tags or markup. The syntax of XML is very exacting because the portable devices will not have to waste processing power guessing how the document should display, but will be able to display information efficiently. XHTML, which combines the language of HTML with the syntax of XML, is a markup language that should adapt to future needs.

An XML document must be **well-formed**. A well-formed document is a document that adheres to the syntax rules of the language. The XHTML examples in the text will guide you in creating well-formed web pages using XHTML. As a starting point, is it recommended that XML documents begin with an XML directive. The basic form of this directive is

```
<?xml version= "1.0" encoding="UTF-8"?>
```

This XML directive indicates that the document is based on the XML 1.0 standard. It also indicates the character encoding (the internal representation of letters, numbers, and symbols) in this document is UTF-8, a form of Unicode. This XML directive will be the first line in each web page that you write. See the section Comparing HTML and XHTML in the *Web Developer's Handbook* for a list of the key syntax rules of XML.

Document Type Definition

Because multiple versions and types of HTML and XHTML exist, the W3C recommends identifying the type of markup language used in a web page document. This text follows the W3C XHTML 1.0 Recommendation. The three types of XHTML 1.0, Transitional, Strict, and Frameset, are defined in Table 2.1.

Table 2.1 XHTML Document Types

Document Type Definition	Description
XTML 1.0 Transitional	The least strict specification for XHTML 1.0. Allows the use of both Cascading Style Sheets and traditional formatting instructions such as fonts. Use this for most of the coding in this text.
XHTML 1.0 Strict	Requires exclusive use of Cascading Style Sheets. Not used in this text.
XHTML 1.0 Frameset	Required for pages using XHTML frames. Use with frames pages later in this text.

The version and type of XHTML is listed in the Document Type Definition (DTD) tag (commonly called the *DOCTYPE*). The DTD identifies the version and type of XHTML contained in your document. Browsers and HTML code validators can use the information in the DTD when processing the web page. The DTD tag is placed at the top of a web page document, even before the **<html>** tag. The DTD for XHTML 1.0 Transitional is

```
<!DOCTYPE html PUBLIC "-//W3C//DTD XHTML 1.0 Transitional//EN"
"http://www.w3.org/TR/xhtml1/DTD/xhtml1-transitional.dtd">
```

You will place the DTD as the second line in each web page document you create. Speaking of creating web pages, are you ready to create your first web page?

Your First Web Page

After the XML directive and the DTD, each web page begins with an opening **<html>** tag and ends with a closing **</html>** tag. These tags indicate that the text between them is HTML formatted. It tells the browser how to interpret the document.

```
<?xml version="1.0" encoding="UTF-8"?>
<!DOCTYPE html PUBLIC "-//W3C//DTD XHTML 1.0 Transitional//EN"
"http://www.w3.org/TR/xhtml1/DTD/xhtml1-transitional.dtd">
<html> an opening tag
.... page information goes here
</html> a closing tag
```

There are two sections on a web page: the **head** and the **body**. The head section, sometimes called the **header**, contains information that describes the web page document. Tags that are located in the head section include the title of the web page, keywords that can be used by search engines, and references to scripts and styles. Many of these do not show directly on the web page. The head section begins with the **<head>** tag and ends with the **</head>** tag.

The body section is used for text and tags that do show directly on the web page. The purpose of the body section is to describe the contents of the web page. You will spend most of your time coding XHTML in the body of a web page. If you type text in the body section, it will appear directly on the page.

The body section begins with the **<body>** tag and ends with the **</body>** tag. The **<body>** tag itself can be used to set attributes such as the color of the page background and the color of hyperlinks (more on this later). The following code sample describes the anatomy of a web page: a header section followed by a body section.

```
<?xml version="1.0" encoding="UTF-8"?>
<!DOCTYPE html PUBLIC "-//W3C//DTD XHTML 1.0 Transitional//EN"
"http://www.w3.org/TR/xhtml1/DTD/xhtml1-transitional.dtd">
<html>
<head>
..... header information goes here
</head>
<body>
..... body information goes here
</body>
</html>
```

Notice that the XHTML tags are lowercase. This is conforms to XML syntax. Notice also that the DTD statement does not follow this syntax. The DTD statement indicates the markup language being used and has its own formatting—mixed case.

In XHTML, the **<html>** tag also needs to describe the location of the documentation for the elements being used (called the **XML namespace** or **xmlns**) and the language being used (in this case English). This additional information is added to the **<html>** tag in the form of attributes. The xmlns attribute points to the URL of the XHTML namespace used in the document, the standard http://www.w3.org/1999/xhtml. You will always use the standard XHTML namespace in this course, but in your career you might use the Math Namespace (to better work with web pages related to mathematical concepts) or even create your own namespace.

The final version of the basic anatomy of a web page is shown as follows. Note that the first five lines will usually be the same on every web page that you create.

```
<?xml version="1.0" encoding="UTF-8"?>
<!DOCTYPE html PUBLIC "-//W3C//DTD XHTML 1.0 Transitional//EN"
"http://www.w3.org/TR/xhtml1/DTD/xhtml1-transitional.dtd">
<html xmlns="http://www.w3.org/1999/xhtml">
<head>
..... header information goes here
</head>
<body>
..... body information goes here
</body>
</html>
```

What are web page editors?

No special software is needed to create an XHTML document—all you need is a text editor. Notepad is a text editor that is included with Microsoft Windows. BBEdit is a popular editing program for Mac users. XHTML documents can also be created with many word processing applications, such as Microsoft Word, by selecting the option to save the document as a web page. An alternative to using a simple text editor or word processor is to use a commercial web authoring tool, such as Microsoft FrontPage, Macromedia Dreamweaver, or Adobe GoLive. There are also many free or shareware editors available, including Netscape Composer, 1st Page 2000, and Emacs. Netscape Composer is a web page editor built right into the Netscape Navigator browser. Regardless of the tool you use, getting a solid foundation in XHTML will be useful. The examples in this text use Notepad.

Launch Notepad or another text editor and type in the following XHTML:

```
<?xml version="1.0" encoding="UTF-8"?>
<!DOCTYPE html PUBLIC "-//W3C//DTD XHTML 1.0 Transitional//EN"
   "http://www.w3.org/TR/xhtml1/DTD/xhtml1-transitional.dtd">
<html xmlns="http://www.w3.org/1999/xhtml">
<head>
<title>My First Web Page</title>
</head>
<body>
Hello World
</body>
</html>
```

Notice that the first lines in the file contain the XML directive and the DTD. The XHTML code begins with an opening **<html>** *tag and ends with a closing* **</html>** *tag. The purpose of these tags is to indicate that the contents in between make up a web page. The head section is delimited by* **<head>** *and* **</head>** *tags, and happens to contain a pair of title tags with the words "My First Web Page" in between. The body section is delimited by* **<body>** *and* **</body>** *tags. The words "Hello World" are typed on a line between the body tags. See Figure 2.1 for a screen shot of the code as it would appear in Notepad. You have just created the source code for a web document.*

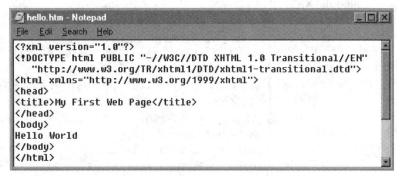

Figure 2.1 *Source code of hello.htm*

Save Your File

You will save the file on your floppy disk with the name of hello.htm. Web pages use either an .htm or .html file extension. Select File from the Menu Bar, then select Save As. The Save As dialog box appears. Using Figure 2.2 as an example, type the file name.

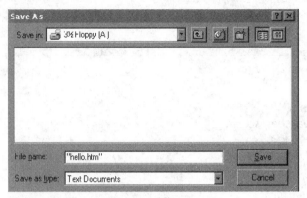

Figure 2.2 *The Save As dialog box*

To prevent Notepad from appending a .txt extension to the file name, you must type the name of the file in quotes. Click the Save button after you type the file name. Sample solutions for the Hands-On Practice exercises are available on this textbook's student disk. If you would like, compare your page with the solution (Chapter2/hello.htm) before you test your work.

Test Your Page

There are two ways to test your page.

1. *Launch Windows Explorer. Select the floppy drive and double-click on hello.htm. The default browser will be launched and will display your hello.htm page. Your page should look similar to the one shown in Figure 2.3.*

Figure 2.3 *Web page displayed by Internet Explorer*

2. *Launch Internet Explorer. Select File, Open, select Browse, then select My Computer, select your floppy drive, double-click on hello.htm, click OK.*

Do I have to start each tag on its own line?

No, you don't. A browser could display the page even if all the tags followed each other on one line with no spaces. Humans, however, find it easier to write and read XHTML if line breaks and indentation (more on this later) are used.

Your page should look similar to Figure 2.3 if you used Internet Explorer. A display of the page using Netscape 6 is shown in Figure 2.4.

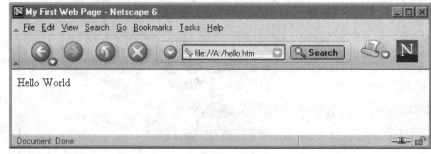

Figure 2.4 *Web page displayed by Netscape 6*

Examine your page. Look carefully at the browser window. What do you think is the purpose of the **<title>** *tag? If you guessed that it's to display the title in the browser window, you are correct! Some search engines need the text surrounded by the* **<title>** *and* **</title>** *tags to help determine relevancy of keyword searches, so make certain that your pages contain descriptive titles. The* **<title>** *tag is also used when viewers bookmark your page or add it to their Favorites. An engaging and descriptive page title may entice a visitor to revisit the page. When the web page is for a company or an organization, it's a good idea to include the name of the company or organization in the title.*

You might be thinking "Hmmm … white background, black text, no images, can't we make the page look more interesting?" Sure you can and that's what you'll begin to learn as you go on to the next section.

XHTML—Body and Text Basics

When you visit web sites have you ever noticed the wide variety of page designs? Whether a web page contains mostly text, uses blocks of color, displays images, uses animation, or is interactive, the foundation of the page is the **<body>** tag.

The Body Tag

The **<body>** tag can be used to set **attributes** (sometimes called *properties*) for your entire web page, such as background color, background image, text color, and link colors.

The following **<body>** tag configures both the background color and text color for the web page.

```
<body bgcolor="#000066" text="#FFFF33">
```

The bgcolor attribute sets the background color of the web page. The value #000066 is the hexadecimal color code that indicates a dark navy blue. The text attribute sets the color of the text on the page and is set to #FFFF33, the hexadecimal color code that indicates yellow. See the color chart on the inside leaf of the back cover for a list of color values and names. Table 2.2 summarizes the **<body>** tag attributes used in the example. Other attributes are discussed later in this text and listed in the XHTML Reference in the *Web Developer's Handbook*.

Table 2.2 *Body Tag bgcolor and text Attributes*

Attribute	Values	Usage
bgcolor	A valid color	Used to configure the background color of the web page.
text	A valid color	Used to configure the color of the text on the web page.

Take a moment now to modify your first web page to use bgcolor and text attributes on the **<body>** tag. Save and test your changes using a browser. Your page should look similar to Figure 2.5.

Figure 2.5 *Web page using* **<body>** *tag attributes to configure the color*

As you noticed when you created your first web page, any text that you type in the body section of a web page document will be displayed by the browser in the actual web page. Often, this text is organized by structural elements that indicate important headings, text paragraphs, and lists. These structural elements control blocks of text such as headings, paragraphs, and lists, and are called **block-level tags**. Tags that affect individual sections of text are called **text-level tags**. Examples of each appear in this section. Web development is a skill—the more you practice, the better you get. Why not try each example as you read?

The Heading Tag

Headings are block-level elements that are organized into levels h1 through h6. The size of the text is largest for **<h1>** and smallest for **<h6>**. Depending on the font being used (more on fonts later), text contained in **<h5>** and **<h6>** tags may be displayed smaller than the default text size.

Hands-On Practice 2.2

Launch Notepad or another text editor and type in the following XHTML:

```
<?xml version="1.0" encoding="UTF-8"?>
<!DOCTYPE html PUBLIC "-//W3C//DTD XHTML 1.0 Transitional//EN"
"http://www.w3.org/TR/xhtml1/DTD/xhtml1-transitional.dtd">
<html xmlns="http://www.w3.org/1999/xhtml">
<head>
<title>Sample Heading Tags</title>
</head>
<body>
  <h1>Heading Level 1</h1>
  <h2>Heading Level 2</h2>
```

continues

How do I choose a color?

You will learn more about the use of color on web pages later in this text. See the XHTML Reference in the *Web Developer's Handbook* for a list of XHTML tags and their attributes. A color chart may be found on the inside leaf of the back cover. This can help you select valid color values. Using color and graphics on web pages is discussed in Chapter 4 and Chapter 7.

```
  <h3>Heading Level 3</h3>
  <h4>Heading Level 4</h4>
  <h5>Heading Level 5</h5>
  <h6>Heading Level 6</h6>
</body>
</html>
```

Save the file as heading.htm. Launch a browser such as Internet Explorer or Netscape to test your page. It should look similar to Figure 2.6. You can compare your work with the solution found on the student disk (Chapter2/heading.htm).

Notice that each heading in Figure 2.6 is on its own line and that there is a blank line between headings. The heading tag is a container tag. Notice how there are always corresponding opening <h#> and closing </h#> tags. It's a good idea to use headings to emphasize important topics or sections on a web page.

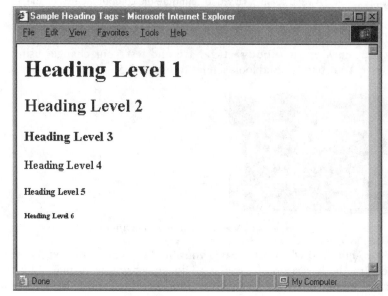

Figure 2.6 *Sample heading.htm*

The Paragraph Tag

Paragraphs tags are block-level elements used to group sentences and sections of text together. Text that is contained by **<p>** and **</p>** tags will have a blank line above and below it.

Hands-On Practice 2.3

Open your heading.htm file in a text editor. Use the following sample code and add a paragraph of text to your page below the line with the <h1> tags and above the line with the <h2> tags. The new code is shown in green. Save your page as heading2.htm.

```
<?xml version="1.0" encoding="UTF-8"?>
<!DOCTYPE html PUBLIC "-//W3C//DTD XHTML 1.0 Transitional//EN"
"http://www.w3.org/TR/xhtml1/DTD/xhtml1-transitional.dtd">
<html xmlns="http://www.w3.org/1999/xhtml" >
<head>
<title>Sample Heading Tags</title>
</head>
<body>
  <h1>Heading Level 1</h1>
  <p>This is a sample paragraph about HTML and XHTML. XHTML is the newest version
     of HTML. XHTML uses the tags and attributes of HTML along with the syntax of
     XML.</p>
```

continues

```
    <h2>Heading Level 2</h2>
    <h3>Heading Level 3</h3>
    <h4>Heading Level 4</h4>
    <h5>Heading Level 5</h5>
    <h6>Heading Level 6</h6>
</body>
</html>
```

Launch a browser such as Internet Explorer or Netscape to test your page. It should look similar to Figure 2.7 and to the solution on the student disk (Chapter2/heading2.htm).

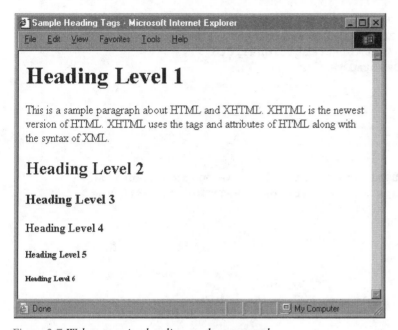

Figure 2.7 *Web page using headings and a paragraph*

Notice how the text wraps automatically as you resize your browser window. If you wanted to have the second sentence in the paragraph begin on its own line, you'd need to add a line break. The next section describes **
**, *the tag used to create line breaks.*

The Line Break Tag

The line break tag, **
**, is used to force a new line when the text on the web page document is displayed by a browser. The line break tag is used alone—it is not used as a pair of opening and closing tags. It is considered to be a stand-alone or self-contained tag. If you were using HTML syntax, the line break tag would be coded as **
**. Because you are using XHTML (which follows XML syntax), the line break tag is coded as **
** (the ending **/>** indicates a self-contained tag).

Open your heading2.htm file in Notepad. Place your cursor after the first sentence in the paragraph (after "This is a sample paragraph about HTML and XHTML."). Press the Enter key. Save your page. Test your page in a browser and notice that even though your source code showed the "This is a sample paragraph about HTML and XHTML." sentence on its own line, the browser did not render it that way—a **
** *tag is needed. Open the heading2.htm file in Notepad and add a* **
** *tag after the first sentence in the paragraph. Save your page as heading3.htm. Your source code should look similar to the following. The* **
** *tag is shown in green.*

```
<?xml version="1.0" encoding="UTF-8"?>
<!DOCTYPE html PUBLIC "-//W3C//DTD XHTML 1.0 Transitional//EN"
   "http://www.w3.org/TR/xhtml1/DTD/xhtml1-transitional.dtd">
<html xmlns="http://www.w3.org/1999/xhtml">
<head>
<title>Sample Heading Tags</title>
</head>
<body>
  <h1>Heading Level 1</h1>
  <p>
  This is a sample paragraph about HTML and XHTML.<br /> XHTML is the newest
  version of HTML. XHTML uses the tags and attributes of HTML along with the
  syntax of XML.</p>
  <h2>Heading Level 2</h2>
  <h3>Heading Level 3</h3>
  <h4>Heading Level 4</h4>
  <h5>Heading Level 5</h5>
  <h6>Heading Level 6</h6>
</body>
</html>
```

Launch a browser such as Internet Explorer or Netscape to test your page. It should look similar to the one shown in Figure 2.8. You can compare your work with the solution found on the student disk (Chapter2/heading3.htm).

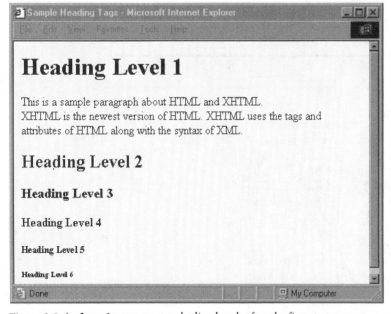

Figure 2.8 *A* **
** *tag creates the line break after the first sentence.*

As you tested your web pages, you may have noticed that the headings and text begin near the left margin. This is called **left alignment** and is the default alignment for web pages. There are times when you want a paragraph or heading to be centered or right-justified. The align attribute can be used for this.

To center an element on a web page use the attribute `align="center"`. To right-justify an element on a web page, use `align="right"`. The default alignment is left. The align attribute can be used with a number of tags, including the paragraph (`<p>`) and heading (`<h1>` through `<h6>`) tags.

Open your heading3.htm file in Notepad. Modify the heading to be centered. Change the `<h1>` tag to `<h1 align="center">` but do not change the closing `</h1>` tag. Also modify the paragraph to be centered on the web page. Change the `<p>` tag to `<p align="center">`, but do not change the closing `</p>` tag. Save your page as heading4.htm and test it in a browser. Your page should look similar to Figure 2.9. You can compare your work with the solution found on the student disk (Chapter2/ heading4.htm).

Why does my web page still look the same?

Often students make changes to a web page but get frustrated because their browser shows an older version of the page. Here are some troubleshooting tips to follow when you know you modified your web page but the changes do not show up in the browser.

1. Make sure you save your page after you make the changes.
2. Verify the location that you are saving your page to—the floppy drive, the hard drive, a particular folder.
3. Verify the location that your browser is requesting the page from—the floppy drive, the hard drive, a folder.
4. Be sure to click the Refresh or Reload button on your browser.

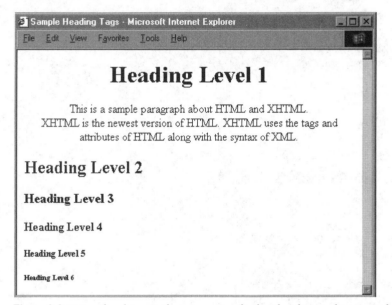

Figure 2.9 *Using the align attribute to center the first heading and paragraph.*

XHTML—List Basics

Lists are used on web pages to organize information. When writing for the web, remember that headings and bulleted lists make your pages clear and easy to read. XHTML can be used to create three types of lists: definition lists, ordered lists, and unordered lists.

Definition Lists

Definition lists help to organize terms and their definitions. The terms stand out and their definitions can be as long as needed to convey your message.

Definition lists are also handy for organizing Frequently Asked Questions (FAQs) and their answers. The questions and answers are offset with indentation. Each defined term begins on its own line at the margin. Each definition begins on its own line and is indented. See Figure 2.10 for an example of a web page that uses a definition list.

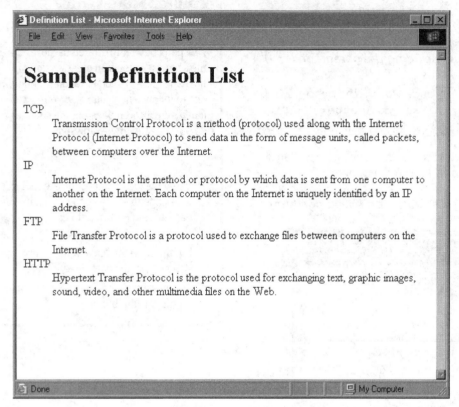

Figure 2.10 *Sample definitionlist.htm*

Any type of information that consists of a number of corresponding terms and longer descriptions is well suited to being organized in a definition list.

Definition lists begin with the **<dl>** and end with the **</dl>** tag. Each defined term in the list begins with the **<dt>** tag and ends with the **</dt>** tag. Each term definition (data definition) begins with the **<dd>** tag and ends with the **</dd>** tag. A definition list is created in Hands-On Practice 2.5.

Hands-On Practice 2.5

Open a new file in Notepad. Use the following sample code to create a definition list.

```
<?xml version="1.0" encoding="UTF-8"?>
<!DOCTYPE html PUBLIC "-//W3C//DTD XHTML 1.0 Transitional//EN"
    "http://www.w3.org/TR/xhtml1/DTD/xhtml1-transitional.dtd">
<html xmlns="http://www.w3.org/1999/xhtml" >
<head>
<title>Definition List</title>
</head>
<body>
  <h1>Sample Definition List</h1>
  <dl>
```
continues

```
<dt>TCP</dt>
   <dd>Transmission Control Protocol is a method (protocol) used along with the
       Internet Protocol (IP) to send data in the form of message units, called
       packets, between computers over the Internet.</dd>
<dt>IP</dt>
   <dd>Internet Protocol is the method or protocol by which data is sent from one
       computer to another on the Internet. Each computer on the Internet is uniquely
       identified by an IP address.</dd>
<dt>FTP</dt>
   <dd>File Transfer Protocol is a protocol used to exchange files between
       computers on the Internet. </dd>
<dt>HTTP</dt>
   <dd>Hypertext Transfer Protocol is the protocol used for exchanging text,
       graphic images, sound, video, and other multimedia files on the Web.</dd>
  </dl>
</body>
</html>
```

*Save your file as definitionlist.htm and test it in a browser. Your
page should look similar to the one shown in Figure 2.10 and to the
solution on the student disk (Chapter2/definitionlist.htm). Don't
worry if the word wrap is a little different—the important
formatting is that each* `<dt>` *term should be on its own line and the
corresponding* `<dd>` *definition should be indented under it. Try
resizing your browser window and notice how the word wrap on
the definition text changes.*

Ordered Lists

Ordered lists use a numbering or lettering system to organize the information contained in the list. An ordered list can be organized by the use of
numerals (the default), uppercase letters, lowercase letters, uppercase roman
numerals, and lowercase roman numerals. See Figure 2.11 for a sample
ordered list.

```
Web Server Intro in an Ordered List

 1.  Apache Web Server
 2.  Microsoft IIS
 3.  iPlanet
```

Figure 2.11 *Sample ordered list*

Ordered lists begin with an `<ol>` tag and end with an `</ol>` tag. Each
list item begins with a `<li>` tag and ends with a `</li>` tag. The type
attribute can be used to change the symbol used for ordering the list. For
example, to create an ordered list organized by uppercase letters, use
`<ol type="A">`. Table 2.3 documents the type attribute and its values
for ordered lists.

Table 2.3 *Type Attributes for Ordered Lists*

Attribute	Value	Symbol
type	1	Numerals (the default)
	A	Uppercase letters
	a	Lowercase letters
	I	Roman numerals
	i	Lowercase roman numerals

The XHTML code to create the ordered list shown in Figure 2.11 is

```
Web Server Intro in an Ordered List
<ol>
   <li>Apache Web Server</li>
   <li>Microsoft IIS</li>
   <li>iPlanet</li>
</ol>
```

Unordered Lists

Unordered lists show a bullet point before each entry in the list. This bullet point can be one of several types: disc (the default), square, and circle. See Figure 2.12 for a sample unordered list.

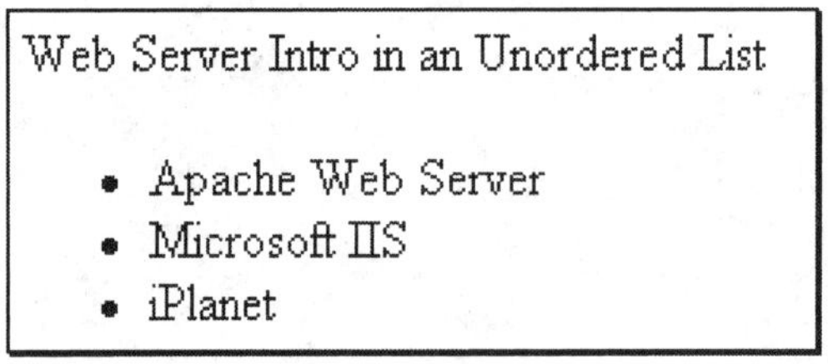

Web Server Intro in an Unordered List

- Apache Web Server
- Microsoft IIS
- iPlanet

Figure 2.12 *Sample unordered list*

Unordered lists begin with an **<ul>** tag and end with an **</ul>** tag. Each list item begins with a **<li>** tag and ends with a **</li>** tag. The type attribute can be used to change the type of bullet point. For example, to create an unordered list organized with square bullet points, use **<ul type="square">**. Table 2.4 documents the type attribute and its values for unordered lists.

Table 2.4 *Type Attributes for Unordered Lists*

Attribute	Value
type	disc (the default)
	square
	circle

The XHTML code to create the unordered list shown in Figure 2.12 is

```
Web Server Intro in an Unordered List
<ul>
   <li>Apache Web Server</li>
   <li>Microsoft IIS</li>
   <li>iPlanet</li>
</ul>
```

Open your heading4.htm file in Notepad. You will modify the text contained between the **<h2>** *tags, create an ordered list, modify the text contained within the* **<h3>** *tags, and create an unordered list. Use your mouse to select the text between the* **<h2>** *and* **</h2>** *tags. Replace the text with "Popular Web Servers". Now place your cursor after the* **</h2>** *tag and press Enter to create a blank line. Type the following code to create an ordered list:*

```
<ol>
  <li>Apache Web Server</li>
  <li>Microsoft IIS</li>
  <li>iPlanet</li>
</ol>
```

Use your mouse to select the text between the **<h3>** *and* **</h3>** *tags. Replace the text with "Popular Web Browsers". Position your cursor after the* **</h3>** *tag and press Enter to create a blank line. Type the following code to create an unordered list:*

```
<ul>
  <li>Internet Explorer</li>
  <li>Netscape</li>
  <li>Opera</li>
</ul>
```

Save your file as heading5.htm. Launch a browser and test your page. It should look similar to Figure 2.13. You can compare your work with the solution on the student disk (Chapter2/heading5.htm).

Figure 2.13 *Web page using both an ordered and unordered list*

Take a few minutes to experiment with the type attribute. Configure the unordered list to use square bullet points. Configure the ordered list to use uppercase letters instead of numerals. Save your page as heading6.htm. Test your page in a browser. It should look similar to Figure 2.14 and the solution on the student disk (Chapter2/heading6.htm).

Figure 2.14 *Using the type attribute with unordered and ordered lists*

XHTML—More Block-Level Tags

So far you have learned to create a basic web page using block-level elements such as the heading, paragraph, and list tags. In this section you will learn to indicate preformatted text and to indent text. These tags are considered to be block-level because they apply to blocks of text.

Preformatted Text

As you have been working through the examples you may have noticed that if you place one or more spaces in your web page XHTML source file, browsers display it as only one space. Also, even if your source file contains text on different lines, the browser will display them on a single line unless you use a **
** tag.

There are times when you need the browser to display *exactly* what you have typed in the web page XHTML source file, preserving spacing and line breaks. One way to accomplish this is to use the preformatted text tag. Preformatted text begins with the **<pre>** tag and ends with the **</pre>** tag. The preformatted text tag preserves your formatting and displays the text in a fixed-width or monospace font.

Experiment with the <pre> *tag by typing the same text with and without* <pre> *tags. Be careful to match the example as closely as possible. Launch Notepad or another text editor and type in the following XHTML:*

```
<?xml version="1.0" encoding="UTF-8"?>
<!DOCTYPE html PUBLIC "-//W3C//DTD XHTML 1.0 Transitional//EN"
    "http://www.w3.org/TR/xhtml1/DTD/xhtml1-transitional.dtd">
<html xmlns="http://www.w3.org/1999/xhtml" >
<head>
<title>Preformatted Text</title>
</head>
<body>
  <pre>
Markup Languages
   HTML       HyperText Markup Language
   DHTML      Dynamic HyperText Markup Language
   XHTML      eXtensible HyperText Markup Language
   XML        eXtensible Markup Language
  </pre>
  <p>Markup Languages
   HTML       HyperText Markup Language
   DHTML      Dynamic HyperText Markup Language
   XHTML      eXtensible HyperText Markup Language
   XML        eXtensible Markup Language </p>
</body>
</html>
```

Save your file as preformat.htm. Launch a browser and test your page. It should look similar to Figure 2.15. You can compare your work with the solution on the student disk (Chapter2/preformat.htm).

Notice that the spacing and line breaks were preserved for the preformatted text. The text that did not use the <pre> *tag wrapped in the browser window and had no special line breaks since none were in the source file.*

Students sometimes ask whether it is a good idea to use the <pre> *tag. The answer is—only when you absolutely need to. Some people find the monospace font to be ugly. However, it can be useful for listing programming or scripting code. There are other, more preferred methods of positioning information on a web page, including the use of tables (Chapter 3) and Cascading Style Sheets (Chapter 9).*

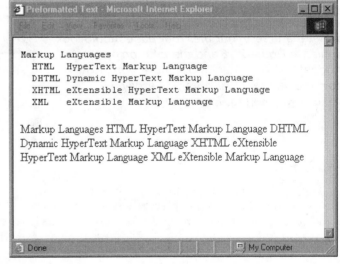

Figure 2.15 *Sample preformat.htm*

Indenting Text

Besides organizing text in paragraphs and lists, sometimes it is useful to indent a block of text for special emphasis. Items often found indented in this manner include quotations, lists, and instructions. A block of indented text begins with a **`<blockquote>`** tag and ends with a **`</blockquote>`** tag.

Hands-On Practice 2.8

Launch Notepad or another text editor and type in the following XHTML:

```
<?xml version="1.0" encoding="UTF-8"?>
<!DOCTYPE html PUBLIC "-//W3C//DTD XHTML 1.0 Transitional//EN"
    "http://www.w3.org/TR/xhtml1/DTD/xhtml1-transitional.dtd">
<html xmlns="http://www.w3.org/1999/xhtml" >
<head>
<title>Blockquote Example</title>
</head>
<body>
  <p>Markup Languages
    <blockquote>
    HTML HyperText Markup Language<br />
    DHTML Dynamic HyperText Markup Language<br />
    XHTML  eXtensible HyperText Markup Language<br />
    XML eXtensible Markup Language
    </blockquote>
  </p>
</body>
</html>
```

Save your file as blockquote.htm. Launch a browser and test your file. Your page should look similar to Figure 2.16 and the solution on the student disk (Chapter2/blockquote.htm). Notice how the text that was entered between **`<blockquote>`** *tags is indented.*

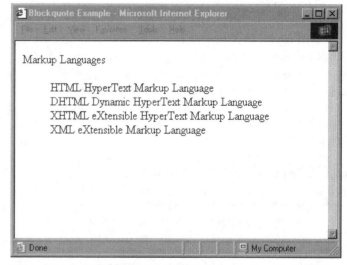

Figure 2.16 *Sample blockquote.htm*

XHTML—Text Formatting

Text can be formatted in various ways using the **<font>** tag, logical style tags, physical style tags, and special characters. These are considered to be text-level tags because they can apply to either a section of text or a single character of text. This is not the only method for formatting text; Cascading Style Sheets (introduced in Chapter 9) can also be used for this purpose.

The <font> Tag

The **<font>** tag allows you to configure the typeface, color, and size of the text between the **<font>** and **</font>** container tags. The use of this tag is deprecated in both HTML 4.01 and XHTML 1.0. A **deprecated tag** is still supported in the current version of the language but will not be supported in a future version of the language. The W3C recommends using Cascading Style Sheets (see Chapter 9) to format text instead of using the **<font>** tag. However, the **<font>** tag is still widely used on the Web, so you need to become familiar with it. Popular web authoring tools such as Microsoft FrontPage and Macromedia Dreamweaver generate web pages that contain the **<font>** tag.

The size attribute of the **<font>** tag sets the size of the text. Font size ranges from 1, the smallest, to 7, the largest, as shown in Figure 2.17. The size attribute of the **<font>** tag can also be set to values such as +1, -2, and so on. These set the size of the font relative to the default size, which is 3.

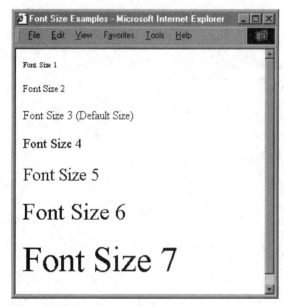

Figure 2.17 *Sample Font Sizes*

The color attribute of the **<font>** tag configures the text color using the same color values used to set the background page color in a **<body>** tag. See the color chart on the inside back cover for a list of values. When you view the color chart, notice that numeric values as well as color names can be used. The numeric values are listed in hexadecimal and correspond to the RGB (red, green, blue) values displayed by monitors. For example, **<font color="#FF0000">** and **<font color="red">** both cause the text to be displayed in the color red. Chapter 4 discusses the use of color and graphical elements on web pages.

The face attribute configures the typeface or font name to be used to display the text. Times New Roman is the default font face displayed by most web browsers. A web browser displays text using the fonts that have been installed on its computer. When a font is specified that is not installed on the web visitor's computer, the default font face is substituted. Table 2.5 shows font categories and some common font typefaces.

Table 2.5 *Common Fonts*

Font Category	Font Typeface
Serif	Century Schoolbook, Garamond, **Times New Roman**
Sans Serif	Arial, Verdana
Monospace	Courier New
Script	*Brush Script Mt.* Lucida Handwriting
Fantasy	Jokerman, Curlz MT

Hands-On Practice 2.9

Let's put it all together! Launch Notepad and open your blockquote.htm page. It should contain the following XHTML:

```
<?xml version="1.0" encoding="UTF-8"?>
<!DOCTYPE html PUBLIC "-//W3C//DTD XHTML 1.0 Transitional//EN"
    "http://www.w3.org/TR/xhtml11/DTD/xhtml11-transitional.dtd">
<html xmlns="http://www.w3.org/1999/xhtml" >
<head>
<title>Blockquote Example</title>
</head>
<body>
  <p>Markup Languages
    <blockquote>
    HTML HyperText Markup Language<br />
    DHTML Dynamic HyperText Markup Language<br />
    XHTML eXtensible HyperText Markup Language<br />
    XML eXtensible Markup Language
    </blockquote>
  </p>
</body>
</html>
```

Configure the text "Markup Languages" to be font color red (#FF0000), font size 4, and use Arial typeface. The opening <font> tag should look like this:

```
<font color="#FF0000" size="4" face="Arial">
```

Place the opening <font> tag before the "Markup Languages" text and a closing </font> tag after the text. The line should look like this:

```
<font color="#FF0000" size="4" face="Arial">Markup Languages</font>
```

Now configure the text within the `<blockquote>` *containers to be slightly smaller than the default text size by using the attribute* `size="-1"` *on the* `<font>` *tag. Remember to place a closing* `</font>` *tag before the closing* `</blockquote>` *tag. Your file should look similar to the this (new code is shown in green):*

```
<?xml version="1.0" encoding="UTF-8"?>
<!DOCTYPE html PUBLIC "-//W3C//DTD XHTML 1.0 Transitional//EN"
"http://www.w3.org/TR/xhtml1/DTD/xhtml1-transitional.dtd">
<html xmlns="http://www.w3.org/1999/xhtml" >
<head>
<title>Blockquote Example</title>
</head>
<body>
  <p> <font color="#FF0000" size="4" face="Arial">Markup Languages</font>
    <blockquote>
    <font size="-1">HTML HyperText Markup Language<br />
    DHTML Dynamic HyperText Markup Language<br />
    XHTML eXtensible HyperText Markup Language<br />
    XML eXtensible Markup Language </font>
    </blockquote>
  </p>
</body>
</html>
```

Save your file as blockquote2.htm and test it in a browser. Your page should look similar to the screen shot in Figure 2.18. You can compare your work with the solution on the student disk (Chapter2/blockquote2.htm).

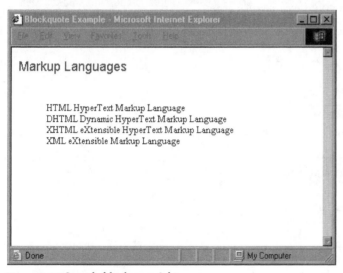

Figure 2.18 *Sample blockquote2.htm*

There are a number of tags that can be used to format text in addition to the font tag. In the next section you will read about logical style tags and physical style tags. Keep in mind that the W3C prefers the use of logical style tags instead of physical style tags.

Logical Style Tags

Logical style tags, sometimes called *phrase elements*, indicate the logical style used to display the text between the container tags. It is up to each browser to interpret that style. For example, the **<strong>** tag indicates that the text associated with it be displayed in a "strong" manner in relation to normal text on the page. Usually, but not always, the browser (or other user agent) will display **<strong>** text in bold. A screen reader might interpret **<strong>** text to indicate that the text should be more strongly spoken. With more and more devices used to access the web, the use of logical style tags instead of physical style tags (whenever possible) is preferred. Both are still used on the Web.

Note that all logical style tags are container tags—an opening and a closing tag should be used. For example, if you wanted the phone number in the following line to have a strong logical style

Call for a free quote for your web development needs: **888.555.5555**

the XHTML would look like

```
<p>Call for a free quote for your web development needs:
<strong>888.555.5555</strong></p>
```

Notice that the **<strong>** opening and closing tags are both contained within the paragraph tags (**<p>** and **</p>**). This XHTML code is nested properly, follows XML syntax, and is considered to be well-formed. An example of improper nesting is shown here:

```
<p>Call for a free quote for your web development needs:
<strong>888.555.5555</p></strong>
```

When improperly nested, the **<p>** and **<strong>** tag pairs overlap each other instead of being nested within each other. The section Comparison of HTML and XHTML in the *Web Developer's Handbook* contains a list of the key syntax rules of XML.

Table 2.6 lists logical style tags and examples of their use.

FAQ

Why do the displays look so similar?

As you look at Table 2.6, you may notice that some tags, such as **<cite>** and **<dfn>**, result in the same type of display (italics) as the **<em>** tag in today's browsers. These tags are logically describing the text as a citation or definition, but the physical display is usually italics in both cases. Cascading Style Sheets (see Chapter 9) are a better way to format the display of elements than logical style tags. However, logical style tags are preferred over physical style tags. If you feel that this a little confusing and that it seems as if there are too many tags with similar purposes, you are correct. Please keep in mind that Cascading Style Sheets can be used to format text instead of physical style and logical style tags and that is the preferred method. We introduce physical style and logical style tags in this chapter because they are still used on the Web.

Table 2.6 *Logical Style Tags*

Element	Example	Usage
<strong>	**strong** text	Causes text to be emphasized or to stand out from surrounding text. Usually displayed in bold.
<em>	*emphasized* text	Causes text to be emphasized in relation to other text on the page. Usually displayed in italics.
<cite>	*cite* text	Identifies a citation or reference. Usually displayed in italics.
<code>	`code` text	Identifies program code samples. Usually a fixed-space font.
<dfn>	*dfn* text	Identifies a definition of a word or term. Usually displayed in italics.
<kbd>	`kbd` text	Identifies user text to be typed. Usually a fixed-space font.
<samp>	`samp` text	Shows program sample output. Usually a fixed-space font.
<var>	*var* text	Identifies and displays a variable or program output. Usually displayed in italics.

Physical Style Tags

Physical style tags are sometimes called *font style elements* because they provide specific font instructions for the browser. This type of tag is still commonly used and often generated by web authoring tools such as Microsoft FrontPage and Macromedia Dreamweaver. Be aware that logical style tags and Cascading Style Sheets provide for a wider range of web access. The physical style tags are covered in this text because many existing web pages use these tags. Table 2.7 lists physical style tags with examples of their use.

Table 2.7 *Physical Style Tags*

Element	Example	Usage
`<b>`	**bold** text	Displays text as bold.
`<i>`	*emphasized* text	Displays text in italics.
`<big>`	big text	Displays text larger than normal size.
`<small>`	small text	Displays text smaller than normal size.
`<sub>`	sub text	Displays text smaller, below the baseline.
`<sup>`	sup text	Displays text smaller, above the baseline.
`<strike>`	~~strike~~ text	Displays text with a line through it.
`<u>`	u text	Displays text underlined. (Avoid using this because underlined text can be confused with hyperlinks.)
`<tt>`	`teletype` text	Displays text in teletype or fixed-space font.

You may have noticed that the `<strong>` logical style tag usually has the same effect as the `<b>` physical style tag. Also, the `<em>` logical style tag usually has the same effect as the `<i>` physical style tag. In order to create XHTML that describes logical styles instead of font instructions for browsers, use `<strong>` instead of `<b>` and use `<em>` instead of `<i>`. As you continue to study web development, you will learn about Cascading Style Sheets and their use in text formatting.

Special XHTML Characters

In order to use special characters such as quotation marks, greater and lesser than signs (`<`, `>`), and the copyright symbol (©) in your web document you need to use **special characters**, sometimes called *entity characters*. For example, if you wanted to include a copyright line on your page, such as

`© Copyright 2001 My Company. All rights reserved.`

You would use the special character `&copy;` to display the copyright symbol. The XHTML would look like

`<p>&copy; Copyright 2001 My Company. All rights reserved.</p>`

Another special character that is useful to know is ` `, which stands for nonbreaking space. You may have noticed that web browsers treat multiple spaces as a single space. If you need a small number of spaces in your text, you may use the ** ** multiple times to indicate multiple blank spaces. This is acceptable if you just need to tweak the position of an element a little. If you find yourself with web pages containing many ** ** special characters in a row, you should use a different method of aligning your page, such as a table or Cascading Style Sheets.

See the Special Characters section in the *Web Developer's Handbook* for a description of Special Characters and their codes.

Hands-On Practice 2.10

The screen shot in Figure 2.19 shows the web page you will be creating.

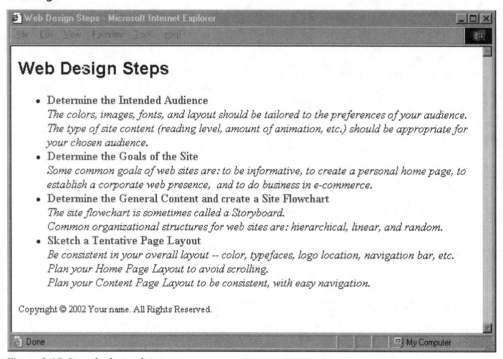

Figure 2.19 *Sample design.htm*

Open Notepad to create the file and save it as design.htm. If it helps, open one of your previous web pages with Notepad to get started. If you do this, be sure to use Save As and give your edited file the name design.htm.

Hints: Use Heading Level 2 and an Arial font for the heading. Create an unordered list. The font color of the bulleted items in the list is a shade of blue (#003366). The bulleted items should be strong, or stand out from the rest of the text. Use line break tags when needed to begin a new line within each bulleted item. The text under each bulleted item should be emphasized. Don't worry if your text wraps a little differently—your screen resolution or browser window size may be different. The line containing the copyright information should be smaller than the rest of the text. Use the special character for copyright.

How did you do? Compare your work to the sample on the student disk (Chapter2/design.htm).

Chapter 2 Review

Summary

This chapter provided an introduction to XHTML. It began with an introduction to HTML, discussed the transition to XHTML, continued with the anatomy of a web page, and introduced text-level and block-level formatting. If you worked along with the samples in the chapter, you should be ready to create some web pages on your own. The Hands-On exercises and Web Case Studies that follow will provide some practice.

Visit the course Web site at http://www.webdevfoundations.net for the links listed in this chapter and for updated information.

Review Questions

Multiple Choice

1. Which tag pair is used to create a new paragraph?
   a. `<new paragraph>    </new paragraph>`
   b. `<paragraph>  </paragraph>`
   c. `<p>  </p>`
   d. `<para>   </para>`

2. Which tag pair is used to create the smallest heading?
   a. `<h1>  </h1>`
   b. `<h9>  </h9>`
   c. `<h type="smallest"> </h>`
   d. `<h6>  </h6>`

3. Which tag is used to force the browser to display the next text or element on a new line?
   a. `<new line />`   c. `<br />`
   b. `<nl />`   d. `<line />`

4. Which attribute can be used to center an element (such as a paragraph) on a web page?
   a. format   c. justify
   b. align   d. none of the above

5. The default alignment for headings and paragraphs is
   a. center
   b. left
   c. right
   d. wherever you type them in the source code

6. Which type of XHTML list will automatically number the items for you?
   a. numbered list   c. unordered list
   b. ordered list   d. definition list

7. Which type of XHTML list contains bullet points?
   a. bullet list   c. unordered list
   b. ordered list   d. definition list

8. Which type of XHTML list would be best for displaying a glossary?
   - a. bullet list
   - b. ordered list
   - c. unordered list
   - d. definition list

9. Which tag pair contains the items in an ordered or unordered list?
   - a. `<item>` `</item>`
   - b. `<li>` `</li>`
   - c. `<dd>` `</dd>`
   - d. none of the above

10. Which tag pair contains the data description or data definition in a definition list?
    - a. `<item>` `</item>`
    - b. `<li>` `</li>`
    - c. `<dd>` `</dd>`
    - d. none of the above

Fill in the Blank

11. The `<blockquote>` tag is used to _____.

12. _____ can be used to display characters such as the coypright symbol.

13. To preserve the spacing and line breaks in your text, use the _____ tag.

14. The _____ is the preferred tag to use when you need to emphasize text.

15. The _____ is used to place a nonbreaking space on a web page.

Apply Your Knowledge

1. **Predict the Result.** Draw and write a brief description of the web page that will be created with the following XHTML code:

```
<?xml version="1.0" encoding="UTF-8"?>
<!DOCTYPE html PUBLIC "-//W3C//DTD XHTML 1.0 Transitional//EN"
"http://www.w3.org/TR/xhtml1/DTD/xhtml1-transitional.dtd">
<html xmlns="http://www.w3.org/1999/xhtml" >
<head>
<title>Predict the Result</title>
</head>
<body>
  <h1><em>Favorite Colors</em></h1>
  <ol>
   <li><font color="#FF0000">Red</font></li>
   <li><font color="#0000FF">Blue</font></li>
   <li><font color="#00FF00">Green</font></li>
  </ol>
  <p align="center">
  <font size="1">Copyright &copy; 2002 Your name
    here</font></p>
</body>
</html>
```

2. **Fill in the Missing Code.** This web page should display a heading and a definition list, but some XHTML tags, indicated by **<_>** are missing. Fill in the missing code.

```
<?xml version="1.0" encoding="UTF-8"?>
<!DOCTYPE html PUBLIC "-//W3C//DTD XHTML 1.0 Transitional//EN"
   "http://www.w3.org/TR/xhtml1/DTD/xhtml1-transitional.dtd">
<html xmlns="http://www.w3.org/1999/xhtml" >
<head>
<title>Door County Wild Flowers</title>
</head>
<body>
  <_>Door County Wild Flowers<_>
  <dl>
    <dt>Trillium<_>
      <_>This white flower blooms from April through June in wooded areas.<_>
    <_>Lady Slipper<_>
      <_>This yellow orchid blooms in June in wooded areas.</dd>
  <_>
</body>
</html>
```

3. **Find the Error**. Why won't this page display in a browser?

```
<?xml version="1.0" encoding="UTF-8"?>
<!DOCTYPE html PUBLIC "-//W3C//DTD XHTML 1.0 Transitional//EN"
   "http://www.w3.org/TR/xhtml1/DTD/xhtml1-transitional.dtd">
<html xmlns="http://www.w3.org/1999/xhtml" >
<head>
<title>Find the Error<title>
</head>
<body>
  <h1>Why don't I display? </h1>
</body>
</html>
```

Hands-On Exercises

1. Write the **<body>** tag that will set the background color to #0000FF and set the text color to #FFFFFF.

2. Create a web page about your favorite movie. Include the name of the movie, the actors and actresses, and a brief description of the movie. Use an unordered list to organize the names of the actors and actresses. Save the page as movie.htm. Open your file in Notepad and print the source code for the page. Display your page in a browser and print the page. Hand in both printouts to your instructor.

3. Create a web page that uses a definition list to display three network protocols (see Chapter 1) and their descriptions. Add an appropriate heading to the page. Save the page as network.htm. Open your file in Notepad and print the source code for the page. Display your page in a browser and print the page. Hand in both printouts to your instructor.

4. Create a web page about your favorite musical group. Include the name of the group, the individuals in the group, your favorite three (or fewer if the group is new) CD releases, and a brief review of each CD.
   - Use an unordered list to organize the names of the individuals.
   - Use a definition list for the names of the CDs and your reviews.

Save the page as band.htm. Open your file in Notepad and print the source code for the page. Display your page in a browser and print the page. Hand in both printouts to your instructor.

5. Create a web page about your favorite recipe. Use an unordered list for the ingredients and an ordered list to describe the steps needed to prepare the food. Save the page as recipe.htm. Open your file in Notepad and print the source code for the page. Display your page in a browser and print the page. Hand in both printouts to your instructor.

Web Site Case Study

Each of these case studies continues throughout most of the text. This chapter introduces the web site scenario, presents the site map or storyboard, and directs you to create a home page for the site.

A. JavaJam Coffee House

Julio Perez is the owner of the JavaJam Coffee House. This is a gourmet coffee shop that serves snacks, coffee, tea, and soft drinks. Local folk music performances and poetry readings are held a few nights during the week. The customers of JavaJam are mainly college students and young professionals. Julio would like a web presence for his shop that will display the services and provide a calendar for the performances. He would like a home page, menu page, performance schedule page, and a page that lists job opportunities.

A site map for the JavaJam Coffee House web is shown in Figure 2.20.

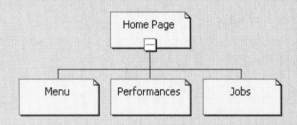

Figure 2.20 *JavaJam site map*

The site map describes the architecture of the web site, a Home page with three main sub-pages: Menu, Performance, and Jobs.

Figure 2.21 displays a sample layout for the Home page of the site. It contains a site logo, area for site content, navigation area, and footer area for copyright information.

Figure 2.21 *JavaJam page layout*

Hands-On Practice Case

You will use Notepad to create a sample Home page for the JavaJam Coffee House web site. The sample page is shown in Figure 2.22.

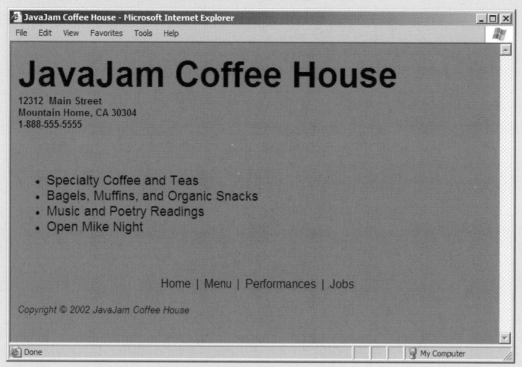

Figure 2.22 *JavaJam Home Page*

Create a folder called javajam on your floppy disk. Launch Notepad and create a web page with the following specifications:

- **Web page:** Use a descriptive page title—the company name is a good choice for a business web site. Choose a background color for the page. If you wish, choose a text color also.

- **Heading area:** Use `<h1>` for the "JavaJam Coffee House" heading. Decide on a font face and font color for the heading. Place the phone number and address in this area also (use a smaller font size for these).

- **Content:** Place the following content in an unordered list:
  "Specialty Coffees and Teas"
  "Bagels, Muffins, and Organic Snacks"
  "Music and Poetry Readings"
  "Open Mike Nights"

- **Navigation:** Place the following text on one line:
  "Home | Menu | Entertainment | Jobs"

- **Footer:** Place the following copyright information in a small font size and emphasized font style.
  "Copyright © 2002 Java Jam Coffee House"

• **Hints:** Yes, the sample page in Figure 2.22 is a little sparse, but don't worry, as you advance your pages will look more professional. White space, or blank space, on the page can be added with **`<br />`** tags where needed. The sample uses a background color of #999966. The font face is set to Arial. The font size is set to 7 on the heading area, 4 on the unordered list, and 1 on the copyright footer. The navigation area is centered. Don't worry if your page does not look exactly the same as the sample. Your goal at this point should be to practice with XHTML.

Save your page in the javajam folder and name it index.htm.

B. Fish Creek Animal Hospital

Magda Patel is a veterinarian and owner of the Fish Creek Animal Hospital. Her customers are local pet owners who range in age from children to senior citizens. Magda would like a web site to provide information to her current and potential customers. She has requested a home page, a page that lists services, an "Ask the Vet" page, and a contact page.

A site map for the Fish Creek Animal Hospital web site is shown in Figure 2.23.

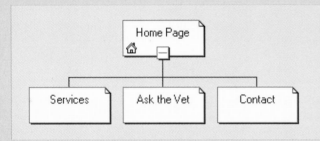

Figure 2.23 *Fish Creek site map*

The site map describes the architecture of the web site, a Home page with three main sub-pages: Services, Ask the Vet, and Contact.

Figure 2.24 illustrates a sample layout for the Home page of the site. It contains a site logo, navigation area, area for site content, and footer area for copyright information.

Figure 2.24 *Page layout*

Hands-On Practice Case

You will use Notepad to create a sample home page for the Fish Creek Animal Hospital web site. The sample page is shown in Figure 2.25.

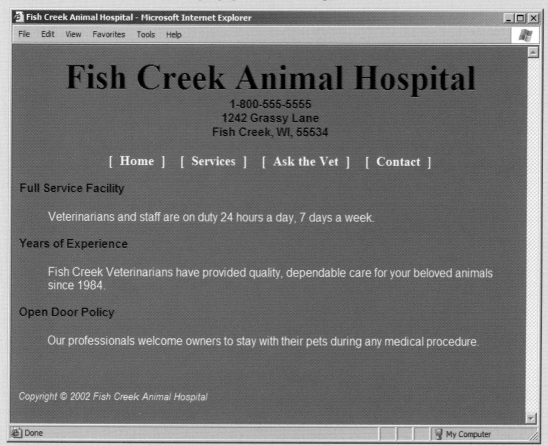

Figure 2.25 *Fish Creek Home page*

Create a folder called fishcreek on your floppy disk. Launch Notepad and create a web page with the following specifications:

- **Web page:** Use a descriptive page title—the company name is a good choice for a business web site. Choose a background color for the page. If you wish, choose a text color also.

- **Heading area:** Use **<h1>** for the "Fish Creek Animal Hospital" heading area. Decide on a font face and font color for the heading. Place the phone number and address in this area also (use a smaller font size for these). Hint: This area is centered in the sample.

- **Navigation:** Place the following text on one line.
  "[Home]   [Services]   [Ask the Vet]   [Contact]"

- **Content:** Place the following content in a definition list format:
  "Full Service Facility
  Veterinarians and staff are on duty 24 hours a day, 7 days a week.
  Years of Experience
  Fish Creek Veterinarians have provided quality, dependable care for your beloved animals since 1984.
  Open Door Policy
  Our professionals welcome owners to stay with their pets during any medical procedure."

- **Footer:** Place the following copyright information in a small font size and using an emphasized font style.
  "Copyright © 2002 Fish Creek Animal Hospital"

- **Hints:** As you gain practice and learn more techniques, your pages will look more professional. Don't worry if this version of the home page (Figure 2.25) seems plain or too simple. White space, or blank space, on the page can be added with **
** tags where needed. The sample uses a background color of #6699FF and a text color of #FFFFFF. The text color in the heading area is set to #000000. The content area and the address area in the heading area use Arial font. The font size is set to 7 on the heading, 3 on the address portion of the heading, and 1 on the copyright footer. The heading and navigation areas are centered. The defined terms (**<dt>** elements) use **<strong>**. Don't worry if your page does not look exactly the same as the sample. Your goal at this point should be to practice with XHTML.

Save your page in the fishcreek folder and name it index.htm.

C. Pete the Painter

Pete Johnson is an independent home painter and decorator. He would like to have a web site to advertise his business. His clients are mainly homeowners in the middle-class suburbs of a large city. They range in age from thirties to fifties. Pete would like a site that contains a home page, a page that lists services, a free estimates page, and a testimonial page.

A site map for "Pete the Painter" is shown in Figure 2.26.

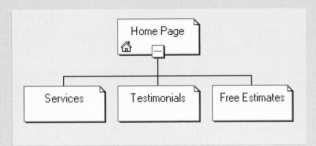

Figure 2.26 *Pete the Painter site map*

The site map describes the architecture of the web site, a Home page with three main sub-pages: Services, Testimonials, and Free Estimates.

Figure 2.24 displays a sample layout for the Home page of the site. It contains a site logo, navigation area, area for site content, and footer area for copyright information.

Hands-On Practice Case

You will use Notepad to create a sample Home page for the Pete the Painter web site. A screen shot of the sample page is shown in Figure 2.27.

Figure 2.27 *Pete the Painter Home page*

Create a folder called painter on your floppy disk. Launch Notepad and create a web page with the following specifications:

- **Web page:** Use a descriptive page title—the company name is a good choice for a business web site. Choose a background color for the page. If you wish, choose a text color also.

- **Heading area:** Use **<h2>** for the "Pete the Painter" heading. Decide on a font face and font color for the heading area. The sample uses the color #336600. Emphasize the motto "Serving the Northwest Chicago Suburbs since 1986". Place the phone number in this area also.

- **Navigation:** Place the following text on one line.

  "Home | Services | Testimonials | Free Estimate"

- **Content:** Include the following text:

  "Pete's Design Specialists will work with you to create the home of your dreams. Specializing in:"
  (Use the **<blockquote>** tag to indent the following block of text.)
  "Interior Painting
  Exterior Painting
  Wallpaper Removal
  Wallpaper Installation
  Drywall"

- **Footer:** Place the following copyright information in a small font size, using an emphasized font style.
  "Copyright © 2002 Pete the Painter"

- **Hints:** The sample page in Figure 2.27 may seem a little sparse, but don't worry, as you gain experience and learn to use more advanced techniques, your pages will look more professional. White space, or blank space, on the page can be added with **
** tags where needed. The sample uses a background color of #FFFFFF. The text in the heading area is set to #336600. The navigation area and content area use Arial font. The font size is set to 7 on the first line of the heading area, 4 in the navigation area, and 1 on the copyright footer. Your page does not need to look exactly the same as the sample. Your goal at this point should be to practice and get comfortable with XHTML.

Save your page in the painter folder and name it index.htm.

Web Research

A. There are many HTML and XHTML tutorials on the Web. Use your favorite search engine to discover them. Choose two that were helpful to you. For each, print out the home page or other pertinent page and create a web page that contains the answers to the following questions.

1. What is the URL of the web site?
2. Is the tutorial geared toward the beginner level, intermediate level, or both levels?
3. Would you recommend this site to others? Why or why not?
4. List one or two concepts that you learned from this tutorial.

Open your file in Notepad and print the source code for the page. (*Hint: Select File, select Print.*) Display your page in a browser and print the page. Hand in both printouts to your instructor.

B. You have begun to learn the syntax of XHTML. However, coding alone does not make a web page—design is very important. Surf the Web and find two web pages—one that is appealing to you and one that is not appealing to you. Print out each page. Create a web page that answers the following questions for each of your examples.

1. What is the URL of the web site?
2. Is this page appealing or unappealing? List three reasons for your answer.
3. If this page is unappealing, what would you do to improve it?

Open your file in Notepad and print the source code for the page. Display your page in a browser and print the page. Hand in both printouts to your instructor.

Chapter Review Answers

1. c
2. d
3. c
4. b
5. b
6. b
7. c
8. d
9. b
10. c
11. indent text
12. special characters
13. `<pre>`
14. `<em>`
15. ` `

Chapter 3

XHTML Links and Tables

Hyperlinks are what makes the Web a web of interconnected resources. Hyperlinks link to other web sites, to other pages on a site, and even within a single web page document. As you create more sophisticated web pages you will often need to organize links and information. Tables can be used to organize web page content. They can also be used to provide structure and format an entire web page.

Learning Outcomes

In this chapter, you will learn how to

▶ Use the anchor tag to link from page to page

▶ Create absolute and relative links

▶ Make a link which opens a new browser window

▶ Build links internal to the same page

▶ Generate e-mail links

▶ Create a table on a web page

▶ Apply attributes to format tables, table rows, and table cells

▶ Format an entire web page within a table

XHTML—Hyperlinks

The Anchor Tag

The **anchor tag** can be used to specify a hyperlink reference (href) to a web page you want to display. The XHTML element **<a>** is the anchor tag. Each hyperlink begins with an **<a>** tag and ends with an **</a>** tag. The opening and closing anchor tags contain or surround the text to click on to perform the hyperlink.

You have probably seen many links on the Web but may have never thought about how they are created. To create an absolute link to a web site such as Yahoo!, you would create a hyperlink with the URL for Yahoo! for the value of the href attribute:

```
<a href="http://yahoo.com">Yahoo!</a>
```

"Yahoo!", the text contained between the anchor tags, is displayed in the browser window. By default, this text is underlined and blue. Figure 3.1 shows an example of a hyperlink to the Yahoo! web site in a browser.

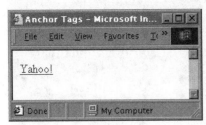

Figure 3.1 *A hyperlink to Yahoo's web site*

Absolute and Relative Links

The link to Yahoo! you just created is an **absolute link**. Notice that the XHTML code for the link indicates the protocol being used, http://, and continues with the domain name, yahoo.com. This indicates the *absolute* location of the web resource. Use absolute links when you are creating links to other web sites.

When you need to link to web pages within your site, use a **relative link**. This link does not begin with http://. It only contains the file name or file name and folder of the web page you want to display. The link location is in relation to or *relative* to the page currently being displayed. For example, if you had a home page called index.htm and wanted to link to a page with your resume (called resume.htm), the XHTML for the relative link would be: **<a href="resume.htm">My Resume</a>**

Hands-On Practice 3.1

The best way to learn XHTML is by writing it. Let's experiment with the anchor tag and create a sample web site to use to practice creating hyperlinks.

Use Windows Explorer to create a new folder called mywebsite. Launch Windows Explorer by selecting Start, Programs, Windows Explorer with your pointing (mouse) cursor. Click on your floppy drive to select it. Select File, New, Folder. See the screen shot in Figure 3.2.

Figure 3.2 *Using Windows Explorer to create a new folder*

Name your folder mywebsite. This site could be a personal web site. It will contain a Home page called index.htm and two content pages called resume.htm and favorites.htm. A sample site map that was created using Macromedia Dreamweaver (Figure 3.3) shows the architecture of the site—a Home page with major links to two pages (resume.htm and favorites.htm).

Now create the Home page for your mywebsite web site. Launch Notepad or another text editor and type in the tags found on every web page (xml declarative, doctype, html, head, title, body). In the body of the Web page create:

- *A heading, "My Web Site"*
- *An absolute link to "Yahoo!"*
- *An absolute link to the web site of your school*
- *A relative link to resume.htm*
- *A relative link to favorites.htm*

Save your page as index.htm in the mywebsite folder. Display your page in a browser. It should look similar to the page shown in Figure 3.4. Compare your work to the sample on the student disk (Chapter3/3.1/index.htm). Hint: Check the Special Characters section in the Web Developer's Handbook for the XHTML code for the "é".

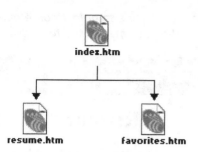

Figure 3.3 *Site map*

Figure 3.4 *Sample index.htm*

Test your page by clicking on each link. When you click the absolute links to Yahoo! and your school you should see those pages displayed if you are connected to the Internet. The relative links should not work yet—let's create those pages next.

Create the resume.htm page. Launch Notepad or another text editor and type in the tags found on every web page (XML directive, doctype, html, head, title, body). In the body of the web page place the following:

- *A heading of "Resumé"*
- *Some text that describes your job objective*
- *A navigation bar that contains a relative link to the home page (index.htm), and a relative link to the favorites page (favorites.htm)*

What if my absolute links don't work?

Check the following:

- Are you currently connected to the Internet?
- Are you certain that you spelled the URLs of the web sites correctly?
- Did you begin with "http://"?
- *Hint:* When you are about to put an absolute link in a web page, display the web site in a browser, then copy and paste the URL. Don't rely on typing the URL accurately.

See Figure 3.5 for a sample Resumé page. Save your Resumé page as resume.htm your mywebsite folder.

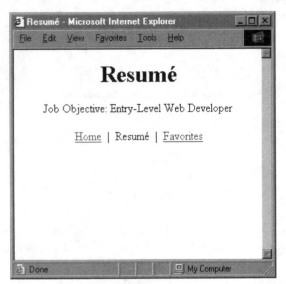

Figure 3.5 *Sample resume.htm*

Test your index.htm page again. This time when you click on the Resumé link, your new page should display. Use the Home link on your resume.htm page to redisplay your Home page.

Create the favorites.htm page. Launch Notepad or another text editor and type in the tags found on every web page (XML directive, doctype, html, head, title, body). In the body of the web page place the following:

* *A heading of "Favorite Sites"*

* *An unordered list that contains the categories "Hobbies", "XHTML", "JavaScript", and "Professional Groups"*

* *A navigation bar that contains a relative link to the Home page (index.htm) and a relative link to the Resumé page (resume.htm).*

See Figure 3.6 for a sample Favorites page. Save your page as favorites.htm in your mywebsite folder.

Figure 3.6 *Sample favorites.htm*

What if my relative links don't work?

Check the following:

* Did you save your index.htm and resume.htm pages in your mywebsite folder?

* Did you save the files with the names as requested? Use Windows Explorer or My Computer to verify the actual names of the files you saved.

* Did you type the file names correctly in the link's href property? Check for typographical errors.

* On many operating systems such as UNIX, file name upper and lowercases matters—make sure that the file name and the reference to it are in the same case. It's a good practice to always use lowercase for file names used on the Web.

* *Hint:* Tiny details such as spelling file names correctly and consistently are very important in web development.

Test your index.htm page again and try the links between the Home page, Resumé page, and Favorites pages. Don't worry if the links don't work perfectly the first time. If you have problems, carefully examine the source code of the pages and verify the existence of the files using Windows Explorer.

Can you share some tips on using links?

- Make your link names descriptive and brief to minimize possible confusion.
- Avoid using the phrase "Click here for" in your links. In the beginning of the Web, this phrase was needed because clicking on links was a new experience for Web users. Now that the Web is an everyday part of our lives, this phrase seems slightly redundant and almost archaic.
- It is more difficult to read web pages than printed pages. Try not to bury links in large blocks of text—use bullet points or definition lists.
- Be careful when linking to external web sites. The Web is dynamic and there is a distinct possibility that the external site may change the name of the page or even delete the page. If this happens, your link will be broken.

Opening a Link in a New Browser Window

The **target attribute** can be used on the anchor tag to open a link in a new browser window. For example,

```
<a href="http://yahoo.com" target="_blank">Yahoo!</a>
```

will open Yahoo!'s home page in a new window. Why not create a test page and try it out? The target attribute **"_blank"** is one of several values that can be used. Later, when the topic of frames is covered in Chapter 5, you will learn additional uses of the target attribute.

By now you should be comfortable with absolute and relative hyperlinks. You may have noticed that these links display the top of the web page. Sometimes it is helpful to link to an exact position on a web page instead of to the top of the page; internal links are used for this function.

Internal Links

Internal links are sometimes called *bookmarks, named anchors*, or *named fragments*. They can be very useful when you need to provide the capability to link to a specific portion of a web page. Lists of frequently asked questions (FAQs) often use this technique.

When using internal links you need to remember that there are two components:

1. The anchor tag that identifies a bookmark or named fragment of a web page. This requires two attributes: the id attribute (supported by newer XHTML-compliant browsers) and the name attribute (used for compatibility with old browsers such as Netscape 4).
2. The anchor tag that links to the bookmark or named fragment of a web page. This uses the href attribute.

To see how these two components are used, consider that Web pages sometimes have links back to the top of a page. This is accomplished in two steps:

1. Type an anchor tag that uses the id and name attributes on a blank line under the **<body>** tag. The value of the id and name attributes should describe the bookmark. It's a good idea to use lowercase letters and avoid punctuation, symbols, and spaces. The value given to the id attribute should be unique within the document. Place the following code near the top of a web page document:

```
<a id="top" name="top"></a>
```

2. At the point of the page where you want to place a link to the top, type another anchor tag. Use the href attribute and place a "#" (sometimes called a hash mark) before the name of the bookmark. The XHTML for a hyperlink to the named anchor "top" is

```
<a href="#top">Top of Page</a>
```

The hash mark indicates that the browser should search for an anchor tag on the same page. If you forget to type the hash mark, the browser will not look on the same web page; it will look for an external file. A bookmark or named anchor does not have to be at the top of a page; it can be just about anywhere.

If you are coding *only* for an XHTML-compliant browser such as Internet Explorer 5 or Netscape 6, you can use the id attribute with any container tag, such as a **<p>** or a **<h1>**, to create a named fragment or bookmark. The top of page example uses the anchor tag to provide for backward compatibility with Netscape 4.

You will modify the favorites.htm web page created in earlier in this chapter in order to practice with internal links. A partial screen shot of the new version of favorites.htm is shown in Figure 3.7.

Launch Notepad and open your favorites.htm file. Examine Figure 3.7 and notice that the heading and unordered list are similar to the original version of favorites.htm. A definition list has been added below the unordered list. This definition list corresponds to topics described in the unordered list.

Modify the page as follows:

1. Create a definition list as indicated in Figure 3.7. The terms "Hobbies", "XHTML", "JavaScript", and "Professional Groups" are the defined terms (`<dt>` tags). Use the following list to create the data definition (`<dd>` tags) content for each. You may substitute your favorite sites for the URLs if you wish. The hyperlinks should all be absolute links.

- Hobbies
  Running
  http://www.runningnetwork.com
  Cooking
  http://www.cooking.com

- XHTML
  Tutorial
  http://www.htmlgoodies.com/
    tutors/xhtml.html
  Specification
  http://www.w3.org/TR/xhtml1/

- JavaScript
  Tutorial
  http://www.pageresource.com/jscript/index.html
  Specification
  http://docs.iplanet.com/docs/manuals/javascript.html#1.3

- Professional Groups
  HTML Writers Guild
  http://www.hwg.org
  The Internet Society
  http://www.isoc.org
  World Organization of Webmasters
  http://www.joinwow.org

2. Create a named anchor for each defined term (`<dt>` tag) in the definition list. For example, place

```
<a id="hobbies" name="hobbies"></a>
```

in front of the `<dt>` tag that corresponds to "Hobbies".

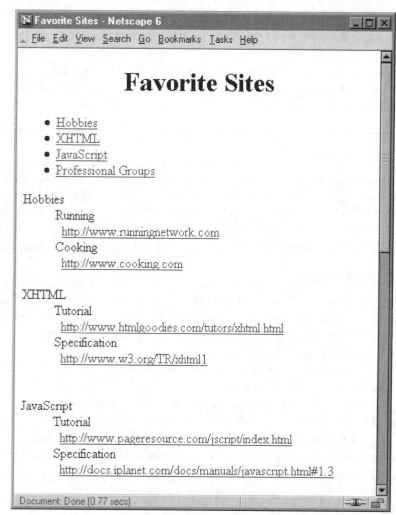

Figure 3.7 *Definition list and internal links added to favorites.htm*

3. *Add hyperlinks to the items in the unordered list so that each entry will link to its corresponding defined term.*

4. *Add a named fragment near the top of the page.*

5. *Near the bottom of the favorites.htm page add a link to the top of the page.*

Save the file in your mywebsite folder and test it. Compare your work with the sample found on the student disk (Chapter3/3.2/favorites.htm).

There may be times when you need to link to a named fragment on another web page. To accomplish this, place the internal link after the file name in the anchor tag. So, to link to the "Professional Groups" (given that it is a named fragment called "groups") from any other page on the mywebsite web, you could use the following XHTML

```
<a href="favorites.htm#groups">Professional Organizations</a>
```

E-mail Links

The anchor tag can also be used to create e-mail links. An e-mail link will automatically launch the default mail program configured for the browser. It is similar to an external hyperlink with two exceptions:

- It uses mailto: instead of http://.
- It launches the default e-mail application for the visitor's browser with your e-mail address as the recipient.

For example, to create an e-mail link to the e-mail address support@ webdevfoundations.net, code the following:

```
<a href="mailto:support@webdevfoundations.net">
Contact Tech Support at support@webdevfoundations.net</a>
```

It is good practice to place the e-mail address both on the web page and within the anchor tag. Not everyone has an e-mail program configured with his or her browser. By placing the e-mail address in both places, you increase usability for all your visitors.

Why don't some of my internal links seem to work?

A web browser cannot display less than the height of the browser window. If there is not enough space left on the bottom of the page below the named reference, it cannot be displayed at the top of the page. Try adding some blank lines (use the `<br />` tag) to the lower portion of the web page. Save your work and test your internal links again.

Open the Home page of your mywebsite web site and add an e-mail link to the bottom of the page. Save and test it in a browser. The page should look similar to Figure 3.8. Compare your work with the sample on the student disk (Chapter3/3.3/index.htm).

This section provided a quick introduction to the anchor tag. You should now be able to code different types of text hyperlinks: e-mail links, links internal to a web page, links relative to a web page, and absolute links to other web sites. As you continue to study, you will learn to use images as hyperlinks (Chapter 4) and to target specific windows and frames (Chapter 5). The next section introduces you to tables—a very powerful formatting and organizational element.

Figure 3.8 *E-mail link added to index.htm*

Using Tables on Web Pages

Tables are commonly used on web pages in two ways:
- To organize information
- To format the entire web page

Take a brief tour of some well-known sites, such as http://ebay.com, http://microsoft.com, and http://sun.com. Each site looks different, but they all use tables to help format their pages.

Overview of an XHTML Table

An XHTML table is composed of rows and columns, like a spreadsheet. Each individual table cell is at the intersection of a specific row and column. Each table begins with a **<table>** tag and ends with a **</table>** tag. There are a number of optional attributes for the **<table>** tag, such as border, width, height, cellspacing, and cellpadding. Each table row begins with a **<tr>** tag and ends with a **</tr>** tag. Each cell (table data) begins with a **<td>** tag and ends with a **</td>** tag. Be very careful to use opening and closing tags when working with tables. If you omit or misplace a tag the results are unpredictable and your page may not display at all. Figure 3.9 shows a sample table with three rows, four columns, and a border:

Name	Birthday	Phone	E-mail
Mary Morris	5/13	857-555-5555	mmorris@hotmail.com
James Baker	11/8	303-555-5555	jbaker@iname.com

Figure 3.9 *Table with three rows, four columns, and a border*

Here is the sample XHTML code for the table:

```
<table border="1">
  <tr>
    <td>Name</td>
    <td>Birthday</td>
    <td>Phone</td>
    <td>E-mail</td>
  </tr>
  <tr>
    <td>Mary Morris</td>
    <td>5/13</td>
    <td>857-555-5555</td>
    <td>mmorris@hotmail.com</td>
  </tr>
  <tr>
    <td>James Baker</td>
    <td>11/8</td>
    <td>303-555-5555</td>
    <td>jbaker@iname.com</td>
  </tr>
</table>
```

Notice how the table is described row by row. Also, each row is described cell by cell. This attention to detail is crucial to the successful use of tables.

What if you don't want a border on your table? The border attribute is optional. The table in Figure 3.9 used a border with its width set to 1. If you omit the border attribute, the table displays with no visible border. Figure 3.10 depicts the same table with the border attribute omitted.

Name	Birthday	Phone	E-mail
Mary Morris	5/13	857-555-5555	mmorris@hotmail.com
James Baker	11/8	303-555-5555	jbaker@iname.com

Figure 3.10 *Table with no visible border*

XHTML Table Headings

The `<th>`, or table heading, tag can be used to distinguish column headings from table content. Figure 3.11 shows a table that uses `<th>` tags.

Name	Birthday	Phone	E-mail
Mary Morris	5/13	857-555-5555	mmorris@hotmail.com
James Baker	11/8	303-555-5555	jbaker@iname.com

Figure 3.11 *Using `<th>` tags on a table*

The XHTML for this table is shown here. Notice that the first row uses `<th>` instead of `<td>` tags.

```
<table border="1">
  <tr>
    <th>Name</th>
    <th>Birthday</th>
    <th>Phone</th>
    <th>E-mail</th>
```

continues

```
  </tr>
  <tr>
    <td>Mary Morris</td>
    <td>5/13</td>
    <td>857-555-5555</td>
    <td>mmorris@hotmail.com</td>
  </tr>
  <tr>
    <td>James Baker</td>
    <td>11/8</td>
    <td>303-555-5555</td>
    <td>jbaker@iname.com</td>
  </tr>
</table>
```

XHTML Table Captions

The **<caption>** tag is often used with a table to describe its contents. The table shown in Figure 3.12 uses **<caption>** container tags to set the caption to Birthday List.

Birthday List

Name	Birthday	Phone	E-mail
Mary Morris	5/13	857-555-5555	mmorris@hotmail.com
James Baker	11/8	303-555-5555	jbaker@iname.com

Figure 3.12 *Birthday List is the caption for this table*

The XHTML for the table is

```
<table border="1">
<caption>Birthday List</caption>
  <tr>
    <th>Name</th>
    <th>Birthday</th>
    <th>Phone</th>
    <th>E-mail</th>
  </tr>
  <tr>
    <td>Mary Morris</td>
    <td>5/13</td>
    <td>857-555-5555</td>
    <td>mmorris@hotmail.com</td>
  </tr>
  <tr>
    <td>James Baker</td>
    <td>11/8</td>
    <td>303-555-5555</td>
    <td>jbaker@iname.com</td>
  </tr>
</table>
```

Notice how the **<caption>** tag was placed after the beginning **<table>** tag but before the first **<tr>** tag.

You will continue to work with the mywebsite web site. Launch Notepad or another text editor and open the resume.htm page from your mywebsite folder. Create a table of three rows and four columns that describes your education. The table headings should be "School Attended", "Years", "Subject", and "Degree Awarded". A sample page is shown in Figure 3.13. Save your page and test it in a browser.

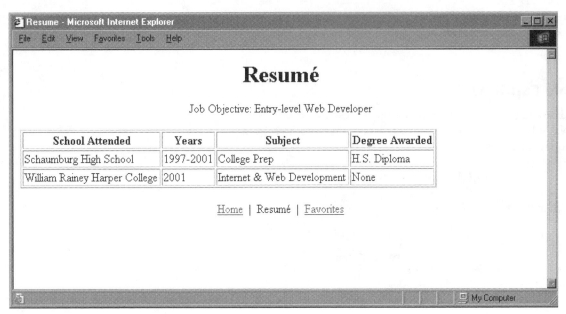

Figure 3.13 *Table added to resume.htm*

XHTML Table Attributes

Common **\<table\>** tag attributes include align, border, bordercolor, width, height, cellspacing, cellpadding, bgcolor, summary, and title. The default display of rows and cells in tables can also be modified using attributes. The most commonly used are bgcolor, valign, rowspan, and colspan. Let's take a closer look at attributes used with **\<table\>** tags.

As you read about each **\<table\>** tag attribute, experiment with the resume.htm page in your mywebsite web site. The best way to learn to write XHTML is to practice it.

Why doesn't my table display?

While Internet Explorer will display a table even if you forget about a closing tag here or there, Netscape is very picky. Be sure to use Netscape to test pages that contain tables. Internet Explorer will often ignore a missing or misspelled tag and display your table. However, when Netscape encounters missing or unmatched table tags, it sometimes will not display parts of your web page or only display a portion of the table.

The align Attribute. This attribute specifies the alignment of the table with the values "right", "center", and "left". The table in Figure 3.14 has the align attribute set to center.

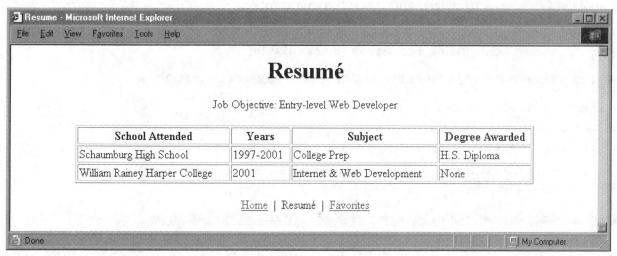

Figure 3.14 *The align attribute was used to center this table*

The W3C has deprecated the use of this attribute with the **<table>** tag. Instead, the W3C suggests that web developers use the division or **<div>** tag with the align attribute to align divisions or sections of web pages. Consider placing your table within **<div>** tags to center it on a web page:

```
<div align="center">
 <table>
  <tr>
    <td>
     table XHTML code goes here...
    </td>
  </tr>
 </table>
</div>
```

The border Attribute. This attribute specifies whether and what type of visible border the table will have. The value ranges from 0 to 100, with 0 indicating that no border will be visible. The values between 1 and 100 determine the thickness of the visible border, where 1 indicates relatively thin and 100 indicates a very thick border. The table in Figure 3.15 has a border set to 10.

School Attended	Years	Subject	Degree Awarded
Schaumburg High School	1997-2001	College Prep	H.S. Diploma
William Rainey Harper College	2001	Internet & Web Development	None

Figure 3.15 *Table with border set to 10*

The browser determines the border color and shading based on the page background color. If you want a specific color, also use the bordercolor attribute.

The bordercolor Attribute. This attribute specifies the color of the border. The values can be a color name or numeric value. See the inside leaf of the back cover for a color chart. The browser displays the border color as a solid color and does not shade the border when the bordercolor attribute is used. The bordercolor attribute is not part of the official W3C Recommendation but is included here because it is widely used and well-supported by browsers. The table in Figure 3.16 has a bordercolor set to a dark color.

School Attended	Years	Subject	Degree Awarded
Schaumburg High School	1997-2001	College Prep	H.S. Diploma
William Rainey Harper College	2001	Internet & Web Development	None

Figure 3.16 *Table with bordercolor set to a dark color*

The width Attribute. This attribute specifies the width of the table in either pixels or in a percentage of the web page. The table will stretch to fit the entire width of the page if 100% is used. If width is not specified, the browser determines the width of a particular table by calculating the width of the elements and text it contains. Use the width attribute when you want more control over your web page. The table in Figure 3.17 has a width set to 75%.

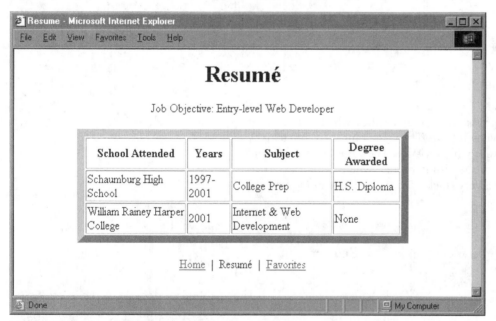

Figure 3.17 *Table with width set to 75%*

The height Attribute. This attribute specifies the height of the table in either pixels or in a percentage of the web page. This is more commonly used on **<tr>** and **<td>** tags. The height attribute is not part of the official W3C Recommendation for the **<table>** tag but is included here because it is widely used and well-supported by browsers.

The cellspacing Attribute. This attribute specifies the distance between the cells in pixels. If you omit the cellspacing attribute, the default value is 2 pixels. The table in Figure 3.18 has a cellspacing set to 10. The XHTML code for the **`<table>`** tag is

```
<table border="1" cellspacing="10">
```

Name	Birthday	Phone	E-mail
Mary Morris	5/13	857-555-5555	mmorris@hotmail.com
James Baker	11/8	303-555-5555	jbaker@iname.com

Figure 3.18 *Table with cellspacing set to 10*

The cellpadding Attribute. This attribute specifies the distance in pixels between the cell contents and the edge of the cell. If you omit the cellpadding attribute, the default value is 1 pixel. An example with cellpadding set to 10 is shown in Figure 3.19. The XHTML code for the **`<table>`** tag is **`<table border="1" cellpadding="10">`**

Name	Birthday	Phone	E-mail
Mary Morris	5/13	857-555-5555	mmorris@hotmail.com
James Baker	11/8	303-555-5555	jbaker@iname.com

Figure 3.19 *Table with cellpadding set to 10*

The bgcolor Attribute. This attribute specifies a background color for the table. The values can be a color name or numeric value. See the inside leaf of the back cover for a color chart. An example with a background color, no border, and cellpadding of 10 is shown in Figure 3.20. The XHTML code for the **`<table>`** tag is:

```
<table border="0" bgcolor="#99CCFF" cellpadding="10">
```

Name	Birthday	Phone	E-mail
Mary Morris	5/13	857-555-5555	mmorris@hotmail.com
James Baker	11/8	303-555-5555	jbaker@iname.com

Figure 3.20 *Borderless table using cellpadding set to 10 along with a background color*

Which is better, specifying width by pixels or by percentage?

It depends. Keep in mind that visitors to your web page will use monitors with different screen resolutions. If you need your table to have a fixed width that you specify, use pixels. If you'd like your table to be flexible and to resize with the browser window, use percentages. It's a good idea to test your web pages using different screen resolutions.

Can I mix and match fixed widths and percentages?

Yes. The width attribute can be applied to table cells (**`<td>`** tags) as well as to the entire table (**`<table>`** tag). If you are using a table to format an entire page, you might want a particular column used for navigation links to have a fixed width while the entire table uses a percentage width. As always, test your web pages using different screen resolutions to make sure that you achieved your desired effect.

The summary Attribute. This attribute specifies a summary of the table contents that can be accessed by a screen reader. This attribute is suggested for use by the Web Accessibility Initiative. For example:

```
<table border="0" width="75%" title="Educational Background" summary="This table
lists my educational background. Graduated Schaumburg High School in 2001. Presently
taking web development classes at William Rainey Harper College.">
```

The title Attribute. This attribute specifies a title of the table that can be accessed by a screen reader. The value of the title attribute is displayed by some browsers, such as Internet Explorer 5.x and Netscape 6, when the mouse passes over the table area. This attribute is suggested for use by the Web Accessibility Initiative.

Applying Attributes to Rows and Cells

Many of the **<table>** tag attributes discussed above can also be applied to the **<tr>** and **<td>** tags to customize the look of your table. In particular, the bgcolor, align, and width attributes are most often used. The following are commonly used attributes for **<tr>** and **<td>** tags.

The bgcolor Attribute. This attribute can be used to apply a background color to a table row or cell. See Figure 3.21 for an example of applying a background color to alternating rows of a table using this attribute.

Name	Birthday	Phone	E-mail
Mary Morris	5/13	857-555-5555	mmorris@hotmail.com
James Baker	11/8	303-555-5555	jbaker@iname.com

Figure 3.21 *Table using a background color on alternate rows*

The XHTML code for the table is

```
<table border="0" cellpadding="10" cellspacing="0">
  <tr bgcolor="#CCCCCC">
    <th >Name</th>
    <th>Birthday</th>
    <th>Phone</th>
    <th>E-mail</th>
  </tr>
  <tr>
    <td>Mary Morris</td>
    <td>5/13</td>
    <td>857-555-5555</td>
    <td>mmorris@hotmail.com</td>
  </tr>
  <tr bgcolor="#CCCCCC">
    <td>James Baker</td>
    <td>11/8</td>
    <td>303-555-5555</td>
    <td>jbaker@iname.com</td>
  </tr>
</table>
```

What if I want a more interesting table?

You can alter the gridlike look of a table by applying the colspan and rowspan attributes to **<td>** tags. As you get into more complex table configurations like these, be sure to sketch out the table on paper *before* you start typing the XHTML code.

The colspan Attribute. This attribute specifies the number of columns that a cell will occupy. Figure 3.22 shows a row that spans two columns.

<table border="1">
<tr><td colspan="2">This spans two columns</td></tr>
<tr><td>Column 1</td><td>Column 2</td></tr>
</table>

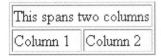

Figure 3.22 *Table with a row that spans two columns*

The XHTML code for the table is

```
<table border="1">
  <tr>
     <td colspan="2">This spans two columns</td>
  </tr>
  <tr>
    <td>Column 1</td>
    <td>Column 2</td>
  </tr>
</table>
```

The rowspan Attribute. This attribute specifies the number of rows that a cell will occupy. An example of a column that spans two rows is shown in Figure 3.23.

<table border="1">
<tr><td rowspan="2">This spans two rows</td><td>Row 1 Column 2</td></tr>
<tr><td>Row 2 Column 2</td></tr>
</table>

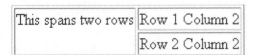

Figure 3.23 *Table with a column that spans two rows*

Here is the XHTML code for the table:

```
<table border="1">
  <tr>
     <td rowspan="2">This spans two rows</td>
     <td>Row 1 Column 2</td>
  </tr>
  <tr>
    <td>Row 2 Column 2</td>
  </tr>
</table>
```

The valign Attribute. This attribute specifies the alignment of the text or image in the cell. The default vertical alignment is "middle", shown in the rowspan example in Figure 3.23. Use the valign attribute when you need the contents of a cell to be vertically aligned at the top or bottom of a cell. Common values for the valign attribute are top, middle, and bottom. Figure 3.24 shows the valign attribute used to top align the contents of the first cell.

<table border="1">
<tr><td rowspan="2" valign="top">This spans two rows</td><td>Row 1 Column 2</td></tr>
<tr><td>Row 2 Column 2</td></tr>
</table>

Figure 3.24 *The first cell in this table uses the valign attribute*

The XHTML code for the table is

```
<table border="1">
  <tr>
    <td rowspan="2" valign="top">This spans two rows</td>
    <td>Row 1 Column 2</td>
  </tr>
  <tr>
    <td>Row 2 Column 2</td>
  </tr>
</table>
```

Hands-On Practice 3.5

You will continue to work with the mywebsite web site. Launch Notepad or another text editor and open the resume.htm page from your mywebsite folder. Center the existing table on the page by using `<div>` tags with the `align="center"` attribute. Add a line break and new table (also centered) to the page below the existing table. The new table will contain work history information. See Figure 3.25 for an example.

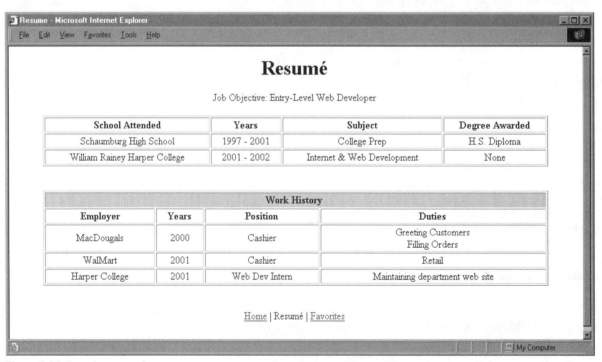

Figure 3.25 *Sample resume.htm*

*Create a table of five rows. The first row will span all four columns and will contain the text **Work History**. The text should be centered and bold. The other rows should contain columns with the headings of **Employer, Years, Position**, and **Duties**. The first row should have a different background color from the others. Either use your own work history or create fictional work history content for the lower three rows of the table. Be sure to use table attributes recommended for accessibility. Save your page and test it in a browser. Compare your work to the sample on the student disk (Chapter3/3.5/resume.htm).*

XHTML—Formatting a Web Page with a Table

Now that you are more familiar with tables, take another look at some well-known sites—http://ebay.com, http://microsoft.com, and http://sun.com — that use tables to format their web pages. As you surf the Web and analyze these and other sites, look for a web page layout that is appealing to you. View the source code and examine how the page was formatted. You will find that many of the pages use tables. It is important not to copy a page, but rather to get ideas from many sources and organize them in a fresh, new way that is all your own. When designing a new web page, it's a good idea to sketch out your ideas on paper.

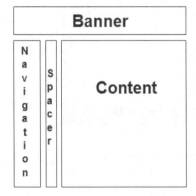

Figure 3.26 *Using a table to format a web page*

Figure 3.26 shows a sketch of a common format consisting of a horizontal banner and three columns. Notice that the middle cell in the second row is used for spacing purposes only—to separate the navigation area from the content area. Sample XHTML code for this type of table layout is as follows:

```
<table border="0" width="80%">
  <tr>
    <td colspan="3"><h2>This is the banner area</h2></td>
  </tr>
  <tr>
    <td width="20%" valign="top">Place Navigation here</td>
    <td width="10"> </td>
    <td>Page content goes here</td>
  </tr>
</table>
```

A web page using this type of table layout is shown in Figure 3.27.

Figure 3.27 *Sample page formatted by a table*

The ** ** character is utilized in Figure 3.27 as a placeholder in the cell used for a spacer. Recall from Chapter 2 that ** ** is a special character that creates a nonbreaking space.

The alignment of the table will be to the left by default. This can sometimes make the page look unbalanced when it is viewed with a monitor set to a higher resolution, such as 800x600 or 1024x768. To prevent this display issue, use a **<div>** tag to center the table. Assign the table a percentage width of the web page. These techniques will cause all browsers of varying resolutions to display the table centered and extending across 80% of the web page.

Several alternate sketches of possible web page design layouts using tables are shown in Figures 3.28, 3.29, 3.30, and 3.31.

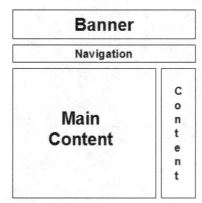

Figure 3.28 *Page layout with banner, horizontal navigation, and two content columns*

Figure 3.29 *Page layout with a banner, left-side navigation, and one large content column*

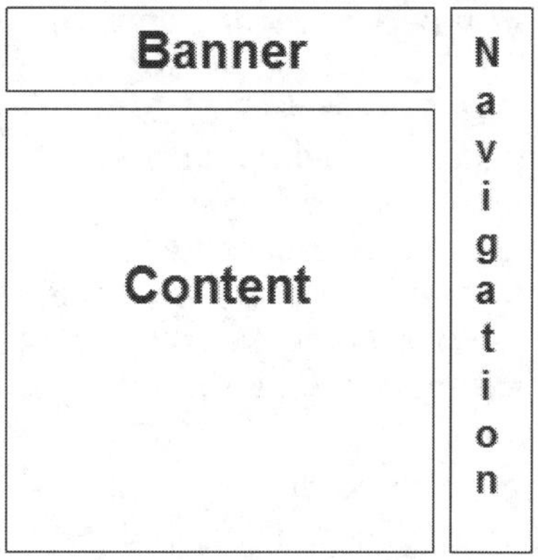

Figure 3.30 *Page layout with a banner, right-side navigation, and one large content column*

The design shown in Figure 3.29 uses a top banner, side navigation, and large main area. This layout design is commonly utilized by web developers.

At this point you should have a basic understanding of the use of tables on web pages. The best way to learn is to practice. Why not create a few experimental pages of your own?

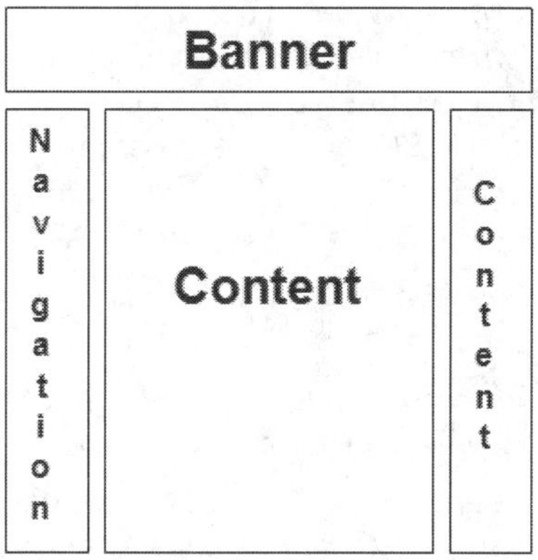

Figure 3.31 *Page layout with a banner, left-side navigation, and two content columns*

Hands-On Practice 3.6

You will continue to work with the mywebsite web site and create an alternate version of the Home page that uses a table for the page layout. Launch Notepad or another text editor and open the index.htm page from your mywebsite folder. Save the file as newindex.htm.

In Notepad, you will modify this page so that it uses a table for layout. See Figure 3.26 for a layout sketch containing a top banner row that spans three columns and an second row with three columns: navigation area, spacer, and main content. The sample page is shown in Figure 3.32.

Compare it with the previous version of index.htm page shown in Figure 3.8. The content is very similar but notice how different the pages look! The table layout and color on the new page visually separate areas. The only change in the actual web page content is the addition of a welcome message. The rest of the content has been moved:

Figure 3.32 *New index.htm using a table for layout*

- The heading "My Web Site" is now placed in the banner area of the table.

- The links to the "My Resumé" and "Fav Sites" pages are in the navigation area.

- The "Yahoo!" link, school link, and e-mail link are in the main content area along with a few sentences that welcome the web page visitor.

The layout of the new version of the Home page is configured as follows:

- The page background color is set to #9999CC (bgcolor attribute on the **<body>** tag).

- The table has border, cellspacing, and cellpadding set to 0; width of 70%, background color (bgcolor attribute) set to #CCCCFF; and is centered on the page (use **<div align="center">**).

- The content in the table cell used for the banner is centered.

- The content in the table cell used for navigation is centered.

- The table cells used for the spacer and main content are configured with a background color of #FFFFFF (bgcolor attribute on the **<td>** tag).

- The table attributes recommended for accessibility (summary and title) have been used.

After making these modifications, save the newindex.htm page and test it in a browser. Your page should be similar to the sample in Figure 3.32. Compare your work to the sample on the student disk (Chapter3/3.6/newindex.htm).

Are you surprised at the way the content of the web page was transformed just by using a table page layout and some color? You will learn more about the use of color and graphics on web pages in the next chapter.

Chapter 3 Review

Summary

This chapter introduced the XHTML techniques used to create hyperlinks and tables. You will use these skills over and over again as you create web pages. Visit the course web site at http://www.webdevfoundations.net for examples, updated information, and the links listed in this chapter.

Review Questions

Multiple Choice

1. Web pages are linked to each other using the
   - a. `<link>` tag
   - b. `<hyperlink>` tag
   - c. `<a>` tag
   - d. `<body>` tag

2. The anchor tag attributes that define an internal bookmark or named reference in a page are
   - a. id and name
   - b. name and bookmark
   - c. internal and id
   - d. id and bookmark

3. How would you link to the bookmark #jobs on the page employ.htm from the home page of the site?
   - a. `<a href="employ.htm#jobs">Employment Opportunities</a>`
   - b. `<a name="employ.htm#jobs">Employment Opportunities</a>`
   - c. `<a link="employ.htm#jobs">Employment Opportunities</a>`
   - d. none of the above

4. When do you need to use a fully qualified URL in a hyperlink?
   - a. when creating an internal link to the same web page
   - b. when linking to a page in another folder on the same site
   - c. when linking to a page on an external web site
   - d. never

5. An e-mail link will
   - a. automatically send you an e-mail message with the visitor's e-mail address as the reply-to field
   - b. launch the default e-mail application for the visitor's browser with your e-mail address as the recipient
   - c. display your e-mail address so that the visitor can send you a message later
   - d. link to your mail server

6. Which attribute is used to specify the distance between the contents of each cell?
   - a. cellpad
   - b. cellpadding
   - c. cellspacing
   - d. cellborder

7. Which attribute is used to specify the distance between the cell text and the cell border?
   - a. cellpad
   - b. cellpadding
   - c. cellspacing
   - d. cellborder

8. What tag pair is used to start and end a table?

   a. `<td> </td>`   c. `<table> </table>`

   b. `<tr> </tr>`   d. none of the above

9. Which tag uses a border attribute to display a table with a border?

   a. `<td>`   c. `<table>`

   b. `<tr>`   d. `<tableborder>`

10. What tag pair is used to specify table headings?

   a. `<td> </td>`   c. `<head> </head>`

   b. `<th> </th>`   d. none of the above

Fill in the Blank

11. The _____ attribute is used to configure the distance between cells in a table.

12. A table with a width set to 600 pixels will look _____ on a monitor with resolution set to 640x480 than on a monitor with resolution set to 1024x768.

13. _____ is an attribute of the `<table>` tag that provides accessibility.

14. _____ is an attribute of the anchor tag that can cause the new web page to open in its own browser window.

Short Answer

15. Explain why it is good practice to place the e-mail address on the web page and within the anchor tag when creating an e-mail link.

Apply Your Knowledge

1. **Predict the Result.** Draw and write a brief description of the web page that will be created with the following XHTML code:

```
<?xml version="1.0" encoding="UTF-8"?>
<!DOCTYPE html PUBLIC "-//W3C//DTD XHTML 1.0 Transitional//EN"
   "http://www.w3.org/TR/xhtml1/DTD/xhtml1-transitional.dtd">
<html xmlns="http://www.w3.org/1999/xhtml" >
<head>
<title>Predict the Result</title>
</head>
<body>
  <div align="center">
    <table border="0" bgcolor="#cccccc" width="80%">
      <tr>
          <td bgcolor="#0000FF" colspan="3">
            <h1><font color="#FFFFFF">Trillium Technologies</font></h1>
          </td>
      </tr>
      <tr>
          <td width="150">
            <p> Home<br /><a href="about.htm"> About</a><br />
            <a href="services.htm">Services</a><br />
            <a href="products.htm">Products</a></p>
          </td>
```

continues

```
            <td>  
            </td>
            <td>
                <p>More than just another web development firm, Trillium Technologies
                    strives to celebrate creativity and the efficient flow of
                    information.</p>
                <p> We aren't satisfied until every site we build is the best in its
                    class.</p>
            </td>
        </tr>
    </table>
  </div>
</body>
</html>
```

2. **Fill in the Missing Code.** This web page should contain an internal
   link at the bottom of the page to that will link back to the top of the
   page. Some XHTML tags, indicated by **<_>** are missing. Fill in the
   missing code.

```
<?xml version="1.0" encoding="UTF-8"?>
<!DOCTYPE html PUBLIC "-//W3C//DTD XHTML 1.0 Transitional//EN"
    "http://www.w3.org/TR/xhtml1/DTD/xhtml1-transitional.dtd">
<html xmlns="http://www.w3.org/1999/xhtml" >
<head>
<title>Trillium Technologies</title>
</head>
<body>
  <_></a>
  <h1>Trillium Technologies</h1>
  <p>More than just another web development firm, Trillium Technologies strives to
     celebrate creativity and the efficient flow of information.</p>
  <p> We aren't satisfied until every site we build is the best in its class.</p>
  <p>Back to <_>Top</a></p>
</body>
</html>
```

3. **Find the Error.** The files index.htm, about.htm, contact.htm, and
   services.htm have been created and saved in the same folder as the
   following page. Why doesn't the link to the home page (index.htm)
   work? What is wrong with the link to the contact page?

```
<?xml version="1.0" encoding="UTF-8"?>
<!DOCTYPE html PUBLIC "-//W3C//DTD XHTML 1.0 Transitional//EN"
    "http://www.w3.org/TR/xhtml1/DTD/xhtml1-transitional.dtd">
<html xmlns="http://www.w3.org/1999/xhtml" >
<head>
<title>Find the Error<title>
</head>
<body>
  <h1>Trillium Technologies </h1>
  <a href="home.htm">Home</a> <a href="about.htm">About</a>
  <a href="services.htm">Services</a>
  <a href="contact.htm>Contact</a>
</body>
</html>
```

Hands-On Exercises

1. Practice writing hyperlinks:
   a. Write the XHTML to create an absolute link to a web site whose domain name is google.com.
   b. Write the XHTML to create a relative link to a web page named contact.htm.
   c. Write the XHTML to create a named anchor or bookmark at the beginning of a web page designated by "top".
   d. Write the XHTML to create an internal link to the named anchor designated by "top".
   e. Write the XHTML to create an e-mail link to me@me.com.

2. Create a web page about your favorite movie that uses a two-column table containing details about the movie. The table should have no border and use background color to organize the information. Include the following in the table:
   - Title of the movie
   - Director or producer
   - Leading actor
   - Leading actress
   - Rating (R, PG-13, PG, G, NR)
   - A brief description of the movie
   - An absolute link to a review about the movie

   Place an e-mail link to yourself on the web page. Save the page as movie2.htm. Hand in printouts of both the source code (print in Notepad) and the browser display of your page.

3. Create a web page that uses a table and describes two organizations that perform work related to Internet/Web standards and guidelines (see Chapter 1). Place the information in a table comprised of at least three columns and three rows. Include links to the web site of each organization. Place an e-mail link to yourself on the web page. Save the page as organization.htm. Hand in printouts of both the source code (print in Notepad) and the browser display of your page.

4. Create a web page about your favorite music CD that utilizes a four-column table. The column headings should be:
   - **Group:** Place the name of the group and the names of its principle members in this column.
   - **Tracks:** List the title of each music track or song.
   - **Year:** List the year the CD was recorded.
   - **Links:** Place at least two absolute links to sites about the group in this column.

   Include an e-mail link to yourself on the web page. Save the page as band2.htm. Hand in printouts of both the source code (print in Notepad) and the browser display of your page.

5. Create a web page about your favorite recipe. Organize the ingredients and directions in single table. Use two columns for the ingredients. Use a row that spans two columns to contain the instructions for creating your culinary delight. Save the page as recipe2.htm. Hand in printouts of both the source code (print in Notepad) and the browser display of your page.

Each of these case studies will continue throughout most of the text. This chapter builds on the Chapter 2 Web Site Case Study activities.

A. JavaJam Coffee House

See Chapter 2 for an introduction to the JavaJam Coffee House case. Figure 2.20 shows a site map for JavaJam. A Home page for the site, index.htm, was created in the Chapter 2 case study. You have two tasks:

1. Add an e-mail link and relative hyperlinks to the Home page.
2. Create the Menu page with the same general page layout as the Home page. See Figure 2.21.

Hands-On Practice Case

1. Add an e-mail link and relative hyperlinks to the Home page.

- Launch Notepad and open index.htm file in the javajam folder that you previously created. Locate the line containing the copyright information. You will add your e-mail link below this line. Place your cursor at the end of the copyright information and press Enter to create a blank line. Now type an e-mail link to yourfirstname@yourlastname.com. The text should be emphasized and use a font size of 2. (Substitute your first name and last name in the e-mail link.)

- View the screen shot of the Home Page (Figure 2.22) and notice the navigation area with the text "Home | Menu | Performances | Jobs". This is the area you will be modifying. Since this is the Home page there is no reason to link to it. Do not modify the "Home" text. Use anchor tags and add relative links to the web page so that the "Menu" text links to menu.htm, "Performances" links to performances.htm, and "Jobs" links to jobs.htm. Save your page. Test it in a browser. Don't worry if your links do not work yet—you'll be creating the pages as you work through this text.

2. Create the Menu page. Figure 3.33 shows a sample Menu page.

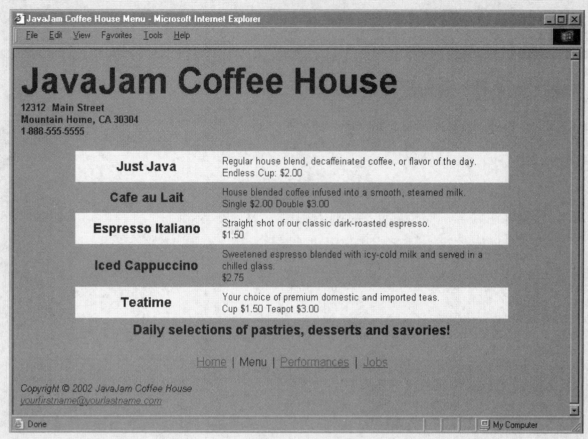

Figure 3.33 *JavaJam Menu page*

A productivity trick is to create new pages based on existing pages—so you can benefit from your previous work. Your new Menu page will use the index.htm page as a starting point. Open the index.htm page for the JavaJam web site in Notepad. Select File, select Save As and save the file with the new name of menu.htm in the javajam folder. Now you are ready to edit the page.

- Modify the page title. Change the text contained between the **<title>** and **</title>** tags to "JavaJam Coffee House Menu".

- Modify the navigation. Add anchor tags to the page to create a relative hyperlink from the text "Home" to index.htm. Remove the hyperlink surrounding the text "Menu".

- Add the menu content to the page. The menu items and menu descriptions are
  "Just Java
  Your choice of regular house blend, decaffeinated coffee, or flavor
     of the day.
  Endless Cup: $2.00
  Cafe au Lait
  House blended coffee infused into a smooth, steamed milk.
  Single $2.00 Double $3.00
  Espresso Italiano
  Straight shot of our classic dark-roasted espresso.
  $1.50
  Iced Cappuccino

Sweetened espresso blended with icy-cold milk and served in a
   chilled glass.
$2.75
Teatime
Your choice of premium domestic and imported teas.
Cup $1.50 Teapot $3.00
Daily selections of pastries, desserts and savories!"

Formatting hints for the menu content: The table has two columns, six
rows, no border, cellspacing of 0, cellpadding of 5, a width of 80% and
should be centered on the page. See the sample screen shot in Figure 3.33.
The text contained in the table should use Arial font. The menu items
("JustJava", "Cafe au Lait", "Espresso Italiano", etc.) should use
size="4", be bold (use the **<strong>** tag), and be centered. The menu
descriptions should use the Arial font with size="2". Use the colspan
attribute when you need to merge columns together (see the last line in the
table).

3. Save your page and test it in a browser. Test the hyperlink from the
   menu.htm page to index.htm. Test the hyperlink from the index.htm
   page to menu.htm. If your links do not work, review your work with
   close attention to these details:

   - Verify that you have saved the pages with the correct names in the
     correct folder.
   - Verify your spelling of the page names in the anchor tags.
   - After you make changes, test again.

B. Fish Creek Animal Hospital

   See Chapter 2 for an introduction to the Fish Creek Animal Hospital
Case. Figure 2.23 shows a site map for Fish Creek. A Home page,
index.htm for the site was created in the Chapter 2 case study. You have
two tasks:

1. Add an e-mail link and relative hyperlinks to the Home page.

2. Create the Services page with the same general page layout (see Figure
   2.24) as the Home page.

Hands-On Practice Case

1. Add an e-mail link and relative hyperlinks to the Home page.

   - Launch Notepad and open index.htm file in the fishcreek folder that
     you previously created. Locate the line containing the copyright
     information. You will add your e-mail link below this line. Place
     your cursor at the end of the copyright information and press Enter
     to create a blank line. Now create an e-mail link to
     yourfirstname@yourlastname.com. The text should be emphasized
     and use a font size of 2. (Substitute your first name and last name in
     the e-mail link.)
   - View the page layout diagram for the Home page (Figure 2.24) and
     notice the navigation area with the text
     "[Home]   [Services]   [Ask the Vet]   [Contact]"
     This is the area you will be modifying. Since this is the Home page
     there is no reason to link to it. Do not modify the "Home" text. Use
     anchor tags and add relative links to the web page so that the "Ser-
     vices" text links to services.htm, "Ask the Vet" links to askvet.htm,
     and "Contact" links to contact.htm. Save your page. Test it in a

browser. Don't worry if your links do not work yet—you'll be creating the pages as you work through this text.

2. Create the Services page. Figure 3.34 shows a sample Services page.

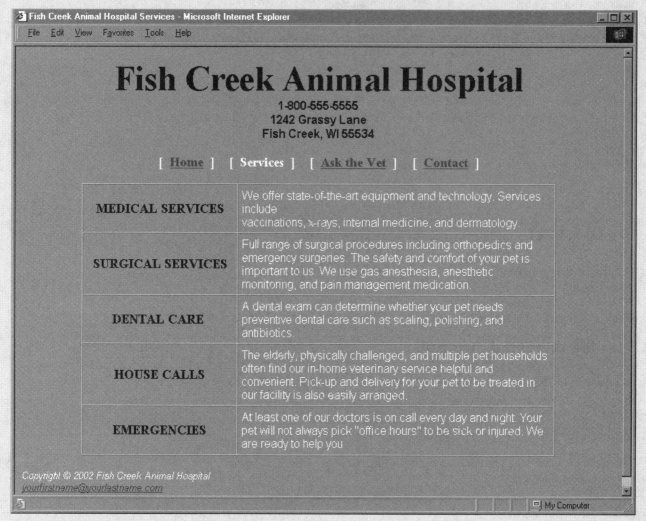

Figure 3.34 *Fish Creek Services page*

As mentioned in the JavaJam case, a productivity technique you can use is to create new pages from existing pages—this way you can benefit from your previous work. (Note that many web authoring tools allow you to create templates of your page layouts.)

Your new Services page will use the index.htm page as a starting point. Open the index.htm page for the Fish Creek web site in Notepad. Select File, select Save As, and save the file with the new name of services.htm in the fishcreek folder. Now you are ready to edit the page.

- Modify the navigation. Add anchor tags to the page to create a relative hyperlink from the text "Home" to index.htm. Remove the hyperlink surrounding the text "Services".

- Add the Services content to the page.

"MEDICAL SERVICES
We offer state-of-the-art equipment and technology. Services include vaccinations, x-rays, internal medicine, and dermatology.

SURGICAL SERVICES
Full range of surgical procedures including orthopedics and emergency surgeries. The safety and comfort of your pet is important to us. We use gas anesthesia, anesthetic monitoring, and pain management medication.
DENTAL CARE
A dental exam can determine whether your pet needs preventive dental care such as scaling, polishing, and antibiotics.
HOUSE CALLS
The elderly, physically challenged, and multiple pet households often find our in-home veterinary service helpful and convenient. Pick-up and delivery for your pet to be treated in our facility is also easily arranged.
EMERGENCIES
At least one of our doctors is on call every day and night. Your pet will not always pick "office hours" to be sick or injured. We are ready to help you."

Formatting hints for the Services content: The table has two columns, five rows, cellpadding of 5, cellspacing of 0, width of 80%, border set to 1, and is centered on the page. See the screen shot in Figure 3.34. The categories of services are formatted to use the default font (Times New Roman), font size of 4, font color of #000000, and are bold (use the `<strong>` tag) and centered. The descriptions of the services use Arial font.

3. Save your page and test it in a browser. Test the hyperlink from the services.htm page to index.htm. Test the hyperlink from the index.htm page to services.htm. If your links do not work, you need to review your work with close attention to these details:

- Verify that you have saved the pages with the correct names in the correct folder.
- Verify your spelling of the page names in the anchor tags.
- After you make changes, test again.

C. Pete the Painter

See Chapter 2 for an introduction to the Pete the Painter case. Figure 2.26 shows a site map for Pete the Painter. A Home page for the site, index.htm, was created in the Chapter 2 case study. You have two tasks:

1. Add an e-mail link and relative hyperlinks to the Home page.

2. Create the Services page with the same general page layout (see Figure 2.24) as the Home page.

Hands-On Practice Case

1. Add an e-mail link and relative hyperlinks to the Home page.

- Launch Notepad and open index.htm file in the painter folder that you previously created. Locate the line containing the copyright information. You will add your e-mail link below this line. Place your cursor at the end of the copyright information and press Enter to create a blank line. Now create an e-mail link to "yourfirstname@yourlastname.com". The text should be emphasized and use a font size of 2. (Substitute your first name and last name in the e-mail link.)

- View the page layout diagram for the Home page (Figure 2.24) and notice the navigation area with the text
"Home | Services | Testimonials | Free Estimate"
This is the area you will be modifying. Since this is the Home page, there is no reason to link to it. Do not modify the "Home" text. Use anchor tags and add relative links to the web page so that the "Services" text links to services.htm, "Testimonials" links to testimonials.htm, and "Free Estimate" links to estimates.htm. Save your page. Test in a browser. Don't worry if your links do not work yet—you'll be creating the pages as you work through this text.

2. Create the Services page. Figure 3.35 shows a sample Services page.

Figure 3.35 *Pete the Painter Services Page*

Creating new pages based on existing pages is a common productivity technique. This allows you to reuse your previous work. Many web authoring tools even provide a feature to create templates to perform this functionality. Your new Services page will use the index.htm page as a starting point. Open the index.htm page for the Painter web site in Notepad. Select File, select Save As, and save the file with the new name of services.htm in the painter folder. Now you are ready to edit the page.

- Modify the navigation. Add anchor tags to the page to create a relative hyperlink from the text "Home" to index.htm. Remove the hyperlink surrounding the text "Services".
- Add Services content to the page. The Services content is

  "Interior Services
  If you need it painted, textured or papered, Pete the Painter can do it! All kinds of interior work including: painting walls, painting ceilings, applying wall textures, drywall, and wallpaper.
  Exterior Services
  If you need it washed, painted, stained, or just touched up, Pete the Painter can do it! All kinds of exterior work including power-washing, painting, staining, and stucco.
  Painting
  Pete has the most dependable and professional painting staff in the area and uses only quality paint.
  Wallcovering
  Pete's design specialists are experts at applying wallpaper and other wallcoverings. They can even help you choose the most appropriate wallcovering for your decorating needs and budget."

Formatting hints for the Services content: The table has one column, eight rows, cellpadding of 0, cellspacing of 5, and a width of 75%. See the screen shot in Figure 3.35. The categories of services ("Interior Services", "Exterior Services", "Painting", and "Wallcovering") use the default font (Times New Roman), font color #336600, and a font size of 4. They are placed in a table cell with a background color of #99FF99. The descriptions of the services use the Arial font.

3. Save your page and test it in a browser. Test the hyperlink from the services.htm page to index.htm. Test the hyperlink from the index.htm page to services.htm. If your links do not work, you need to review your work with close attention to these details:
   - Verify that you have saved the pages with the correct names in the correct folder.
   - Verify your spelling of the page names in the anchor tags.
   - After you have made changes, test again.

Web Research

A. Search the Web and find a web page formatted with one or more XHTML tables. Print the browser view of the page. Print out the source code of the web page. (Hint: To print the source code, display the page using Internet Explorer, and select View Source. Notepad will launch and display the page. Select File and Print.) On the printout, highlight or circle the tags related to tables. On a separate sheet of paper create some XHTML notes by listing the tags and attributes related to tables found on your sample page, along with a brief description of their purpose. Hand in the browser view of the page, source code printout, and your XHTML notes page.

B. Good artists view and analyze many paintings. Good writers read and evaluate many books. Similarly, good web developers view and scrutinize many web pages. Surf the Web and find two web pages, one that is appealing to you and one that is unappealing to you. Print out each page. Create a web page that answers the following questions for each of your examples.

1. What is the URL of the web site?

2. Does this page use tables? If so, for what purpose—page layout, organization of information, or another reason?

3. Is this page appealing or unappealing? List three reasons for your answer.

4. If this page is unappealing, what would you do to improve it?

Open your file in Notepad and print the source code for the page. Display your page in a browser and print the page. Hand in both printouts to your instructor.

Chapter Review Answers

1. c

2. a

3. a

4. c

5. b

6. c

7. b

8. c

9. c

10. b

11. cellspacing

12. larger

13. summary or title

14. target

15. Not everyone has an e-mail program configured with their browser. By placing the e-mail address in both places, you increase usability for all your visitors.

Chapter 4

XHTML Color and Visual Elements

A key component of a compelling web site is the use of interesting and appropriate graphics. This chapter introduces you to working with color and visual elements on web pages. When you include images on your web site, it is important to remember that not all web users are able to view them. Some users may have vision problems and need assistive technology such as a screen reader application that reads the web page to them. In addition, search engines send out spiders and robots to walk the web and catalog pages for their indexes and databases; such programs do not access your images. As a web developer, you should create pages that are enhanced by graphical elements but that are usable without them.

Learning Outcomes

In this chapter, you will learn how to:

▶ **Use color on web pages**

▶ **Create and format horizontal rules on web pages**

▶ **Decide when to use graphics and what graphics are appropriate**

▶ **Apply the image tag to add graphics to web pages**

▶ **Select images as backgrounds on tables and web pages**

▶ **Place images as hyperlinks**

▶ **Find both free and fee-based sources of graphics**

▶ **Follow recommended web design guidelines when using graphics on web pages**

Using Color on Web Pages

Monitors display color as a combination of different intensities of red, green, and blue, also known as RGB color. RGB intensity values are numerical from 0 to 255. Each RGB color will have three values, one each for red, green, and blue. These are always listed in that order (red, green, blue) and specify the numerical value of each color used. For example, the RGB values for the color red are (255,0,0)—all red, no green and no blue. The RGB values for blue are (0, 0, 255)—no red, no green, and all blue. These colors can also be specified using hexadecimal values.

Hexadecimal is the name for the Base 16 numbering system, which uses the characters 0, 1, 2, 3, 4, 5, 6, 7, 8, 9, A, B, C, D, E, and F to specify numeric values. When a hexadecimal is used to specify RGB color, the numeric value pairs range from 00 to FF (0 to 255 in Base 10). The hexadecimal value contains three numeric value pairs written sequentially as one number. Each pair is associated with the amount of red, green, and blue displayed. Using this notation, the color red would be specified as #FF0000 and the color blue as #0000FF. The # symbol signifies that the value is in hexadecimal.

Don't worry—you won't need to do calculations to work with web colors, just become familiar with the numbering scheme. See Figure 4.1 for an excerpt from the color chart on the inside leaf of the back cover.

#FFFFFF	#FFFFCC	#FFFF99	#FFFF66	#FFFF33	#FFFF00
#FFCCFF	#FFCCCC	#FFCC99	#FFCC66	#FFCC33	#FFCC00
#FF99FF	#FF99CC	#FF9999	#FF9966	#FF9933	#FF9900

Figure 4.1 *Partial color chart*

Take a few moments to examine the color chart. You will observe a display of colors and their associated hexadecimal RGB values in hexadecimal. You may notice that there is a pattern to the hexadecimal numbers (pairs of 00, 33, 66, 99, CC, or FF). This pattern is signifies a color on the Web Safe Color Palette (more on this later). As you further examine the color chart on the inside leaf of the back cover, you will see a list of colors using color names. Some web developers find it easier to use the color names. However, the names are not uniformly supported by all versions of all browsers, so the W3C recommends using numeric color values instead of color names.

Web Color Palette

A web developer usually has no way of knowing what type of computer or browser the web site visitors will be using. The various operating systems and browsers display colors differently, and sometimes not at all. The Web Safe Color Palette, also known as the Web Color Palette, is a collection of 216 colors that display the same on both the Mac and PC platforms. It is easy to tell if a color is on the Web Color Palette when you consider the individual the hexadecimal RGB value pairs. The values of 00, 33, 66, 99, CC, and FF are the only values for hexadecimal RGB value pairs on the Web Color Palette. Take another look at the color chart on the inside leaf of the back cover and note that all the colors listed by RGB follow this numbering scheme—they comprise the Web Color Palette. See Figure 4.2 for a comparison of a Web Safe Color, #CC0000, and a non-Web Safe Color, #880000. They both are a shade of red; however, the Web Safe Color will display predictably across platforms and the other color will not.

| bgcolor="#CC0000" This cell background is on the Web Color Palette and should display the same on all platforms. | bgcolor="#880000" This cell background is NOT on the Web Color Palette. Expect this cell background to display differently on some platforms. |

Figure 4.2 *Web Safe Colors display in a predictable manner.*

Color and the Body Tag

You already have used attributes with the **<body>** tag to configure the page background color (bgcolor) and the text color (text). The link, alink, and vlink attributes can be used with the **<body>** tag to configure the hyperlink color, active link color, and visited link color on the web page. Table 4.1 shows attributes of the **<body>** tag that are related to color.

Table 4.1 **<body>** *Tag Color Attributes*

Attribute	Values	Usage
bgcolor	Valid color	Configures the background color.
text	Valid color	Configures the color of the text.
link	Valid color	Configures the color of the hyperlinks.
vlink	Valid color	Configures the color of the visited hyperlinks.
alink	Valid color	Configures the color of the active hyperlinks.

Even though it is possible to use body tag attributes to change the default colors of links, active links, and visited links, this doesn't mean that you should do so. Noted web design and usability expert Jakob Nielsen (http://www.useit.com) suggests that web developers not change the default link colors. He states that most web users expect hyperlinks to be blue, active links to be red, and visited links to be purple. Nielsen has found that web pages become more difficult to use when these default colors are changed.

Horizontal Rules

A horizontal rule or line can be helpful to separate areas of a page. Horizontal rule or **<hr />** tags place a horizontal line across a web page. The horizontal rule tag is used alone, not in a pair of opening and closing tags.

What color value should I use?

It depends. Use a color that is not on the Web Color Palette if you want the maximum color selectivity for your web page. Be aware that on certain combinations of browsers and operating systems, your colors may not be displayed or may be dithered. If a browser cannot display a requested color it will *dither*, or attempt to replace it with an approximation composed of two or more other colors it can produce. Figure 4.3 shows an image that was created using a color not on the Web Color Palette. Notice how grainy it is.

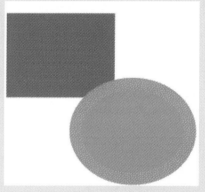

Figure 4.3 *Dithering*

Use colors on the Web Color Palette if you want to be certain that your site will look similar on all platforms. If you use other values, some combinations of browsers and operating systems will approximate your color by dithering. The choice is yours.

Open your index.htm file from your mywebsite web site in a text editor. Add an <hr /> tag after the "Contact me" line but before the line with the </body> tag. Add a line of text with "Date Last Updated" and today's date below the line with the <hr /> line.

Save your page and test it in a browser. It should look similar to the screen shot shown in Figure 4.4. Compare your work with the solution on the student disk (Chapter4/4.1/index.htm).

Figure 4.4 *index.htm with an* <hr /> *tag*

Horizontal Rule Attributes

Horizontal rules are centered on the web page by default. You can modify this with the align attribute. A number of other optional attributes appear in Table 4.2.

Table 4.2 *Horizontal Rule Attributes*

Attribute	Value
width	Percentage of the width of the web page `<hr width="85%" />`
	Width of the rule in pixels `<hr width="60" />`
color	A valid color `<hr color="#0000FF" />` The W3C recommends using hexadecimal color values.
align	Configures the alignment of the rule. `<hr align="right" />` left center (default) right
size	Height of the rule in pixels `<hr size="10" />`

Table 4.2 *Horizontal Rule Attributes (continued)*

Attribute	Value
border	Size of the rule border in pixels `<hr border="3" />`
noshade	Removes shadow from the rule. `<hr noshade="noshade" />` *Note:* If you were following HTML syntax, the correct coding for this tag is `<hr noshade>`. Since XHMTL documents follow the syntax of XML, all attributes must have values.

Hands-On Practice 4.2

Modify your index.htm page in the mywebsite folder and select a width of 75%, the color #0000FF (blue), and a size of 5 for your horizontal rule. Test in both Netscape and Internet Explorer browsers. Expect your page to look different in Netscape than in Internet Explorer. Netscape browsers usually support the width and align attributes but do not support the other horizontal rule attributes. See Figure 4.5 for a screen shot of the page using Internet Explorer. Figures 4.6 and 4.7 show the page displayed in Netscape 4.7 and Netscape 6. The student disk contains a sample solution (Chapter4/4.2/index.htm).

My page looks different in various browsers. What can I do?

Web pages looking different depending on the browser is a frustrating fact of life in the world of web development. The good news is that browser manufacturers are finally beginning to be less inventive and more compliant with the W3C standards. Also, organizations such as The Web Standards Project at http://www.webstandards.org/ have lobbied for standards compliance in browsers. Look for more compliance in the future!

Figure 4.5 *Internet Explorer display of revised index.htm*

Notice how a tag even as simple as
`<hr />` appears differently depending
upon the way the browsers display the
page. To avoid this,

- Design for the browser you think most
  of your visitors will use,

- Design the page so that it "degrades
  gracefully" (looks OK) in other
  browsers.

You have had an introduction to the use
of color on web pages, the horizontal
rule tag, and browser display issues
related to color and graphical elements.
The next section continues with a
discussion of types of graphics used on
web pages.

Figure 4.6 *Notice that the* **`<hr  />`** *tag is rendered differently in Netscape 4.*

Figure 4.7 *Netscape 6 also renders the* **`<hr  />`** *tag in different way than
Internet Explorer.*

Types of Graphics

Graphics help to make web pages compelling. Unfortunately, they can also make pages very slow to load. This section discusses types and features of graphic files used on the Web: GIF, JPEG, and PNG.

Browsers render, or display, web page documents in order, line-by-line, starting at the top of the document. They also display standard images as the files are read in order from top to bottom. The top of a standard image begins to display after 50% of the image has been read by a browser. As you read about types of images, look for techniques you can use to make your pages load faster.

GIF Images

Graphic interchange format (GIF) is best used for flat line drawings containing solid tones and simple images such as clip art. The maximum number of colors in a GIF file is 256 (although most do not use more than the 216 colors in the Web Color Palette). GIF images have a .gif file extension.

Transparency. The format GIF89A supports image transparency. In a graphics application such as Adobe Photoshop or a web authoring tool such as Microsoft FrontPage, one color (usually the background color) of the image can be set to be transparent. This helps the image to blend in with the web page background or table background. Figure 4.8 shows two GIF images, one that does not use transparency and one with a background color configured to be transparent.

Figure 4.8 *Comparison of nontransparent and transparent gifs*

When working with transparent GIFs you should also be aware of the halo effect—a fringe of color around parts of the transparent image. Transparent GIFs are usually optimized for display on a particular background color. Displaying them on a background other than the type they were designed for can produce the halo effect.

The GIF used in Figure 4.9 was created to display on a light background. When it is shown on a dark background, the halo of light pixels is noticeable. This halo can only be fixed by modifying the image in a graphics application such as Adobe Photoshop or Macromedia Fireworks and saving a version that is optimized for display on a dark background.

Figure 4.9 *Notice the halo effect on the dark background*

Animation. Animated GIF images also use the .gif file extension. They are contained in a GIF file that consists of several images or frames, each of which is slightly different. When the frames flash on the screen in order, the image appears animated, animated GIF images can be created in a graphics application such as Macromedia Fireworks or Adobe ImageReady. Shareware GIF animation applications such as the GIF Construction Set are also commonly used. There are advantages to using an animated gif to add action to your web page. This format is widely supported, does not require a browser plug-in, and is relatively easy to create.

When you decide to add an animated GIF to your web page, try to use the image only for special emphasis. If you're like most people, at some time you have been annoyed by a flashing ad banner at the top of a web page. Use animated gifs sparingly.

Compression. When a GIF file is saved, **lossless** compression is used. This means that nothing in the original image is lost and that the compressed image, when rendered by a browser, will contain the same pixels as the original.

Interlacing. When a GIF graphic file is created it can be configured as **interlaced**. This changes the way that browsers render the image. Remember that browsers display standard (noninterlaced) images as the file is read from top to bottom and only begin to display the image after 50% of the file has been downloaded by a browser. An interlaced image progressively displays and seems to fade in as it downloads. The image first appears fuzzy but

FAQ

Why does my text image look jagged?

If your image looks jagged, your graphic designer did not use **antialiasing** (sometimes called smoothing). Antialiasing is the process of creating a slight blur to smooth the jagged (stair-step) edges found in digital images. In Figure 4.10, the top image was created using antialiasing and the bottom was not. Note the jagged edges in the bottom image. The only letters not affected are the "I" and "i", because the shapes of these letters are perfectly horizontal and vertical.

Figure 4.10 *Notice the smoother look of the top line of text*

gradually becomes clearer and sharper. Interlaced images are repeatedly scanned from left to right. The first time about 13% of the image is displayed. The next pass renders about 25%. This process continues until the image is completely displayed. When you are using complex GIF images, consider interlacing to improve the perceived load time of your page.

JPEG Images

Joint Photographic Experts Group (JPEG) images are best used for photographic images. In contrast to a GIF image, a JPEG image can contain 16.7 million colors. But, JPEG images cannot be made transparent and they cannot be animated. JPEG images usually have a .jpg or .jpeg file extension.

Compression. Another difference between GIF and JPEG images is that JPEG images are **lossy** compressed. This means that some pixels in the original image are lost or removed from the compressed file. When a browser renders the compressed image, the display is similar but not exactly the same as the original image.

There are trade-offs between quality of the image and the amount of compression. An image with less compression will have higher quality and result in a larger file size. An image with more compression will have lower quality and result in a smaller file size. Most graphics applications allow you to preview the quality/compression trade-off and choose the image that best suits your needs.

Figure 4.11 shows a JPEG image (photograph taken by Karen Felke) that is stored in a 42K file. The same image was saved at various quality levels: Figure 4.12 was saved with 70% quality and is 36K; Figure 4.13 used 50% quality and is 18K; Figure 4.14 used 10% quality and is 5K. View these images to gain a perspective on the quality/size trade-off. You should notice that the quality of the image degrades as the file size decreases. The square blockiness you see in the smallest file is called **pixelation**.

Figure 4.11 *Initial JPEG image (42K file size) photo courtesy of Karen Felke*

Figure 4.12 *JPEG saved at 70% quality (36K file size)*

Figure 4.13 *JPEG saved at 50% quality (18K file size)*

Figure 4.14 *JPEG saved at 10% quality (5K file size)*

Progressive JPEG. When a JPEG file is created it can be configured as **progressive**. A progressive JPEG is similar to an interlaced GIF in that the image progressively displays and seems to fade in as it downloads. Consider using this for complex images since the general shapes will initially appear and then sharpen as the file is progressively scanned and displayed by the browser.

PNG Images

PNG, pronounced "ping", stands for **portable network graphic**. Browsers have only recently begun to support this type of image. It combines the best of GIF and JPEG images and will be a replacement for the GIF in the future. PNG graphics can support millions of colors. They can support variable transparency levels and use lossless compression. PNG images also support interlacing. PNG is the native file format of some graphics applications, such as Macromedia Fireworks.

Using Graphics

Now that you've been introduced to the use of color on web pages and different types of images, we get to the part you really want to know—how to place graphics on your web pages.

The <img> Tag

The **<img>**, or image, tag is used to place graphics on a web page. These graphics can be photographs, banners, company logos, navigation buttons —you are limited only by your creativity and imagination.

The image tag is used alone, not in a pair of opening and closing tags. The src (pronounced source) attribute is the only required attribute on an image tag. The image file should be in either the same folder as your web site or in a subfolder of your site. For example, to place an image called logo.gif on your web page, you would use the XHTML code

```
<img src="logo.gif" />
```

A number of optional attributes that can be applied to images. It is a good idea to include the height, width, and alt attributes. The height and width attributes can cause the web page to load more efficiently and quickly. The alt attribute provides a text description of the image. A better version of the logo XHTML code would be

```
<img src="logo.gif" height="200" width="500"  alt="CircleSoft Logo" />
```

Table 4.3 lists attributes and their values. Commonly used attributes are shown in bold.

Table 4.3 *Image Attributes*

Attribute	Value
align	right, left (default), center, top, texttop, middle, absmiddle, bottom
alt	Text phrase that describes the image
border	Image border size in pixels (0 will prevent the border from being displayed.)
height	Height of image in pixels
hspace	Amount of space that is blank to the left and right of the image in pixels
id	Text name, alphanumeric, beginning with a letter, no spaces, The value must be unique and not used for other id values on the same XHTML document.
longdesc	URL of a web page that contains a text description of the image.
name	Text name, alphanumeric, beginning with a letter, no spaces, This attribute names the image so that it can be easily accessed by client-side scripting languages such as JavaScript. This attribute is deprecated in XHTML but is used to provide backward compatibility with browsers that support HTML.
src	The URL or file name of the image
vspace	Amount of space that is blank above and below the image in pixels
width	Width of image in pixels

What if I don't know the height and width of an image?

Most graphics applications can display the height and width of an image. If you have a graphics application such as Adobe Photoshop or Macromedia Fireworks handy, launch the application and open the image. These applications include options that will display the properties of the image, such as height and width.

If you don't have a graphics application available, you can determine the dimensions of an image using Internet Explorer. Display the image on a web page. Right-click on the image to display the context-sensitive menu. Select properties and view the dimensions (height and width) of the image. (*Warning:* if the height and width are specified on the web page, those values will be displayed even if the image's actual height and width are different.)

Use height and width attributes to help the browser render your page more efficiently. If you omit the attributes, the browser must often adjust and shift the other page elements after your images load. This slows down the loading of your web page. The browser reserves the correct amount of space for your image if you use the height and width attributes with values either equal to or approximately the size of the image.

Use the alt attribute to provide accessibility. The alt attribute configures an alternative text description of the image. This alt text is used by the browser in two ways. The browser will show the alt text in the image area before the graphic is downloaded and displayed. The browser will also show the alt text as a tool tip whenever the web page visitor places a mouse over the image area. Applications such as screen readers will read the text in the alt attribute out loud. Macromedia's Accessibility Techniques Guidelines (http://www.trainingcafe.com/macromedia/accessibility/) recommend that alt text be no more than 50 characters long.

Standard browsers such as Internet Explorer and Netscape Navigator are not the only type of application or user agent that can access your web site. Major search engines run programs called *spiders* or *robots*; these programs index and categorize web sites. They cannot process images, but some do process the value of the alt attributes in image tags.

The longdesc attribute is used to provide accessibility when the alt text description is too short to convey the meaning of the image. The value of the longdesc attribute is the URL of a web page that contains a detailed text description and explanation of the image. Most current browsers do not support this attribute but you can expect expanded support in the future.

The align, vspace, and hspace attributes help position the image on the page relative to text. Examples of formatting images and text using vertical alignment properties are shown in Figure 4.15.

Vertical Alignment

align="top"

default alignment

align="middle"

Figure 4.15 *Examples of vertical alignment*

Figure 4.16 provides examples of horizontal alignments, the hspace attribute and the vspace attribute. The hspace and vspace attributes are used to symmetrically add space around an image.

Horizontal Alignment

The XHTML tag for this coffee cup image is coded with align="right". This causes the text to be placed to the left and wrap around the image. If text continues, it will wrap around the image. This should wrap under the image.

 The XHTML tag for this coffee cup image is coded with align="left". This causes the text to be placed to the right and wrap around the image. If text continues it will wrap around the image.

Figure 4.16 *Examples of horizontal alignment*

Page Backgrounds

Using the bgcolor attribute to configuring the background color of a web page was introduced in Chapter 2. The W3C recommends that web developers use the hexadecimal numeric value rather than the color name when setting a background color. For example, the XHTML code to configure the background of a web page to be a soft yellow is

```
<body bgcolor="#FFFF99">
```

You also can choose to use an image for the background of a web page. Be careful not to choose an image that is too busy; it could interfere with your text and graphics. Use the background attribute to configure a background image for a web page. For example, the XHTML code to configure the background of a web page to be the image background1.gif located in the same folder as the web page is

```
<body background="background1.gif">
```

You can use a graphics application to create your own backgrounds or find a free background image on the web.

Can I use *both* a bgcolor and a background attribute on the <body> tag?

Yes, you can! The background color (specified by the bgcolor attribute) will display first. Then the image specified as the web page background will be loaded and tiled across the page. It's a good idea to choose a background color of a hue similar hue to the major color in your web page background image. By coding both a background color and a background image you provide your visitor with a more pleasing visual experience. If the background image does not load for some reason, the page background will still have the expected contrast with your text color. XHTML for a page with both a background color and a background image is

```
<body bgcolor="#FFFF99"
  background="background1.gif">
```

You may think that a graphic created to be the background of a web page would always be about the size of a browser window. While this can be done, often the background image is actually much smaller than the typical browser window. The shape of a background image is usually either a long, thin rectangle or a small rectangular block. Web browsers repeat, or tile, these images to cover the page background. The images have small file sizes so that they download as quickly as possible. Figure 4.17 shows a long, thin rectangular image that will repeat down the page.

The web page shown in Figure 4.18 uses a small rectangular image that is repeated or tiled on the page.

In each of these cases, the small background image has the effect of a much larger image that fills the screen.

Figure 4.17 *A long, thin, background image tiles down the page.*

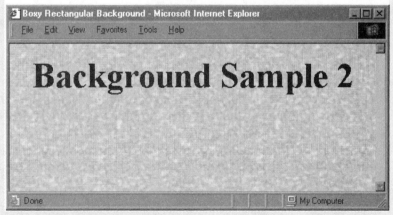

Figure 4.18 *A small rectangular background is repeated to fill the web page window.*

You will be creating a few web pages for a fictional web design company called CircleSoft. Create a new folder called circlesoft on a floppy disk. Obtain the images used in this Hands-On Practice from the textbook's student disk in the Chapter4/starters folder. Save the images in your circlesoft folder.

Launch Notepad and create the Home page, named index.htm, for your circlesoft web site. A sample screen shot is shown in Figure 4.19.

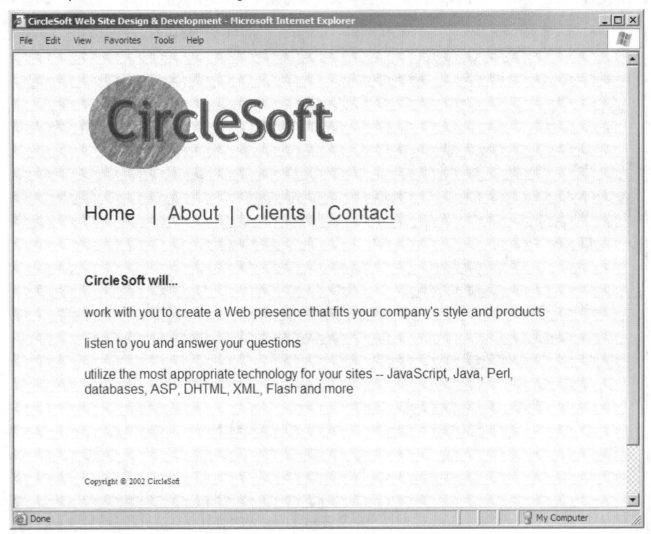

Figure 4.19 *CircleSoft index.htm*

The page should be configured as follows:

1. *Use a background image. Choose one of the following images from the textbook's student disk to use as your page background: background.gif, background1.gif, or background2.gif. Save the file in your circlesoft folder.*

2. *Display a logo for CircleSoft. Choose one of the following images from the textbook's student diskto use as your logo: logo1.gif or circlelogo.gif. Save the file in your circlesoft folder.*

3. *Include text that consists of a few sentences about CircleSoft. The sample uses Arial font. Either create your own text or use the following sample:*

   "CircleSoft will... work with you to create a Web presence that fits your company's style and products, listen to you and answer your questions, utilize the most appropriate technology for your sites— JavaScript, Java, Perl, databases, ASP, DHTML, XML, Flash and more."

4. *Include links to pages named about.htm, contact.htm, and clients.htm. The links in the sample use Arial font.*

5. *Save your file as index.htm in the circlesoft folder. Test it in a browser. Compare your results with the sample in Figure 4.19. The student disk contains a sample solution (Chapter4/4.3/index.htm).*

What if my images don't show?

Here are common reasons for images not displaying on a web page:

- Are your images *really* in the web site folder? Use Windows Explorer to double check.
- Did you code the XTHML correctly? Check for common mistakes such as typing "scr" instead of "src" and missing quotation marks.
- Do your images have the *exact* file names that you have used in the background or src attributes in your XHTML code? Attention to detail and consistency will be very helpful here.

Hints for naming image files:

- Use all lowercase letters.
- Do not use punctuation symbols and spaces.
- Do not change the file extensions (should be .gif, .jpg, .jpeg, or .png).
- Keep your file names short but descriptive.
  i1.gif is probably too short
  myimagewithmydogonmybirthday.gif is too long
  dogbday.gif may be just about right

Image Links

The XHTML to make an image function as a hyperlink is very easy. All you need to do is surround your `<img>` tag with anchor tags. For example, to place a link around an image called home.gif, use the following XHTML code:

```
<a href="index.htm"><img src="home.gif"
  height="19" width="85" alt="Home"
/></a>
```

When an image is used as a hyperlink, the default is to show a blue outline (border) around the image. If you would prefer not to display this outline, use the border="0" attribute in your image tag.

```
<a href="index.htm"><img src="home.gif"
  height="19" width="85" alt="Home"
  border="0" /></a>
```

What if my images are in their own folder?

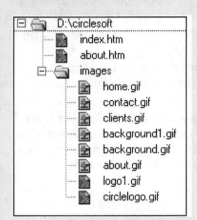

Figure 4.20

It's a good idea to organize your web site by placing all your images in a folder separate from your web pages. Notice that the circlesoft web site shown in Figure 4.20 has a folder called images that contains a number of gif files. To refer to these files in an `<img>` or `<body>` tag, you also need to refer to the images folder. Here are some examples:

- The XHTML code to configure the background.gif file from the images folder as the page background:

```
<body background="images/background.gif">
```

- The XHTML to place the logo1.gif file from the images folder:

```
<img src="image/logo1.gif"
  alt="CircleSoft Logo" width="500"
  height="100" />
```

Hands-On Practice 4.4

You will continue to work on your CircleSoft web site and replace the text links with image links. Obtain the images used in this Hands-On Practice from the textbook's Student disk in the Chapter4/starters folder. If you have not done so already, save the images in your "circlesoft" folder. (Note: These image files are images of text. Web developers often use images containing text when they want to use a special font that many visitors will not have installed on their computers.)

Launch Notepad and open your index.htm file. It's time to organize the web site by placing all the images in a single folder. See Figure 4.19 for an example. Add a folder called images to the web. (Hint: Launch Windows Explorer and select the circlesoft folder. Select File, New, and Folder. Name the folder images. Use Windows Explorer to move all your image files to the images folder.

Modify your index.htm page to refer to the background image in its new location; for example

```
<body background="images/background1.gif">
```

Modify the index.htm page to refer to the logo image in its new location; for example

```
<img src="images/circlelogo.gif" alt="CircleSoft Logo"
  height="40" width="100" />
```

Next, modify the index.htm page to use images as navigation links instead of the text links. The image named about.gif should link to the page about.htm; clients.gif should link to the page clients.htm; and contact.gif should link to the page contact.htm. The sample page uses a border value of 0 on all images used as hyperlinks. Save and test your page in a browser. The sample Home page uses a table to control the page layout and is shown in Figure 4.21.

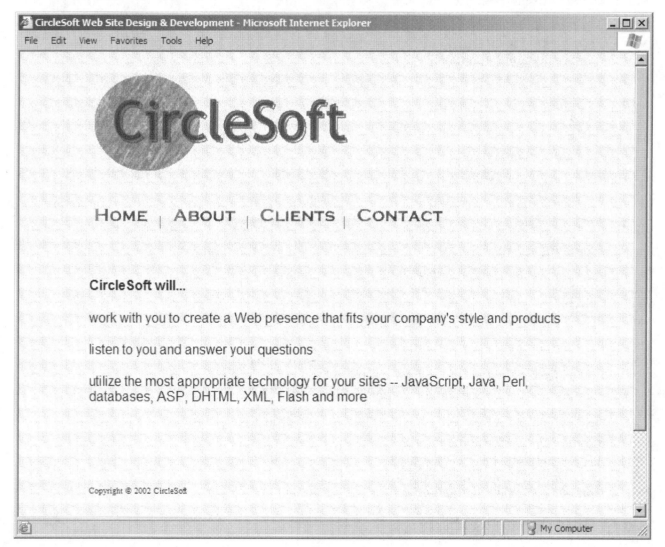

Figure 4.21 *CircleSoft index.htm with image links in a table*

Wouldn't it be a good idea to test your links? Next, you'll create another page for the CircleSoft site, the about.htm page shown in Figure 4.22.

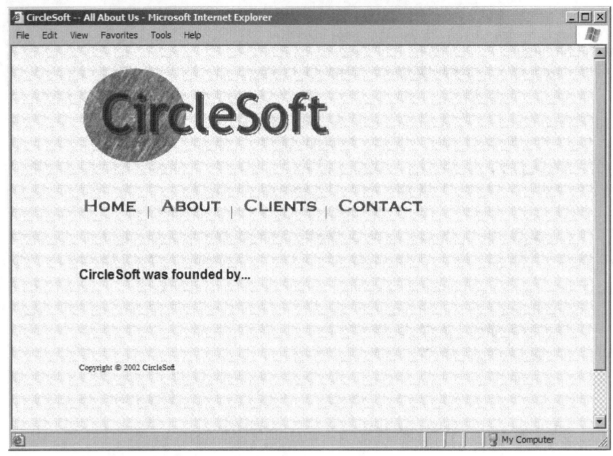

Figure 4.22 *CircleSoft about.htm*

You will use the index.htm page as the basis for your new page. Launch Notepad and open the index.htm file in your circlesoft folder. Select File, select Save As and save the file in the circlesoft folder with the name about.htm. Using Notepad, modify the about.htm file as follows:

1. *Modify the page title.*

2. *Modify the image links. Create a link from the home.gif image to the index.htm page. Remove the link from the about.gif to the about.htm page. Since this is the about.htm page there is no need to link to it.*

3. *Modify the content in the body of the web page to describe the founding of our fictional company. Either create some text yourself or use the text in the sample "CircleSoft was founded by ...".*

4. *Save the page and test it in a browser. Try hyperlinking back and forth between the index.htm and about.htm pages. You've got image links! See the Chapter4/4.4 folder in the student disk for sample pages.*

XHTML Images and More

This section introduces additional XHTML coding techniques associated with using images on web pages. Topics discussed include the **<nobr>** tag, using a table to format images, image maps, thumbnail images, and image slicing.

The <nobr> Tag

There are times when you might be using images in a navigation bar and you would like to keep the images in a horizontal row no matter what the screen resolution settings are or browser window size is on your visitor's computer. That's when the **<nobr>** tag can be useful. The web page shown in Figure 4.23 did not use the **<nobr>** tag.

Figure 4.23 *Undesirable effect of resizing the browser window*

When the browser is resized, the images move to the next line. This is usually not desirable when using a horizontal row of images for site navigation. Figure 4.24 shows a web page with this problem corrected.

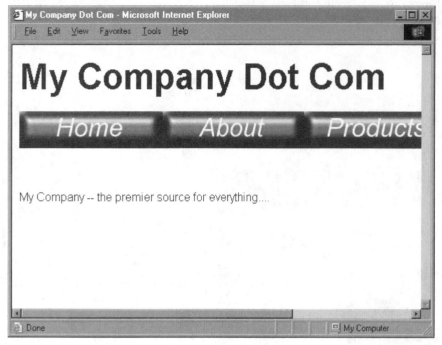

Figure 4.24 *Using the* **<nobr>** *tag to keep the images in a horizontal line*

The page in Figure 4.24 used the opening **<nobr>** tag before the images that are to remain on the same line and the closing **</nobr>** tag after the images that are to remain on the same line. Notice that the browser now has a horizontal scroll bar and displays the images in a straight line. Here's the XHTML code for this example:

```
<nobr>
<a href="index.htm"><img src="home.gif" alt="Home" width="200" height="50"
  border="0 /"></a>
<a href="about.htm"><img src="about.gif" alt="About" width="200" height="50"
  border="0" /></a>
<a href="products.htm"><img src="products.gif" alt="Products" width="200"
  height="50" border="0" /></a>
<a href="contact.htm"><img src="contact.gif" alt="Contact" width="200" height="50"
  border="0" /></a>
</nobr>
```

Using a Table to Format Images

Another technique to force the images into a horizontal line across the page is to place the images in a table. (Refer to Chapter 3 for information on tables.) An example of this is shown in Figure 4.25.

Using a Table to Format the Navigation Bar

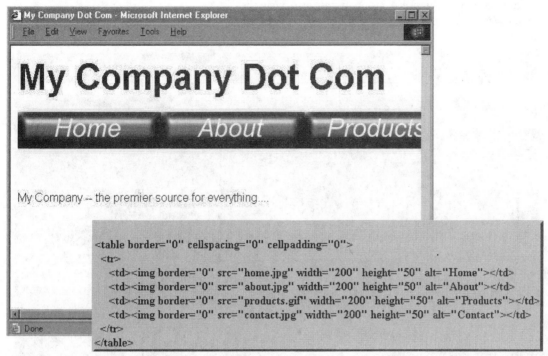

Figure 4.25 *A table keeps the images in a horizontal line.*

Why would you choose one technique over the other? It depends. If you are using tables to format your web page, it would seem appropriate to also use one to format your image navigation as well. Using tables to format a web page gives you greater control over the placement of text and images. Here is XHTML for a table used for this purpose.

```
<table border="0" cellspacing="0" cellpadding="0">
  <tr>
    <td><img border="0" src="home.gif" alt="Home" width="200" height="50" /></td>
    <td><img border="0" src="about.gif" alt="About" width="200" height="50" /></td>
    <td><img border="0" src="products.gif" alt="Products" width="200"
      height="50" /></td>
    <td><img border="0" src="contact.gif" alt="Contact" width="200"
      height="50" /></td>
  </tr>
</table>
```

Image Maps

An **image map** is an image that can be used as one or more hyperlinks. An image map will have at least one clickable area and usually multiple clickable areas that link to another web page or web site. The clickable areas are sometimes called **hotspots**. You have probably used image maps many times but never realized it. The web site for the Museum of Science and Industry in Chicago, http://www.msichicago.org/, usually uses an image map on their home page. See Figure 4.26. You can also visit the text's web site at http://webdevfoundations.net/chapter4 to try out an image map.

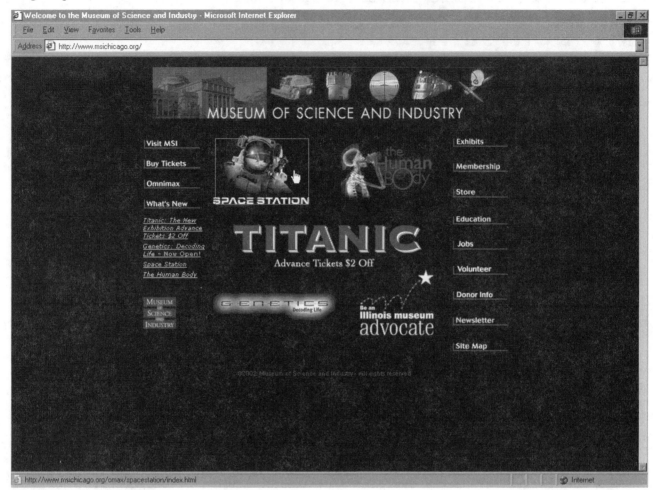

Figure 4.26 *An image map is used to highlight popular exhibits on this web site.*

Most web authoring software, such as Microsoft FrontPage or Macromedia Dreamweaver, have wizards or other tools to help you create image maps quickly and easily. If you don't have access to a web authoring tool to create an image map, the most difficult part is determining the pixel coordinates of the hyperlink area. The coordinates are in pairs of numbers that signify the number of pixels from the top and the number of pixels from the left edge of the image. If you are working with a graphic artist, he or she may be able to supply you with the coordinates. Another option is to open the image in a graphics application such as Macromedia Fireworks, Adobe Photoshop, or even MS Paint to obtain approximate coordinates. You can modify these coordinate values as you work with the XHTML on your web page. Image maps can be used to create clickable areas in three shapes: rectangles, circles, and polygons.

An image map uses two new tags: **<map>** and **<area>**. The **<map>** tag is a container tag and is used to begin and end the image map. The name attribute is used to correspond the **<map>** tag with its associated image. The **<img>** tag uses a new attribute, usemap, to indicate which **<map>** to use. For example, **<img src="fishingboat.jpg" usemap="#boat" />** will be associated with the image map described by **<map name="boat" id="boat">**. The id attribute is part of XHTML. The name attribute is required for backward compatibility with older browsers that were written to process HTML.

The **<area>** tag is used to define the coordinates or edges of the map area and uses shape, coords, alt, and href attributes. Table 4.4 describes the type of coordinates (coords) needed for each shape value.

Table 4.4 *Shape Coordinates*

Shape	coords	Meaning
rect	"x1,y1, x2, y2"	The coordinates at point (x1,y1) represent the upper-left corner of the rectangle. The coordinates at point (x2,y2) represent the lower-right corner of the rectangle.
circle	"x,y,r"	The coordinates at point (x,y) indicate the center of the circle. The value of r is the radius of the circle in pixels.
polygon	"x1, y1, x2, y2, x3, y3", etc.	The values of each (x,y) pair represent the coordinates of a corner point of the polygon.

This text focuses on rectangular image maps. For a rectangular image map, the value of the shape attribute is "rect" and the coordinates indicate the pixel positions as follows: upper-left corner distance from top of image, upper-left corner distance from left side of image, lower-right corner distance from top of image, lower-right corner distance from left edge of image.

Figure 4.27 shows an image with a fishing boat. The dotted rectangle around the fishing boat indicates the location of the hotspot. The coordinates shown (24, 188) indicate the top left corner is 24 pixels from the left edge of the image and 188 pixels from the top of the image. The pair of coordinates in the lower right corner (339, 283) indicates this corner is 339 pixels from the left image edge and 283 pixels from the image top. The XHTML to create this image map is as follows.

```
<map name="boat" id="boat">
<area href="http://www.doorcountyvacations.com" shape="rect"
  coords="24, 188, 339, 283" alt="Door County Fishing" />
</map>
<img src="fishingboat.jpg" usemap="#boat" alt="Door County"
  width="416" height="350" />
```

Figure 4.27 *Sample image map*

This example is for a client-side image map. No special web server processing is needed for this image map to work. Another, more complex type of Image Map is a server-side image map. This type requires a program on the web server to coordinate the linking. Server-side maps are no longer commonly used because they require resources on the web server. It is more efficient to distribute processing to be on the web browser client whenever possible. This way, the resources of the web server can be reserved for the tasks that only it can perform.

Most web developers do not hand-code image maps. As mentioned previously, the easiest way to create a client-side image map is to use a web authoring tool. Some shareware programs, such as CoffeCup Image Mapper 3.0 (http://www.coffeecup.com/mapper) and HTML Map Designer Pro 2.0 (http://www.imagecure.com/) also provide this feature.

Thumbnail Images

A **thumbnail image** is a smaller version of an image you would like to include on your site. It usually is placed within anchor tags that link to the larger, more detailed version of the image. Large images can significantly increase the load time of a web page. If you are creating a page with multiple detailed images, consider displaying thumbnail images instead. This way, visitors who are interested in the images and willing to wait can use the thumbnail image to link to the larger image.

Most graphics applications can create thumbnail images. Microsoft FrontPage is one authoring tool that provides this feature.

Advanced Techniques: Image Slicing

Graphic artists and designers can create complex web page images. Sometimes parts of these images are better optimized as GIFs than as JPEGs. Some parts of these images may be better optimized as JPEGs rather than as GIFs. By **slicing** the single, complex images into multiple smaller images, you can optimize all portions for the most efficient display. There may be times when you plan special mouse rollover effects for parts of a large, complex, image. In this case, parts of the image need to be individually accessible to scripting languages and the image needs to be sliced. When an image is sliced, it is broken into multiple graphic files. These multiple graphic files are formatted using an XHTML table. Most graphics applications, such as Macromedia Fireworks and Adobe Photoshop, have features for image slicing that automatically create the XHTML for you. Visit the text's web site at http://webdevfoundations.net/chapter4 for more information on image slicing.

Sources and Guidelines for Graphics

How do you obtain graphics for your pages? What are recommended ways to use graphics? This section will help you answer these questions and discuss sources of graphics as well as guidelines for using images on web pages.

 ## Sources of Graphics

There are many ways to obtain graphics: you can create them yourself using a graphics application, download them from a free site, purchase and download them from a graphics site, purchase a graphics collection on a CD, take digital photographs, scan photographs, scan drawings, or hire a graphic designer to create graphics for you. Popular graphic applications include Adobe Photoshop, Macromedia Fireworks, and Jasc PaintShop Pro. These applications usually include tutorials and sample images to help you get started. Visit the text's web site, http://webdevfoundations.net/chapter4, for a tutorial on using Macromedia Fireworks to create a logo banner image.

However, one thing that you should definitely not do is right-click and download graphics that others have created without their permission. Materials on a web site are copyrighted (even if a copyright symbol or notice is not visible) and not free for use by others unless the owner of the site permits it.

There are many web sites that offer free graphics, although some graphics are free for nonprofit use only. Choose any search engine and search for "free graphics"—you'll get more results than you have time to view. Here are a few sites that you may find helpful when looking for images:

- Microsoft Design Gallery Live: http://dgl.microsoft.com/
- Big Nose Bird: http://www.bignosebird.com/sets.shtml
- Free Stock Photos: http://free-stock-photos.com/
- Free Images: http://www.freeimages.co.uk/

Some sites offer graphics and photographs for a fee. A selection is listed here. Search for "stock photos" to find others.

- Photos To Go: http://www.photostogo.com/default.asp
- The Stock Solution: http://www.tssphoto.com/
- SuperStock: http://www.superstock.com/
- Photo Disc: http://photodisc.com

Recently Adobe began offering free online graphics tools at http://webservices.adobe.com. As you might expect, the number of options offered by this free service are limited. However, Adobe's online functions may help you get started creating banners and other graphics.

Guidelines for Using Images

Images can help your web page by creating an engaging, interesting user experience. Images can hurt your web pages by slowing down their performance to a crawl and discouraging visitors.

Consider Image Load Time. Be careful when using images on web pages—it takes time for them to load. A suggested maximum file size for both the web page and all the media files used by it is 60K. If your banner graphic is 25K, that does not leave much room for other images or even for your web page XHTML. Use images when they are necessary to convey a message or a web site's look and feel. Table 4.5 lists the download time for file sizes of 30K, 60K, and 90K at various connection speeds.

Table 4.5 *Download Times*

File Size	Connection Speed				
	28.8K	33.6K	56K	128K ISDN	T-1 (1.544Mb)
30K	8 seconds	7 seconds	4 seconds	1 second	Less than 1 second
60K	17 seconds	14 seconds	8 seconds	3 seconds	Less than 1 second
90K	25 seconds	21 seconds	13 seconds	5 seconds	Less than 1 second

Reuse Images. Once an image from your site is requested for a web page, it is stored in the cache on your visitor's hard drive. Subsequent requests for the image will use the file from the hard drive instead of another download. This results in faster page loads for all pages that also use the image. It is recommended that you reuse common graphics such as logos and navigation buttons on multiple pages instead of creating multiple different versions of these common graphics.

The Size/Quality Issue. When using a graphics application to create an image, you can choose between varying levels of image quality. There is a correspondence between the quality of the image and the size of the image file—the higher the quality, the larger the file size. Choose the smallest file that gives you appropriate quality. You may need to experiment until you get the right match. Also be aware of the file size when using graphics created by others—the image may look great but if it is 300K, you really shouldn't use it on a web page.

Resolution. Web browsers display images at 72ppi (pixels per inch) resolution. Many digital cameras and scanners can create images with much higher resolution. Of course, higher resolution means larger file size. Even though the browser does not display the depth of resolution, more bandwidth is still used for the large file size. Be careful when taking digital photographs or scanning. Use a resolution setting appropriate for web pages. A one-inch image saved at 150ppi will appear close to two inches wide on a 72ppi monitor.

Specify Dimensions. Always use accurate height and width attributes on image tags. This will allow the browser to allocate the appropriate space on the web page for the image and load the page faster. Do not try to resize the appearance of an image by modifying the settings of the height and width attributes. While this will work, your page will load slower and your image quality may suffer. Instead, use a graphics application to create a smaller or larger version of the graphic when needed.

Gamma. Gamma refers to the brightness and contrast of the monitor display. Monitors used with Macintosh and Windows operating systems use a different default gamma setting (Macintosh 1.8, Windows 2.2). Images that have good contrast on a computer running Windows may look slightly washed out on a Macintosh. Images created on a Macintosh may look darker with less contrast when displayed on a computer with a Windows operating system. Be aware that even monitors on the same operating system may have slightly different gamma values than the default for the platform. A web developer cannot control gamma, but should be aware that images will look different on various platforms because of this issue.

Web Accessibility

Even though images help to create a compelling, interesting web site, remember that not all your visitors will be able to view your images. The Web Accessibility Initiative has a number of guidelines for web developers in the use of color and images.

- Don't rely on color alone. Some visitors may have color perception deficiencies. Use high contrast between background and text color.
- Avoid using the colors red and brown next to each other—they are difficult for individuals with the most common color perception deficiency to differentiate.
- Provide a text equivalent for every nontext element. Use the alt attribute on your image tags.
- If your site navigation uses image links, provide simple text links at the bottom of the page.

Vinton Cerf, the coinventor of TCP/IP and the former Chairman of the Internet Society, has said, "The Internet is for everyone." Follow web accessibility guidelines to ensure this is true.

Chapter 4 Review

Summary

This chapter introduced the use of color and graphical elements on web pages. As you continue to create web pages, look back at the guidelines and accessibility issues related to graphics. The number one reason visitors leave web pages is long download times. When using images, be careful to minimize download time. Also, provide alternatives to images (such as text links) and use the alt attribute on your pages.

Visit the text's web site at http://www.webdevfoundations.net for examples, updated information, and the links listed in this chapter.

Review Questions

Multiple Choice

1. Why should you include height and width attributes on an **`<img>`** tag?
   a. They are required attributes and must always be included.
   b. To help the browser render the page faster because it reserves the appropriate space for the image.
   c. To help the browser display the image in its own window.
   d. None of the above

2. If you place both the background and the bgcolor attributes on the **`<body>`** tag, the browser will
   a. display the background color instead of the background image.
   b. display no background for the page because it is confused.
   c. display the background color while the background image loads and before the background image is displayed.
   d. do none of the above

3. Choose the item that creates an image link to the index.htm page when the home.gif graphic is clicked.
   a. `<a href="index.htm" src="home.gif"></a>`
   b. `<a href="index.htm"><img src="home.gif" /></a>`
   c. `<img src="home.gif" href="index.htm">`
   d. none of the above

4. What tag is used to place in image on a web page?
   a. `<a href>`   c. `<image>`
   b. `<img>`   d. `<graphic>`

5. What attribute specifies text that is available to browsers and other user agents that do not support graphics?
   a. alt   c. src
   b. text   d. none of the above

6. One method to display a group of images all on one line, even if the browser window is resized, is to
   a. place all the **`<img>`** tags on one line in the source code.
   b. place multiple src attributes on a single **`<img>`** tag.
   c. surround the group of images with **`<nobr>`** and **`</nobr>`** tags.
   d. none of the above

7. A type of graphic that is best-suited to photographs is
   a. GIF
   b. photo
   c. PNG
   d. none of the above

8. A type of graphic that can be made transparent and is commonly used on the Web is
   a. GIF
   b. JPG
   c. PNG
   d. photo

9. The Web Safe Color Palette is a collection of 216 colors that
   a. display quicker than other colors.
   b. display the same on both the Mac and PC platforms.
   c. relate to the fashion industry and change each year.
   d. none of the above

10. Choose the color that is considered a Web Safe Color:
    a. #0045FF
    b. #123456
    c. #000022
    d. #33CC99

Fill in the Blank

11. When displaying an image to the left of a block of text on a web page, use the align attribute with the value of _____.

12. If your web page uses graphic links, include _____ at the bottom of the page to increase accessibility.

13. A _____ image is a smaller version of a larger image that usually links to the larger image.

14. One method to obtain graphics for your web site is to _____.

15. A(n) _____ is an image that can be used as one or more hyperlinks.

Apply Your Knowledge

1. **Predict the Result.** Draw and write a brief description of the web page that will be created with the following XHTML code:

```
<?xml version="1.0" encoding="UTF-8"?>
<!DOCTYPE html PUBLIC "-//W3C//DTD XHTML 1.0 Transitional//EN"
   "http://www.w3.org/TR/xhtml1/DTD/xhtml1-transitional.dtd">
<html xmlns="http://www.w3.org/1999/xhtml" >
<head>
<title>Predict the Result</title>
</head>
<body>
  <div align="center">
    <img src="logo.gif" alt="Trillium Technologies" height="150" width="600" />
    <br />
    <p>Home <a href="about.htm">About</a> <a href="services.htm">Services</a>
    </p>
  </div>
```

continues

```
<p><img src="people.jpg" alt="Professionals at Trillium Technologies"
    height="300" width="300" align="right" /> Our professional staff takes pride
    in its working relationship with our clients by offering personalized services
    which listen to their needs, develop their target areas, and incorporate these
    items into a well presented Web Site that works.</p>
  <p> </p>
  <p> </p>
<div align="center">
  <p> <font size="1">
   Contact <a href="mailto:web@trilliumtechnologies.biz">
    web@trilliumtechnologies.biz</a>
    <br />
   Copyright &copy; 2003 Trillium Technologies</font></p>
</div>
</body>
</html>
```

2. **Fill in the Missing Code.** This web page contains an image link and should be configured so that the background and text colors have good contrast. The image used on this web page should link to a page called services.htm. Some XHTML tags and their attributes, indicated by **<_>**, are missing. Some XHTML attribute values, indicated by "_" are missing.

```
<?xml version="1.0" encoding="UTF-8"?>
<!DOCTYPE html PUBLIC "-//W3C//DTD XHTML 1.0 Transitional//EN"
   "http://www.w3.org/TR/xhtml1/DTD/xhtml1-transitional.dtd">
<html xmlns="http://www.w3.org/1999/xhtml" >
<head>
<title>Trillium Technologies</title>
</head>
<body bgcolor="#0066CC" text="_" link="_" vlink="_">
  <_><img src="logo.gif" alt="_" height="100" width="600" /></a><br />
  <a href="services.htm">Enter Trillium Technologies</a>
</body>
</html>
```

3. **Find the Error**. This page displays an image called trillium.jpg. This image is 100 pixels wide by 200 pixels high. When this page is displayed, the image does not look right. Find the error. Describe the attributes that you would code in the **<img>** tag to provide accessibility.

```
<?xml version="1.0" encoding="UTF-8"?>
<!DOCTYPE html PUBLIC "-//W3C//DTD XHTML 1.0 Transitional//EN"
   "http://www.w3.org/TR/xhtml1/DTD/xhtml1-transitional.dtd">
<html xmlns="http://www.w3.org/1999/xhtml" >
<head>
<title>Find the Error<title>
</head>
<body>
  <img src="trillium.jpg" height="100" width="100" />
</body>
</html>
```

Hands-On Exercises

1. Practice writing XHTML for images

   a. Write the XHTML to place an image called mylogo.gif on a web page. The height of the image is 100 pixels. The width of the image is 600 pixels.

   b. Write the XHTML to create an image hyperlink. The image is called myfamily.jpg. It is 200 pixels high by 300 pixels wide. The image should link to a web page called family.htm. There should be no border on the image.

   c. Write the XHTML to create a row of three images used as navigation links. Because they are used in this manner, write code that will ensure that they always appear on the same line of the web page. Table 4.6 gives information about the images and their associated links.

Table 4.6

Image Name	Link Page Name	Image Height	Image Width
home.gif	index.htm	50	200
products.gif	products.htm	50	200
order.gif	order.htm	50	200

2. Create a new web page about your favorite movie. This page will use a table for layout (review sample table layouts in Chapter 3), a background color for the page, and either background images or background colors for at least two sections of the table. Search the Web for a photo of a scene from the movie, an actress in the movie, or an actor in the movie.

(*Note:* It is not ethical to steal an image from another web site. Some web sites have a link to their copyright policy. Most web sites will give permission for you to use an image in a school assignment. If there is no available policy, e-mail the site's contact person and request permission to use the photo. If you are unable to obtain permission, you may substitute with clip art or an image from a free site instead.) Include the following information on your web page:

- Title of the movie
- Director or producer
- Leading actor
- Leading actress
- Rating (R, PG-13, PG, G, NR)
- A brief description of the movie
- An absolute link to a review about the movie

Place an email link to yourself on the web page. Save the page as movie3.htm. Hand in printouts of both the source code (print in Notepad) and the browser display of your page.

3. Create a web page that includes a table and provides a list of resources for free clip art and free photographs. The list should contain at least five different web sites. Use your favorite graphic sites, the sites suggested in this chapter, or sites you have found on the Web. The table should be centered on the page, use 60% of the width of the page, and have two columns. Each row will display the URL of a graphic site in the first column and a sample image from the site in the second column. Place an e-mail link to yourself on the web page. Save the page as freegraphics.htm. Hand in printouts of both the source code (print in Notepad) and the browser display of your page.

4. Create a Web page about your favorite musical group. Use a table for layout (review sample table layouts in Chapter 3), a background color for the page, and either background images or background colors for at least two sections of the table. Search the Web for a photo of the group.

(*Note:* It is not ethical to steal an image from another web site. Some web sites have a link to their copyright policy. Most web sites will give permission for you to use an image in a school assignment. If there is no available policy, e-mail the site's contact person and request permission to use the photo. If you are unable to obtain permission, you may substitute clip art or an image from a free site.) Include the following information about the group on your web page:

- Name of group
- Type of music
- Names of principle group members
- Photo of group
- Link to another web page with information about the group.

Include an e-mail link to yourself on the web page. Save the page as band3.htm. Hand in printouts of both the source code (print in Notepad) and the browser display of your page.

5. Visit the text's web site at http://webdevfoundations.net/chapter4 and follow the link to the Macromedia Fireworks tutorial. Follow the instructions to create a logo banner. Hand in the printouts described in the tutorial to your instructor.

Each of these case studies will continue throughout most of the text. The case study activities in this chapter include adding images to the web site, creating a new page, and modifying existing pages.

A. JavaJam Coffee House

See Chapter 2 for an introduction to the JavaJam Coffee House case. Figure 2.20 shows a site map for JavaJam. The Home page and Menu page were created in earlier chapters. You will continue to work with this web site in this case study, creating the Performances page, shown in Figure 4.28.

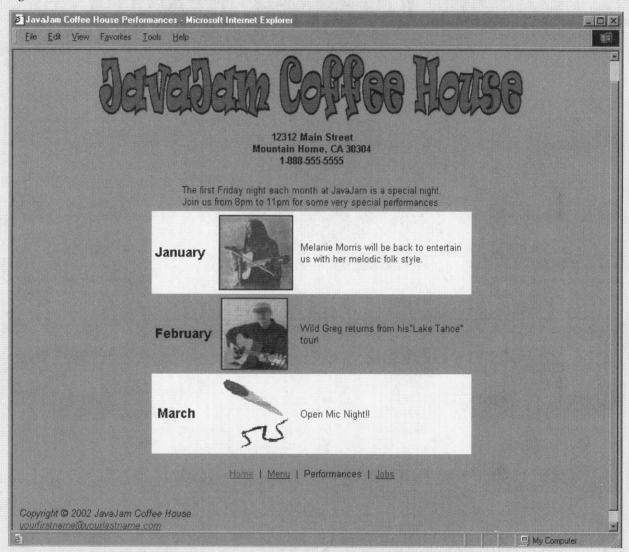

Figure 4.28 *JavaJam performances.htm*

Hands-On Practice Case

1. Obtain the images used in this case study from the textbook's student disk. The images are located in the Chapter4/CaseStudyStarters folder. The images are: javalogo.gif (Figure 4.29), melanie.jpg (Figure 4.30), melaniethumb.jpg (Figure 4.31), greg.jpg (Figure 4.32), gregthumb.jpg (Figure 4.33), and mic.gif (Figure 4.34). Save them in your javajam folder.

Figure 4.29 *JavaJam logo (javalogo.gif)*

Figure 4.30 *Melanie Morris (melanie.jpg)*

Figure 4.32 *Greg (greg.jpg)*

Figure 4.31 *Melanie Morris thumbnail (melaniethumb.jpg)*

Figure 4.33 *Greg thumbnail (gregthumb.jpg)*

Figure 4.34 *Microphone graphic (mic.gif)*

2. Use the Menu page as the starting point for the performances page. Launch Notepad and open the menu.htm file in the JavaJam folder that you previously created. Save the file as performances.htm.

3. Center the page content by placing a **`<div align="center">`** tag below the **`<body>`** tag and a **`</div>`** tag directly above the **`</body>`** tag.

4. Modify your file to be similar to the Performances page, shown in Figure 4.28:

- Change the page title to an appropriate phrase.
- Replace the "JavaJam Coffee House" heading with the javalogo.gif, Figure 4.29. Be sure to include the alt, height, and width attributes on the **<img>** tag for the graphic.
- Modify the text links at the bottom of the page. The "Menu" text should link to the menu.htm page. Remove the link on the "Performances" text.
- The page content will consist of a table with three rows and three columns. Either modify the existing table or delete the existing table and create a new one with the specified format.
- The content of the table is as follows:

  Line 1 Column 1: "January"

  Line 1 Column 2: Use the melaniethumb.jpg as an image link to melanie.jpg. Use appropriate attributes on the **<img>** tag.

  Line 1 Column 3: "Melanie Morris will be back to entertain us with her melodic folk style."

  Line 2 Column 1: "February"

  Line 2 Column 2: Use the gregthumb.jpg as an image link to greg.jpg. Remember to use the alt, height, and width attributes on the **<img>** tag. Line 2 Column 3: "Wild Greg returns from his 'Lake Tahoe' tour!"

  Line 3 Column 1: "March"

  Line 3 Column 2: Insert the mic.gif image. This image is not used as a hyperlink.

  Line 3 Column 3: "Open Mic Night!!"

- The text contained in the table should use the Arial font. The names of the months ("January, February, March") should use size="4", be bold (use the **<strong>** tag), and be centered. Configure the remaining text in the table to use Arial font with size="2".
- Configure the table with no border, width of 448 pixels, cellpadding set to 5 and cellspacing set to 0. As indicated in Figure 4.28, the table rows should use alternating background colors. You may configure the table cell widths using pixels or percentages to obtain a pleasing effect. The **<td>** tags in the sample are configured using the width set to a pixel value. Experiment until you achieve a look that you like.

5. Save your page and test it in a browser. If your images do not appear or your image links do not work, examine your work carefully. Use Windows Explorer to verify that the images are saved in your javajam folder. Examine the src attribute on the **<img>** tags to be sure you spelled the image names correctly.

6. Modify the Home page (index.htm) and Menu page (menu.htm) to look similar to the Performances page you just created. Save and test your pages. Isn't it interesting how just a few images can add a professional look to a web site?

B. Fish Creek Animal Hospital

See Chapter 2 for an introduction to the Fish Creek Animal Hospital case. Figure 2.23 shows a site map for Fish Creek. The Home page and Services page were created in earlier chapters. You will continue to work with this web site in this case study, creating the Ask The Vet page, shown in Figure 4.35.

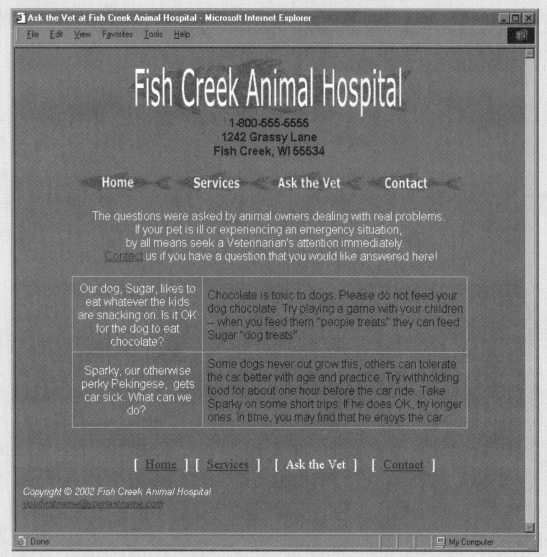

Figure 4.35 *Fish Creek askthevet.htm*

Hands-On Practice Case

1. Obtain the images used in this case study from the student disk. The images are located in the Chapter4/CaseStudyStarters folder. The images are: fishcreeklogo.gif (Figure 4.36), home.gif (Figure 4.37}, services.gif (Figure 4.38), askthevet.gif (Figure 4.39), and contact.gif (Figure 4.40) files and save them in your fishcreek folder.

Figure 4.36 *Fish Creek logo (fishcreeklogo.gif)*

Figure 4.37 *Home button (home.gif)*

Figure 4.38 *Services button (services.gif)*

Figure 4.39 *Ask the Vet button (askthevet.gif)01*

Figure 4.40 *Contact button (contact.gif)*

2. Use the Services page as the starting point for the Ask the Vet page. Launch Notepad and open the services.htm file in the fishcreek folder that you previously created. Save the file as askvet.htm.

3. Center the page content by placing a `<div align="center">` tag below the `<body>` tag and a `</div>` tag directly above the `</body>` tag.

4. Modify your file to be similar to the Ask The Vet page shown in Figure 4.35.

   Change the page title to an appropriate phrase.

   - Replace the "Fish Creek Animal Hospital" heading with the fishcreeklogo.gif, Figure 4.36. Be sure to include the alt, height, and width attributes on the `<img>` tag for the graphic.

   - Move the text links to the bottom of the page right above the copyright information (see Figure 4.35). Next, modify the text links so that they are appropriate for this page. The "Services" text should link to the services.htm page. Remove the link from the "Ask the Vet" text.

   - See Figure 4.35 and add image links under the logo area. The home.gif (Figure 4.37) should link to index.htm. The services.gif (Figure 4.38) should link to services.htm. The askthevet.gif (Figure 4.39) should not link to another web page. The contact.gif (Figure 4.40) should link to contact.htm. Use appropriate attributes on the `<img>` tag: alt, height, width, border.

   - Delete the table that was part of the services.htm page.

   - The page content consists of a paragraph of text followed by a table that contains frequently asked questions and answers.

   - The text in the paragraph is as follows:

   - "The questions were asked by animal owners dealing with real problems. If your pet is ill or experiencing an emergency situation, by all means seek a Veterinarian's attention immediately. Contact us if you have a question that you would like answered here!"

   The paragraph should be centered. Use line breaks (`<br />`) where appropriate. This text should be Arial font and use the page text color of white (#FFFFFF). The word "Contact" should link to the contact.htm page.

     - The table consists of two rows and two columns and is configured to have a border set to 1, a width of 80%, cellpadding set to 5, and cellspacing set to 0.

- The content of the table is as follows:

  Line 1 Column 1: "Our dog, Sugar, likes to eat whatever the kids are snacking on. Is it OK for the dog to eat chocolate?"

  Line 1 Column 2: "Chocolate is toxic to dogs. Please do not feed your dog chocolate. Try playing a game with your children—when you feed them "people treats" they can feed Sugar "dog treats"."

  Line 2 Column 1: "Sparky, our otherwise perky Pekingese, gets car sick. What can we do?"

  Line 2 Column 2: "Some dogs never out grow this, others can tolerate the car better with age and practice. Try withholding food for about one hour before the car ride. Take Sparky on some short trips. If he does OK, try longer ones. In time, you may find that he enjoys the car."

  The text contained in the table should use the Arial font. Each cell should use center alignment (`<td align="center">`). The text in the second column of each row should be configured to the color black (#000000) as the text color.

5. Save your page and test it in a browser. If your images do not appear or your image links do not work, examine your work carefully. Use Windows Explorer to verify that the images are saved in your fishcreek folder. Examine the src attribute on the `<img>` tags to be sure you spelled the image names correctly.

6. Modify the Home page (index.htm) and Services page (services.htm) to look similar to the Ask the Vet page you just created. Save and test your pages. Notice how the use of coordinating logo and navigation images helped to unite the web site visually. To provide accessibility, the original text navigation links were not deleted. Instead they were moved to the bottom of the page. It is common for sites that use images for main navigation to provide simple text links at the lower portion of each web page.

C. Pete the Painter

See Chapter 2 for an introduction to the Pete the Painter case. Figure 2.26 shows a site map for Pete the Painter. The Home page and Services page were created in earlier chapters. You will continue to work with this web site in this case study and create the Testimonials page, shown in Figure 4.41.

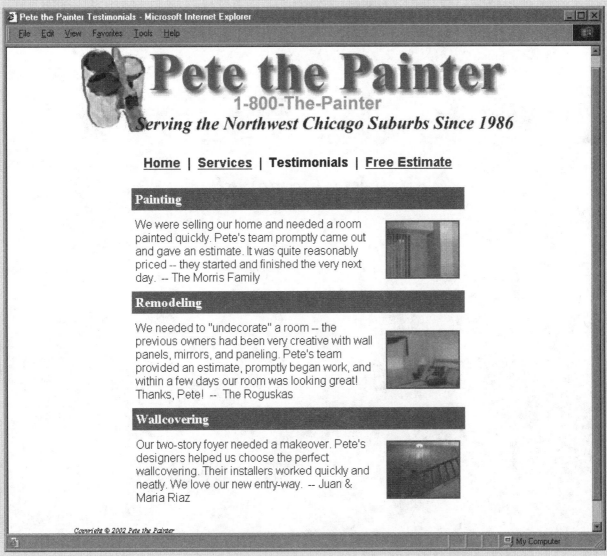

Figure 4.41 *Pete the Painter testimonials.htm*

Hands-On Practice Case

1. Obtain the images used in this Case Study from the student disk. The images are located in the Chapter4/CaseStudyStarters folder. The images are: painterlogo.gif (Figure 4.42), paintroom.jpg (Figure 4.43), paintroom_small.jpg (Figure 4.44), undecorate.jgp (Figure 4.45), undecorate_small.jpg (Figure 4.46), foyer.jpg (Figure 4.47), and foyer_small.jpg (Figure 4.48) files and save them in your painter folder.

Figure 4.42 *Pete the Painter logo (painterlogo.gif)*

Figure 4.43 *Painted room (paintroom.jpg)*

Figure 4.44 *Painted room thumbnail (paintroom_small.jpg)*

Figure 4.45 *Undecorated room (undecorated.jpg)*

Figure 4.46 *Undecorated room thumbnail (undecorated_small.jpg)*

Figure 4.47 *Foyer (foyer.jpg)*

Figure 4.48 *Foyer thumbnail (foyer_small.jpg)*

2. Use the Services page as the starting point for the Testimonials page. Launch Notepad and open the services.htm file in the painter folder that you previously created. Save the file as testimonials.htm.

3. All the content in this page (images, text, tables, etc.) will be centered and contained within a single layout table that uses a percentage width. This will allow the page to be very fluid and resize with different browser window sizes and screen resolutions. Usually this results in a web page document that looks good on a wide variety of browsers. Center the page content by placing a **`<div align="center">`** tag below the **`<body>`** tag and a **`</div>`** tag directly above the **`</body>`** tag. Directly under the **`<div align="center">`** tag, begin a table with no border, width set to 80%, one row, and one column. The XHTML sample is below:

```
<div align="center">
<table width="80%">
  <tr>
    <td>
```

Code the closing tags for this single row and cell table directly above the closing **`</div>`** tag. The XHTML sample is below:

```
    </td>
  </tr>
</table>
</div>
```

4. Modify your file to be similar to the Testimonials page, shown in Figure 4.41:

- Change the page title to an appropriate phrase.

- Replace the "Pete the Painter" heading with the painterlogo.gif, Figure 4.42. Be sure to include the alt, height, and width attributes on the `<img>` tag for the graphic.

- Modify the text links so that they are appropriate for this page. The "Services" text should link to the services.htm page. Remove the link from the "Testimonials" text.

- Delete the table that was copied as part of the services.htm page.

- Keep the copyright and contact information on the bottom of the page. Add a new table to contain the testimonial information between the text navigation links and the copyright information configured as follows.

- The text related to the testimonials and their images will be contained within a table with six rows. A sketch of the table is shown in Figure 4.49.

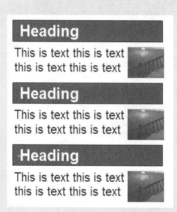

Figure 4.49 *Table layout sketch*

- The table should be configured to have no border, a width of 75%, cellspacing of 5 and cellpadding of 5. Table rows that contain headings ("Painting", "Remodeling", "Wallcovering") should have a background color of #336600. Note that this is a different color than was used for the Services page in the Chapter 3 case study. Your graphic designer suggested the color change to correspond with the logo image for the site. These heading rows will also contain a single table cell that spans two columns. The table rows that contain descriptions and graphics will contain two columns.

- The content of the table is as follows:

  Line 1 Column 1: "Painting" *(Note: This table cell spans two columns.)*

  Line 2: Column 1: "We were selling our home and needed a room painted quickly. Pete's team promptly came out and gave an estimate. It was quite reasonably priced—they started and finished the very next day. —The Morris Family"

  Line 2 Column 2: Use the paintroom_small.jpg as an image link to paintroom.jpg. Remember to use the alt, height, and width attributes on the `<img>` tag.

  Line 3 Column 1: "Remodeling" *(Note: This table cell spans two columns.)*

Line 4 Column 1: "We needed to "undecorate" a room—the previous owners had been very creative with wall panels, mirrors, and paneling. Pete's team provided an estimate, promptly began work, and within a few days our room was looking great! Thanks, Pete! — The Roguskas"

Line 4 Column 2: Use the undecorated_small.jpg as an image link to undecorated.jpg. Use appropriate attributes on the **<img>** tag.

Line 5 Column 1: "Wallcovering" (*Note: This table cell spans two columns.*)

Line 6 Column 1: "Our two-story foyer needed a makeover. Pete's designers helped us choose the perfect wallcovering. Their installers worked quickly and neatly. We love our new entry-way. —Juan & Maria Riaz"

Line 6 Column 2: Use the foyer_small.jpg as an image link to foyer.jpg. Remember to use the alt, height, and width attributes on the **<img>** tag.

- The text that is used for headings ("Painting", "Remodeling", "Wallcovering") should be the color white (#FFFFFF), Times New Roman font, and have font size set to 4. The remaining text in the table should use the Arial font.

5. Save your page and test it in a browser. If your images do not appear or your image links do not work, examine your work carefully. Use Windows Explorer to verify that the images are saved in your painter folder. Examine the src attribute on the **<img>** tags to be sure you spelled the image names correctly.

6. Modify the Home page (index.htm) and Services page (services.htm) to look similar to the Testimonials page you just created. Save and test your pages. Try resizing your browser window or changing screen resolutions. Notice how the page content is centered and attempts to use 80% of the browser window at different resolutions.

Web Research

A. Providing access to the Web for all people is an important issue. Visit the W3C's Web Accessibility Initiative and explore their Checklist of Checkpoints for Web Content Accessibility Guidelines at http://www.w3.org/TR/WCAG10/full-checklist.html (The text's web site at http://webdevfoundations.net/chapter4 has an updated link if needed). View additional pages at the W3Cs site as necessary. Explore the difference between Priority 1, Priority 2, and Priority 3 Checkpoints. Find an example of each that is related to the use of color and images on web pages. Create a web page that contains a table, uses color, and includes the information that you discovered. Print both the source code (from Notepad) and the browser view of your web page.

B. Visit any of the web sites referenced in this chapter that interested you. Print the home page or one other pertinent page from the site. Create a web page that discusses the web site you visited. Your new web page will use a table for layout and include the use of color and images. Write a one-page summary and reaction to the web site you chose to visit. Address the following topics:

1. What is the purpose of the site?

2. Who is the intended audience?

3. Do you believe the site reaches its audience?

4. Was this site useful to you? Why or why not?

5. List the colors that were used on the home page of this web site: background, backgrounds of page sections, text, logo, navigation buttons, and so on.

6. How did the use of color enhance the web site?

Chapter Review Answers

1. b

2. c

3. b

4. b

5. a

6. c

7. d

8. a

9. b

10. d

11. left

12. text links

13. thumbnail

14. Create them yourself using a graphics application, download them from a free site, purchase and download them from a graphics site, purchase a graphics collection on CD, take digital photographs, scan photographs, scan drawings, or hire a graphic designer to create graphics.

15. image map

Chapter

5

XHTML Frames

*H*ave you ever visited a web site and noticed that a portion of the browser window remains stationary while other parts can scroll? If so, you were probably visiting a web site that used XHTML to create frames, or separate areas of a browser window. This chapter introduces you to this technique.

Overview of Frames

Multiple, independently controllable sections in a browser window are called **frames** and are created as separate XHTML files. A "master" **frame-set file**, which controls the configuration of the entire browser window, is requested when the user types the URL of a web page that uses frames.

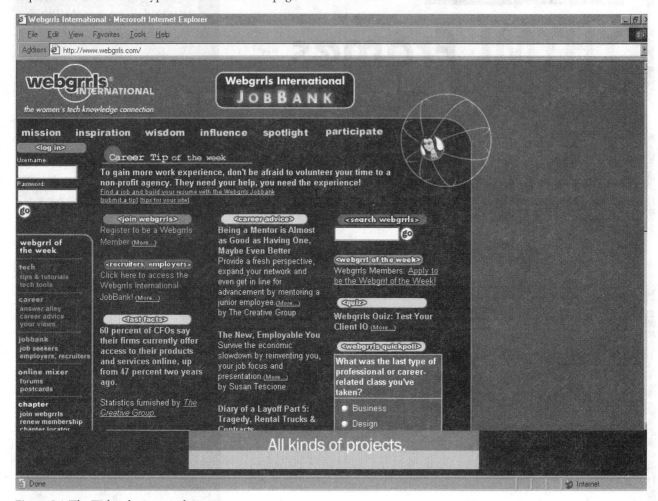

Figure 5.1 *The Webgrrls site uses frames.*

The home page of the Webgrrls site (http://www.webgrrls.com/), shown in Figure 5.1, has a frameset file that supports two frames.
(*Note:* If you visit the Webgrrls site today, it may look different.) Notice that the top portion (frame) of the browser window can scroll vertically (see scroll bar on the right) while the bottom portion (frame) is stationary. The browser has actually downloaded and rendered *three* web page files:

- A file that contains the frameset XHTML to configure the window
- An XHTML file to display the content that displays in the top portion of the browser
- An XHTML file to display the ad banner in the bottom portion

If you displayed this web site in a browser, you could examine the XHTML for the frameset page by clicking on View, Source. The XHTML source code would contain **<frameset>** and **<frame>** tags. Each **<frame>** tag describes a separate portion or frame of the browser window. The **<frameset>** tag provides instructions on how to configure the frames in the browser window. These XHTML tags will be discussed in detail later.

To display the XHTML for the individual frames, or portions of the entire frameset, right-click on the page and select View, Source. Each frame is a web page that could stand on its own!

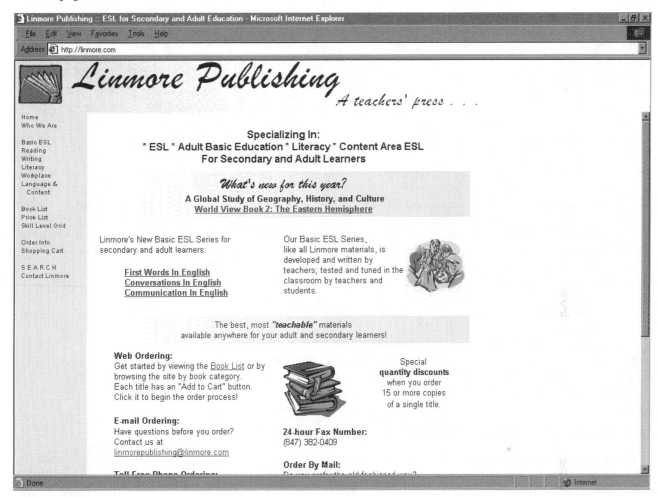

Figure 5.2 *This ESL book publishing site also uses frames.*

The home page of Linmore Publishing (http://linmore.com), is shown in Figure 5.2, also uses frames, but it looks quite unlike the Webgrrls' page. (*Note:* If you visit the Linmore site today, it may look different.) Notice that the top and left portions (frames) of the browser window are stationary, while the right portion is scrollable. The browser has downloaded and rendered *four* web page files to display this page:

- The frameset page, which you don't see, that configures the browser window
- The XHTML file that displays the "Linmore Publishing" banner in the top portion of the browser window
- The XHTML file that displays the navigation in the left portion of the browser window
- The XHTML file that displays the content in the right portion of the browser window

As you can see, framesets are quite versatile! Both Linmore Publishing and Webgrrls used frames but the look and feel of each web site is very different. Let's take a look at the pros and cons of using frames.

Advantages of Using Frames

You've seen two examples of web sites that use frames to organize the browser window. Earlier chapters covered the use of tables to format web pages. You may be asking, why should I choose frames instead of tables to format my web pages? This section discusses some advantages of frames.

Ease of Navigation. Frames generally provide easier navigation for web site visitors. When your main site navigation appears in a stationary frame, visitors always know exactly where to look for it and do not need to scroll to the top or bottom of long web pages to find it.

Ease of Maintenance. Frames save web developers time and effort. The main navigation for the site is only placed on a single page—instead of on each of many (possibly hundreds) of pages. Because all the main navigation is in a single XHTML file, site maintenance is less tedious. When new navigation links need to be added or current navigation links need to be changed, the web developer only updates a single file.

Degrades Gracefully. Web sites that use frames can be written to provide content for applications that do not support frames, such as older browsers, search engine robots, and other user agent applications. You can utilize the **<noframes>** tag (more on that later) to create text and links for these applications to process. XHTML that works great in the current standard technology but still functions in older or simpler technologies is said to **degrade gracefully**.

Unifies Resources. Because the only URL that displays in the browser's address bar is the URL of the frameset page, you can display pages from multiple servers within a single web site as part of a unified whole. Your web page visitors will be unaware that the document files may reside on different servers.

Disadvantages of Using Frames

Using frames has a downside, too. This section discusses reasons not to use frames.

Frames Are Deprecated. The use of frames has been deprecated by the W3C. This means that web sites created using frames may not be supported in the future by browsers. Since web standards are followed on a voluntary basis it most likely will be quite some time before browsers drop their support for them. Be aware that frames have been deprecated and you should consider not developing new web sites using them. However, as a web developer you will probably run across web sites that use frames. They are included in this text for this reason.

Not Universally Supported. While frames are supported in Netscape and Internet Explorer (version 4 and later), they are not uniformly supported by technologies such as screen readers and search engine robots. Appropriate use of the **<noframes>** tag should help in this matter. To enhance the processing of search engine robots on sites using frames, place the following within the **<noframes>** tags: site name, heading, sentences using pertinent keywords, and navigation links. This will allow search engine robots, screen readers, and other applications that do not process frames to access your site. Hands-On Practice 5.1 demonstrates the use of these tags.

Bookmark Issues. It's happened to many of us—you spend 20 minutes on someone's site and bookmark or add to favorites the one page you found useful. If the site uses frames, you've just bookmarked the home

Why would I want to display pages from different servers?

This probably won't happen very often, but it can be useful. For example, a client may need to use a database that its web host does not support. Using a frameset, you could create the database access on your own server and display it as part of their site—that is until you convince your client to switch to a host that offers what they truly need....

page—happy hunting! Here's the good news—newer browsers, such as Internet Explorer 5, bookmark directly to the useful page you found. This will quickly become a nonissue as more browsers become frame-friendly.

Accessibility Issues. Individuals using screen readers often cannot use framesets and must access the **<noframes>** content. The Web Accessibility Initiative offers suggestions for dealing with frames at http://www.w3.org/TR/WCAG10-HTML-TECHS/#frames. These suggestions range from placing titles on frames (discussed later) that clarify the purpose of each window portion to creating a separate navigation page for the site. Another technique is to place a text navigation bar at the bottom of each page. This may remove the advantage of single site navigation but it will allow visitors to navigate the site even if their user-agent does not support frames.

XHTML—Using Frames

Frames—some web developers embrace them and others shy away from them. Like them or not, you will encounter web sites developed with frames in your role as a web developer and will need to understand the XHTML code used to configure them. This section focuses on the XHTML code to create frames pages. The **<frameset>** tag, **<frame>** tag, **<noframes>** tag, and target attribute are discussed while you create a sample frameset page and web site. Once you've experimented a little with a frameset, you will be ready for the detailed explanation of the tags and attributes used in this technique later in the chapter. Using frames may be a little confusing at first, but stick with it—this powerful technique can come in handy in your future role as a web developer.

Your First Frameset

The frameset web page—the silent partner behind every frames page—uses a combination of **<frameset>**, **<frame>**, and **<noframe>** tags to configure the browser display. The **<frameset>** tag defines the structure of the frames displayed on the web page. The **<frame>** tag is used to configure a portion of the browser window and identify which page should initially be displayed there. The **<noframes>** tag describes what will display if the browser does not support frames.

The best way to learn XHTML is by writing it. In this Hands-On Practice you will create a frames version of the CircleSoft web site. The Home page is shown in Figure 5.3.

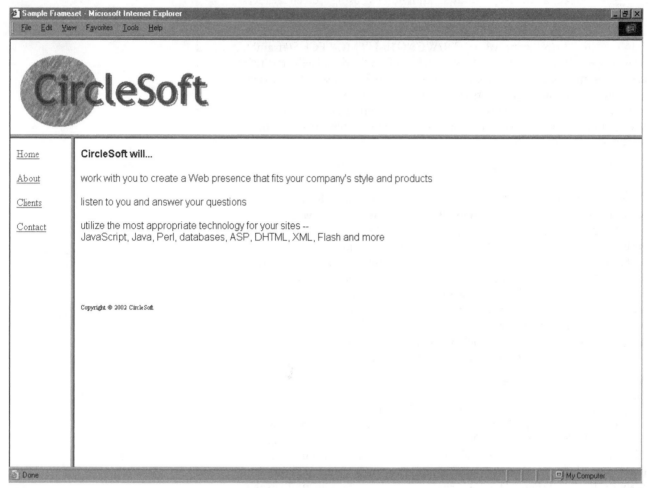

Figure 5.3. *CircleSoft new Home page (index.htm)*

The browser has to render four web pages to create the display shown in Figure 5.3: the frameset page (which you don't see), the banner page, the navigation page, and the main or content page. The following instructions guide you in creating your version of the CircleSoft Home page using frames. It's a good idea to sketch out your frameset before you try to code it. A sample sketch is shown in Figure 5.4.

The banner frame (banner.htm) will occupy the first 150 rows of pixels in the browser window. The rest of the window will be divided as follows: the navigation frame (nav.htm) will occupy the first 100 columns of pixels, and the main content (main.htm) will be displayed in the remaining area of the browser window.

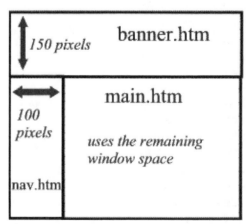

Figure 5.4 *Page layout for the new CircleSoft Home page*

Now you are ready to create your frameset. Begin with the web page document that describes the frames and that is not visible in the browser window—the frameset page. The frameset page uses a special DTD specified by the W3C for framesets. This DTD should be placed on the frameset web page document. Web pages that are opened in the frames contained in the frameset use the Transitional or Strict DTD. The Frameset DTD is

```
<!DOCTYPE html PUBLIC "-//W3C//DTD XHTML 1.0 Frameset//EN"
"http://www.w3.org/TR/xhtml1/DTD/xhtml1-frameset.dtd">
```

Another difference between frameset pages and standard web pages is that **<frameset>** *tags are not contained within* **<body>** *tags; instead,* **<body>** *tags are used within* **<noframes>** *tags. The* **<frameset>** *container tags are used to describe the division of the rows and columns in the browser window.*

Create a folder called sampleframe on your floppy disk. Launch Notepad and get ready to create your frameset page. Type the following XHTML code in your text file:

```
<?xml version="1.0" encoding="UTF-8"?>
<!DOCTYPE html PUBLIC "-//W3C//DTD XHTML 1.0 Frameset//EN"
"http://www.w3.org/TR/xhtml1/DTD/xhtml1-frameset.dtd">
<html xmlns="http://www.w3.org/1999/xhtml">
<head>
<title>Sample Frameset</title>
</head>
<frameset rows = "150, *">
```

This sets aside the first 150 rows of pixels for the first frame described. The asterisk (*) reserves the rest of the window for whatever frames or framesets are specified later in the document.

Now type the **<frame>** *tag for the banner:*

```
<frame name="banner" title="CircleSoft Company Logo" src="banner.htm"
  scrolling="no" />
```

This defines a frame named banner. The src attribute specifies the web page document that will be displayed in this frame— banner.htm. The scrolling attribute is set to "no", which means that scroll bars will not appear. The title attribute provides a text description that could be used by assistive technologies such as screen readers. Notice that the **<frame>** *tag is a self-contained tag.*

Refer to Figure 5.4 and observe that columns are used to organize the remaining portion of the browser window. Another frameset will be needed to configure this. The first column is 100 pixels wide and will be used for main navigation. The second column will occupy the remaining portion of the browser window and is reserved for the main content page. The value "" is used to reserve the remaining portion of the browser window. The frames to contain the nav.htm (navigation) and main.htm (main) web pages also need to be defined. Continue working on your page and type the following code:*

```
<frameset cols="100,*">
<frame name="navigation" title="CircleSoft Site Navigation" src="nav.htm" />
<frame name="main" title="CirclSoft Site Content" src="main.htm" />
</frameset>
```

Next, you will specify content for browsers that don't support frames. Note that the `<body>` tag is used within the `<noframes>` tags. Type the following:

```
<noframes>
<body>
  <h1>CircleSoft Web Design</h1>
  <a href="nav.htm">Site Links</a>
</body>
</noframes>
```

Type another closing `</frameset>` tag to close the first frameset. Now type your closing tag:

```
</html>
```

Save your file as index.htm in the sampleframe folder.

The frameset page specified three web page documents: banner.htm, nav.htm, and main.htm. Your next task is to create these files. First, create the banner web page document, shown in Figure 5.5.

Obtain the image, logo1.gif, from the student disk. The image is located in the Chapter5/5.1 folder. Save the image in your sampleframe folder.

Once you've obtained the file, launch Notepad and create a page similar to the one shown in Figure 5.5, with a white background and

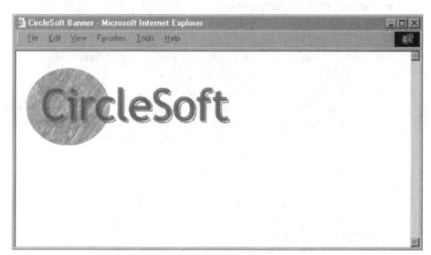

Figure 5.5 *CircleSoft banner.htm*

the logo graphic. Save the file as banner.htm in the sampleframe folder. Test your page in a browser to verify that the page displays the logo image.

Next, create the navigation web page document, nav.htm, shown in Figure 5.6.

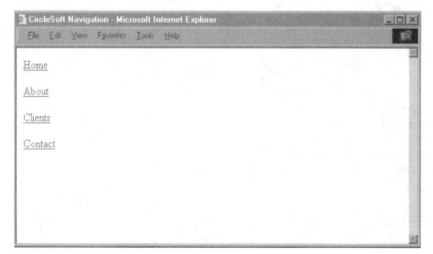

Figure 5.6 *CircleSoft nav.htm*

Launch Notepad and create a page similar to the one shown in Figure 5.6. It should have a white background and contain four text hyperlinks as indicated in Table 5.1.

Table 5.1

Text	Hyperlink Reference
Home	main.htm
About	about.htm
Clients	clients.htm
Contact	contact.htm

When visitors click on these links, the new web page should be displayed in the main content frame, which initially contains the page main.htm. However, the default behavior of hyperlinks is to change the contents of the frame that they are in—in this case the navigation frame. Since all the links in the navigation frame should modify the contents of the main content frame, we will need to target that frame. There are two techniques available to accomplish this: use target attributes on each anchor tag (discussed later in the chapter) or use a **<base>** *tag in the header section of the web page to modify the default target for the entire document.*

The **<base>** *tag is a self-contained tag that can be used to configure the default target for every link in the web page document. The XHTML code to configure the default behavior for all of the links on this page to target the frame called main is:*

```
<base target="main" />
```

Add the base tag to the header section of your nav.htm page. Your header section should now look like this:

```
<head>
<title>CircleSoft Navigation</title>
<base target="main" />
</head>
```

Save the web page document as nav.htm in the sampleframe folder. Test your page in a browser. Don't expect the links to work (you haven't created those pages yet), just verify that your page displays.

Now you are ready to create the main frame page, main.htm, shown in Figure 5.7.

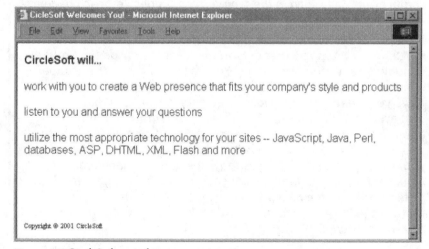

Figure 5.7 *CircleSoft main.htm*

Launch Notepad and create a page similar to Figure 5.7. It should have a white background and contain this text:

"CircleSoft will…
work with you to create a Web presence that fits your company's style and products
listen to you and answer your questions
utilize the most appropriate technology for your sites—JavaScript, Java, Perl, databases, ASP, DHTML, XML, Flash and more"

Save the web page document as main.htm in the sampleframe folder. Test your page in a browser to verify that it displays.

Now you are ready to create shell versions of the other content pages: about.htm, clients.htm, and contact.htm. If this were a real project web site, each page would have meaningful content.

First create a shell version of the about.htm page. Launch Notepad and create the web page document shown in Figure 5.8.

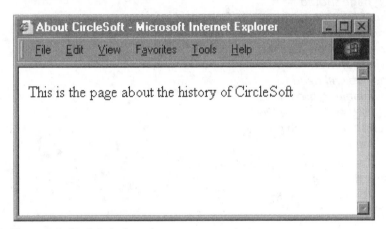

Figure 5.8 *CircleSoft about.htm*

The page should have a white background and contain the text "This is the page about the history of CircleSoft". Save this document as about.htm in your sampleframe folder.

Next, use Notepad and create shell pages for clients.htm and contact.htm. Save each in the sampleframe folder. Test each page to verify that it displays.

Review what you have done: You first created the frameset page, index.htm. This page works behind the scenes to divide the browser window into sections, or frames. You have configured the browser window to contain three frames—banner, navigation, and main. Next, you created the individual web page documents that will be displayed in the frameset—banner.htm, nav.htm, main.htm, about.htm, contact.htm, and clients.htm. You are now ready to test your frameset. Launch a browser and display the index.htm page in your sampleframe folder. You should see a frames page similar to Figure 5.3, with your banner, navigation, and main pages displayed. Click on a link in the navigation frame to change the main frame. Compare your work with the sample solution found on the student disk at Chapter5/5.1/index.htm.

What if my frameset doesn't work?

Some very careful troubleshooting is in order.

- Check the index.htm page first. Did you spell all the file names correctly?

- Use Windows Explorer to verify that the files are saved in the sampleframe folder.

- Use Windows Explorer and check the file names to make sure they are correctly spelled.

Usually at this point patience and attention to detail will find the error or errors.

The <frameset> Tag

The **<frameset>** tag divides up the browser window with either the rows or cols attribute. The values for these attributes can be numeric pixels, a percentage, or an asterisk (*). The special value * reserves the remaining portion of the browser window. The exact size of this area varies depending on the size of the browser window and the monitor resolution being used. The **<frameset>** tag is a container tag and should be closed with a **</frameset>** tag. As demonstrated in Hands-On Practice 5.1, **<frameset>** tags can be nested when you need to divide the browser window into both rows and columns.

The **rows attribute** reserves horizontal areas (rows) of the browser window. For example, the value **rows="150,*   "** will configure the browser window shown in Figure 5.9. It contains two horizontal frames; the top frame has a height of 150 pixels and the lower frame takes up the remaining portion of the browser window.

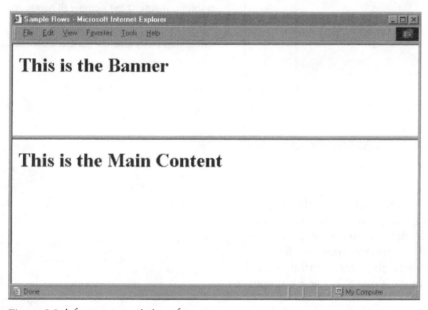

Figure 5.9 *A frameset consisting of two rows*

The **cols attribute** reserves vertical areas (columns) of the browser window. For example, the value **cols="200,*,100"** will configure the browser window shown in Figure 5.10. It contains three vertical frames; the left frame has a width of 200 pixels, the right frame has a width of 100 pixels, and the middle frames takes up the remaining portion of the browser window.

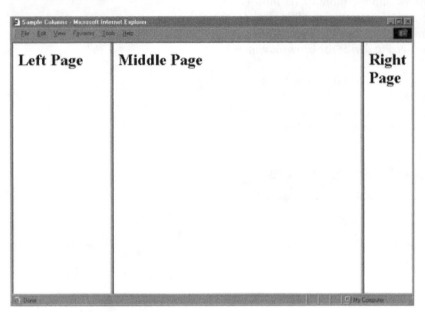

Figure 5.10 *A frameset consisting of three columns*

You will always use either a rows or cols attribute to configure your frameset. In Figures 5.9 and 5.10, you may have noticed the gray border surrounding each frame; it is placed there by default. To remove the border, use the frameborder and framespacing attributes: frameborder="0", framespacing="0". The frameborder attribute and other attributes used with the **<frameset>** tag are described in the Table 5.2. The most commonly used attributes are shown in bold.

Table 5.2 **<frameset>** *Tag Attributes*

Attribute	Value	Purpose
bordercolor	Valid hexadecimal color value or color name	Specifies the color of the frame borders in the frameset. Default color is gray.
cols	Number of pixels, percentage, or * to indicate remaining window area	Reserves vertical areas (columns) of the browser window.
frameborder	0 or 1	0 indicates that no frame borders will be visible in the frameset. 1 indicates that frame borders will display in the frameset (default).
framespacing	Number of pixels. Set to 0 to remove frame borders.	Specifies the width of the frameborders in the frameset.
rows	Number of pixels, percentage, or "*" to indicate remaining window area	Reserves horizontal areas (rows) of the browser window.
title	A brief text description	Provides a text description of the frameset that can be used by assistive technologies.

The <frame> Tag

The **<frame>** tag is used to configure a single frame or portion of the browser window. It specifies items such as the file to be displayed, the name of the frame, the target of links, and the title of the frame. A **<frame>** tag is a self-contained tag—it does not have a closing **</frame>** tag. Table 5.3 lists attributes of the **<frame>** tag. The most commonly used attributes are shown in bold.

Table 5.3 **<frame>** *Tag Attributes*

Attribute	Values	Purpose
bordercolor	Valid hexadecimal color value or color name	Configures the color of the border of this frame.
frameborder	0 indicates no visible borders. 1 indicates borders display (default).	Determines whether borders should be displayed around this frame.
id	Alphanumeric, no spaces. The value must be unique and not used for other id values on the same XHTML document.	Provides a unique identifier for the frame.
longdesc	Detailed text description of the frame may be accessed by assistive technologies	Gives URL of web page with a detailed description of the frame.
marginheight	Number of pixels	Configures the top and bottom margins of the frame.
marginwidth	Number of pixels	Configures the width of the right and left margins of a frame.
name	Alphanumeric, no spaces, begins with a letter	Configures the name of the frame. This is required when the target attribute is used to configure hyperlinks. Deprecated in XHTML but is used to provide backward compatibility with browsers that support HTML.
noresize	Indicates that the frame cannot be resized. If this attribute is not used, web page visitors can resize the frame.	Determines whether the web page visitor can resize a frame by dragging the frame border with the mouse.
scrolling	"yes" indicates that scrollbars are always present. "no" indicates that scrollbars are never displayed. "auto" indicates that scrollbars appear when needed (default)	Determines whether scrollbars will appear if the document displayed is larger than the size of the frame.
src	Valid file name of a web page document (required)	Configures the name of the file to be displayed in the frame.
target	"_top", "_blank", "_self" (default), valid frame name, valid window name	Sets the default window for all links in the frame to use. See the section on the target attribute later in this chapter.
title	Text phrase that describes the frame	Configures the title of the frame. This can be accessed by screen readers and is recommended by the W3C to improve accessibility.

In this Hands-On Practice you will modify the frameset created earlier in the chapter. Open the index.htm file in your sampleframe folder. You will modify the document to configure the frameset to display similar to the sample in Figure 5.11.

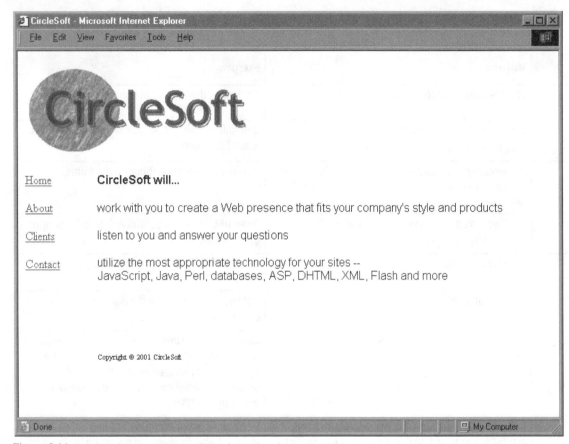

Figure 5.11 *CircleSoft Home page without frame borders*

Notice that there are no borders between the separate portions of the browser window.

Modify the `<frameset>` tag on the index.htm page to have the attributes `frameborder="0"` and `framespacing="0"`. Also configure the scrolling attribute on the banner frame so that scroll bars will not appear in the frame (use `scrolling="no"` on the `<frame>` tag). Save your page and test in a browser. Your page should look similar to Figure 5.11. You can compare your work with the solution found on the student disk at Chapter5/5.2/index.htm.

Experiment with resizing the browser window. You should be able to resize the window to be smaller so that scrolling bars appear for the main and navigation frames as shown in Figure 5.12.

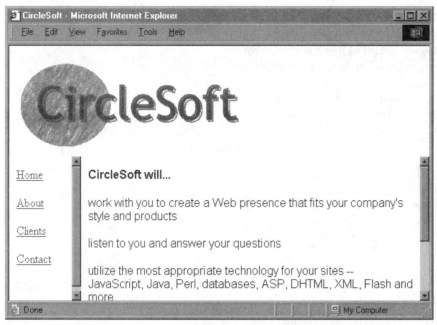

Figure 5.12 *The scroll bars automatically appear for the nav and main frames when the window is resized.*

Notice that the banner frame still takes up the first 100 rows of the browser window, but that scroll bars appear in the other frames. The content of the navigation and main frames will be scrollable no matter how tiny the browser window is. Because the banner frame has scrolling set to no, its contents can become inaccessible if the browser window is resized enough, as shown in Figure 5.13.

Figure 5.13 *Because the banner frame has scrolling set to no, a portion of the frame disappears when the window is resized.*

The <noframes> Tag

The **<noframes>** tag should be placed within your frameset, after the last frame (indicated by the last **<frame>** tag) and before the outermost **</frameset>** tag. Any content that you want displayed if your visitor's browser does not support frames should be placed between the **<noframes>** and **</noframes>** tags. Suggestions for content include your organization name, sentences that use keywords pertinent to your site, and main navigation links.

Keep in mind that browsers are not the only applications that can be used to access your web site. Search engines run programs (called robots or spiders) that walk the web in search of pages to categorize and index. Place navigation links in your **<noframes>** area to assist them in their task. The **<noframes>** area may also be used by devices such as PDAs and web-aware phones.

The Target Attribute

Now that you are familiar with the **<frameset>**, **<frames>**, and **<noframes>** tags, we will turn our attention to the target attribute. Using the target attribute with a value of **"_blank"** was discussed in Chapter 3 as technique to open a web page in a new window. The target attribute was also just used in the **<base>** tag and **<frame>** tags.

The default target of a link is the same frame in the same browser window that contains the link. The target attribute applies to the anchor tag, the base tag, and the frame tag. It is used to configure the window that will open a hyperlink. When the target attribute is used on the anchor tag it only applies to that specific link. When the target attribute is used on the **<base>** tag, it configures the default for all the links on the specific web page. When the target attribute is used on the **<frame>** tags, it configures the default for any web pages that are displayed in that specific frame. Table 5.4 lists attribute values.

Table 5.4 *Target Attribute Values*

Value	Purpose
_blank	Opens the linked page in a new browser window.
_self	Opens the linked page in the same browser window (default).
_top	Opens the linked page in the entire browser window. This is often used to "bust out of" a frameset. The visitor can return to the previous page by selecting the Back button on his or her browser application.
Text name of a frame	Opens the linked page in the named frame. If a frame with that name does not exist, most browsers will open a new window (similar to _blank).
_parent	Opens the linked page in the parent frame (used with nested framesets).

The <base> Tag

The **<base>** tag, a self-contained tag located in the header section of a web page, configures the default target for all the links on an entire web page. The value of the target attribute determines the default window. If the **<base>** tag is omitted, all links open in the current window by default. In Hands-On Practice 5.1 the navigation page, nav.htm, was configured with a base target set to the frame named main. This caused all the links in nav.htm to open in the main frame. The XHTML code for setting the target to a frame named "main" is **<base target="main" />**.

Inline Frames

An **inline frame** does not need to be part of a frameset. An inline frame (sometimes called a *floating frame*) can be placed on the body of any web page, similar to the way you would place an image on a web page. What is special about the inline frame is that it embeds another web page in within a scrolling area. Figure 5.14 shows the use of an inline frame. The white scrolling area is the inline frame—it displays *another web page* that contains the image of the flower and a text description.

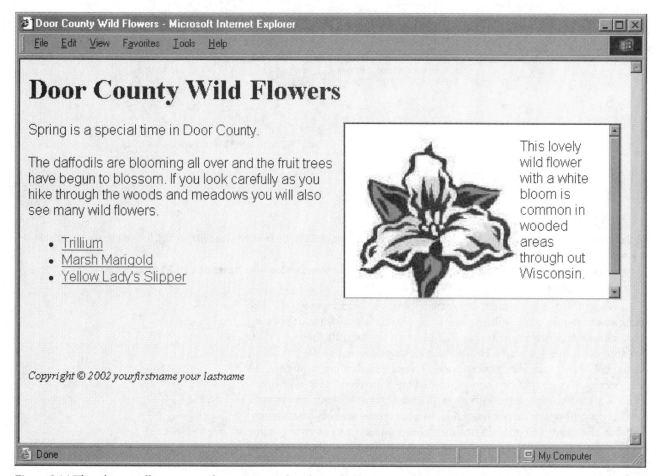

Figure 5.14 *The white scrolling area on the page is an inline frame displaying a separate web page.*

The screen shots in Figure 5.15 are both of the same web page with different pages displayed in the inline frame area.

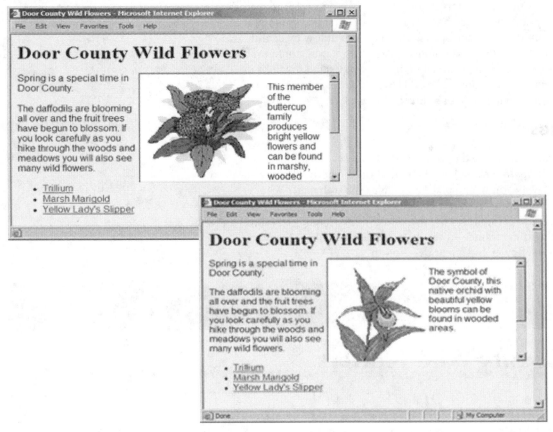

Figure 5.15 *The same page with different content in the inline frame area*

The code for the inline frame used to create this effect is

```
<iframe src="trillium.htm" title="Trillium Wild Flower" height="200" align="right"
  name="flower" width="330">
  Description of the lovely Spring wild flower, the <a href="trillium.htm"
  target="_blank">Trillium</a></iframe>
```

As shown, an inline frame is created using the **<iframe>** tag. The **<iframe>** tag is a container tag. It is always used with its closing **</iframe>** tag. Any content that should be displayed if the browser does not support inline frames (such as a text description or link to the actual page) should be placed between the tags. The **<iframe>** tag configures an area on a web page that can be used to display a different web page document. This inline area is 150 pixels high and 300 pixels wide by default. The height and width attributes can be used to configure the exact dimensions. In the example code, the align attribute was used to align the inline frame to the right of the text on the web page. The name attribute was used so that the inline frame could be targeted by links. Table 5.5 lists attributes for **<iframe>** tags. Commonly used attributes are shown in bold.

Table 5.5 **<iframe>** *Tag Attributes*

Attribute	Values	Purpose
align	right, center, left (default)	Specifies the horizontal alignment of the inline frame.
frameborder	0 indicates no visible borders. 1 indicates borders display (default).	Determines whether borders should be displayed around this inline frame.
height	Number of pixels	Gives height of the inline frame in pixels.
id	Alphanumeric, no spaces. The value must be unique and not used for other id values on the same XHTML document.	Provides a unique identifier for the inline frame.
longdesc	Provides a detailed text description of the frame. May be accessed by assistive technologies	Gives URL of web page with detailed description of the contents of the inline frame.
marginheight	Number of pixels	Configures the top and bottom margins of the inline frame.
marginwidth	Number of pixels	Configures the width of the right and left margins of a inline frame.
name	Alphanumeric, no spaces, begin with a letter	Configures the name of the inline frame. Required when using the target attribute to configure hyperlinks. This attribute is deprecated in XHTML but is used to provide backward compatibility with browsers that support HTML.
scrolling	"yes" indicates that scrollbars are always present. "no" indicates that scrollbars are never displayed. "auto" indicates that scrollbars appear when needed (default).	Determines whether scrollbars will appear if the document displayed is larger than the size of the inline frame.
src	Valid file name of a web page document (required)	Configures the name of the file to be displayed in the inline frame.
title	Text phrase that describes the inline frame	Configures the title of the inline frame. This can be accessed by screen readers and is recommended by the W3C to improve accessibility.
width	Number of pixels	Specifies width of the inline frame in pixels.

While inline frames are supported by the most recent versions of Internet Explorer and Netscape, they not supported by all browsers and are not part of the W3C Recommendation. A web developer should carefully consider a decision to use this technique.

In this Hands-On Practice you will create a new Home page for CircleSoft that uses inline frames and three web pages that display in the inline frame. To begin, create a new folder called circlesoftinline on a floppy disk. Obtain the logo1.gif image used in this Hands-On Practice from the student disk. The image is located in the Chapter5/5.3 folder. Save the image in your circlesoftinline folder.

Launch Notepad and create the Home page, named index.htm, for your circlesoftinline web site. A sample is shown in Figure 5.16.

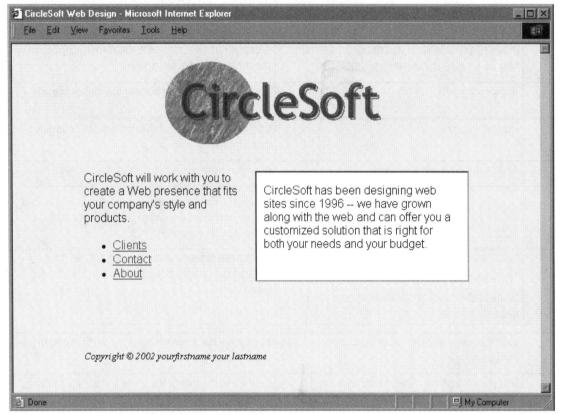

Figure 5.16 *The CircleSoft inline frames Home page (index.htm)*

Configure the page as follows:

1. *Set the background color to #FFFFCC. Give the page an appropriate title.*

2. *Place the content on the page in a table with one row and one column. The table should have no border, be centered (use the* **<div>** *tag), and have the width set to 75%. (See Chapter 3 for a review on tables).*

3. *Use the logo1.gif image found on the student disk.*

4. *Add a paragraph that contains the following text: "CircleSoft will work with you to create a Web presence that fits your company's style and products."*

5. Add an unordered list that contains the following text:
   "Clients"
   "Contact"
   "About"

   You will code text hyperlinks in a later step.

6. Add the copyright line. It should be emphasized (use **\<em>**) and have a smaller font size.

7. All text on the page should use the Arial font.

8. Add the **\<iframe>** tags before the first paragraph. The inline frame should use **align="right"**, initially display the about.htm page, have the name set to circlesoftinfo, and contain descriptive content between the **\<iframe>** tags. For example:

```
<iframe src="about.htm" title="About CircleSoft" align="right"
  name="circlesoftinfo" >Find out more about <a href="about.htm"
  target="_blank">Circlesoft</a></iframe>
```

9. Create hyperlinks out of the "Clients", "Contact", and "About" text. Set the target attribute on the links to the name of the inline frame, target="circlesoftinfo". Table 5.6 shows the text and the name of the linked page.

Table 5.6

Text	Hyperlink Reference
Clients	clients.htm
Contact	contact.htm
About	about.htm

10. Save your index.htm page in the circlesoftinline folder.

Next, you will create the web pages that will display in the inline frame: about.htm, clients.htm, and contact.htm.

1. Create a web page called about.htm with the following text:

   "CircleSoft has been designing web sites since 1996—we have grown along with the web and can offer you a customized solution that is right for both your needs and your budget."

   Use the Arial font. Save the page in the circlesoftinline folder.

2. Create a web page called clients.htm with the following text:

   "CircleSoft has many satisfied Fortune 500 clients. Join their ranks and contact us today!"

   Use the Arial font. The text "contact" should link to the contact.htm (do not use a target attribute). Save the page in the circlesoftinline folder.

3. Create a web page called contact.htm with the following text:

"Contact Circlesoft today!
E-mail: yourfirstname@yourlastname.com
Phone: 888-555-5555"

Use the Arial font. Create an e-mail link for yourfirstname@yourlastname.com. Substitute your own first and last name for yourfirstname and yourlastname. Save the page in the circlesoftinline folder.

You are ready to test your inline frames page. Launch a browser and display the index.htm page. You page should be similar to Figure 5.16. Try out the links; they should change the contents of the inline frame. The student disk contains a sample solution at Chapter5/5.3/index.htm.

 Since inline frames are not supported by all browsers and assistive technologies such as screen readers, use them with caution. If you choose to use inline frames on your web site, be sure to provide alternate means of accessing the content. Consider including both a description of the inline frame and a link to a text page between the **<iframe>** and **</iframe>** tags.

Frames, Links, and Ethics

In a frameset it is common to open links within a named frame or in the same frame that contains the link. This is a good practice for links to pages internal to the web site. However, linking to an external web site and displaying the page within a frame on your web site can be construed as passing off the work as your own. While this may be far from what you intended, you could incur a legal liability. To avoid this problem when using framesets, always open external web sites in their own window (use **target="_blank"** on the anchor tag).

Keep in mind that some web development and web usability professionals recommend that frames not be used. Visit noted web usability expert Jakob Nielsen's site, http://www.useit.com, and search for "frames" to read his opinion on why frames usually should not be used. Even though frames are not recommended for the design of new web sites, many existing web sites use frames. Since web developers often need to maintain and update existing web sites, it is important to be familiar with frames.

Chapter 5 Review

Summary

This chapter introduced the use of frames on web pages. You created a new, frame version of the CircleSoft web site and gained some experience with inline frames. You also learned that there is a controversy surrounding the use of frames on web pages.

Visit the text web site at http://www.webdevfoundations.net for examples, updated information, and the links listed in this chapter.

Review Questions

Multiple Choice

1. Which tag contains the structure for a web page that uses frames?

   a. `<noframes>` tag
   b. `<frame>` tag
   c. `<frameset>` tag
   d. `<window>` tag

2. Which attribute is used to divide a web page into horizontal frames?

   a. horizontal
   b. cols
   c. rows
   d. none of the above

3. Which attribute is used to specify the content of a frame?

   a. border
   b. target
   c. src
   d. none of the above

4. Which attribute is used to specify the frame that hyperlinks will be displayed in?

   a. border
   b. target
   c. link
   d. base

5. The purpose of the `<frame>` tag is to

   a. define the number of columns or rows in a frameset
   b. identify the content of each frame in a frameset
   c. define the percentage or pixel value of each frame
   d. none of the above

6. Select the statement that is true about inline frames.

   a. Inline frames are supported by all browsers.
   b. There is no way to specify content to display if inline frames are not supported.
   c. Inline frames may not be accessible to all visitors to your web site.
   d. None of the above is true.

7. Select the link that will display the about.htm page in a frame with the name content.

   a. `<a href="about.htm" target="content">About</a>`
   b. `<a href="content" target="about.htm">About</a>`
   c. `<a href="about.htm#content" target="_blank">About</a>`
   d. None of the above will work.

8. Select the statement that is true about frames.

    a. Framesets can be nested inside frames.
    b. Framesets can be nested inside other framesets.
    c. The frames tag divides up the web page into portions.
    d. None of the above is true.

9. Choose the rows attribute that would configure a frameset with four rows, the top row using 50 pixels and the other rows taking the available space on the page.

    a. `rows="*, *, *,50"`
    b. `rows="50, *, *, *"`
    c. `rows="50,25%,*, *"`
    d. None of the above will work.

10. Select the attribute used on the `<frameset>` tag to eliminate the display of frame borders on the web page.

    a. border
    b. frameborder
    c. borderspacing
    d. More than one attribute needs to be configured.

Fill in the Blank

11. If you want your frames to be a specific height or width, use _____ to specify their size.

12. To open a web page in a new browser window, use the value of _____ on the target attribute.

13. The ____ attribute on a frameset tag causes the browser window to be divided into vertical portions or frames.

Short Answer

14. List one reason why new web sites should not be designed using frames.

15. List one reason why the `<iframe>` tag should be avoided.

Apply Your Knowledge

1. **Predict the Result.** Draw and write a brief description of the web page that will be created with the following XHTML code:

```
<?xml version="1.0" encoding="UTF-8"?>
<!DOCTYPE html PUBLIC "-//W3C//DTD XHTML 1.0 Transitional//EN"
   "http://www.w3.org/TR/xhtml1/DTD/xhtml1-transitional.dtd">
<html xmlns="http://www.w3.org/1999/xhtml" >
<head>
<title>Predict the Result</title>
</head>
<body>
  <div align="center">
    <iframe src="about.htm" title="About Trillium" align="right"
      name="Trillium" >Find out more about <a href="about.htm"
      target="_blank">Trillium</a></iframe>
```

continues

```
    <p> Our professional staff takes pride in its working relationship with our
       clients by offering personalized services that meet their needs, develop their
       target areas, and incorporate these items into a well-presented Web Site that
       works.</p>
    <br />
    <p><a href="services.htm" target="Trillium">Services</a><br />
     <a href="contact.htm" target="Trillium">Contact</a><br />
    </p>
    <p> <font size="1">
     Contact <a href="mailto:web@trilliumtechnologies.biz">
     web@trilliumtechnologies.biz</a>
     <br />
     Copyright &copy; 2003 Trillium Technologies</font></p>
  </div>
</body>
</html>
```

2. **Fill in the Missing Code.** This web page configures a frameset with two
   columns—a navigation column and a main content column. The
   navigation column should take up 25% of the page and initially display
   nav.htm. The main content column should take up the rest of the page
   and initially display content.htm. Some XHTML tags and their
   attributes, indicated by <_>, are missing. Some XHTML attribute
   values, indicated by "_", are missing.

```
<?xml version="1.0" encoding="UTF-8"?>
<_>
<html xmlns="http://www.w3.org/1999/xhtml" >
<head>
<title>Trillium Technologies</title>
</head>
<frameset  cols="_">
<frame src="_" name="_" />
      <_>
<noframes>
  <body>
    <h1>Trillium Technologies</h1>
    <a href="nav.htm">Site Links</a>
  </body>
<_>
<_>
</html>
```

3. **Find the Error.** The files nav.htm, about.htm, and contact.htm have
   been created and saved in the same folder as the following page. How
   can the frame borders be configured so they do not display? Why
   doesn't the nav.htm page initially display? What could be modified to
   cause the frame named nav to open any links (such as one to
   contact.htm) in the frame called main?

```
<?xml version="1.0" encoding="UTF-8"?>
<!DOCTYPE html PUBLIC "-//W3C//DTD XHTML 1.0 Frameset//EN"
"http://www.w3.org/TR/xhtml1/DTD/xhtml1-frameset.dtd">
<html xmlns="http://www.w3.org/1999/xhtml">
<head>
<title>Trillium Technologies</title>
```

continues

```
</head>
<frameset  rows="100,* ">
  <frame src="nav" name="nav.htm" />
  <frame src="about.htm" name="main" />
  <noframes>
    <body>
      <h1>Trillium Technologies</h1>
      <a href="nav.htm">Site Links</a>
  </body>
  </noframes>
</frameset>
</html>
```

Hands-On Exercises

1. Write the XHTML to create a frameset (shown in Figure 5.17) that
   separates the browser window into three horizontal portions. The top
   portion will use the first 100 rows of pixels, the bottom portion will use
   75 rows, and the middle portion will use all the remaining browser
   window area. Code the **<frame>** tags so that the web page document
   mybanner.htm displays in the top portion, main.htm displays in the
   middle portion, and mynav.htm displays in the bottom portion. All
   hyperlinks in nav.htm should target the middle portion of the browser
   window. Be sure to use the appropriate DTD on your frameset page.

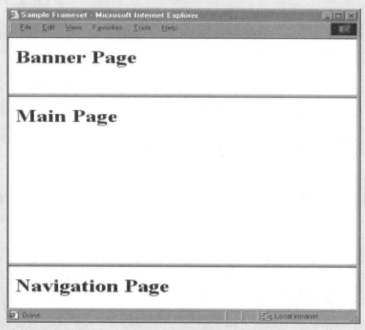

Figure 5.17 *A frameset page with three horizontal frames*

2. Write the XHTML to create a frameset (shown in Figure 5.18) that separates the browser window into three portions: two columns with a single row underneath.

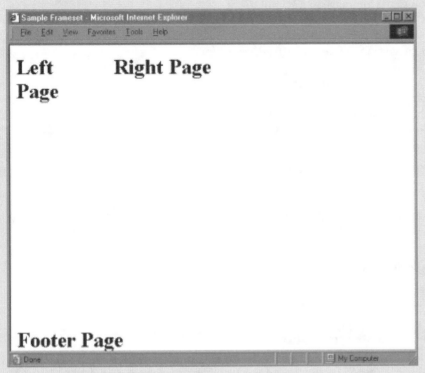

Figure 5.18 *Sample frameset with no borders*

The left column should be 150 pixels wide, the right column will use the remaining width of the browser window, and the bottom row should be 50 pixels high. Code the frame tags so that nav.htm displays in the left portion, main.htm displays in the right portion, and footer.htm displays in the bottom portion of the web page. All hyperlinks in nav.htm should target the right portion of the browser window. There should be no frame borders. Make certain that web page visitors cannot resize the nav or footer frames.

3. Create a group of frame pages about your favorite movie. The frameset page should be named index.htm. Use the diagram in Figure 5.4 as a guide. The banner frame (banner.htm) should contain the name of the movie. The navigation frame (nav.htm) should contain a link to the Main page (main.htm), the Review page (named review.htm), and the Image page (named image.htm).

- The Main page should briefly describe the movie and list its stars.

- The Review page should contain your opinion of the movie.

- The Image page should display an image about the movie or a star in the movie. Search the Web for a photo of a scene from the movie, an actress in the movie, or an actor in the movie.

(*Note:* It is not ethical to steal an image from another web site. Some web sites have a link to their copyright policy. Most web sites will give permission for you to use an image in a school assignment. If there is no available policy, e-mail the site's contact person and request permission to use the photo. If you are unable to obtain permission, you may substitute clip art or an image from a free site instead.)

Place an e-mail link to yourself on the Main page, Review page, and Image page. Test your index.htm page in a browser. The banner.htm, nav.htm, and main.htm pages should display. Print the source view of the index.htm page. Do a screen print of the browser window. Continue to test your frameset and select the Review link. Do a screen print of the browser window. Hand in all three printouts.

4. Create a group of frame pages about your favorite musical group. Name the frameset page index.htm. Use the screen shot in Figure 5.17 as a guide. The banner frame (banner.htm) should contain the name of the music group. The navigation frame (nav.htm) should contain a link to the Main page (main.htm), the Review page (named review.htm), and the Image page (named image.htm).

- The Main page should briefly describe the music group and list its members.

- The Review page should contain your opinion of the music group.

- The Image page should display an image of the musical group. Search the Web for a photo of the music group or graphic of a CD jacket.

(*Note:* It is not ethical to steal an image from another web site. Some web sites have a link to their copyright policy. Most web sites will give permission for you to use an image in a school assignment. If there is no available policy, e-mail the site's contact person and request permission to use the photo. If you are unable to obtain permission, you may substitute clip art or an image from a free site instead.)

Place an e-mail link to yourself on the Main page, Review page, and Image page. Test your index.htm page in a browser. The banner.htm, nav.htm and main.htm pages should display. Print the source view of the index.htm page. Do a screen print of the browser window. Continue to test your frameset and select the link to the Review page. Do a screen print of the browser window. Hand in all three printouts.

Each of these case studies will continue throughout most of the text. In this chapter, you will create new version of each case study web site that uses frames.

A. JavaJam Coffee House

See Chapter 2 for an introduction to the JavaJam Coffee House case. Figure 2.20 shows a site map for the JavaJam site. The pages were created in earlier chapters. You will use the existing web site to help create a new version that uses frames.

Hands-On Practice Case

1. Create a folder called javajamframes. Copy all the files from your javajam folder into the javajamframes folder.

2. Save your index.htm page as main.htm in the javajamframes folder.

3. You will now create a new index.htm page that will be the frameset page for the web site. Launch Notepad and create a frameset page that is similar in layout to Figure 5.4. The page will contain three frames: a banner frame (banner.htm) a navigation frame (nav.htm), and a main content frame (main.htm). Write the XHTML to create this frameset. Be sure to use the frameset DTD and to include appropriate `<noframes>` content. The banner frame should be 120 pixels high. The nav frame should be 150 pixels wide. The main frame can take up the remaining area on the web page. Configure the frameset so it does not display any borders (use both the framespacing and frameborder attributes on the `<frameset>` tag). Save your page as index.htm in the javajamframes folder.

4. Next you will create the pages to initially display in the frameset. You will base them on the existing JavaJam pages. When you are done and test your frameset the new Home page (index.htm) will be similar to Figure 5.19.

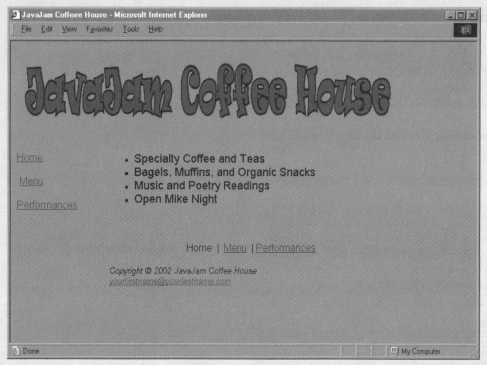

Figure 5.19 *New JavaJam Home page (index.htm)*

Use Notepad and create a new page called banner.htm. See Figure 5.20 for an example. This page will have the same background color (#999966) as the other JavaJam pages. Place the javalogo.gif on the page. Save the banner.htm in the javajamframes folder.

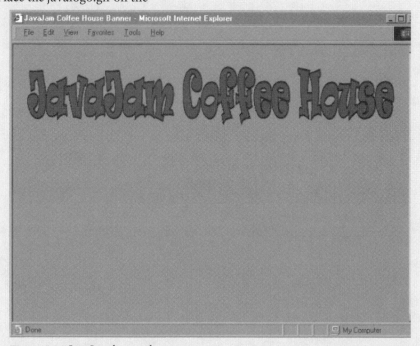

Figure 5.20 *JavaJam banner.htm*

5. Use Notepad and create a new page called nav.htm. See Figure 5.21 for an example. This page will have the same background color (#999966) as the other JavaJam pages. The text should use the Arial font. Place text links on this page as indicated in Table 5.7. Save the nav.htm page in the javajamframes folder.

Table 5.7

Text	Hyperlink Reference
Home	main.htm
Menu	menu.htm
Performances	performances.htm

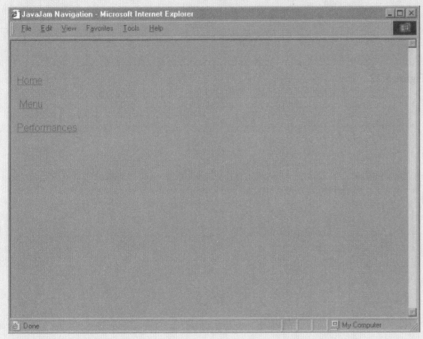

Figure 5.21 *JavaJam nav.htm*

6. Open the main.htm page in Notepad. Delete the top logo and address area. See Figure 5.22 for an example. Save the main.htm page in the javajamframes folder.

7. Open the menu.htm page in Notepad. Delete the top logo and address area on this page also. Modify the link to the home page to link to main.htm instead of index.htm. Save the menu.htm page in the javajamframes folder.

8. Open the performances.htm page in Notepad. Delete the top logo and address area on this page also. Modify the link to the home page to link to main.htm instead of index.htm. Save the performances.htm page in the javajamframes folder.

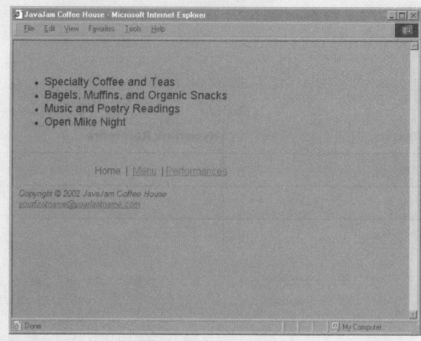

Figure 5.22 *JavaJam main.htm*

9. Now you are ready to test your new javajamframes web site! Launch a browser and open the index.htm page—it should look similar to Figure 5.19. The links on the nav.htm page should change the appearance of the main content page. Note: The javajamframes web site will not be used in the rest of the book.

B. Fish Creek Animal Hospital

See Chapter 2 for an introduction to the Fish Creek Animal Hospital case. Figure 2.23 shows a site map for the Fish Creek site. The pages were created in earlier chapters. You will use the existing web site as a start while you create a new version of this web site that uses frames.

Hands-On Case Practice

1. Create a folder called fishcreekframes. Copy all the files from your fishcreek folder into the fishcreekframes folder.

2. Save your index.htm page as main.htm in the fishcreekframes folder.

3. You will now create a new index.htm page that will be the frameset page for the web site. Launch Notepad and create a frameset page that is similar in layout to Figure 5.4.

The page will contain three frames—a banner frame (banner.htm) a navigation frame (nav.htm) and a main content frame (main.htm). Write the XHTML to create this frameset. Be sure to use the frameset DTD and to include appropriate **<noframes>** content. The banner frame should be 90 pixels high. The nav frame should be 168 pixels wide. The main frame can take up the remaining area on the web page. Configure the frameset so it does not display any borders (use both the framespacing and frameborder attributes on the **<frameset>** tag). Save your page as index.htm in the fishcreekframes folder.

4. Next you will create the pages to initially display in the frameset. You
   will base them on the existing Fish Creek pages. When you are done and
   test your frameset, the new Fish Creek Home page (index.htm) will be
   similar to Figure 5.23.

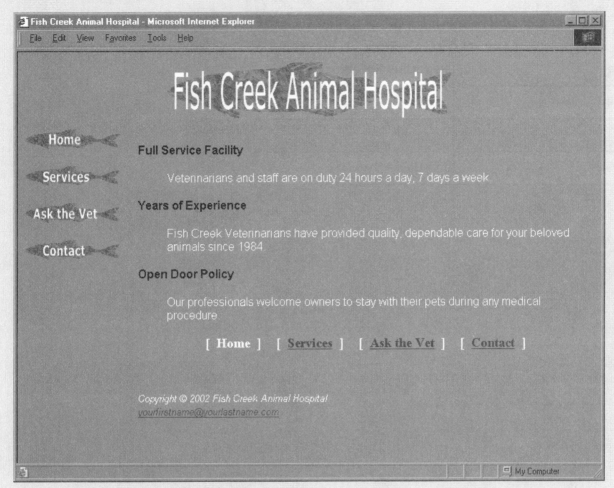

Figure 5.23 *New Fish Creek Home page (index.htm)*

Launch Notepad and create a new page called banner.htm. See Figure
5.24 for an example. This page will have the same background color
(#6699FF) as the other Fish Creek
pages. Place the fishcreeklogo.gif
centered on the page. Save the
banner.htm in the fishcreekframes
folder.

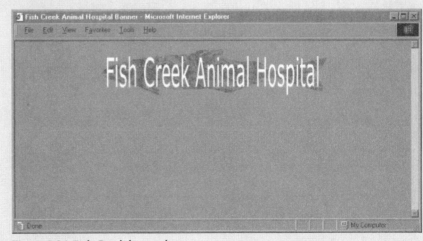

Figure 5.24 *Fish Creek banner.htm*

5. Launch Notepad and create a new page called nav.htm. See Figure 5.25 for an example. This page will have the same background color (#6699FF) as the other Fish Creek pages. Place the image links (home.gif, services.gif, askthevet.gif, and contact.gif) on this page as indicated in Table 5.8.

Table 5.8

Image	Hyperlink Reference
home.gif	main.htm
services.gif	services.htm
askthevet.gif	askvet.htm
contact.gif	contact.htm

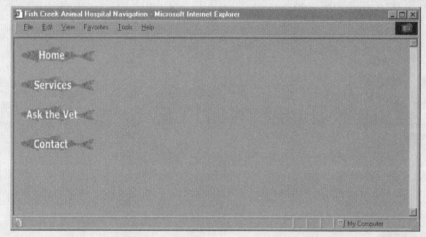

Figure 5.25 *Fish Creek nav.htm*

Hint: The image links will look better if you place each one in its own paragraph. Save the nav.htm page in the fishcreekframes folder.

6. Open the main.htm page in Notepad. Delete the top logo and image link area. See Figure 5.26 for an example. Save the main.htm page in the fishcreekframes folder.

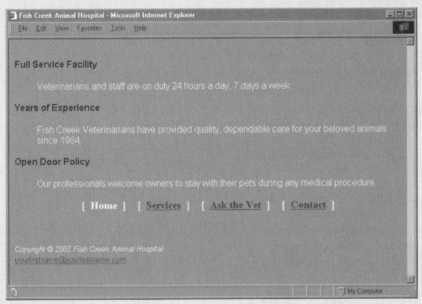

Figure 5.26 *Fish Creek main.htm*

7. Open the services.htm page in Notepad. Delete the top logo and image link area on this page also. Modify the link to the Home page to link to main.htm instead of index.htm. Save the services.htm page in the fishcreekframes folder.

8. Open the askthevet.htm page in Notepad. Delete the top logo and image link area on this page also. Modify the link to the Home page to link to main.htm instead of index.htm. Save the askthevet.htm page in the fishcreekframes folder.

9. Now you are ready to test your new fishcreekframes web site! Launch a browser and open the index.htm page—it should look similar to Figure 5.23. The links on the nav.htm page should change the appearance of the main content page. *Note:* The fishcreekframes web site will not be used in the rest of the book.

C. Pete the Painter

See Chapter 2 for an introduction to the Pete the Painter case. Figure 2.26 shows a site map for the Pete the Painter web site. The Home page, Services page, and Testimonials page were created in earlier chapters. You will use the existing web site to create a new frames version.

Hands-On Practice Case

1. Create a folder called painterframes. Copy all the files from your painter folder into the painterframes folder.

2. Save your index.htm page as main.htm in the painterframes folder.

3. You will now create a new frameset index.htm page for the web site. Launch Notepad and create a frameset page that is similar in layout to Figure 5.4.

   The page will contain three frames—a banner frame (banner.htm) a navigation frame (nav.htm), and a main content frame (main.htm). Write the XHTML to create this frameset. Be sure to use the frameset DTD and to include appropriate **\<noframes\>** content. The banner frame should be 163 pixels high. The nav frame should be 164 pixels wide. The main frame can take up the remaining area on the web page. Configure the frameset so it does not display any borders (use both the framespacing and frameborder attributes on the **\<frameset\>** tag). Save your page as index.htm in the painterframes folder.

4. Next you will create the pages to initially display in the frameset. You will base them on the existing painter pages. When you are done and test your frameset the new painterframes Home page (index.htm) will be similar to Figure 5.27.

Figure 5.27 *New Painter Home page (index.htm)*

Use Notepad and create a new page called banner.htm. See Figure 5.28 for an example. Place the painterlogo.gif on the page. Save the banner.htm in the painterframes folder.

Figure 5.28 *Painter banner.htm*

5. Use Notepad to create a new page called nav.htm. See Figure 5.29 for an example. The text should use the Arial font. Place text links on this page as indicated in the Table 5.9.

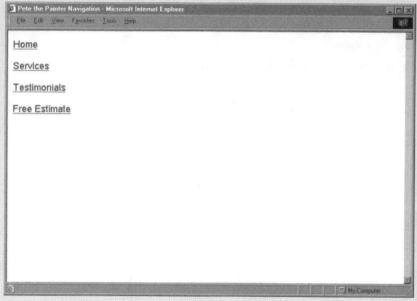

Figure 5.29 *Painter nav.htm*

Table 5.9

Text	Hyperlink Reference
Home	main.htm
Services	services.htm
Testimonials	testimonials.htm
Free Estimate	estimates.htm

Hint: The links will look better if you place each one in its own paragraph. Save the nav.htm page in the painterframes folder.

6. Open the main.htm page in Notepad. Delete the top logo and link area. See Figure 5.30 for an example. Save the main.htm page in the painterframes folder.

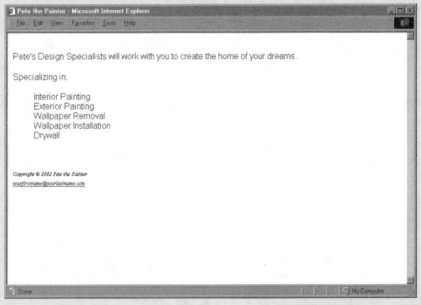

Figure 5.30 *Painter main.htm*

7. Open the testimonials.htm page in Notepad. Delete the top logo and link area on this page also. Save the testimonials.htm page in the painterframes folder.

8. Open the services.htm page in Notepad. Delete the top logo and link area on this page also. Save the services.htm page in the painterframes folder.

9. Now you are ready to test your new painterframes web site! Launch a browser and open the index.htm page—it should look similar to Figure 5.27. The links on the nav.htm page should change the appearance of the main content page. Note: The painterframes web site will not be used in the rest of the book.

Web Research

A. This chapter introduced using frames to organize web pages. Some web developers do not use frames because they are not particularly user-friendly and can reduce the accessibility of a web site. Other web developers find them helpful for quickly creating a web site or when there is a strong possibility of future changes in the way the site is organized. Use a search engine and search for online articles about the use of frames, or about guidelines for using frames. Here are a few resources to get you started:

- http://www.htmlhelp.com/design/frames/guidelines/
- http://www.useit.com/alertbox/9612.html
- http://realtytimes.com/rtnews/rtapages/20010801_frames.htm
- http://builder.cnet.com/webbuilding/pages/Authoring/Frames/ss05.html
- http://www.alistapart.com/stories/frames/
- http://www.evolt.org/article/rating/22/293/

As you read the articles, decide whether you are in favor of using frames (following the guidelines) or against using frames. Create a web page that supports your position. If you are in favor of using frames, state why and also include guidelines that constitute appropriate usage of frames. If you are against using frames, state why and list specific examples of the inappropriateness of frames. Whatever your opinion, be sure to list and link to the web sites that you referenced to create your position. Your web page should contain a table and use color. Place your name in the e-mail address at the bottom of the web page. Print both the source code (from Notepad) and the browser view of your web page.

B. Search the Web for a web page that uses XHTML frames. Print the browser view of the page. Print out the source code of the web page. Using the printout, highlight or circle the tags related to frames. On a separate sheet of paper create some XHTML notes by listing the tags and attributes related to frames found on your sample page along with a brief description of their purpose. Hand in the browser view of the page, source code printout, and your XHTML notes page.

Chapter Review Answers

1. c

2. c

3. c

4. b

5. b

6. c

7. a

8. b

9. b

10. d

11. numeric pixels

12. _blank

13. cols

14. Frames are deprecated. Frames are not universally supported. Frames are difficult to bookmark. Frames may be difficult for individuals with accessibility problems to access.

15. Not all browsers support inline frames. If a web page visitor is using one of these browsers or an assistive technology that does not support frames, he or she may get frustrated and leave the web site.

XHTML Forms

*F*orms are used for many purposes all over the Web. They are used by search engines to accept keywords and by online stores to process e-commerce shopping carts. Web sites use forms to help with a variety of functions—accepting visitor feedback, encouraging visitors to send a news story to a friend or colleague, collecting e-mail addresses for a newsletter, and accepting order information. This chapter introduces a very powerful tool for web developers—forms that accept information from web page visitors.

Learning Outcomes

In this chapter, you will learn how to:

▶ **Describe common uses of forms on web pages**

▶ **Describe the elements used in forms**

▶ **Create forms on web pages using the `<form>`, `<input>`, `<textarea>`, and `<select>` tags**

▶ **Create forms that provide additional accessibility features using the accesskey and tabindex attributes**

▶ **Associate form elements and element groups using the `<label>`, `<fieldset>`, and `<legend>` tags**

▶ **Create custom image buttons and use the `<button>` tag to include more variety and richer content than the standard form button**

▶ **Invoke server-side processing to handle form data**

Overview of Forms

Every time you use a search engine, place an order, or join a mailing list online, you are using a form. A form is an XHTML element that contains and organizes other objects—such as text boxes, check boxes, and buttons —that can accept information from web site visitors.

For example, look at Yahoo!'s search form in Figure 6.1. You may have used this many times but never thought about how it works. The form is quite simple; it contains just two elements: the text box that accepts the keywords used in the search, and the search button that submits the form and gets the search started.

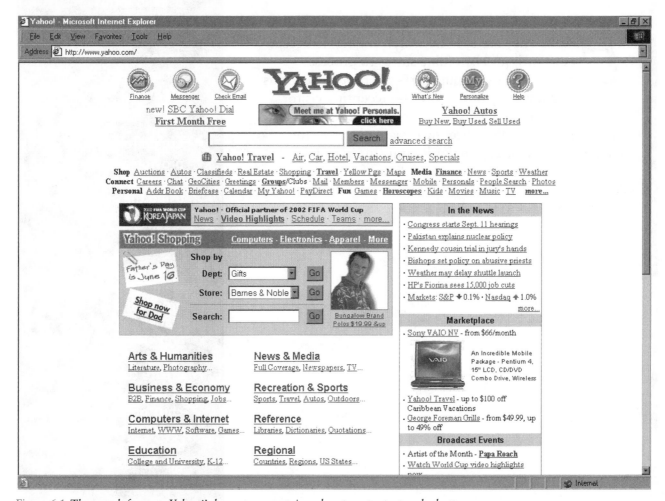

Figure 6.1 *The search form on Yahoo!'s home page contains a box to enter text and a button.*

Figure 6.2 shows a more detailed form, used to process credit card information for orders placed at Amazon.com. This form uses text boxes to accept information such as a credit card number and the cardholder's name. **Select lists** (sometimes called drop-down boxes) are used to capture information with a limited number of correct values, such as the type of credit card and expiration date information. The lozenge-shaped Continue graphic is a form button. When a visitor clicks the graphic, the form information is submitted and the ordering process continues. Whether a form is used to search for web pages or to purchase a book, the form alone cannot do all the processing. The form needs to invoke a program or script on the server in order to search a database or record an order. There are usually two components to using a form:

1. The XHTML form itself, which is the web page user interface
2. The server-side processing, called Common Gateway Interface (CGI), which works with the form data and sends e-mail, writes to a text file, updates a database, or performs some other type of processing on the server

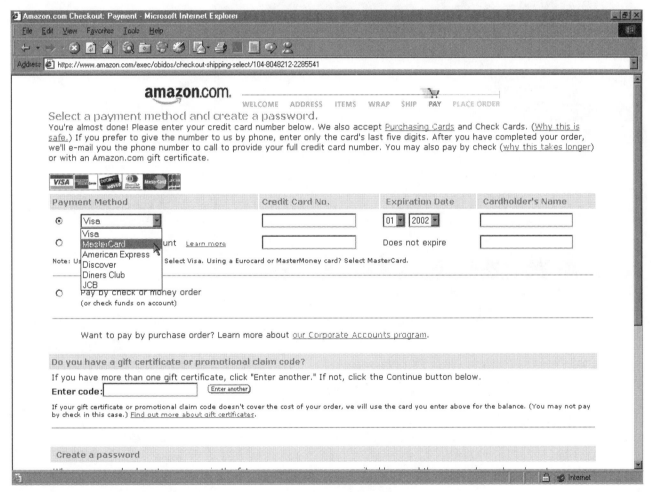

Figure 6.2 *This form accepts credit card information for an e-commerce web site.*

XHTML—Using Forms

Now that you have a basic understanding of what forms do, let's focus on the XHTML code to create a form. The **<form>** tag, **<input>** tag, and their attributes will be introduced while you create a sample form page. Once you've experimented a little with this form, you will be ready for a detailed discussion of the tags and attributes.

Hands-On Practice 6.1

In this Hands-On Practice session you will add a form to the sampleframe CircleSoft web site created in Hands-On Practice 5.1 and Hands-On Practice 5.2. The form will allow web page visitors to request that CircleSoft contact them. This sample form, shown in Figure 6.3, is very simple and only contains two elements: a text box to accept the visitor's e-mail address, and a submit button.

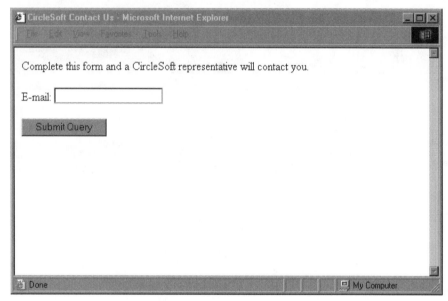

Figure 6.3 *The initial version of the CircleSoft contact form*

The form will be added to the contact.htm page. A shell version of this page was created in Hands-On Practice 5.1. When you display this form in your frameset, your browser window will look similar to Figure 6.4.

Figure 6.4 *The CircleSoft contact form displayed within the frameset*

Let's get started. Launch Notepad and open the contact.htm page that you created in Hands-On Practice 5.1. Replace the text you added to the page in the earlier exercise with a paragraph that says "Complete this form and a CircleSoft representative will contact you."

You are ready to configure the form area. The first XHTML in a form is the **<form>** *tag. Place your cursor on a blank line under the paragraph you just added and type in a* **<form>** *tag:*

<form>

As you read through the chapter you will find that a number of attributes can be used with the **<form>** *tag. In your first form, we are using the minimal XHTML needed to create the form.*

To create the area for the visitor's e-mail address to be entered, type the following XHTML:

**E-mail: <input type="text" name="CustomerEmail" />
**

This places the text "E-mail:" in front of the text box used to enter the visitor's e-mail address. The **<input>** *tag has a type attribute with the value of text that causes the browser to display a text box. The name attribute assigns the name CustomerEmail to the information entered into the text box (the value) and could be used by server-side processing. Since the* **<input>** *tag is a self-contained tag, it needs to be closed with /*>. *The* **
** *configures a line break.*

Now you are ready to add the submit button to the form. The XHTML code is

```
<input type="submit" />
```

This causes the browser to display a button with the default value of "Submit Query". Finally, you are ready to enter the closing form tag, `</form>`. A sample with all of the XHTML for the form is shown below.

```
<form>
E-mail:
<input type="text" name="CustomerEmail" />
<br />
<input type="submit" />
</form>
```

Save your contact.htm file in the sampleframe folder and test it in a browser. It should look similar to Figure 6.3. Experiment with the frameset you created in Chapter 5: Display the sampleframe index.htm page in a browser and select the "Contact" link. Your display should be similar to Figure 6.4. You can compare your work with the solution found on the student disk in the Chapter6/6.1 folder. Try entering some information into your form. Try clicking the button. Don't worry if the form redisplays but nothing seems to happen when you click the button—you haven't configured this form to work with any server-side processing. Connecting forms to server-side processing is demonstrated in Hands-On Practice 6.4. First, let's take a detailed look at the tags and attributes used to create forms.

But what if I need my form to really do something?

Forms usually need to invoke some type of server-side processing to perform functions such as sending e-mail, writing to text files, updating databases, and so on. Another option is to set up a form to send information using the e-mail program configured to work with the web page visitor's browser. In what is sometimes called using a mailto: URL, the `<form>` tag is coded to use your e-mail address in the action attribute:

```
<form method="post"
action="mailto:lsnblf@yahoo.com">
```

When a form is used in this manner the web visitor will see a warning message. The content of the warning message depends on how the visitor's browser is configured. If the visitor's browser is configured to work with an e-mail application, he or she will receive a message that states: "This form is being submitted using e-mail. Submitting this form will reveal your e-mail address to the recipient, and will send the form data without encrypting it for privacy." If the visitor's browser is not configured to work with an e-mail application, a different warning will appear. In either case, the warning message presents a nonprofessional image and is not the best way to inspire trust and confidence in your web site or business.

There are other reasons not to use the mailto: URL. For example, when people share a computer—they may not be using the default e-mail application. In this case, filling out the form has been a waste of time for them. Even if the person using the computer also uses the default e-mail application, perhaps he or she may not want to give out this particular e-mail address. Perhaps he or she has another e-mail address that is used for forms and newsletters, and does not want to waste time filling out your form. In either case, the result is not a happy visitor to your web site. So, while using the mailto: URL is easy, it does not always create the most usable web form for your visitors. What's a web developer to do? Use server-side processing (see Hands-On Practice 6.4) to handle form data instead of the mailto: URL.

The <form> Tag

The **<form>** tag specifies the beginning of a form area on a web page. Its closing tag, **</form>**, specifies the ending of a form area on a web page. There can be multiple forms on a web page, but they cannot be nested inside each other. The **<form>** tag can be configured with attributes that specify what server-side program or file will process the form, how the form information will be sent to the server, and the name of the form. Attributes such as name, method, and action are used to configure these options. These attributes are listed in Table 6.1. The most commonly used attributes are shown in bold.

Table 6.1 **<form>** *Tag Attributes*

Attribute	Values	Purpose
action	When used to invoke server-side processing, the value should be a valid file name on a web server. This is often a Perl script (.pl extension), a Microsoft Active Server Pages (.asp extension), or Sun's Java Server Pages (.jsp extension).	This attribute is optional. It is commonly used to specify what server-side program or script will process your form data using CGI.
	When used to send an e-mail, the value should be mailto: followed by a valid e-mail address.	Although not recommended, this attribute can also be used to specify an email address that the form information will be sent to.
		If no action attribute is present, the web page containing the form is requested and redisplayed by the browser.
id	Alphanumeric, no spaces. The value must be unique and not used for other id values on the same XHTML document.	This attribute is optional. It provides a unique identifier for the form.
method	"get"	This attribute is optional, but defaults to a value of "get" if omitted. The value of "get" causes the form data to be appended to the URL and sent to the web server.
	"post"	The post method is more private and transmits the form data in the body of the HTTP response. This method is preferred by the W3C.
name	Alphanumeric, no spaces, begins with a letter. Choose a form name value that is descriptive but short. For example, OrderForm is better than Form1 or WidgetsRUsOrderForm.	This attribute is optional. It names the form so that it can be easily accessed by client-side scripting languages, such as JavaScript, to edit and verify the form information before the server-side processing is invoked. This attribute is deprecated in XHTML but is used to provide backward compatibility with browser that still support HTML.

For example, to configure a form with the name of orderform, using the post method, and invoking a script called order.pl in a folder called cgi-bin on your web server, the XHTML is

```
<form name="orderform" method="post"
   action="cgi-bin/order.pl">
form elements go here....
</form>
```

Basic Form Elements

The purpose of a form is to gather information from a web page visitor; form elements are the objects that accept the information. Types of form elements include text boxes, scrolling text boxes, select lists, radio buttons, check boxes, and buttons. XHTML tags that configure these form elements include the `<input>`, `<textarea>`, `<select>`, and `<option>` tags. Most form elements are configured with the `<input>` tag, which is self-contained. The text box, password box, check box, radio button, scrolling text box, select list, submit button, reset button, button, and hidden fields are introduced in Tables 6.2 through 6.11.

What's the difference between the get and post methods?

You should usually use post as the value of the method on your forms. When you use get as the value the form data is appended to the end of the URL. This URL area (called the HTTP_REFERER) can be captured and stored in web site logs. You probably don't want your visitor's form data showing up in someone else's web server logs. This makes the get method much less private than the post message, which sends the form data in the entity body of the HTTP Request.

Table 6.2

Text Box
This form element is configured by the `<input>` tag and accepts text or numeric information such as names, e-mail addresses, phone numbers, and other text. See Figure 6.5 for a sample text box.

Sample Text Box

E-mail: [   ]

Figure 6.5 The `<input>` tag with `type="text"` configures this form element.

The XHTML code is **E-mail: `<input type="text" name="email" />`**

Common Attributes	Values	Usage
type	text	Configures the text box.
name	Alphanumeric, no spaces, begins with a letter	Names the form element so that it can be easily accessed by client-side scripting languages (such as JavaScript) or by server-side processing. The name should be unique.
size	Numeric	Configures the width of the text box as displayed by the browser. If size is omitted, the browser displays the text box with its own default size.
maxlength	Numeric	Configures the maximum length of data accepted by the text box.
value	Text or numeric characters	Assigns an initial value to the text box that is displayed by the browser. Accepts the information typed in the text box. This value can be accessed by client-side scripting languages and by server-side processing.

Table 6.3

Password Box

The `<input>` tag configures this element. The password box is similar to the text box but it accepts information that needs to be hidden as it is entered, such as a password. When the user types information in a password box, asterisks (*) are displayed instead of the characters that have been typed, as shown in Figure 6.6. This hides the information from someone looking over the shoulder of the person typing. The actual characters typed are sent to the server and the information is not really secret or hidden. See Chapter 13 for a discussion of encryption and security.

Sample Password Box

Password: ▮▮▮▮▮▮▮▮▮

Figure 6.6 *Although the characters secret999 were typed, the browser displays* *********

The XHTML code is **Password: <input type="password" name="myPassword" />**

Common Attributes	Values	Usage
type	password	Configures the password box.
name	Alphanumeric, no spaces, begins with a letter	Names the form element so that it can be easily accessed by client-side scripting languages or by server-side processing. The name should be unique.
size	Numeric	Configures the width of the password box as displayed by the browser. If size is omitted, the browser displays the password box with its own default size.
maxlength	Numeric	Optional. Configures the maximum length of data accepted by the password box.
value	Text or numeric characters	Assigns an initial value to the text box that is displayed by the browser. Accepts the information typed in the password box. This value can be accessed by client-side and by server-side processing.

Table 6.4

Check Box

This form element is configured by the `<input>` tag and allows the user to select one or more of a group of predetermined items. Figure 6.7 shows a sample check box.

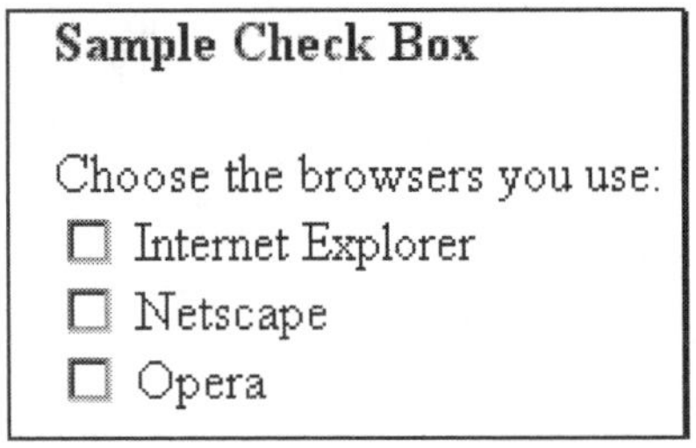

```
Sample Check Box

Choose the browsers you use:
  ☐ Internet Explorer
  ☐ Netscape
  ☐ Opera
```

Figure 6.7 *Use a check box when one or more selections is appropriate.*

The XHTML code is

```
Choose the browsers you use:<br />
<input type="checkbox" name="IE" value="yes" /> Internet Explorer<br />
<input type="checkbox" name="Netscape" value="yes" /> Netscape<br />
<input type="checkbox" name="Opera" value="yes" /> Opera
```

Note that the value of all the check boxes just happened to be yes. You can set the value to be any meaningful word or phrase. The name of each checkbox should be unique.

Attribute	Values	Usage
type	checkbox	Configures the check box.
name	Alphanumeric, no spaces, begins with a letter	Names the form element so that it can be easily accessed by client-side scripting languages or by server-side processing. The name of each checkbox should be unique.
checked	"checked"	Configures the check box to be checked by default when displayed by the browser.
value	Text or numeric characters	Assigns a value to the check box that is triggered when the check box is checked. This value can be accessed by client-side and by server-side processing.

Table 6.5

Radio Button

The `<input>` tag configures this element. Radio buttons allow the user to select exactly one item from a group of predetermined items. Each radio button in a group is given the same name and a unique value. Because the name is the same, the elements are identified as part of a group and only one may be selected. Figure 6.8 shows a sample radio button group.

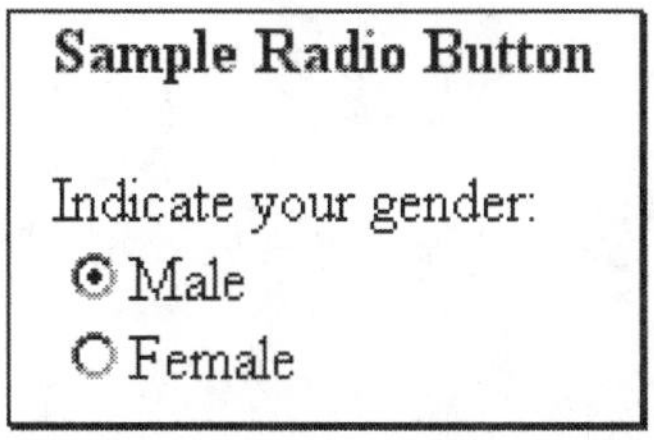

Sample Radio Button

Indicate your gender:
- ⊙ Male
- ○ Female

Figure 6.8 *Use radio buttons when only one choice is an appropriate response.*

The XHTML code is

```
Indicate your gender:<br />
<input type="radio" name="Gender" value="Male" checked="checked" /> Male<br />
<input type="radio" name="Gender" value="Female" /> Female
```

Notice that the name attributes all have the same value—Gender. This is what creates the group. Each radio button in the same group can be uniquely identified by its value attribute. Each radio button in the same group is configured with a different value.

Attribute	Values	Usage
type	radio	Configures the radio button.
name	Alphanumeric, no spaces, begins with a letter	Required. All radio buttons in a group must have the same name. This attribute also names the form element so that it can be easily accessed by client-side scripting languages or by server-side processing.
checked	"checked"	Configures the radio button to be selected by default when displayed by the browser.
value	Text or numeric characters	Assigns a value to the radio button that is triggered when the radio button is selected. This should be a unique value for each radio button in a group. This value can be accessed by client-side and by server-side processing.

Table 6.6

Scrolling Text Box

The **<textarea>** container tag configures a scrolling text box. A scrolling text box is used for accepting free-form comments, questions, or descriptions. See Figure 6.9 for a sample scrolling text box.

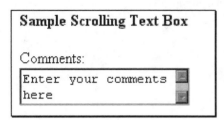

Figure 6.9 *Scrolling text boxes accept free-form comments from web page visitors.*

The XHTML code is

```
Comments:<br />
<textarea name="ordercomments" cols="40" rows="2">Enter your comments
here</textarea>
```

Notice that the **<textarea>** tag is a container tag. The text that you place between the opening **<textarea>** and closing **</textarea>** will be initially displayed in the scrolling text box.

Common Attributes	Values	Usage
name	Alphanumeric, no spaces, begins with a letter	Names the form element so that it can be easily accessed by client-side scripting languages (such as JavaScript) or by server-side processing. The name should be unique.
cols	Numeric	Configures the width in character columns of the scrolling text box. If cols is omitted, the browser displays scrolling text box with its own default width.
rows	Numeric	Configures the height in rows of the scrolling text box. If rows is omitted, the browser displays the scrolling text box with its own default height.
value	Text or numeric characters	Accepts the information typed in the scrolling text box. This value can be accessed by client-side scripting languages and by server-side processing.

Table 6.7

Select List

The **\<select\>** container tag (along with **\<option\>** tags) configures a select list. This form element has several names: select list, select box, drop-down list, drop-down box, and option box. It allows the visitor to select one or more items from a list of predetermined choices. The **\<option\>** container tag configures the choices in a select list. Sample select lists are shown in Figure 6.10 and 6.11.

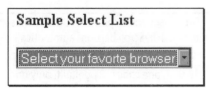

Figure 6.10 *A select list with size set to 1 will function as a drop-down box when the arrow is clicked.*

The XHTML code is

```
<select size="1" name="favbrowser">
  <option selected="selected" >Select your favorite browser</option>
  <option value="Internet Explorer">Internet Explorer</option>
  <option value="Netscape">Netscape</option>
  <option value="Opera">Opera</option>
</select>
```

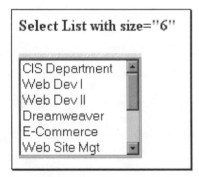

Figure 6.11 *This select list has size set to 6. Since there are more than six choices, the browser displays a scroll bar.*

The XHTML code is

```
<select size="6" name="jumpmenu">
  <option value="cisdept.htm">CIS Department</option>
  <option value="webdev1.htm">Web Dev I</option>
  <option value="webdev2.htm">Web Dev II</option>
  <option value="dreamweaver.htm">Dreamweaver</option>
  <option value="ecommerce.htm">E-Commerce</option>
  <option value="webmgt.htm">Web Site Mgt</option>
  <option value="perl.htm">Perl Intro</option>
</select>
```

Table 6.7 (continued)

Select List <select> tag

Common Attributes	Values	Usage
name	Alphanumeric, no spaces, begins with a letter	Names the form element so that it can be easily accessed by client-side scripting languages (such as JavaScript) or by server-side processing. The name should be unique.
size	Numeric	Configures the number of choices the browser will display. If set to 1, element functions as a drop down list (see Figure 6.10). Scroll bars are automatically added by the browser if the number of options exceeds the space allowed.
multiple	"multiple"	Configures a select list to accept more than one choice. By default, only one choice can be made from a select list.

Select List <option> tag

Common Attributes	Values	Usage
value	Text or numeric characters	Assigns a value to the option. This value can be accessed by client-side and by server-side processing.
selected	"selected"	Configures an option to be initially selected when displayed by a browser.

Table 6.8

Submit Button

This form element is configured by the `<input>` tag and is used to submit the form. It triggers the action method on the `<form>` tag and causes the browser to send the form data (the name and value pairs for each form element) to the web server. The web server will invoke the server-side processing program or script listed on the form's action property. Figure 6.12 shows a sample submit button.

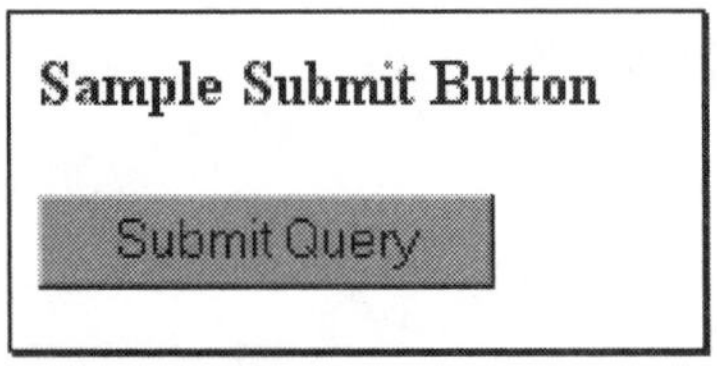

Sample Submit Button

Submit Query

Figure 6.12 *Clicking the submit button will invoke the server-side processing configured in the action property of the* `<form>` *tag.*

The XHTML code is

```
<input type="submit" />
```

Common Attributes	Values	Usage
type	submit	Configures the submit button.
name	Alphanumeric, no spaces, begins with a letter	Names the form element so that it can be easily accessed by client-side scripting languages (such as JavaScript) or by server-side processing. The name should be unique.
value	Text or numeric characters	Configures the text displayed on the submit button. By default, the text "Submit Query" is displayed.

Table 6.9

Reset Button

This form element is configured by the **`<input>`** tag and is used to reset the form fields to their initial values. See Figure 6.13 for a sample reset button.

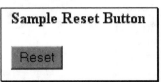

Figure 6.13 *Use the reset button to give web page visitors a chance to reset or clear their mistakes.*

The XHTML code is

```
<input type="reset" />
```

Common Attributes	Values	Usage
type	reset	Configures the reset button.
name	Alphanumeric, no spaces, begins with a letter	Names the form element so that it can be easily accessed by client-side scripting languages (such as JavaScript) or by server-side processing. The name should be unique.
value	Text or numeric characters	Configures the text displayed on the reset button. By default, the text "Reset" is displayed.

Table 6.10

Button

This form element is configured by the `<input>` tag and offers a flexible user interface. There is no default action when the button is clicked. Form information is not sent to the web server when this button is clicked.

This element is usually used with client-side scripting such as JavaScript, to cause some processing to occur on the client (see Chapter 12). Types of client-side processing may include calculations, edits, or other functions such as displaying a different page. A sample button is shown in Figure 6.14.

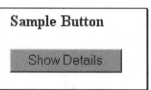

Figure 6.14 *This button has no default action. It is often used with client-side scripting such as JavaScript.*

The XHTML code is

```
<input type="button" value="Show Details" />
```

Common Attributes	Values	Usage
type	button	Configures the button.
name	Alphanumeric, no spaces, begins with a letter	Names the form element so that it can be easily accessed by client-side scripting languages (such as JavaScript) or by server-side processing. The name should be unique.
value	Text or numeric characters	Configures the text displayed on the button.

Table 6.11

Hidden

This form element is configured by the `<input>` tag and is not displayed on the web page. Hidden form fields can be accessed by both client-side and server-side scripting and sometimes contain information needed as the visitor moves from page to page.

The XHTML to create a hidden form element with the name sendto and the value of an e-mail address is

```
<input type="hidden" name="sendto" value="order@site.com" />
```

Common Attributes	Values	Usage
type	hidden	Configures the hidden element.
name	Alphanumeric, no spaces, begins with a letter	Names the form element so that it can be easily accessed by client-side scripting languages (such as JavaScript) or by server-side processing. The name should be unique.
value	Text or numeric characters	Assigns a value to the hidden element. This value can be accessed by client-side scripting languages and by server-side processing.

As you have seen, there are a number of form elements, each with a specific purpose. This would be a good time to visit a few web sites and examine how they use forms. Why not take a look at a few sites such as http://yahoo.com, http://amazon.com, http://ebay.com, or one of your favorites and identify when and how they use forms and form elements?

In this Hands-On Practice session you will modify the form you created in Hands-On Practice 6.1 (see Figure 6.3). Recall that the purpose of the form is to allow web page visitors to request that CircleSoft contact them. You will modify the form to include a reset button and to accept the Customer's name, phone number, and a question or comment in addition to the e-mail address. This modified form is shown in Figure 6.15.

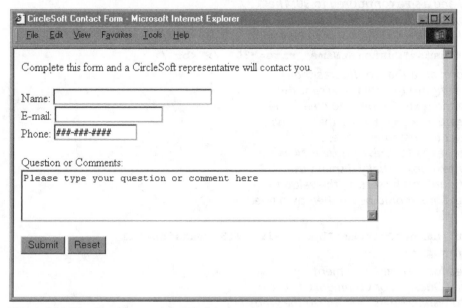

Figure 6.15 *The new version of the CircleSoft contact form*

When you display this form in your frameset, your browser window will look similar to Figure 6.16.

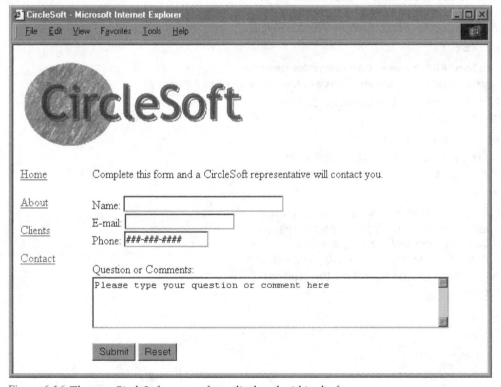

Figure 6.16 *The new CircleSoft contact form displayed within the frameset*

Let's get started. Launch Notepad and open the contact.htm page that you created in Hands-On Practice 6.1. Perform the following edits.

1. *Place the cursor after the* **<form>** *tag and press Enter to create a new line. Configure the area where the customer name will be entered. Type the text "Name: " to create the label for the text box. Now create an* **<input>** *tag that has type configured to text, a name set to CustomerName, and a size configured to 30. The label and text box should be on their own line. (Hint: Use a* **
** *tag at the end of the line.) The XHTML is shown below.*

```
Name: <input type="text" name="CustomerName" size="30" /> <br />
```

2. *Create a new line under the form area that configures the CustomerEmail text box and configure the area to accept the customer phone number. Type the text "Phone: " to create the label for the text box. Now create an* **<input>** *tag that has type configured to "text", a name set to CustomerPhone, a size configured to 15 and a maxsize set to 11. View Figure 6.14 and notice that the phone number text box initially displays the characters ###-###-####. Configure this by setting the value to ###-###-####. The label and text box should be on their own line. The XHTML is*

```
Phone: <input type="text" name="CustomerPhone" size="15" maxsize="11
    value="###-###-####" /><br />
```

3. *Now you will configure the area for customer comments or questions. On its own line, type "Question or Comments: ". Use a* **
** *tag to cause this text to display on its own line in the web browser. Next, configure a scrolling text box with 4 rows, 60 columns and the name CustomerComment. Set rows to 4, cols to 60, and the name to CustomerComment. Configure the default text to display between the* **<textarea>** *and* **</textarea>** *tags as "Please type your question or comment here". Configure a blank line underneath the scrolling text box. Sample The XHTML is*

```
Question or Comments:<br />
<textarea rows="4" cols="60" name="CustomerComment">
    Please type your question or comment here</textarea><br /><br />
```

4. *Notice that in Figure 6.14 the submit button displays "Submit". Use the value attribute to configure this:*

```
<input type="submit" value="Submit" />
```

5. *Add a blank space next to the submit button, then add a reset button. to the form. The XHTML is*

```
<input type="reset" />
```

6. *Save your contact.htm file and test it in a browser. It should look similar to Figure 6.15. Experiment with the frameset you created in Chapter 5, display the sampleframe index.htm page in a browser and select the link for "Contact". Your display should be similar to Figure 6.16. The solution can be found on the student disk in the Chapter6/6.2 folder.*

As you view your form (or Figure 6.16) you may notice that it looks a little messy—the form elements don't align under each other. A technique often used to align form elements is to format the form area with a table. See Figure 6.17 for a more orderly version of the form formatted by a table.

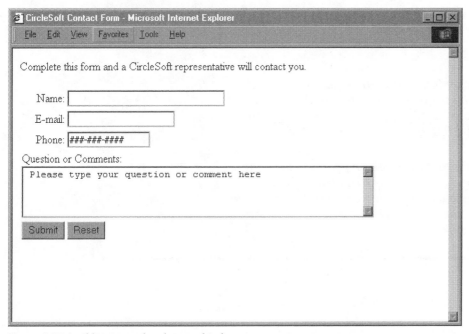

Figure 6.17 *A table was used to format this form.*

A table with five rows and two columns was added to the page in Figure 6.17, within the **<form>** *and* **</form>** *container tags. The text labels for the "Name:", "E-mail:", and "Phone:" form elements were each placed in their own table cell and right-aligned. Each text box and button was placed in its own table cell. The scrolling text box was placed in a table cell that spanned two columns. (See Chapter 3 to review tables.) The table was configured to have no border and to take up 75% of the browser window. The first column was configured to take up 10% of the table width. The revised XHTML for the entire form is shown here with the table code in green. Notice that since a table is used to format the form, fewer* **
** *tags are needed.*

```
<form>
  <table border="0" width="75%">
    <tr>
      <td align="right" width="10%">Name: </td>
      <td><input type="text" name=CustomerName size="30" /> </td>
    </tr>
    <tr>
      <td align="right" width="10%">E-mail: </td>
      <td><input type="text" name="CustomerEmail" /></td>
    </tr>
    <tr>
      <td align="right" width="10%">Phone: </td>
      <td><input type="text" name="CustomerPhone"
        size="15" maxsize="11" value="###-###-####" /></td>
    </tr>
```

continues

```
<tr>
  <td colspan="2">Question or Comments:<br />
  <textarea rows="4" cols="60" name="CustomerComment">Please type your question
  or comment here</textarea></td>
</tr>
<tr>
  <td align="right" width="10%"><input type="submit" value="Submit" /></td>
  <td><input type="reset" /></td>
</tr>
</table>
```

Tables are often used to organize forms on web pages. Modify your page as indicated here. Save the page as contact.htm in the sampleframe folder, test in a browser and compare your result with Figure 6.17. The solution can be found on the student disk at Chapter6/6.2/contact2.htm.

You are now familiar with using forms on web pages, with different elements that can be placed on forms, and with using a table to format a form. Additional detailed information on these form elements and their attributes may be found in the XHTML Reference in the Web Developer's Handbook.

Form Enhancements

There are additional XHTML tags that can enhance your forms by associating text labels with form elements and by visually grouping form elements together. These enhancements are supported by Internet Explorer but may not be supported by other popular browsers. Use them with caution.

The <label> Tag

The **<label>** tag is a container tag that is used to associate a text description with a form element. It can serve as a fragment identifier or bookmark and allow the form element to be directly linked to from other parts of the web page (or other web pages, if needed).

There are two ways to associate a label with a form element. The first method places the **<label>** tag as a container around both the text description and the form element. The code is

```
<label>E-mail: <input type="text" name="CustomerEmail" /><label>
```

The second method uses the id attribute to associate the label with a particular form element. This is more flexible and is better suited for forms that are formatted with a table. The code is

```
<label for="email">E-mail: </label><input type="text"
  name="CustomerEmail" id="email" />
```

Notice that the value of the for attribute on the **<label>** tag is the same as the value of the id attribute on the **<input>** tag. This creates the association between the **<label>** and the form element. The **<input>** tag uses both the name and id attributes for different purposes. The name attribute can be used by client-side and by server-side scripting. The id attribute creates an identifier that can be used by the **<label>** and anchor tags.

The <fieldset> and <legend> Tags

You have seen an example using a table to format a form. Another technique that can be used to create a more visually pleasing form is to group elements with the **<fieldset>** tag. Browsers that support this feature will place a visual cue, such as an outline or a border, around form elements grouped in a **<fieldset>**. The **<legend>** tag can be used to provide a label for this grouping. Figure 6.18 shows the CircleSoft contact form (contact.htm) with the CustomerName, CustomerEmail, and Customer Phone elements grouped in this manner.

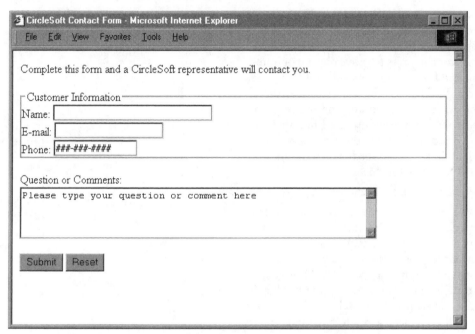

Figure 6.18 *The CircleSoft contact form (contact.htm) using a* **<fieldset>**

The XHTML to create the grouping shown in Figure 6.18 follows:

```
<fieldset><legend>Customer Information</legend>
Name: <input type="text" name=CustomerName" size="30" /><br/>
E-mail: <input type="text" name="CustomerEmail" /><br />
Phone: <input type="text" name="CustomerPhone" size="15" maxsize="11"
  value="###-###-####" />
<br /></fieldset>
```

The grouping and visual effect of the **<fieldset>** tag can be used to create a more appealing web page containing a form. Be aware that older browsers, such as Netscape 4, do not support the **<fieldset>** and **<legend>** tags. If you decide to use them, make certain that your form is easy to use and understand even if the visual grouping is not displayed.

The Tabindex Attribute

Some of your web page visitors may have difficulty using the mouse and will access your form with a keyboard. They may use the Tab key to move from one form element to another. The default action for the Tab key is to move to the next form element in the order the form elements are coded in the XHTML. This is usually appropriate. However, if the tab order needs to be changed for a form, use the **tabindex attribute** on each form element. For each form element (**<input>**, **<select>**, **<textarea>**), code a tabindex attribute with a numeric value, beginning with 1, 2, 3, etc. in numerical order. The XHTML code to configure the CustomerEmail text box as the initial position of the cursor is: **`<input type="text" name="CustomerEmail" tabindex="1" />`**. The tabindex attribute is not supported in older browsers such as Netscape 4. If you assign a form element with **`tabindex="0"`**, it will be visited after all other form elements that are assigned tabindex. If you happen to assign two elements the same tabindex value, the one that is coded first in the XHTML will be visited first.

The Accesskey Attribute

Another technique that can make your form keyboard-friendly is the use of the **accesskey** attribute on form elements. Assigning the accesskey a value of one of the characters (letter or number) on the keyboard will create a hot key that your web page visitor can press to move the cursor immediately to a form element. The method used to access this hot key varies depending on the operating system. Windows users will press the Alt key and the character key. The combination is the Cmd key and the character key for Mac users. For example, if the form in Figure 6.18 had the CustomerEmail text coded with an **`accesskey="E"`**, the web page visitor using Windows could press the Alt and e keys to immediately move the cursor to the Email text box. The XHTML code for this is

```
<input type="text" name="CustomerEmail" accesskey="E" />
```

The accesskey attribute is not supported in older browsers such as Netscape 4. Even when browsers do support the accesskey feature, you cannot rely on the browser to indicate that a character is an accesskey. You will have to manually code information about the hot key. A visual cue may be helpful. The W3C suggests underlining the letter in each text label that is used as a hot key. Other options include displaying the hot key in bold or by placing a message such as Alt+E after a form element that uses a hot key. Hands-On Practice 6.3 will provide you with some experience using the accesskey attribute.

Image Buttons and <button> Tag

As you have worked with forms in this chapter, you may have noticed that the standard submit button (see Figure 6.12) is a little plain. You can make the form area that you click to submit the form more compelling and visually interesting in two ways: by creating custom images that are configured with the **`<input>`** tag or by using the **`<button>`** tag.

Figure 6.19 shows an image used in place of the standard submit button. This is called an image button. When an image button is clicked, the form is submitted. The image button is coded using the **`<input>`** tag along with **`type="image"`** and a src attribute with the value of the name of the image file. For example, to use the image called login.gif as an image button the XHTML code is

```
<input type="image" src="login.gif" />
```

Figure 6.19 *The web page visitor will click the "Log in" graphic to submit the form.*

Another way to add more interest to a form is to use the **<button>** tag. This tag can be used to configure not only images but also blocks of text as the clickable area that can submit or reset a form. The **<button>** tag is a container tag. Any web page content that is between the **<button>** and **</button>** tags is configured to be part of the button. Table 6.12 lists common attributes of the **<button>** tag.

Table 6.12

Common Attributes	Values	Usage
type	submit	Functions as a submit button.
	reset	Functions as a reset button.
	button	Functions as a button.
name	Alphanumeric, no spaces, begins with a letter	Names the form element so that it can be easily accessed by client-side scripting languages (such as JavaScript) or by server-side processing. The name should be unique.
value	Text or numeric characters	A value given to a form element that is passed to the form handler

Figure 6.20 shows a version of the CircleSoft contact page that has an image (contact.gif) and text description configured as a submit button using the **<button>** tag.

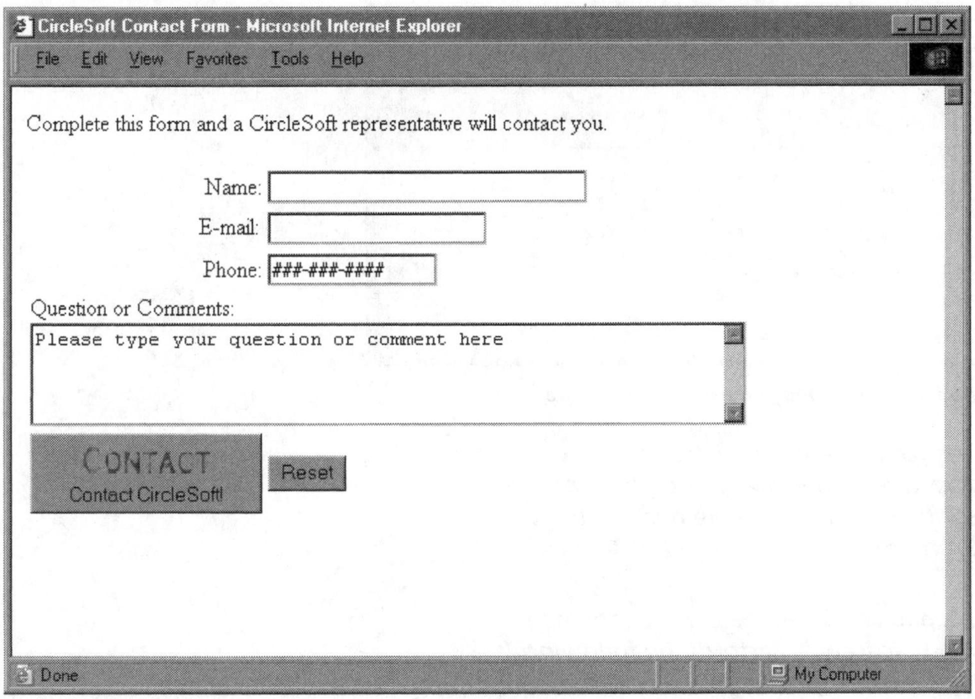

Figure 6.20 *The* **<button>** *tag configured as a submit button*

The XHTML code to create the button shown in Figure 6.20 is

```
<button type="submit">
<p align="center">
<img src="contact.gif" width="100" height="30" alt="Submit form" />
<br />Contact CircleSoft!</p>
</button>
```

As you visit web pages and take a look at their source code, you will find that the **<button>** tag is not used as often as the standard submit button or the image button.

Hands-On Practice 6.3

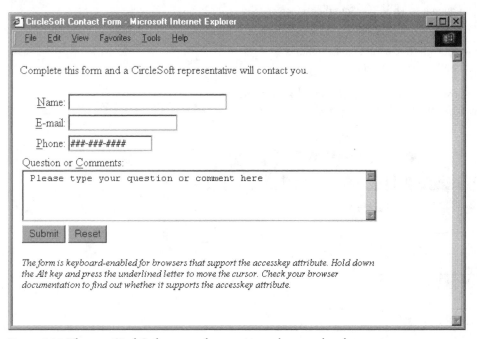

In this Hands-On Practice session you will modify the contact form you worked with in Hands-On Practice 6.2 to use the accesskey attribute (See Figure 6.21).

Figure 6.21 *The new CircleSoft contact form supports the accesskey feature*

Recall that the purpose of the form is to allow web page visitors to request that CircleSoft contact them. You will add hot keys that will immediately move the cursor to a specific form element. You will also add a comment to the form that explains this feature to your web page visitors.

Let's get started. Launch Notepad and open the contact.htm page that you created in Hands-On Practice 6.2. Perform the following edits.

1. *Add the accesskey attribute to each form element (`<input>` and `<textarea>` tags). Assign the value of the accesskey as shown in Table 6.13.*

Table 6.13

Form Element	accesskey
CustomerName	N
CustomerEmail	E
CustomerPhone	P
CustomerComment	C
Submit Button	S
Reset Button	R

2. *Use the `<u>` tag to display each hot key character as underlined when it appears in the label for a form element.*

3. *Add a row to the table (remember the `<td>` tag and use `colspan="2"`) at the bottom of the page below the form. Enter the following text:*

   "The form is keyboard-enabled for browsers that support the accesskey attribute. Hold down the Alt key and press the underlined letter to immediately move the cursor. Check your browser documentation to find out whether it supports the accesskey attribute."

   This text should be emphasized and have font size set to "2".

4. *Save your contact.htm file in the sampleframe folder and test in a recent browser such as Internet Explorer 5 (or later) or Netscape 6 (or later). It should look similar to Figure 6.21. You can compare your work with the solution found on the student disk (Chapter6/6.3). As you try out the hot keys and move around the form, you may notice that when you activate the Submit button, the form redisplays. That is because there is no action property in the `<form>` tag. The next section focuses on the second component of using forms on web pages—server-side processing.*

Server-Side Processing

Your web browser requests web pages and their related files from a web server. The web server locates the files and sends them to your web browser. The web browser then renders the returned files and displays the requested web pages. Figure 6.22 illustrates the communication between web browser and web server.

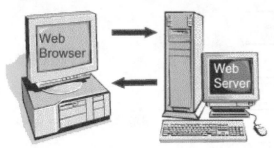

Figure 6.22 *The web browser (client) works with the web server.*

Sometimes a web site needs more functionality than static web pages—possibly a site search, order form, e-mail list, database display, or other type of processing. That is when server-side processing is needed, commonly known as the **Common Gateway Interface (CGI)**. The term Common Gateway Interface refers to the fact that the two computers communicating do need not have the same hardware or operating system —there is a common gateway between the different platforms.

CGI is a protocol, or standard method, for a web server to pass a web page user's request (which is typically initiated through the use of a form) to an application program and to accept information to send to the user. The web server typically passes the form information to a small application program that processes the data, and it usually sends back a confirmation web page or message. This specification for passing data back and forth between the server and the application is called CGI and is part of the Hypertext Transfer Protocol (HTTP) specification.

A web page invokes CGI by either an action method on a form or a hyperlink—the URL of the CGI script or program is used. Any form data that exists is passed to the CGI script. The CGI script completes its processing and may create a confirmation or response web page with the requested information. The web server returns this page to the web browser. Every time you perform a search using Yahoo! or other search engines, you are using CGI.

CGI programs or scripts can be written in many languages; Perl, C, and C++ are just a few. Server-side scripts usually end in the .pl or .cgi extension. At this writing, Perl is the most common language for CGI processing.

There are other technologies that perform server-side processing. Sun's Java Server Pages (JSP), Microsoft's Active Server Pages (ASP), and Microsoft's ASP.Net are a few that are commonly used. Instead of a program executing on the server, a web page containing a script is invoked. This web server executes the script before the response page is sent to the web browser. In Hands-On Practice 6.4, you will invoke an Active Server Pages script to perform the server-side processing.

In this Hands-On Practice you will modify the contact.htm page that you created earlier in this chapter, modifying the form so that it uses the post method to invoke a server-side script. Please note that your computer must be connected to the Internet when you test your work.

Launch Notepad and open the contact.htm file from your sample-frame folder. Modify the `<form>` tag to use the post method. The XHTML is shown below

```
<form method="post">
```

The post method is recommended by the W3C and is more private than the get method. The post method does not pass the form information in the URL; it passes it in the entity-body of the HTTP Request, which makes it more private.

When using a server-side script you will need to obtain some information, or documentation, from the person or organization providing the script. You will need to know the location of the script, whether it requires any specific names for the form elements, and whether it requires any hidden form elements. The action attribute is used on the `<form>` tag to invoke a server-side script. A server-side script has been created at http://webdevfoundations.net/scripts/formdemo.asp for students to use for this exercise. The documentation for the server-side script is listed in Table 6.14 below.

Table 6.14

Location of Script:	http://webdevfoundations.net /scripts/formdemo.asp
Purpose of Script:	This script will place all input from a form in the body of a web page that is displayed. This is a sample script for student assignments. It demonstrates that server-side processing has been invoked. A script used by an actual web site would perform a function such as sending an e-mail message or updating a database.

Now you will add the configuration required to use the formdemo.asp server-side processing with your form. Launch Notepad and open the contact.htm file from your sampleframe folder. Modify the `<form>` tag again by adding an action attribute with a value of "http://webdevfoundations.net/scripts/formdemo.asp". The XHTML code for the revised `<form>` tag is

```
<form  method="post" action="http://webdevfoundations.net/scripts/formdemo.asp" >
```

*Save your page as contact.htm in the sampleframes folder. Display
the page in the frameset you created in Chapter 5 by displaying the
sampleframe index.htm page in a browser and selecting the link for
Contact. Your screen should look similar to Figure 6.23.*

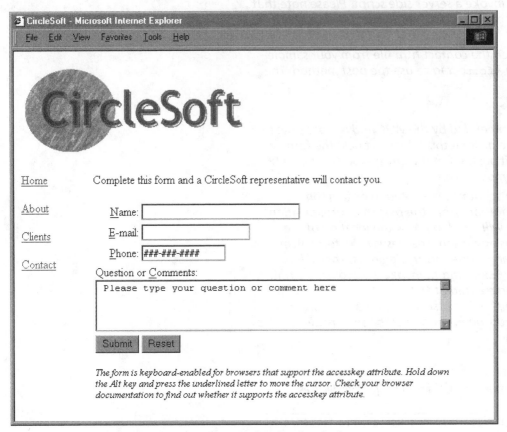

Figure 6.23 *The final CircleSoft contact form displayed within the frameset*

Now you are ready to test your form. You must be connected to the Internet to successfully test your form. Enter information in the form elements and click the submit button. You should see a confirmation page similar to the one shown in Figure 6.24.

Figure 6.24 *The server-side script has created this page in response to your form.*

The formdemo.asp script creates a web page that displays a message and the form information you entered. Where did this confirmation page originate? This confirmation page was created by the server-side script on the action attribute in the <form> tag. Sometimes students wonder what code is used in the formdemo.asp file. Writing scripts for server-side processing is beyond the scope of this course. However, if you are curious visit http://webdevfoundations.net/ chapter6 to see the source code for this script.

What do I do if nothing happened when I tested my form?

Try these troubleshooting hints:
- Verify that your computer is connected to the Internet.
- Verify the spelling of the script location in the action attribute.
- Attention to detail is crucial!

Sources of Free Server-Side Processing

Of course, you could be lucky and have a best friend who does CGI programming or server-side scripting. However, if you are like most beginning web developers you may need to find free sources of server-side processing. Many web host providers offer free scripts for their clients. Contact their support area or FAQs to learn more about their services. They often have examples showing you how to use their scripts.

There are also web sites that offer remotely hosted scripts such as http://formbuddy.com, http://hostedscripts.com, http://response-o-matic.com, and http://master.com. These offer a limited number of scripts that you may invoke for free. They usually have sample pages and FAQ pages to help you get started. What's the catch? The catch is that the web pages generated by the hosted scripts often contain site logos or even ads.

What is FrontPage?

Microsoft FrontPage is a web authoring tool that has its own server-side processing—the FrontPage Server Extensions. These are CGI in disguise—you point and click your way to sending form data in e-mails, saving form data in files, and saving form data in databases. FrontPage creates the method and action attributes for you. It also creates any needed hidden form fields automatically. This can be a real time-saver, but you should be aware of some constraints. If you use FrontPage and depend on its server extensions be sure you *always* use FrontPage to publish your site and never use FTP. If you forget and use FTP, the forms on your web pages may not function correctly and you will need to ask your web host provider to reinstall the FrontPage Server Extensions for your web site.

Chapter **6** Review

Summary

This chapter introduced the use of forms on web pages. You learned how to configure form elements and provide for accessibility. You also learned how to configure a form to access server-side processing. Visit the text web site at http://www.webdevfoundations.net for examples, updated information, and the links listed in this chapter.

Review Questions

Multiple Choice

1. Which XHTML tag configures a button that can be clicked to automatically reset form fields to their default values?

   a. `<input type="reset" />`
   b. `<button type="reset">`Reset`</button>`
   c. `<input type="button" value="Reset" />`
   d. both a and b

2. Which attribute of the `<form>` tag is used to specify the name and location of the script that will process the form field values?

   a. action   c. method
   b. process   d. none of the above

3. Which of the following form elements does not use the `<input>` tag?

   a. text box   c. check box
   b. select list   d. radio button

4. Choose the XHTML tag that would configure a textbox with the name "email" and a width of 40 characters.

   a. `<input type="text" id="email" width="40" />`
   b. `<input type="text" name="email" size="40" />`
   c. `<input type="text" name="email" space="40" />`
   d. `<input type="text"  width="40"/>`

5. Which of the following form elements would be appropriate for an area that your visitors can use to type in comments about your Web site?

   a. select list   c. scrolling text box
   b. text box   d. none of the above

6. You would like to conduct a survey and ask your web page visitors to vote for their favorite search engine. Select the form element that is best to use for this purpose.

   a. check box   c. text box
   b. radio button   d. scrolling text box

7. You would like to conduct a survey and ask your web page visitors to indicate the web browsers that they use. Select the form element that is best to use for this purpose.

    a. check box
    b. radio button
    c. text box
    d. scrolling text box

8. An order form contains an area for web visitors to select their preferred method of shipping. You need to limit the amount of space on the form that is used for this feature. Select the form element that is best to use for this purpose.

    a. check box   c. text box
    b. radio button   d. select list

9. Which XHTML tag would configure a scrolling text box with the name comments, 2 rows, and 30 characters?

    a. `<textarea name="comments" width="30" rows="2"></textarea>`
    b. `<input type="textarea" name="comments" size="30" rows="2" />`
    c. `<textarea name="comments" rows="2" cols="30"></textarea>`
    d. none of the above

10. Choose the XHTML that would associate a label displaying the text "Phone Number" with the text box named orderPhone. The letter P should function as a hot key for the text box.

    a. `Phone Number: <input type="textbox" name="orderPhone" />`
    b. `<label>Phone Number: <input type="text" name="orderPhone" accesskey="P" /> </label>`
    c. `<label for="Phone">Phone Number: </label><input type="text" name="orderPhone" id="Phone" accesskey="P" />`
    d. both b and c

Fill in the Blank

11. If you to limit the number of characters that a text box will accept, use the _____ attribute.

12. To group a number of form elements visually on the page, use the _____ tag.

13. To cause a number of radio buttons to be treated as a single group, the value of the _____ attribute must be identical.

Short Answer

14. Explain why a web developer should avoid using mailto: to process form information.

15. List one purpose of using a form on a web page.

Apply Your Knowledge

1. **Predict the Result.** Draw and write a brief description of the web page that will be created with the following XHTML code.

```
<?xml version="1.0" encoding="UTF-8"?>
<!DOCTYPE html PUBLIC "-//W3C//DTD XHTML 1.0 Transitional//EN"
   "http://www.w3.org/TR/xhtml1/DTD/xhtml1-transitional.dtd">
<html xmlns="http://www.w3.org/1999/xhtml" >
<head>
<title>Predict the Result</title>
</head>
<body>
  <div align="center">
    <h1>Contact Trillium</h1>
    <form>
      <fieldset><legend>Complete the form and a consultant will contact you</legend>
        Email: <input type="text" name="E-mail" size="40" /><br />
        Please indicate which services you are interested in:<br />
        <select name="inquiry" size="1">
          <option value="development">Web Development</option>
          <option value="redesign">Web Redesign</option>
          <option value="maintain">Web Maintenance</option>
          <option value="info">General Information</option>
        </select>
        <br />
        <input type="submit">
      </fieldset>
    </form>
    <p><a href="index.htm">Home</a> <a href="services.htm"
      target="Trillium">Services</a> Contact</p>
    <p><font size="1">
    Contact <a href="mailto:web@trilliumtechnologies.biz">
      web@trilliumtechnologies.biz</a> <br />
    Copyright &copy; 2003 Trillium Technologies</font></p>
  </div>
</body>
</html>
```

2. **Fill in the Missing Code.** This web page configures a survey form to collect information on the favorite search engine used by web page visitors. The form action should submit the form to the server-side script, called survey.pl. Some XHTML tags and their attributes, indicated by <_>, are missing. Some XHTML attribute values, indicated by "_", are missing.

```
<?xml version="1.0" encoding="UTF-8"?>
<!DOCTYPE html PUBLIC "-//W3C//DTD XHTML 1.0 Transitional//EN"
   "http://www.w3.org/TR/xhtml1/DTD/xhtml1-transitional.dtd">
<html xmlns="http://www.w3.org/1999/xhtml" >
<head>
<title>Trillium Technologies</title>
</head>
<body>
  <h1>Vote for your favorite Search Engine</h1>
  <form method="_" action="_">
    <input type="radio" name="_" value="Yahoo" /> Yahoo!<br />
```

continues

```
    <input type="radio" name="survey" value="Google" /> Google<br />
    <input type="radio" name=" _" value="AltaVista" />Alta Vista<br />
    <_>
  </form>
</body>
</html>
```

3. **Find the Error.** Find the coding errors in this subscription form.

```
<?xml version="1.0" encoding="UTF-8"?>
<!DOCTYPE html PUBLIC "-//W3C//DTD XHTML 1.0 Frameset//EN"
"http://www.w3.org/TR/xhtml1/DTD/xhtml1-frameset.dtd">
<html xmlns="http://www.w3.org/1999/xhtml">
<head>
<title>Trillium Technologies</title>
</head>
<body>
  <p>Subscribe to our monthly newsletter and receive free coupons!</p>
  <form action="get" method="cgi-bin/newsletter">
    E-mail: <input type="textbox" name="email" char="40"><br />
    <input type="button" /> <input type="reset" />
  </form>
</body>
</html>
```

Hands-On Exercises

1. Write the XHTML to create a text box named city that will be used to accept the name of a city from web page visitors. The text box should allow a maximum of 30 characters to be entered.

2. Write the XHTML to create a group of radio buttons that web site visitors can check to vote for their favorite day of the week.

3. Write the XHTML to create a select list that asks web site visitors to select their favorite day of the week.

4. Write the XHTML to create a form that accepts requests for a brochure to be sent in the mail. Sketch out the form on paper before you begin.

5. Write the XHTML to create a form that accepts feedback from web site visitors. Sketch out the form on paper before you begin.

6. Create a web page that contains a music survey form similar to the example in Figure 6.25.

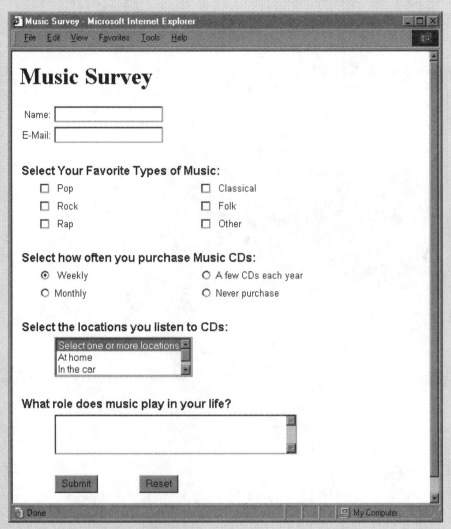

Figure 6.25 *Sample music survey form*

Include the following form elements:
- Text boxes for name and e-mail address
- A scrolling text box that is 60 characters wide and 3 rows high (*Hint:* `<textarea>`)
- A radio button group with at least three choices
- A check box group with at least three choices
- A select box that initially shows three items but contains at least four items
- A submit button
- A reset button

Use a table to organize your form. Place your e-mail address at the bottom of the web page. *Hint:* Draw a sketch of your form and the table before you begin coding the XHTML. Hand in printouts of both the source code (print in Notepad) and the browser display of your page.

Web Site Case Study

Each of these case studies will continue throughout most of the text. In this chapter, a page containing a form that invokes server-side processing is added to the web sites.

A. JavaJam Coffee House

See Chapter 2 for an introduction to the JavaJam Coffee House case. Figure 2.20 shows a site map for the JavaJam site. The Home page, Menu page, and Performances page were created in earlier chapters. You will work with the web pages in the original javajam folder in this case study —creating the Jobs page, shown in Figure 6.26, of the site.

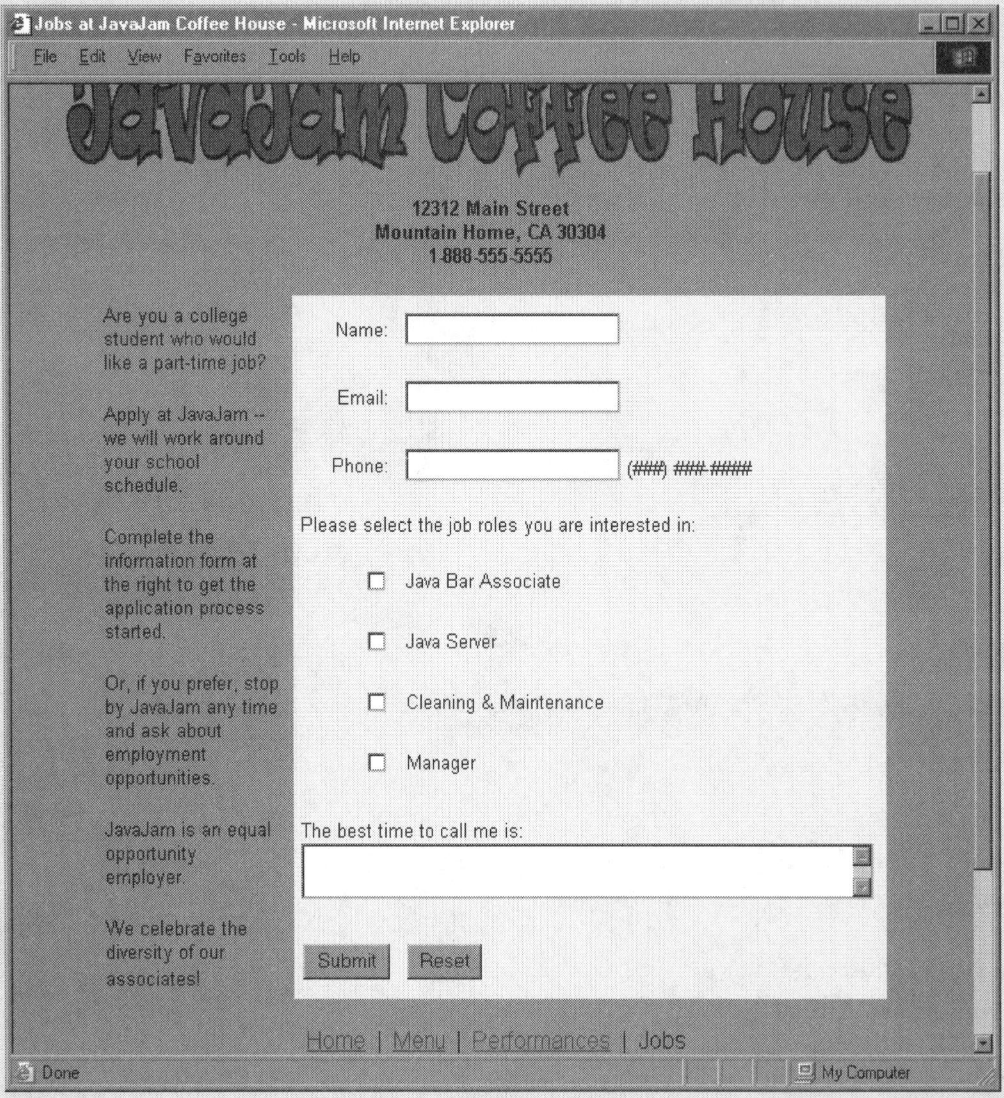

Figure 6.26 *JavaJam jobs.htm page*

Hands-On Practice Case

1. Use the Performances page as the starting point for the Jobs page. Launch Notepad and open the performances.htm file in the javajam folder that you previously created. Save the file as jobs.htm.

2. Modify your file to be similar to the Jobs page, shown in Figure 6.26, as follows

   - Change the page title to an appropriate phrase.

   - Modify the text links at the bottom of the page. The "Performances" text should link to the performances.htm page. Remove the link on the "Jobs" text.

   - The Jobs page content will be placed in a table with different formatting than the table used on the Performances page. Delete the table from the page. In its place create a new table, following the formatting indicated by Figure 6.27.

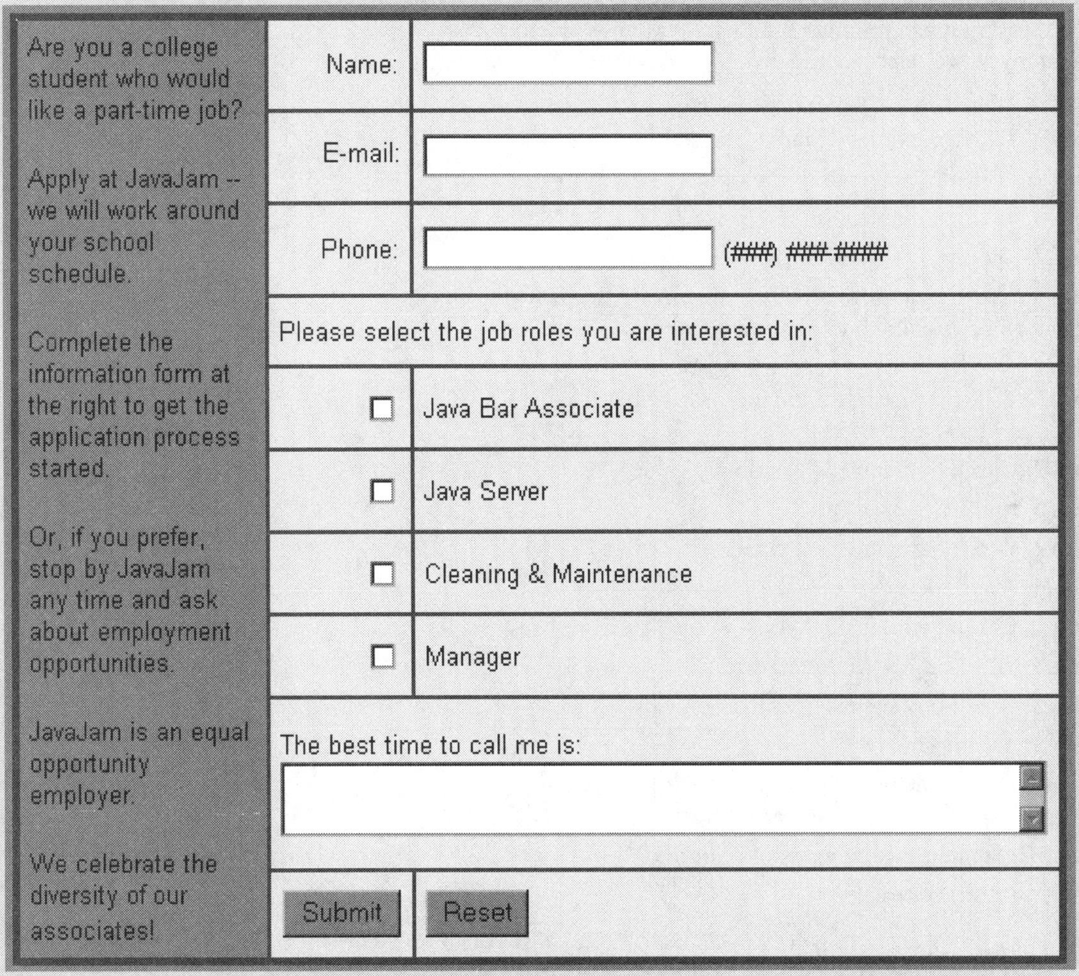

Figure 6.27 Close-up of the jobs.htm form showing table borders

   - The page content will consist of a form that is organized by a table with 10 rows and three columns. Notice that the first column of the table spans all 10 rows. Code the XHTML for this form area by beginning with a **<form>** tag, then a **<table>** tag.

- The **`<form>`** tag should use the post method and the action attribute to invoke server-side processing. Unless directed otherwise by your instructor, configure the action attribute to send the form data to http://webdevfoundations.net/scripts/javajam.asp.

- The table in the sample is configured to be 554 pixels wide with cell-padding of 5. The cells in the first column are 126 pixels wide and have a background color of #99966. The detailed example in Figure 6.27 shows a table border to clearly define the rows and columns. *Hint:* As you work on your table, use **`border="1"`**. This will help you to identify and resolve problems with formatting. Once you are satisfied with your table layout, set the table border to 0.

- The text in the table should use the Arial font, size 2. The content of the table is as follows

  Line 1 Column 1: "Are you a college student who would like a part-time job? Apply at JavaJam—we will work around your school schedule. Complete the information form at the right to get the application process started. Or, if you prefer, stop by JavaJam any time and ask about employment opportunities. JavaJam is an equal opportunity employer. We celebrate the diversity of our associates!"

  Line 1 Column 2: "Name:", aligned to the right

  Line 1 Column 3: Text box named "Name", size=20

  Line 2 Column 2: "E-mail:", aligned to the right

  Line 2 Column 3: Text box named "Email", size=20

  Line 3 Column 2: "Phone:", aligned to the right

  Line 3 Column 3: Text box named "Phone", size=20 (Also provide a sample of the format showing how the phone number should be entered.)

  Line 4 Columns 2 & 3: "Please select the job roles you are interested in:"

  Line 5 Column 2: Check box named "JavaBar", value "Yes"

  Line 5 Column 3: "Java Bar Associate"

  Line 6 Column 2: Check box named "JavaServer", value="Yes"

  Line 6 Column 3: "Java Server"

  Line 7 Column 2: Check box named "Maintenance", value="Yes"

  Line 7 Column 3: "Cleaning & Maintenance"

  Line 8 Column 2: Check box named "Manager", value="Yes"

  Line 8 Column 3: "Manager"

  Line 9 Columns 2 & 3: "The best time to call me is :" Text area named "bestTime", width of 48 characters, 2 lines

  Line 10 Column 2: Submit button, value of "Submit"

  Line 10 Column 3: Reset button

3. Save your page and test it in a browser. It should look similar to the screen shot in Figure 6.26. If you are connected to the Internet, submit the form. This will send your form information to the server-side script configured in the **`<form>`** tag. A confirmation page that lists the form information and their corresponding names will be displayed.

B. Fish Creek Animal Hospital

See Chapter 2 for an introduction to the Fish Creek Animal Hospital case. Figure 2.23 shows a site map for the Fish Creek site. The Home page, Services page, and Ask the Vet page were created in earlier chapters. You will work with the web pages in the original fishcreek folder in this case study—creating the Contact page, shown in Figure 6.28, of the site.

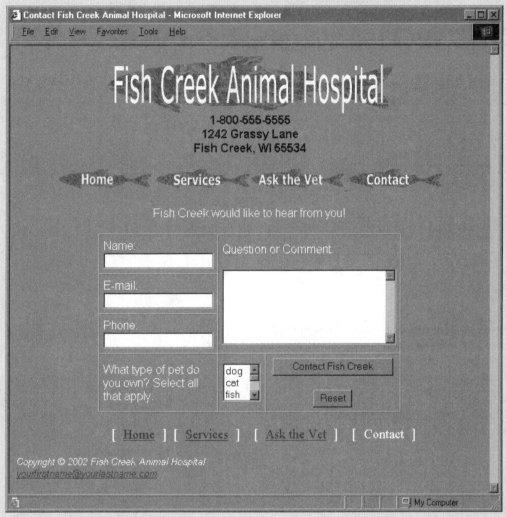

Figure 6.28 *Fish Creek contact.htm*

Hands-On Practice Case

1. Use the Ask The Vet page as the starting point for Contact page. Launch Notepad and open the askthevet.htm file in the fishcreek folder that you previously created. Save the file as contact.htm.

2. Modify your file to be similar to Contact page, shown in Figure 6.28, as follows
   - Change the page title to an appropriate phrase.
   - Modify the text links so that they are appropriate for this page. The "Ask the Vet" text and image should link to the askthevet.htm page. Remove the link from the "Contact" text and "Contact" image.
   - Delete the table that was part of the askthevet.htm page.

- The page content consists of a paragraph of text followed by a form that is organized by a table. The text in the paragraph is as follows: "Fish Creek would like to hear from you!" The paragraph should be centered. This text should be in the Arial font and use the page text color of white (#FFFFFF).

- The **`<form>`** tag should use the post method and the action attribute to invoke server-side processing. Unless directed otherwise by your instructor, configure the action attribute to send the form data to http://webdevfoundations.net/scripts/fishcreek.asp.

- The table consists of four rows and three columns, and is configured to have a border set to 1, a width of 60%, cellpadding set to 5, and cellspacing set to 0.

- Refer to Figure 6.28 as you create the content of the table described as follows:

  Line 1 Column 1: "Name:", followed by a text box named "Name", size=20

  Line 1 Column 2 & 3: "Question or Comment", followed by a textarea named "Comment", 28 characters wide, 6 lines high. This cell spans three rows.

  Line 2 Column 1: "E-mail:", followed by a text box named "Email", size=20

  Line 3 Column 1: "Phone:", followed by a text box named "Phone", size=20

  Line 4 Column 1: "What type of pet do you own? Select all that apply."

  Line 4 Column 2: A select box named "Pet" that allows multiple choices and shows three options. The options should include "dog", "cat", "bird", "fish", "turtle", "lizard", and "other".

  Line 4 Column 3: A submit button with the value of "Contact Fish Creek" followed by a reset button.

  - The text in the table should be in the Arial font and use the color #FFFFFF. The cell containing the buttons should use center alignment (**`<td align="center">`**).

3. Save your page and display it in a browser. It should look similar to Figure 6.28. If you are connected to the Internet, submit the form. This will send your form information to the server-side script configured in the **`<form>`** tag. A confirmation page that lists the form information and their corresponding names will be displayed.

C. Pete the Painter

See Chapter 2 for an introduction to the Pete the Painter case. Figure 2.26 shows a site map for the Pete the Painter site. The Home page, Services page, and Testimonials page were created in earlier chapters. You will work with the web pages in the original painter folder in this case study, creating the Free Estimate page, shown in Figure 6.29.

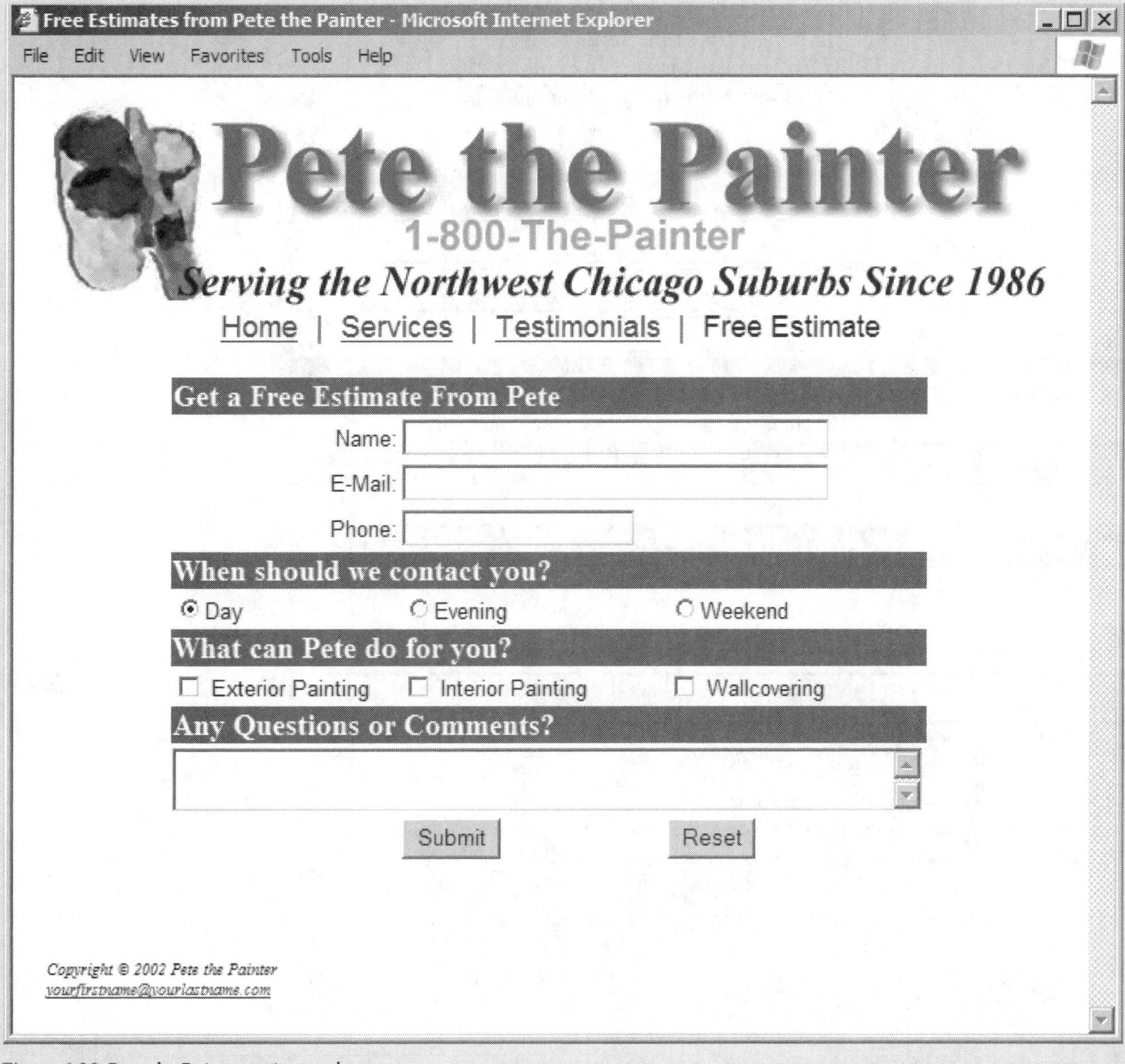

Figure 6.29 *Pete the Painter estimates.htm*

Hands-On Practice Case

1. Use the Testimonials page as the starting point for the Free Estimate page. Launch Notepad and open the testimonials.htm file in the painter folder that you previously created. Save the file as estimates.htm.

2. Modify your file to be similar to Free Estimate page, shown in Figure 6.29, as follows

- Change the page title to an appropriate phrase.

- Modify the text links so that they are appropriate for this page. The "Testimonials" text should link to the testimonials.htm page. Remove the link from the "Free Estimate" text.

- The Free Estimate page content will be placed in a table with slightly different formatting than the table used on the Testimonials page. Delete the table containing the Testimonials information from the page. In its place create a new table, following the formatting indicated by Figure 6.30.

Get a Free Estimate From Pete		
Name:		
E-Mail:		
Phone:		
When should we contact you?		
⊙ Day	○ Evening	○ Weekend
What can Pete do for you?		
☐ Exterior Painting	☐ Interior Painting	☐ Wallcovering
Any Questions or Comments?		
	Submit	Reset

Figure 6.30 *Close-up of the estimates.htm form*

- The page content will consist of a form that is organized by a table with 11 rows and three columns. Notice that some table rows display one column and others display two columns. Code the XHTML for this form area by beginning with a **`<form>`** tag, then a **`<table>`** tag.

- The **`<form>`** tag should use the post method and the action attribute to invoke server-side processing. Unless directed otherwise by your instructor, configure the action attribute to send the form data to http://webdevfoundations.net/scripts/painter.asp.

- The table in the sample is configured to a width of 75%, cellpadding set to 1, and no border. The cells containing headings ("Get a Free Estimate From Pete", "When should we contact you?", "What can Pete do for you?", "Any Questions or Comments?") should span three columns and have a background color of #999966. Configure the text contained in these cells to use the default font, **`size="4"`**, and be bold. The text in all other rows of the table should be in the Arial font, **`size="2"`**. Figure 6.30 shows a table border to clearly define the rows and columns. *Hint:* As you work on your table, use **`border="1"`**. This will help you to identify and resolve problems with formatting. Once you are satisfied with your table layout, set the table border to 0.

- The content of the table is as follows:

Line 1 Columns 1, 2, 3: "Get a Free Estimate From Pete"

Line 2 Column 1: "Name:", aligned to the right

Line 2 Columns 2, 3: Text box named "Name", size=40

Line 3 Column 1: "E-mail":, aligned to the right

Line 3 Columns 2,3: Text box named "Email", size=40

Line 4 Column 1: "Phone:", aligned to the right

Line 4 Columns 2,3: Text box named "Phone", size=20

Line 5 Columns 1, 2, 3: "When should we contact you?"

Line 6 Column 1: Radio Button named "Contact", value="Day" followed by the text " Day"

Line 6 Column 2: Radio Button named "Contact", value="Evening" followed by the text " Evening"

Line 6 Column 3: Radio Button named "Contact", value="Weekend" followed by the text " Weekend"

Line 7 Column 1, 2, 3: "What can Pete do for you?"

Line 8 Column 1: Check box named "Exterior", value="Yes" followed by the text " Exterior Painting"

Line 8 Column 2: Check box named "Interior", value="Yes" followed by the text " Interior Painting"

Line 8 Column 3: Check box named "Wallcovering", value="Yes" followed by the text " Wallcovering"

Line 9 Column 1, 2, 3: "Any Questions or Comments?"

Line 10 Column 1, 2, 3 Textarea named "Questions", 55 characters wide, two rows high

Line 11 Column 1: **" "** or ** ** *Hint:* Table cells that are empty or have no contents sometimes are not displayed properly by all browsers. To avoid this, place either a blank space or the special character for nonbreaking space, ** ** in the cell.

Line 11 Column 2: Submit button, value of "Submit"

Line 11 Column 3: Reset button

3. Save your page and test it in a browser. It should look similar to the screen shot in Figure 6.29. If you are connected to the Internet, submit the form. This will send your form information to the server-side script configured in the **<form>** tag. A confirmation page that lists the form information and their corresponding names will be displayed.

Web Research

A. This chapter mentioned a number of sources of free remotely hosted scripts, including http://formbuddy.com, http://hostedscripts.com, http://response-o-matic.com, and http://master.com. Either visit two of these sites or use a search engine to find other resources for free remotely hosted scripts. Register (if necessary) and examine the web site to see exactly what is offered. Most sites that provide remotely hosted scripts have a demo you can view or try out. If you have time (or your instructor asks you to) follow the directions and access a remotely hosted script from one of your web pages. Now that you've at least been through a demo of the product or tried it yourself (even better!), it's time to write your review.

Create a web page that lists the two resource sites you chose and provides a comparison of what they offer. Use a table to list the following:
- Ease of registration
- Number of scripts or services offered
- Type of scripts or services offered
- Site banner or advertisement
- Ease of use
- Recommendation (Would you recommend this site to others?)

Provide links to the resource sites you reviewed and place your name in the e-mail address at the bottom of the page. Print both the source code (from Notepad) and the browser view of your web page.

B. Search the Web for a web page that uses an XHTML form. Print the browser view of the page. Print out the source code of the web page. Using the printout, highlight or circle the tags related to forms. On a separate sheet of paper, create some XHTML notes by listing the tags and attributes related to forms found on your sample page along with a brief description of their purpose. Hand in the browser view of the page, source code printout, and your XHTML notes page.

Chapter Review Answers

1. d

2. a

3. b

4. b

5. c

6. b

7. a

8. d

9. c

10. d

11. maxsize

12. `<fieldset>`

13. name

14. This technique should be avoided because it presents an unprofessional image and can be inconvenient for web page visitors. Its success depends on the visitor wanting to use the e-mail application configured with their browser. The visitor may not have configured an e-mail application or may not want to use the e-mail application that was configured. This technique can decrease the usability of a form.

15. Forms accept information from web page visitors, such as a search keyword, newsletter subscription information, online ordering information, general feedback, and others.

Web Site Design

A s a web site visitor, you have probably found that certain web sites are appealing and easy to use while others seem awkward or just plain annoying. What separates the good from the bad? This chapter discusses recommended web site design practices. The topics include site organization, site navigation, page design, text design, graphic design, and accessibility considerations.

Whatever your personal preferences, your web site should be designed to appeal to your target audience— the people who will use your web site. They may be teens, shoppers, college students, young couples, the list goes on and on. You should follow all of the recommended web site design practices with an eye on your target audience.

For example, a site that showcases an exotic vacation destination, http://www.atlantis.com (Figure 7.1), should have a different look and feel from a site whose purpose is to sell books and other commodities (see http://www.amazon.com, Figure 7.2).

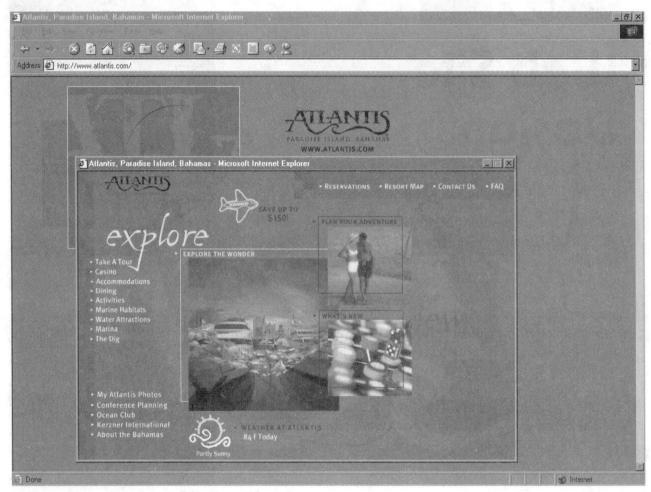

Figure 7.1 *This web site for a vacation resort draws you in.*

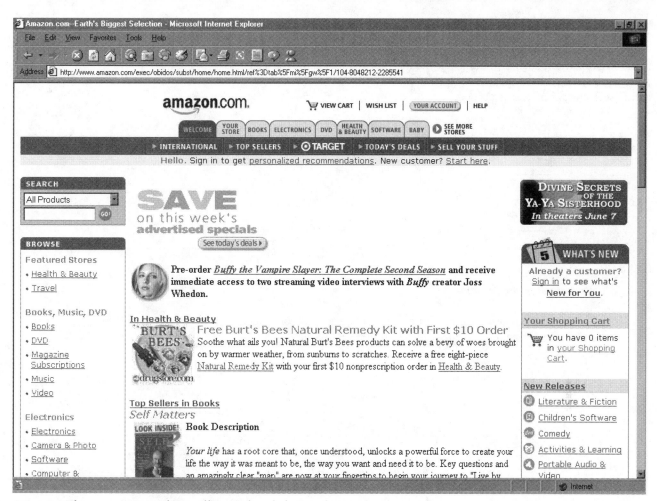

Figure 7.2 *This e-commerce web site offers quick and obvious choices.*

The first engages you and draws you in. The second provides you with choices of products so that you can quickly get down to the business of shopping. (*Note:* Amazon.com isn't strictly all business—more on this in Chapter 11.) With your target audience in mind, take a look at some common recommended web site design practices.

Web Site Organization

How will visitors move around your site? How will they find what they need? This is largely determined by the web site's organization or architecture. There are three common types of web site organization:

- Hierarchical
- Linear
- Random (sometimes called Web organization).

A diagram of the organization of a web site is called a **site map** or **storyboard**. Creating the site map is one of the initial steps in developing a web site (more on this in Chapter 8).

Hierarchical Organization

Most Web sites use **hierarchical organization**. A site map for hierarchical organization, such as the one shown in Figure 7.3, is characterized by a clearly defined home page with links to major site sections. Web pages within sections are placed as needed.

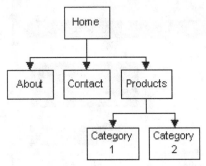

Figure 7.3 *Hierarchical site organization*

It is important to be aware of pitfalls of hierarchical organization. Figure 7.4 shows a site design that is too shallow—there are too many major site sections.

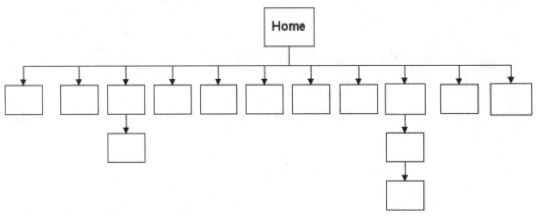

Figure 7.4 *This site design uses a shallow hierarchy.*

This site design needs to be broken down into small, easily managed topics or units, a process called **chunking**. In the case of web page design, each unit of information is a page. George A. Miller, a research psychologist for Princeton University's WorldNet (http://www.cogsci.princeton.edu/~wn/) found that humans can store only five to nine chunks of information at a time in short-term memory (see http://www.well.com/user/smalin/miller.html). He called this the "seven plus or minus two" principle. Following this principle, many web designers try not to place more than nine major navigation links on a page, unless they are creating a very large site. Even then, they may try to chunk the navigation links into visually separate sections on the page with each group having no more than nine links.

Another design pitfall is designing a site that is too deep. Figure 7.5 is an example of this.

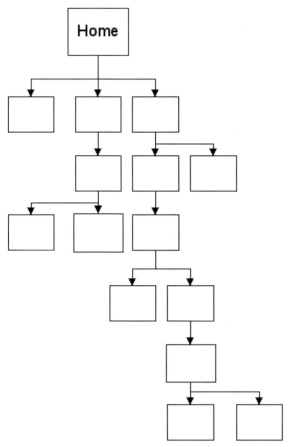

Figure 7.5 *This site design uses a deep hierarchy.*

The interface design "three click rule" says that a web page visitor should be able to get from any page on your site to any other page on your site with a maximum of three hyperlinks. In other words, a visitor who cannot get what they want in three mouse clicks will begin to feel frustrated and may leave your site. This rule may be very difficult to satisfy on a large site, but in general the goal is to organize your site so that your visitors can easily navigate from page to page within the site structure.

An example of a hierarchical site is Wizarding World at http://wizardingworld.com. The original site map is shown in Figure 7.6.

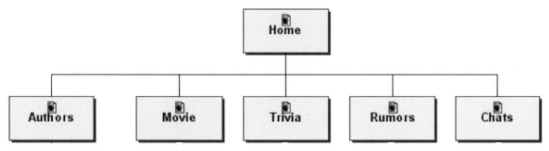

Figure 7.6 *Original wizardingworld.com site map*

The Home page introduces the site and contains navigation to the main sections. It functions as and even looks like a map to the site (see Figure 7.7) and it is intentionally different from the content pages.

Figure 7.7 *Wizarding World home page*

The main section content pages of a site usually have a similar look and feel. Two content pages for the Wizarding World site are shown in Figure 7.8.

Figure 7.8 *Sample content pages*

Each main section may have one or more subpages. Some sites with a hierarchical organization may use a consistent design for the home page *and* the content pages. Either method is acceptable. Most commercial sites, such as http://amazon.com and http://ebay.com use hierarchical site organization.

Linear Organization

When the purpose of a site or series of pages on a site is to provide a tutorial, tour, or presentation that needs to be viewed in a sequential fashion, linear organization, shown in Figure 7.9, is useful.

Figure 7.9 *Linear site organization*

In linear organization, the pages are viewed one after another. Some web sites use hierarchical organization in general, but with linear organization in a few small areas. An example of this is the Macromedia site at http://macromedia.com. The main site organization is hierarchical with linear organization used for product feature tutorials. Notice the "Next Feature" link in the Figure 7.10; the link to the next page in the linear presentation of Dreamweaver features.

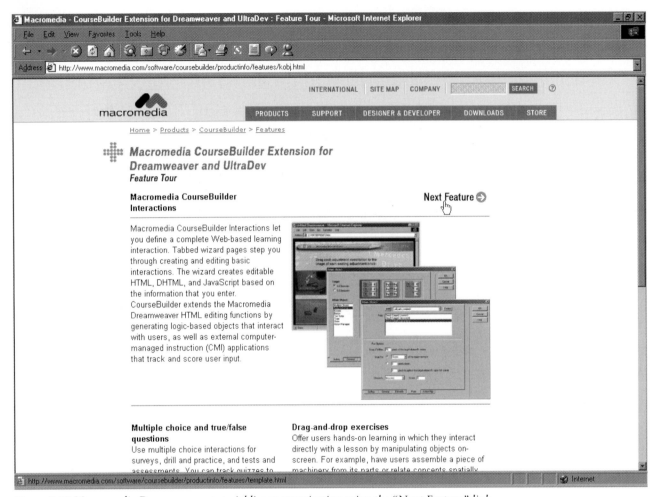

Figure 7.10 *Macromedia Dreamweaver tutorial linear organization using the "Next Feature" link*

Random Organization

Random organization (sometimes called Web organization) offers no clear path through the site, as shown in Figure 7.11.

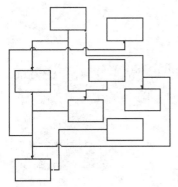

Figure 7.11 *Random site organization*

There is often no clear home page and no discernable structure. Random organization is not as common as hierarchical or linear organization and is usually found only on artistic sites or sites that strive to be especially different and original. This type of organization is typically not used for commercial web sites.

Web Site Navigation— Recommended Practices

Ease of Navigation

Sometimes web developers are so close to their sites that they can't see the forest for the trees. A new visitor will wander into the site and not know what to click or how to find out what it offers. Clearly labeled navigation on each page is helpful—it should be in the same location on each page for maximum usability. A visitor should not feel lost in the site. Jakob Nielson, a well-known web usability and web design professional, favors

Where do I begin?

Sometimes it is difficult to begin creating a site map for a web site. What some design teams do is meet in a room with a blank wall and a package of large Post-it® Notes. They write the titles of topics and subtopics needed on the site on the Post-it® Notes. They arrange the notes on the wall and discuss until the site structure becomes clear and there is consensus within the group. If you are not working in a group, you can try this on your own and then discuss the way you have chosen to organize the web site with a friend or fellow student.

what he calls "breadcrumb trails" for larger sites. Figure 7.12 shows a page from http://realtor.com, a site that has a well-organized navigation area near the top of each page in addition to personalized "breadcrumb trails" for each visitor. Note the horizontal row of text links—"Home", "Find a Home", "California", "Tahoe Sierra", and so on under the main navigation area. These breadcrumbs can help a visitor retrace his or her steps within the site or easily jump back to a previously viewed section.

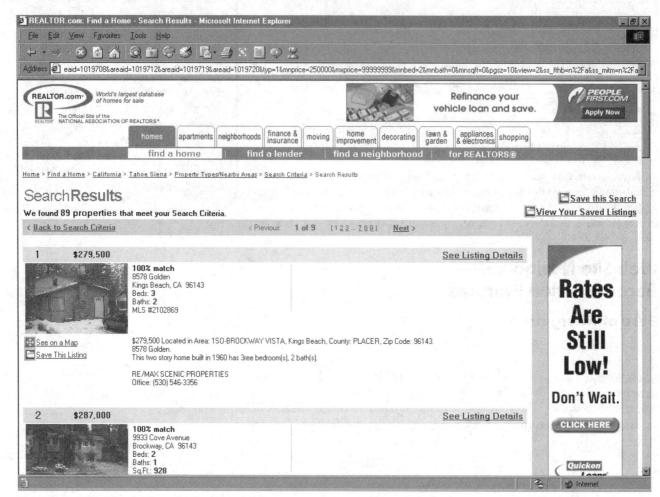

Figure 7.12 *Visitors can follow the "breadcrumbs" to retrace their steps through the site.*

Navigation Bars

Clear navigation bars, either graphic- or text-based, make it obvious to your users where they are and where they can go next. The CNN site, http://cnn.com, shown in Figure 7.13, includes a vertical text navigation bar down the left side of the page.

Figure 7.13 *Vertical text-based navigation*

The display of the link "Weather", shown in contrasting white text with red background and an arrow, provides a clear visual cue that the visitor is at that location. The navigation bar also indicates other choices available to the web site visitor.

Sometimes graphics are used to convey navigation, as in the web site for Harper College (http://www.harpercollege.edu), shown in Figure 7.14.

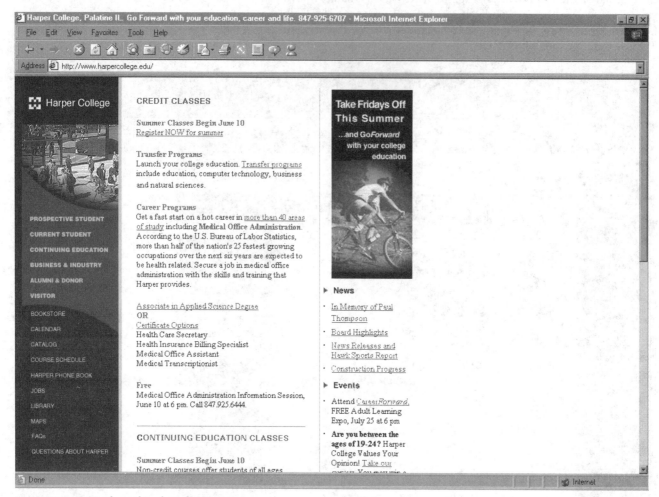

Figure 7.14 *Vertical graphics-based navigation*

The "text" for the navigation is actually stored in image files. This technique of placing text in navigation images is used to create interactive web pages. In this case, JavaScript is used to detect when the web page visitor has placed the mouse over an image of text, which then displays an alternate image. If you visit the Harper College site and the design hasn't been modified since this was written, notice how the "text" changes when you place the mouse over the left navigation area.

Combinations of text with graphic images can be helpful to your visitors. The Saturn site, http://saturn.com, shown in the screen shot in Figure 7.15, displays a graphic of the car model when you place the mouse over a specific model number.

Technologies such as Macromedia Flash can be combined with XHTML to create interactive, interesting navigation. See the screen shot in Figure 7.16 of http://www.project514.com, a page from the web site of a media design company called Project 514. This page uses both text-based (along the bottom of the screen) and image-based (the file folders will open and display information on the "monitor") navigation.

Figure 7.15 *The car image changes as you move the mouse over each model number.*

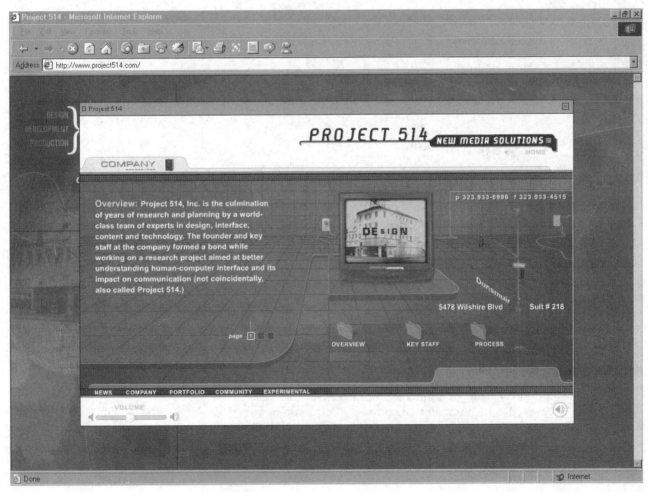

Figure 7.16 *Flash navigation*

Java applets and Dynamic HTML (DHTML) can also be used to create similar interactive effects. Chapter 12 discusses using these technologies to create interactive web pages. At the time this was written, Microsoft's site at http://microsoft.com (Figure 7.17) checked for the browser used by each visitor. The site then displayed a web page that was designed to utilize DHTML and look good in the visitor's browser.

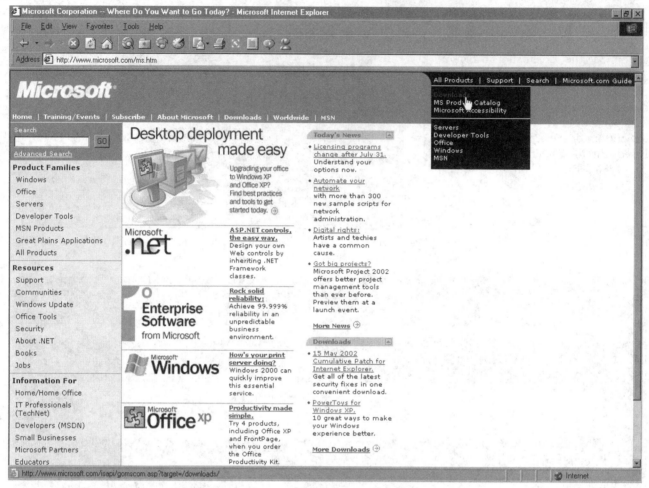

Figure 7.17 *Microsoft's web site uses DHTML to create dynamic navigation menus.*

In Figure 7.17, "All Products" has been selected causing the vertical black menu to appear. This type of navigation on a large complex site keeps the visitor from feeling overwhelmed by choices. The visitor first chooses a major menu category, then sees the individual additional choices that can be made.

Short Pages

A web page is considered long if it is three or more screen lengths. Long pages are usually slow to load. Your visitors are probably only interested in portions of a long page, so consider breaking a long page into multiple short pages—possibly using linear organization to link the ideas together.

Table of Contents

When a long web page must be kept as a single file, a table of contents or bulleted list at the top of the page can provide links to specific parts of the page. This will help visitors find exactly what they need. An example of this is the Welcome page for an online class shown in Figure 7.18. Note the list of questions near the top of the page—they all link to corresponding answers at another location on the same page.

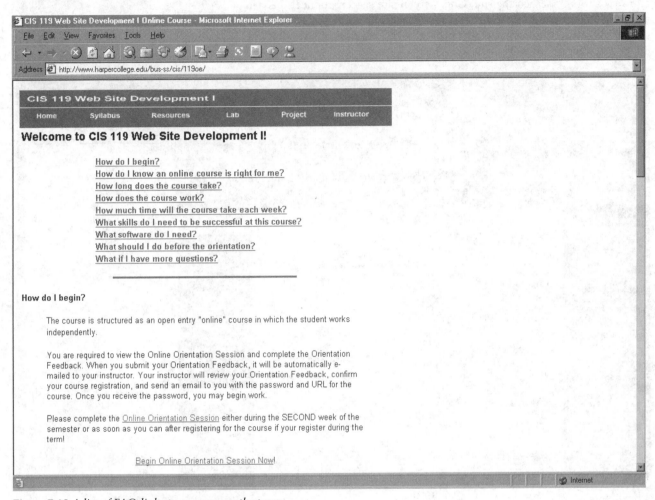

Figure 7.18 *A list of FAQ links to answers on the page*

Site Map and Site Search Features

The *Los Angeles Times* web site is shown in Figure 7.19. The *LA Times* has a site search and site map on the same page. The site map allows a visitor to visually scan the contents of the site. The search helps visitors find information that is not apparent from the navigation or the site map features. Some web authoring tools, such as Microsoft FrontPage, offer a site search wizard that indexes the site and creates a search form web page that allows visitors to search the site. Commercial site search applications are also available, including Atomz (http://www.atomz.com) and FusionBot (http://www.fusionbot.com), which provide a free service for sites that are under a certain number of pages.

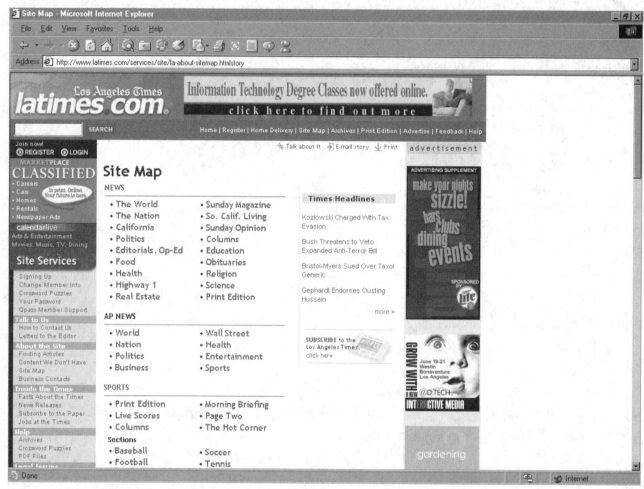

Figure 7.19 *This large site offers both a site search and a site map to their visitors.*

You are now familiar with web site organization and navigation. The next section continues with a discussion of recommended web site design practices related to page layout, text, graphic, and accessibility design.

Web Page Design—Recommended Practices

The major components of web page design are

- Page layout design
- Text design
- Graphic design
- Accessibility considerations

Web sites that look great and are easy to use don't happen by accident. Outstanding web sites are carefully planned and created by using recommended design practices (and a little bit of talent!).

Load Time

The last thing you want to happen is for your visitors to leave your page before it has even finished loading! Make sure your pages load as quickly as possible. How long do *you* generally wait for a page to load? Many web page visitors will not wait more than several seconds. It's a good practice to limit the total file size of a web page and all of its associated images and media files to under 60KB. It takes about 8 seconds at 56K for a browser to display a web page and associated files of 60KB.

Recent studies have shown that only 22% of U.S. Internet users have broadband (cable, T1, etc.) access. This means that almost 80% of your web site's potential visitors could have a slow telephone connection. Other nations have an even lower percentage of broadband users. Visit http://www.nua.com/surveys/ and http://cyberatlas.internet.com for the most current Internet usage statistics. The chart in Figure 7.20 compares file sizes and connection speed download times.

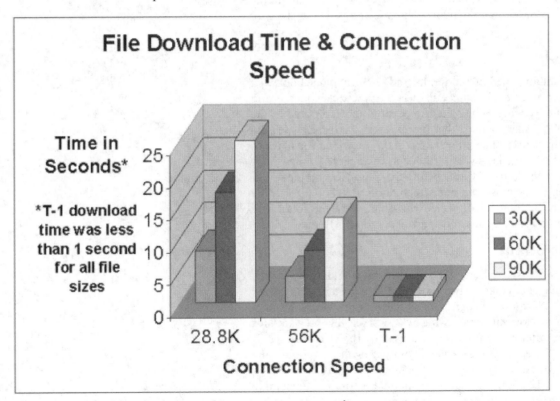

Figure 7.20 *File size download times and Internet connection speeds*

The 60KB per page limit is a guideline—it's better if the file size of your home page and associated media files is smaller. Go over the limit for content pages only when you are sure your visitors will be interested enough to wait to see what your site is presenting.

One method to help determine if the load time of your page is acceptable is to view the size of your web site files in Windows Explorer. Calculate the total file size of your web page plus all its associated images and media. If the total file size for a single page and its associated files is over 60KB, take a closer look at your design. Consider if you really need to use all the images to convey your message. Perhaps the images can be better optimized for the web or the content of the page should be divided into multiple pages. This is a time for some decision-making!

Popular web authoring tools such as Microsoft FrontPage and Macromedia Dreamweaver will calculate load time at various transmission speeds.

Perceived Load Time

Perceived load time is the amount of time a web page visitor is aware of waiting while your page is loading. Since visitors often leave a web site if a page takes too long to load, it is important to shorten their perception of waiting. A common technique is to shorten the perceived loading time by breaking the long page into multiple smaller pages using the methods described earlier. This might even aid in the organization of your web site.

Web pages containing large graphics may appear to load very slowly. Image slicing—dividing or slicing large images into multiple smaller images (see Chapter 4), divides large images into several smaller graphics. Since each graphic displays as it loads, the perceived load time is shorter than it is for a single large graphic. Even though the total download time is about the same, the visitor sees the browser window changing and perceives the wait as being shorter.

Above the Fold

Placing important information "above the fold" is a technique borrowed from the newspaper industry. When newspapers are placed on counters and in vending machines waiting to be sold, the portion above the fold in the page is viewable. Publishers noticed that more papers were sold when the most important, attention-getting information in this location. You may use this technique to attract and keep visitors on your web pages. Arrange interesting content above the fold—the area before the visitor sees before scrolling down the page. At the most common screen resolution, 800 pixels wide by 600 pixels high, the amount of screen viewable above the fold (after accounting for web browser menus and controls) is about 410 pixels.

Horizontal Scrolling

In order to make it easy for web page visitors to view and use your web pages, avoid creating pages that are too wide to be displayed in the browser window. These pages require the user to scroll horizontally. Using the most common screen resolution, 800 pixels wide by 600 pixels high, the amount of viewable screen (after accounting for area used by the web browser) is about 760 pixels. An easy way to make sure your page will not require horizontal scrolling is to place the page contents in a layout table that uses a percentage width of 100% or less. Another method is to use a fixed table width set to 760 pixels or less. If you expect your pages to be printed often, set the width to 560 or less pixels.

Page Layout

Using tables and style sheets to create interesting page layouts can keep visitors interested in your web site. Web authoring tools such as Microsoft FrontPage and Macromedia Dreamweaver offer templates and example sites to assist you with layout ideas.

See Figures 7.21, 7.22, and 7.23 for diagrams of three possible web page layouts. Note that the exact content (text, images, logo, navigation) does not need to be placed in the diagram in order to illustrate this concept. The page area where the content will appear is indicated. This type of sketch can be used to experiment with page structures and find the one that will work the best for a site. Figure 7.21 shows a diagram of a web site with a logo, navigation area, and content area.

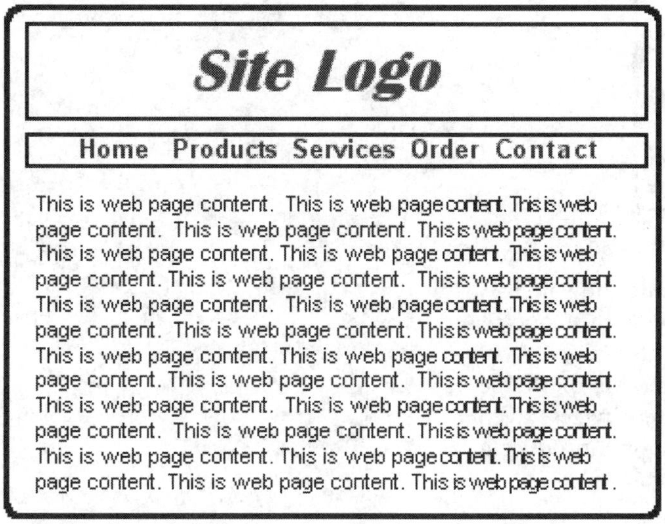

Figure 7.21 *An adequate page layout*

While this is adequate and may be appropriate for some content, it is not very interesting. Figure 7.22 depicts a diagram of a page containing the same content, but with a table formatting it in three columns.

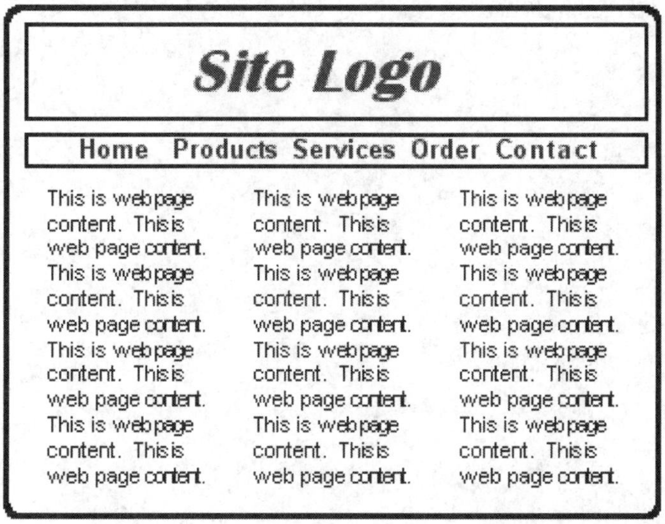

Figure 7.22 *The columns make this page layout more interesting.*

This is an improvement, but something is still missing. Figure 7.23 displays a diagram of the same content but in three columns of varying widths, with graphics interspersed.

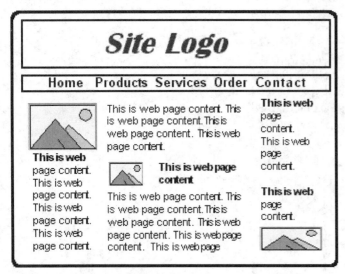

Figure 7.23 *Page layout using images and columns of varied widths*

This is the most interesting page layout of the three. Notice how images and tables make the same content more appealing. Try using this concept when designing your pages.

Often the page layout (sometimes called a *storyboard*) for the home page is different from the page layout used for the content pages. Even when this is the case, a consistent logo and color scheme will produce a more cohesive web site.

Adequate White Space

This term *white space* is also borrowed from the publishing industry. Placing blank or white space (because paper is usually white) in areas around blocks of text increases the readability of the page. Placing white space around graphics helps them to stand out. Allow for some blank space between blocks of text and images. How much is adequate? It depends—experiment until the page is likely to look appealing to your target audience.

Target Audience

Use of color. Younger audiences, such as children and preteens, prefer bright, lively colors. Nickelodeon's home page, at http://nickelodeon.com, shown in Figure 7.24, features bright graphics, lots of color, and interactivity.

Figure 7.24 *A typical site for children*

The home page displays both a poll and an interactive movie created with Macromedia Flash.

Individuals in their late teens and early twenties generally prefer dark background colors with occasional use of bright contrast, music, and dynamic navigation. Figure 7.25 depicts http://www.korn.com, a web site for a popular music group.

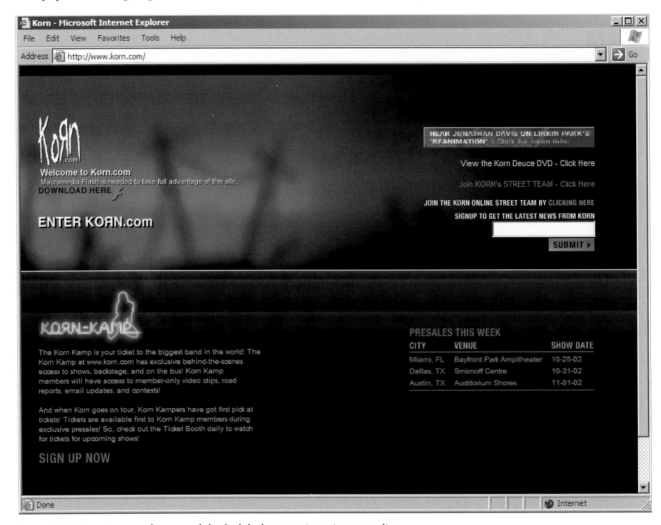

Figure 7.25 *Many teens and young adults find dark, mysterious sites appealing.*

Note how it has a completely different look and feel from the Nickelodeon site.

Individuals in their thirties and beyond usually prefer light backgrounds with good contrasting text. The popular Amazon.com and eBay.com sites are prime examples of sites that appeal to this market and, because they are so easy to use, to all markets.

For an older target audience, light backgrounds, well-defined images and large text are appropriate. The screen shot of the AARP site, http://www.aarp.org shown in Figure 7.26 is an example of a site intended for the over 50 group.

Figure 7.26 *A site designed specifically for the 50 and over age range*

Another issue related to color is the fact that many individuals experience color deficiency (color blindness). The inability to differentiate between red and green, called *deuteranopia*, is the most common type of color deficiency. To increase the accessibility of web pages for these individuals, a web designer can use high contrast between background and text. The choice of colors is important—avoid using red, green, brown, gray, or purple next to each other. White, black, and shades of blue and yellow are easier for these individuals to differentiate. To see what your pages looks like to a person with color blindness, try the online simulator at http://www.vischeck.com/chooseType.shtml.

Reading Level. Match the reading level and style of writing to your target audience. Use vocabulary that they will be comfortable with.

Animation. Use animation only if it adds to your site. Don't include an animated GIF just because you found one. In general, animation appeals more to younger audiences than to older audiences. The Nickelodeon site

(Figure 7.24) is geared to children and uses lots of animation. This would be too much animation for a web site targeted to adults or shoppers. However, a well-done navigation animation or an animation that describes a product could be appealing to almost any target group. Macromedia Flash is frequently used on the web to add animation to web pages and even to create entire animated web sites.

Browser-Friendly

Just because your web page looks great in your favorite browser, doesn't automatically mean that all browsers will render it well. Determine the browser most likely to be used by your target audience. A good source of statistics is NUA Surveys at http://www.nua.com. Develop the site so that it looks great in your target audience's most popular browser and acceptable (sometimes this is called degrading gracefully) in other browsers. Visit http://www.upsdell.com/BrowserNews/ for timely information about current browsers.

Always try to test your pages in the most popular versions of browsers and in the newest versions. At the time of this writing, these would be Internet Explorer 5, Internet Explorer 6, Netscape 4.7, and Netscape 6. While it is possible to install both Netscape 4.x and Netscape 6 on the same computer, dual installs cannot be done with Internet Explorer. Unless you have multiple computers to work with, test with the most popular version of Internet Explorer. If you can, it is also a good idea to test your pages on both the Mac and PC platforms.

Large information technology departments and web design firms will dedicate a number of computers with various operating systems and browser versions for compatibility testing. Many web page components, including default text size and default margin size, are different among browsers, browser versions, and operating systems.

Screen Resolution

Most users have their monitors configured for 800 by 600 screen resolution. You should design your page to avoid horizontal scrolling at this resolution. Higher resolutions are becoming more popular, so your page should look acceptable at 1024 by 768 (and higher) screen resolutions. You can accomplished this by placing the entire page in a table that is centered using a **<div>** tag:

```
<html>
<head>
… Header section of web page document
</head>
<body>
  <div align="center">
    <table>
…… Page content goes here. The table may be given either a percentage width or an
exact width using pixels.
    </table>
  </div>
</body>
</html>
```

Which browser is everyone using?

A recent survey by Statmarket found that 86% of Internet users prefer Internet Explorer and only 13.9% prefer Netscape. Another survey by Statmarket showed that Internet Explorer 6 earned 2.4% of the market within the first week of its launch —already exceeding the market share of Netscape 6. However, even though Internet Explorer seems to have the market cornered, it is still important to test your site in the major browsers (and versions). You never know which browser your next client will favor!

If you are developing for an intranet, ask what browser (and version) is installed at the organization. If you are developing for a client, ask what browser he or she regularly use.

Text Design—Recommended Practices

Long blocks of text and long paragraphs are difficult to read on the web. Use the text equivalent of sound-bytes—short sentences and phrases. It is important to be concise. Bulleted lists stand out on the page and are easily read. While long-winded sentences and explanations are often found in academic textbooks or romance novels, they really are not appropriate for a web page.

You may be wondering how to know if a page is easy to read. Here are some suggestions that will help increase the readability of your pages:

- Use common fonts such as Arial and Times New Roman. Remember that the web page visitor must have the font installed on his/her computer in order for that particular font to appear. Your page may look great with Gill Sans Ultra Bold Condensed, but if your visitor doesn't have the font, a default font will be used.
- Be careful with the size of the fonts—12 point font size is the same as "Normal" size and is the same as **size="3"**. Be aware that fonts display smaller on a Mac than on a PC. Even within the PC platform, the default font size for Netscape is larger than the default font size for Internet Explorer. As you become more comfortable with style sheets (more on this in Chapter 9), set font size by pixels to create web pages that display in a more consistent manner on different platforms.
- Use appropriate color combinations. Students often choose color combinations for web pages that they would never dream of using in their wardrobe. An easy way to choose colors that contrast well and look good together is to select colors from an image or logo you will use for your site. Make sure your page background color properly contrasts with your text, link, visited link, and active link colors.
- Be aware of line length and alignment—use white space and multiple columns if possible. Review Figures 7.21, 7.22, and 7.23 for examples of text placement on a web page.
- Bold (use the **<strong>** tag) or emphasize (use the **<em>** tag) important text.
- Hyperlink keywords or phrases—do not hyperlink entire sentences.
- Avoid the use of the words "click here"—everyone knows that by now.

Finally, check spelling and grammar. Many web sites every day contain misspelled words. Most web authoring tools have built-in spelling checkers; consider using this feature. Also, be sure that you proofread and test your site thoroughly. It is very helpful if you can find web developer buddies—you check their sites and they check yours. It's always easier to see someone else's mistake than your own.

Graphic Design—Recommended Practices

Chapter 4 discussed the use of graphics on web pages. This section summarizes and adds to the recommended practices discussed in that chapter.

- **Choose colors on the Web Color Palette.** If you would like your site to look consistent when displayed on various monitors using various computer platforms, choose from the 216 colors on the Web Color Palette.

- **Use antialiased text in images.** Antialiasing introduces intermediate colors to smooth jagged edges in digital images. Graphic applications such as Adobe Photoshop and Macromedia Fireworks can be used to create antialiased text images. The graphic shown in Figure 7.27 was created using antialiasing.

Antialiased

Figure 7.27 *Antialiased text*

Figure 7.28 contains an image that did not use antialiasing; note the jagged edges.

Aliased

Figure 7.28 *This graphic has a jagged look and was not saved using antialiasing.*

The only letters not affected are the *i* and *I* because the edges of these letters are perfectly horizontal and vertical.

- **Use only necessary images.** Don't use extra images, just because you found them. Oh, by the way, isn't my dog (see Figure 7.29) cute?

Figure 7.29 *It's Sparky. Only use necessary images—do you really need to see a picture of my dog in this book?*

- **Keep images as small as possible.** Try to display only exactly what is needed to get your point across. Use a graphic application to crop an image or create a thumbnail image that links to a larger version of the image.

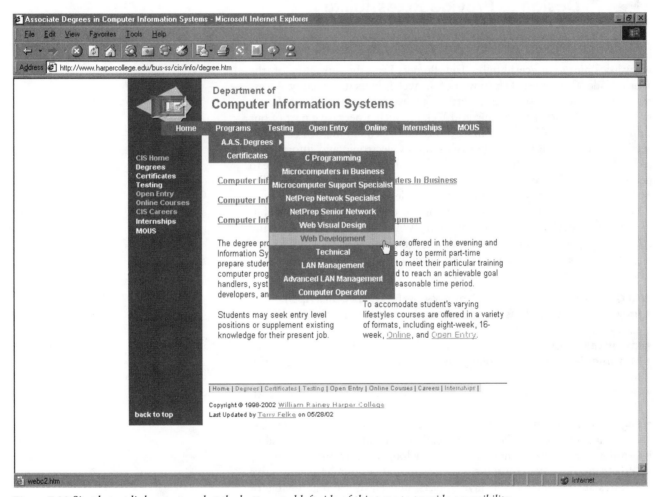

• Make sure the site is usable if images are not displayed. If a web page visitor is using an assistive technology, such as screen reader, he or she will not see your images but will still want to navigate your web site. If your main navigation uses images, DHTML, Flash, or other interactive technologies, place a plain text navigation bar at the bottom of each page. This is becoming the unofficial standard for usability. The Harper College CIS Department web site, htttp://www.harpercollege.edu/bus-ss/cis/info/, shown in Figure 7.30, uses this technique.

Figure 7.30 *Simple text links were used at the bottom and left side of this page to provide accessibility.*

An interactive menu is placed near the top under the "Computer Information Systems" logo area. As the web page visitor moves the mouse over the menu categories, drop-down lists appear with additional choices. There are plain text links to the main site categories both on the left side of the page and at the bottom of the page.

It is also a good idea to include text descriptions of important concepts or key points that your site is trying to communicate. Don't rely on images alone—some individuals may not be able to see them—they may have set their browser to not display images or be using an assistive technology such as a screen reader to visit your page.

- **Use alternate text for images.** Place the alt attribute with descriptive text on each **`<img>`** tag. (See Chapter 4 for a discussion of the **`<img>`** tag and use of the alt attribute.)
- **Limit the use of animated items.** Only use animation if it makes the page more effective. Consider limiting how long an animation plays.
- **Create a text only version of the page.** If there are a large number of images, or the images are integral to your content, consider creating an alternate version of the page that contains only text. Keep in mind that this means double maintenance for all future page modifications.

Design to Provide Accessibility

Vinton Cerf, the coinventor of TCP/IP and the former chairman of the Internet Society, proclaimed, "The Internet is for everyone" (see http://www.isoc-chicago.org/cerf.html). Tim Berners-Lee, the inventor of the World Wide Web, states, "The power of the web is in its universality. Access by everyone regardless of disability is an essential aspect" (see http://www.w3.org/WAI/). The Internet and Web are such a pervasive part of our culture that accessibility is becoming protected by laws in the United States. Section 508 of the Rehabilitation Act requires electronic and information technology, including web pages, used by federal agencies to be accessible to people with disabilities. The federal government is promoting accessibility by law and the private sector is following their lead.

The W3C is also active in this cause and has created the Web Accessibility Initiative (WAI) (see http://www.w3.org/WAI/) to create guidelines and standards applicable to web content developers, authoring tool developers, and browser developers. The WAI has developed a collection of materials designed to promote accessibility, including the following quick tips.

WAI Quick Tips (http://www.w3.org/WAI/References/QuickTips/)
- **Images and animations.** Use the alt attribute to describe the function of each visual.
- **Image maps.** Use the client-side map and text for hotspots.
- **Multimedia.** Provide captioning and transcripts of audio, and descriptions of video.
- **Hypertext links.** Use text that makes sense when read out of context. For example, avoid "click here."
- **Page organization.** Use headings, lists, and consistent structure. Use Cascading Style Sheets (see Chapter 9) for layout and style where possible.
- **Graphs and charts.** Summarize or use the longdesc attribute.
- **Scripts, applets, and plug-ins.** Provide alternative content in case active features such as JavaScript, Java applets, and Flash are inaccessible or unsupported.
- **Frames.** Use the **`<noframes>`** element and meaningful titles.
- **Tables.** Make line-by-line reading sensible. Summarize.
- **Check your work.** Validate. Use the tools, checklists, and guidelines at http://www.w3.org/TR/WCAG.

Developing accessible web sites is an important aspect of web site design. Web authoring tools such as Macromedia Dreamweaver provide extensions that will help you create accessible sites. Bobby (see http://www.cast.org/bobby/) is a free web page validator that will check your web page for common accessibility issues. The online version will only test one page at a time. An application that will do batch testing of an entire web site is also available for download at http://www.cast.org.

Chapter 7 Review

Summary

This chapter introduced recommended web site design practices. The choices you make in the use of color, graphics, and text should be based on your particular target audience. Developing an accessible web site should be the goal of every web developer.

Visit the text web site at http://www.webdevfoundations.net for examples, updated information, and the links listed in this chapter.

Review Questions

Multiple Choice

1. Choose the recommended design practice that applies to a web site that uses images for its main site navigation.

   a. Provide alternative text for the images.
   b. Place text links at the bottom of the page.
   c. Both a and b
   d. No special considerations are needed.

2. The three most common methods of organizing web sites are

   a. horizontal, vertical, and diagonal
   b. hierarchical, linear, and random
   c. accessible, readable, maintainable
   d. none of the above

3. To avoid overly long load times for your pages, try not to let the file size of the page and its associated media exceed

   a. 30KB   c. 1MB
   b. 60KB   d. 60MB

4. Which of the following is not a web design recommended practice?

   a. Design your site to be easy to navigate.
   b. Use frames whenever possible.
   c. Design your pages to load quickly.
   d. Limit the use of animated items.

5. A consistent web site design would have all of the following except

   a. the same fonts on each content page
   b. the same logo in the same location on each content page
   c. a similar navigation area on each content page
   d. a different background color on each page

6. The intended or target audience of a site will help to determine

   a. the amount of color used on the site
   b. the font size and styles used on the site
   c. the overall look and feel for the site
   d. all of the above

7. The main site navigation or a section offering navigation choices should contain

   a. no more than nine links
   b. as many links as you need
   c. only the most important pages
   d. none of the above

8. White space means

   a. the empty screen area around blocks of text and images
   b. the background color of white used for a page
   c. both a and b
   d. none of the above

9. When creating text hyperlinks, you should

   a. create the entire sentence as a hyperlink
   b. include the words "click here" in your text
   c. use a key phrase as a hyperlink
   d. none of the above

10. The most commonly used screen resolution is

    a. 640 by 480   c. 1024 by 768
    b. 800 by 600   d. none of the above

Fill in the Blank

11. _____ web site organization is the most common web site structure used for commercial web sites.

12. Placing _____ around graphics and headings helps them to stand out.

13. Animation should be used only if it _____ to your web site.

14. All browsers and browser versions _____ display web pages in exactly the same way.

15. The _____ is a group whose mission is to create guidelines and standards for web accessibility.

Hands-On Exercises

1. Practice creating site maps for the following situations. You may either draw your site map using a pencil and a ruler or use software such as Microsoft Visio, Microsoft Word, or Microsoft PowerPoint.

   a. Doug Kowalski is a freelance photographer specializing in nature photography. He often gets work on contract, shooting photos for textbooks and journals. Doug would like a web site that showcases his talents and that provides publishers with an easy way to contact him. He would like a home page, a few pages with samples of his nature photographs, and a contact page. Create a site map based on this scenario.

   b. Mary Ruarez owns a business, named Just Throw Me, that hand-crafts specialty pillows. She currently sells at craft fairs and local gift shops but would like to expand her business to the Web. She would like a web site with a home page, a page that describes her products, a page for each of her seven pillow styles, and an order page. She has been advised that since she is collecting information from individuals, a page describing her privacy policy would be a good idea. Create a site map based on this scenario.

c. Prakesh Khan owns a dog-grooming business named A Dog's Life. He would like a web presence that includes a home page, a page about grooming services, a page with a map to his shop, a contact page and a section that explains how to select a good pet. The content for the part of the web site on selecting a pet will be a step-by-step presentation. Create a site map based on this scenario.

2. Practice creating page layouts with the following situations. Use the style for page layout composition shown in Figures 7.21, 7.22, and 7.23, where places for logo, navigation, text, and images are indicated. Do not worry about exact wording or exact images. Use a pencil, ruler, and paper to draw the diagrams.

a. Create sample page layout diagrams for Doug Kowalski's photography business, described in 1a. Create one page layout diagram for the home page. Create another page layout diagram for the content pages.

b. Create sample page layout diagrams for the Just Throw Me web site described in 1b. Create one page layout diagram for the home page. Create another page layout diagram for the content pages.

c. Create sample page layout diagrams for the A Dog's Life web site described in 1c. Create one page layout diagram for the home page and the regular content pages. Create another page layout diagram for the presentation pages.

Each of these Case Studies will continue throughout most of the text. This chapter asks you to analyze the design of the web sites.

A. JavaJam Coffee House

See Chapter 2 for an introduction to the JavaJam Coffee House case. Figure 2.20 shows a site map for the JavaJam web site. The pages for this site were created in earlier chapters. In this case study you will review the site for recommended web site design practices.

Hands-On Practice Case

1. Examine the site map in Figure 2.20. What type of site organization is used for the JavaJam web site? Is it the most appropriate organization for the site? Why or why not?

2. Review the recommended web page design practices from this chapter. Evaluate the JavaJam site that you created in earlier chapters. Cite three design practices that have been well implemented. Cite three design practices that could be implemented in a better way. How else would you improve the web site?

B. Fish Creek Animal Hospital

See Chapter 2 for an introduction to the Fish Creek Animal Hospital Case. Figure 2.23 shows a site map for the Fish Creek web site. The pages for the site were created in earlier chapters. In this case study you will review the site for recommended web site design practices.

Hands-On Practice Case

1. Examine the site map in Figure 2.23. What type of site organization is used for the Fish Creek web site? Is it the most appropriate organization for the site? Why or why not?

2. Review the recommended web page design practices from this chapter. Evaluate the Fish Creek site that you created in earlier chapters. Cite three design practices that have been well implemented. Cite three design practices that could be implemented in a better way on the Fish Creek site. How else would you improve the web site?

C. Pete the Painter

See Chapter 2 for an introduction to the Pete the Painter Case. Figure 2.26 shows a site map for the Pete the Painter web site. The pages for the site were created in earlier chapters. During this case study you will review the site for recommended web site design practices.

Hands-On Practice Case

1. Examine the site map in Figure 2.26. What type of site organization is used for the Pete the Painter web site? Is it the most appropriate organization for the site? Why or why not?

2. Review the recommended web page design practices from this chapter. Evaluate the Pete the Painter site that you created in earlier chapters. Cite three design practices that have been well implemented. Cite three design practices that could be implemented in a better way on the Pete the Painter web site. How else would you improve the web site?

Web Research

A. This chapter offered suggestions for organizing text on web pages. In this research exercise take this topic a step further and investigate writing for the web. A few resources are listed here.

- http://useit.com. Search for an article called "Writing for the Web".
- Visit http://www.webreference.com/content/writing/. If you cannot find that page, visit webreference.com and search for "writing for the web".
- http://www.newarchitectmag.com/documents/s=4579/ new1013637064/. If you cannot find that page, visit newartchitectmag.com and search for "Effective Web Writing".

If these resources are no longer available, search the Web for information on "writing for the web". Read one or more articles. Select five techniques that you would like to share with others. Create a web page that presents your findings. Include a link to the source of each technique. Your web page should contain a table and use color. Place your name in the e-mail address at the bottom of the web page. Print both the source code (from Notepad) and the browser view of your web page.

B. This chapter discusses recommended web design practices. Sometimes it is helpful to learn about good design by examining poor design. Visit http://www.webpagesthatsuck.com and read about their examples of poor design. Try to think of web sites that you have visited on the Web. Do any of them have similar qualities? Find two web sites that use poor web design practices. Create a web page that includes an introduction about the design practices not followed at the web sites, a link to each site, and a description of how each site has practiced poor web site design. Your web page should contain a table and use color. Place your name in the e-mail address at the bottom of the web page. Print both the source code (from Notepad) and the browser view of your web page.

C. Visit any of the web sites referenced in this chapter that interested you. Print the home page or one other pertinent page from the site. Create a web page that discusses the web site you visited. Your new web page should use a table for layout, and include the use of color and images. Write a one-page summary and reaction to the web site you chose to visit. Address the following topics:

1. What is the purpose of the site?

2. Who is the intended audience?

3. Do you believe the site reaches the intended audience?

4. List three examples of how this web site uses recommended web design guidelines.

5. How could this site be improved?

Chapter Review Answers

1. c

2. b

3. b

4. b

5. d

6. d

7. a

8. a

9. c

10. b

11. hierarchical

12. white space

13. adds

14. will not

15. Web Accessibility Initiative (WAI)

Chapter 8

Web Site Development

Thial chapter discusses the skills needed for successful large-scale project development and introduces you to common web development methods. It is important to realize that each project is unique; each has its own needs and requirements. Choosing the right people to work on a web project team can make or break it.

Successful Large-Scale Project Development

Large-scale projects are not completed by only one or two individuals. They are created by a group of people working together as a team. The job roles of project manager, information architect, marketing representative, copywriter and editor, graphic designer, database administrator, network administrator, and web developer are usually needed for large projects. In smaller companies or smaller organizations each person can wear many hats and juggle his or her job roles. In a smaller-scale project one of the web developers may double as the project manager, graphic designer, database administrator, and/or information architect. Job roles necessary for successful projects are discussed in this section.

Project Manager

The project manager oversees the web site development process and coordinates team activities. Project managers create the project plan and schedule. This individual is accountable for reaching project milestones and producing results. Excellent organizational, managerial, and communication skills are required.

Information Architect

The role of the information architect is to clarify the mission and goals of the site, assist in determining the functionality of the site, and be instrumental in defining the site organization, navigation, and labeling. Web developers and/or the project manager sometimes take on this role themselves.

Marketing Representative

The marketing representative handles the organization's marketing plan and goals. Marketing representatives work with the web designers to create a **web presence**, or look and feel, that aligns with the marketing goals of the organization. The marketing representative also helps to coordinate the web site with other media used for marketing such as print, radio, and television marketing.

Copywriter and Editor

The copywriter prepares and evaluates copy. When material from existing brochures, newsletters, and white papers will be used on the web site, it must be repurposed or reworked for the web media. An editor may work with the copywriter, checking the text for grammar and consistency.

Graphic Designer

The graphic designer determines appropriate use of color and graphics on the site, creates page layouts, and designs graphics. Graphic designers may work closely with the web developers to create graphic buttons used in mouseover effects.

Database Administrator

A database administrator is needed if the site accesses information stored in databases. Database administrators create databases, create procedures to maintain databases (including backup and recovery), and control access to databases.

Network Administrator

This network administrator configures and maintains the web server, installs and maintains system hardware and software, and controls access security.

Web Developer

The web developer writes XHTML code and client-side scripting such as JavaScript. Web developers may develop server-side processing such as CGI or ASP. There will typically be multiple web developers assigned to a large project, each with his or her area of expertise.

Project Staffing Criteria

Whether the project is large or small, finding the right people to work on it is crucial. When selecting staff for a project, take into consideration each individual's work experience, portfolio, formal education, and industry certifications.

Another option to staffing a web project (or developing an entire web site) is to outsource the project; that is hire another company to do the work for you. Sometimes portions of a project are outsourced, such as graphics creation or multimedia aspects. Other times server-side scripting is outsourced. When this option is chosen, communication between the project manager and the external organization is crucial. The outsource team needs to be aware of the goals and deadlines of the project.

Large or small, developed in-house or outsourced, the success of a web site project depends on planning and communication. Formal project development methodology is used to coordinate and facilitate the planning and communication needed for a successful web project.

The Development Process

Large corporate and commercial web sites don't just happen. They are carefully built, usually by following a project development methodology. A methodology is a step-by-step plan that encompasses the life cycle of a project from start to finish. It is comprised of a series of phases, each having specific activities and deliverables. Most modern methodologies have their roots in the **System Development Life Cycle (SDLC)**, a process that has been used for several decades to build large-scale information systems. The SDLC is composed of a set of **phases**, sometimes called *steps* or *stages*. Each phase is usually completed before beginning the activities in the next phase. The basic phases of the standard SDLC (shown in Figure 8.1) are: systems investigation, systems analysis, systems design, systems implementation, and maintenance.

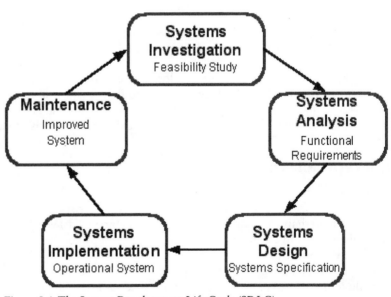

Figure 8.1 *The System Development Life Cycle (SDLC)*

Web sites are often developed using a variation of the SDLC that is modified to apply to web projects. Large companies and web design firms usually create their own special methodology for use on projects. The Web Site Development Cycle is a guide to successful web project management.

Depending on the scope and complexity of a particular project, some steps can be completed in a single meeting, other steps can take weeks or months.

The Web Site Development Cycle, shown in Figure 8.2, usually consists of the following steps: Conceptualization, Analysis, Design, Production, Testing, Launch, Maintenance, and Evaluation.

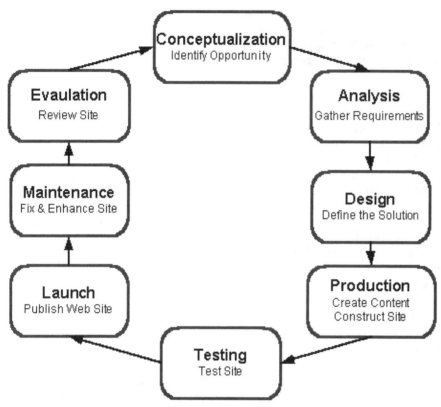

Figure 8.2 *The Web Site Development Cycle*

An important aspect of web site development is that you are never finished—the site needs to be kept fresh and up-to-date, there will be errors or omissions that need to be corrected, and new components and pages will be needed on the site. The very first step is to decide why the site is needed in the first place.

Conceptualization

What opportunity or issue is the site addressing? What is the motivation for the site? Perhaps your client owns a retail store and wishes to sell over the Internet. Perhaps your client's competitor just completed a web site and your client needs to create one just to keep up. Perhaps you have a great idea that will be the next eBay!

Because the focus of your work will be to make the site usable and appealing to your target audience, you must determine the intended audience of the site. It is crucial to be aware of who your audience is and what their preferences are.

Another task during this step is to determine the long-term and short-term goals or mission of the site. Perhaps a short-term goal is simply to publish a home page. Perhaps a long-term goal would be for 20% of your product sales to be made on your web site. Or you may simply want a certain number of web site visitors each month. Whatever they are, it is better if the objectives are measurable. Decide how you will measure the success (or failure) of your web site.

Determining the purpose and goals of a site is usually done with the cooperation of the client, project manager, and information architect. In a formal project environment, a document that details the results of this step would be created and would need to be approved by the client development could proceed.

Analysis

The Analysis phase involves meetings and interviews with key client personnel. The tasks are usually completed by the project manager, information architect or other analyst, and the client's marketing representative and related personnel. The network administrator and database administrator may be interviewed depending on the scope of the project. Common tasks are listed here:

- **Determine information topics.** Organize the information to be presented on the site into categories and create a hierarchy. This will be used later as a starting point for developing the site navigation.
- **Determine functionality requirements.** State what the site will do, not how it will do it. For example, state "the site will accept credit card orders from customers", not "the site will perform order processing using Active Server Pages to look up each price and sale tax information in Oracle databases and use real-time credit card verification supplied by somewebsite.com." Note the difference in the level of detail.
- **Determine environmental requirements.** What hardware, operating system, memory capacity, screen resolution, and bandwidth will your site visitors be using? What type of hardware and software requirements will the Web server need? (See Choosing a Web Host, toward the end of this chapter, for help with this question.)
- **Determine content requirements.** Does content already exist in another format—brochures, catalogs, white papers? Determine who is responsible for creating and repurposing content for the site. Does the client company or marketing department have any requirements that must be met? For example, is there a specific look and feel or corporate branding component that must be present on the site?
- **Compare the old approach to the new approach.** Perhaps you are not creating a new web site but modifying an existing one. What benefits or added value will the new version provide?
- **Review your competitor's sites.** A careful review of your competitors' web presence will help you to design a site that will stand out from the crowd and be more appealing to your shared customer base. Note both the good and bad components of their sites.
- **Estimate costs.** Create an estimate of the costs and time involved to create the site. A formal project plan is often created or modified at this point.
- **Do a cost/benefit analysis.** Create a document that compares the costs and benefits of the site. Measurable benefits are the most useful and most appealing to clients.

In a formal project environment, a document that details the results of this analysis would need to be approved by the client before the team could proceed.

Design

Once everyone knows what is needed, it is time to determine how that can be accomplished. The Design phase involves meetings and interviews with key client personnel. This phase is usually completed by the project manager, information architect or other analyst, graphic designer(s), senior web developer(s), and the client's marketing representative and related personnel. Common tasks are listed here:

- **Choose a site organization.** As discussed in Chapter 7, common web site organizational forms are hierarchical, linear, and random. Determine which is best for the project site and create a site map (sometimes called a *flowchart* or *storyboard*).
- **Prototype the design.** Often a graphics application is used to create sample web page mock-ups as page layouts are created. These can be shown to clients as a prototype, or working model, of the system for approval. They can also be shown to focus groups for usability testing.
- **Create a page layout design.** The overall layout, or look and feel, of the site should be designed. This is used as a guideline for Home page and Content page layouts. Items such as the site color scheme, size of logo graphics, button graphics, and text should be determined. Using the page layout design and site map, create sample layouts for the Home page and Content pages. Use a graphic application to create mock-ups of these pages to get a good idea of how the site will function. If you use a web authoring tool instead, you run the risk of your manager or client thinking you already have the site half done and insisting on earlier delivery.
- **Document each page.** While this may seem unnecessary, lack of content is a frequent cause of web site project delays. Prepare a content sheet, such as the one shown in Figure 8.3, for each page that describes the

Page Title:

Basic Description:

Suggested Graphic Elements:

Other Special Features:

Special Informational Needs:

Information Sources:

Content Provider(s):

File Format of Provided Content:
Deadline for Content:
Content Approval:

Figure 8.3 *Sample content sheet*

functionality of the document, text and graphic content requirements, source of content, and approver of content.

The site map and page design prototypes are usually approved by the client before the team can continue with the Production phase.

Production

During this step all the previous work comes together (hopefully) in a usable and effective web site. During the Production phase the web developers are on the critical path—their work must be done as scheduled or the project will be late. The other project members are consulted on an as-needed basis for clarification and approval. Common tasks are listed here:

- **Choose a web authoring tool.** The use of a web authoring tool such as Macromedia Dreamweaver or Microsoft FrontPage can greatly increase productivity. Specific productivity aids include designer notes, page templates, task management, and web page check-in and check-out to avoid overlapping page updates. The use of an authoring tool will serve to standardize the XHTML used in the project pages. Any standards related to indentation, comments, and so on should be determined at this time.
- **Organize your site files.** Consider placing images and media in their own folder. Also place server-side scripts in a separate folder. Determine naming conventions for web pages, images, and media.
- **Develop and individually test components.** During this task the graphic designers and web developers create and individually test their contributions to the site. As the images, web pages, and server-side scripting are developed, they are individually tested. This is sometimes called **unit testing**. On some projects, a senior web developer or the project manager will review the components for quality and standards compliance.

Once all components have been created and unit tested, it's time to put them all together and begin the Testing phase.

Testing

The components should be published to a test web server. This test web server should have the same operating system and web server software that the production (actual) web server will be using. Some common site testing considerations are listed here:

- **Test on different browsers and browser versions.** Many web pages look fine on Internet Explorer but will not even *display* on Netscape Navigator. It is very important to test your pages on commonly used browsers and versions of those browsers.
- **Test with different screen resolutions.** Not everyone uses 1228 by 1024 screen resolution. The most commonly used screen resolution at the time of this writing is 800 by 600. Be sure to test your web pages on various resolutions—you might be surprised at the results.
- **Test using different bandwidths.** If you live and work in a metropolitan area, everyone you know may have broadband access to the Internet. However, most people still are using dial-up phones to access the Web. It is important to test your site on both slow and fast connections. Images that look great over your school's T3 line may load very slowly over a 56K modem.
- **Test from another location.** Be sure to test your web site using a computer other than the one the web site was developed on. This way you are more closely simulating the web page visitor experience.

- **Test, test, test.** There is no such thing as too much testing. We are human and make mistakes. It is much better for you and your team to find the errors than for your client to point them out to you when they review the web site.

Does this sound like a lot to keep track of? It is. That's why it's a good idea to create a **test plan**. A test plan is a document that describes what will be tested on each page of a web site. A sample test plan for a web page, shown in Figure 8.4, can help you organize your testing as you check your document in different browsers and screen resolutions. The document validation section covers content, links, and any forms or scripting that may be required for the page. The search engine optimization meta tags are discussed in Chapter 11. However, at this point you should be able to verify that the page title is descriptive and includes the company or organization name. Testing your page using different bandwidths is important because web pages that take too long to download are often abandoned.

Web Page Document Test Plan

File Name:							Date:		
Title:							Tester:		

Browser Compatibility

	800x600	1024x768	1280x1024	PC	Mac	Images Off	Print	Other
Netscape 6								
Netscape 4								
IE 6								
IE 5								
IE 4								
Opera								
AOL								
WebTV								
Other								

Document Validation

	Check Spelling
	Required Content
	Required Graphics
	Check Alt Attributes
	Test Links
	HTML Validation
	Form Processing
	Scripting / Dynamic Effects
	Usability / Accessibility

Search Engine Optimization

	Page Title
	Meta Tag (Description)
	Meta Tag (Keyword)
	Other

Bandwidth Check

	28.8K
	56.6K
	Broadband
	Other

Notes

Figure 8.4 *Sample test plan*

Automated Testing Tools and Validators. The web authoring tool your project is using will have some built-in site reporting and testing features—be sure to use them. There are also other automated testing tools that are available. Some are free, such as the W3C Validator and HTML Tidy. The W3C Validator (http://validator.w3.org/) can be used to validate both HTML and XHTML. HTML Tidy (http://www.w3.org/ People/Raggett/tidy/) will convert an HTML page to an XHTML page –correcting the tag syntax and replacing font tags with formatting using Cascading Style Sheets (see Chapter 9). An online version of HTML Tidy is available at http://valet.htmlhelp.com/tidy/. Other testing tools that offer additional features such as page load time and broken link checking are available from http://www.netmechanic.com/ and others. See http:// www.softwareqatest.com/qatweb1.html for a partial list.

Besides validating HTML and testing for broken links, consider using a tool such as Rational SiteLoad (http://www.rational.com/products/siteload/ index.jsp) to stress-test the web server or using an application like WebKing (http://www.thewebking.com/products/webking/index.htm) to test all possible paths through the site. The scope and complexity of your site will determine the amount of testing needed. For a simple site, validation and link checking will probably be sufficient. Other types of sites will benefit from more rigorous testing.

Usability Testing. Testing how actual web page visitors use a web site is called **usability testing**. It can be conducted at any phase of a web site's development and is often performed more than once. A usability test is conducted by asking users to complete tasks on a web site, such as placing an order, looking up the phone number of a company, or finding a product. The exact tasks will vary depending on the web site being tested. The users are monitored while they try to perform these tasks. They are asked to think out loud about their doubts and hesitations. The results are recorded (often on video tape) and discussed with the web design team. Often changes are made to the navigation and page layouts based on these tests.

If usability testing is done early in the development phase of a web site, it may use the paper page layouts and site map. If the web development team is struggling with a design issue, sometimes a usability test can help to determine which design idea is the better choice.

When usability is done during a later phase, such as the Testing Phase, the actual web site is tested. This can lead to either a confirmation that the site is easy to use and well-designed, to last minute changes in the web site, or to a plan for web site enhancements in the near future.

Launch

Your client—whether another company or another department in your organization—needs to review and approve the test web site before the files are published to the live web site. Sometimes this approval takes place at a face-to-face meeting. Other times, the test URL is given to the client and the client e-mails approval or requested changes.

Once the test web site has been approved, it is published to your live production web site. If you think you are all through—think again! It is crucial to test all site components after publishing to make sure the site functions properly in its new environment. Marketing and promotion activities for the web site (see Chapter 11) usually take place at this time.

Maintenance

A web site is never finished. There are always errors or omissions that were overlooked during the development process. Clients usually find many new uses for a web site once they have one and request modifications, additions, and new sections. So at this point, the project team identifies the new opportunity or enhancement and begins another loop through the development process.

Other types of updates needed are relatively small—perhaps a link is broken, a word misspelled, or a graphic needs to be changed. These small changes are usually made as soon as they are noticed. The question of who makes the changes and who approves them is often a matter of company policy. If you a freelance web developer working on your own the situation is more straightforward—you will make the changes and your client will approve them.

Evaluation

Remember the goals set for the web site way back in the Conceptualization phase? It's time to take a look at them and determine whether your web site is meeting them. If it is not, consider how you can enhance the site, and you'll begin another loop through the development process.

Web Hosting

Where is the appropriate place for your web project to "live"? Choosing the most appropriate web host provider for your business or client could be one of the most important decisions you make. A good web hosting service will provide a robust, reliable home for your web site. A poor web hosting service will be the source of problems and complaints. Which would you prefer to have?

Types of Web Host Providers

The types of web host providers range from local ISPs who have some empty space on their servers and web developers who host sites on the side, to local hosting companies and national companies that guarantee 99.999% uptime of your web site. Understandably, the fees and the level of service for each of these will be different. What does your business or client need? This section looks at needs of various size businesses.

One word of caution: Never consider using a "free" web host provider for your business. These sites are great for kids, college students, and hobbyists, but they are unprofessional. The last thing you or your client wants is to be perceived as not serious or unprofessional.

As you consider different web host providers, be sure to check references. Also try contacting their support phone numbers and e-mail addresses to determine just how responsive they really are. It is common for web host providers to charge a setup fee in addition to the monthly hosting fee. Hosting fees vary widely. The cheapest hosting provider is not necessarily the one to use. Word of mouth, web searches, the local phone directory, and online directories such as http://webhosts.thelist.com/business are all resources in your quest for the perfect web host provider.

Hosting Needs

Small to Medium Web Site. Suggested requirements include unlimited data transfer, 60MB or more of hard disk space, e-mail, and support of Microsoft FrontPage Extensions (unless you know a good CGI programmer). This type of hosting is usually **virtual hosting**. The web host provider's server is divided into a number of virtual domains, and multiple web sites are set up on the same computer.

Keep in mind that over time your web site will grow and your processing needs will increase. Do you have access to your web site log or will automatic reporting be included? Does the web host provider offer an e-commerce package that you could use when you are ready? Do they offer CGI or database support? You may not need these technologies now, but

What about other web site development methodologies?

The development methodology presented in this chapter is a version of the traditional SDLC modified for web site development. Other development methods include the following:

- **Prototyping.** A small working model is created and shown to the client. It is continually revised by the developer until it is usable for the intended purpose. This method can easily be included in the Web Development Life Cycle during the Design step.

- **Spiral System Development.** This is excellent for very large-scale or phased projects where it is important to reduce risk. Small portions of the project are completed one after the other in a spiral of development.

- **Joint Application Development (JAD).** This type of development focuses on group meetings and collaboration between the users and developers of a web site or system. It is generally only used for in-house development.

- **Agile Software Development.** This development methodology is viewed as innovative in that it stresses responsiveness based on generating and sharing knowledge within a development team and with the client. The philosophy emphasizes code over documentation and results in the project being developed in many small, iterative steps.

- **Organization-specific Development Methodologies.** Large companies and web development firms often create their own version or interpretation of site development methodology to be used on projects.

try to keep your options open for the future. Moving a site from one web host provider to another is not always an easy process. Choose a web host provider that will most likely meet your future as well as present needs.

Also consider the operating system and web server application that your host offers. The UNIX operating system running an Apache web server is quite common and very efficient. However, if the skill set of your organization is mainly Microsoft technologies, your staff will be more comfortable and more productive with a web host that offers Microsoft 2000 running Internet Information Server 5.0 as the web server.

Consider local web hosting providers as well as national web host providers in your search.

Large to Enterprise Web Site. If you are expecting a high traffic site that may support a chat room or streaming media content, consider large national web hosting services. These generally provide a high bandwidth Internet connection (typically OC-1 or higher), 24-hour staffing, hardware and media redundancy, and enhanced security. Determine the guaranteed level of service and response time. Also consider using a dedicated or co-located web server at a national web host provider. A dedicated or co-located web server will be running *only* your web site—you do not share the processor or hard drive with any other organization. There is an additional charge for this but the added security and guarantee of processing may be worth it to your organization.

A **dedicated web server** refers to the rental and exclusive use of a computer and connection to the Internet that is housed in the Web hosting company's premises. A dedicated server is usually needed for a web site that may develop a considerable amount of traffic, such as tens of millions of hits a day. The server can usually be configured and operated remotely from the client company or you can pay the web host provider to administer it for you.

A **co-located web server,** sometimes referred to as *colocated* or *collocated*, is a computer that your organization has purchased and configured. Your organization effectively rents space at the web host provider's location. Your server is kept and connected to the Internet at their location. Your organization administers this computer. This provides your organization with additional control over the web server, but it also means that you need to staff or contract an individual with web server administration experience.

Large, national web host providers can supply dedicated T1 or T3 Internet access, 24/7 support, network utilization statistics and log access, hardware and media redundancy, and the ability to cluster web servers, support web farms, e-commerce, and streaming media delivery. A **service-level agreement (SLA)** that details the level of support and response time is also usually supplied by large, national web host providers.

Small, medium, or large—selecting the right web host can be crucial to the success of your web site.

Why do I care about knowing which operating system my web host provider uses?

Knowing the operating system used by your web host provider is important because it can help you with troubleshooting your web site. Often students' web sites work great on their own PC (usually with a Windows-based operating system) but fall apart (with broken links and images that do not load) after being published to a free web server that uses a different operating system.

Some operating systems, such as Windows, treat upper and lowercase letters in exactly the same way. Other operating systems, such as UNIX and Linux, consider upper and lowercase letters to be different. This is called being *case-sensitive*. For example, when a web server running with on a Windows operating system receives a request generated by an anchor tag coded as `<a href="MyPage.htm">My Page</a>`, it will return a file named with any combination of upper or lowercase letters. The values MyPage.htm, mypage.htm, myPage.htm could all be used. However, when the request generated by the same anchor tag is received by a web server running on a UNIX system (which is case-sensitive) the file would only be found if it were really saved as MyPage.htm. If the file were named mypage.htm, a 404 (not found) error would result. This is a good reason to always be consistent when naming files—consider always using lowercase letters for file names.

Chapter 8 Review

Summary

This chapter introduced the system development life cycle and its application to web development projects. The job roles related to web site development and issues related to web hosting were also discussed.

Visit the text web site at http://www.webdevfoundations.net for examples, updated information, and the links listed in this chapter.

Review Questions

Multiple Choice

1. Testing a site should include
   a. checking all of the hyperlinks within the site
   b. viewing the site in a variety of web browsers
   c. viewing the site in a variety of screen resolutions
   d. all of the above

2. The role of an information architect includes
   a. being instrumental in defining the site organization, navigation, and labeling
   b. attending all meetings and collecting all information
   c. mangaging the project
   d. none of the above

3. A methodology long used to develop information systems is the
   a. System Development Life Cycle
   b. Service Delivery Life Cycle
   c. System Development Life Chain
   d. none of the above

4. The methodology used by web project teams is usually
   a. the SDLC
   b. a derivative of the SDLC similar to the one discussed in this chapter
   c. decided on as the project is built
   d. web sites do not require the use of a development methodology

5. In the Analysis Phase of a web site project, team members
   a. determine what the site will do—not how it will be done
   b. determine the information topics of the site
   c. determine the content requirements of the site
   d. all of the above

6. A prototype of the web site will often be created in
   a. the Design Phase
   b. the Conceptualization Phase
   c. the Production Phase
   d. the Analysis Phase

7. During the Production Phase
    a. a web authoring tool is often used
    b. the graphics, web pages, and other components are created
    c. the web pages are individually tested
    d. all of the above

8. The Evaluation Phase
    a. is a time to review the goals for the site
    b. may result in another loop through the development process
    c. both of the above
    d. none of the above

9. A web hosting option appropriate for the initial web presence of an organization is
    a. virtual hosting
    b. free web hosting
    c. dedicated hosting
    d. co-located hosting

10. A web hosting option appropriate for a large to enterprise web site is
    a. virtual hosting
    b. free web hosting
    c. dedicated hosting
    d. none of the above

Fill in the Blank

11 _____ can be described as testing how actual web page visitors use a web site.

12. The _____ determines appropriate use of graphics on the site, and creates and edits graphics.

13. The _____ operating system(s) treat uppercase and lowercase letters differently.

Short Answer

14. Describe why the web sites of competitors should be reviewed when designing a web site.

15. Why should you try to contact the technical support of a web host provider before you are one of its customers?

Hands-On Exercises

1. In this exercise you will validate a web page. Choose one of the web pages that you have created. Launch a browser and visit the W3C HTML Validator page at http://validator.w3.org/. Click on the "Upload Files" link to display the HTML Validation Service: Upload files page (http://validator.w3.org/file-upload.html). Click on the "Browse" button, select a file from your computer, and click OK to upload the file to the W3C site. Do not change the default settings for the document type drop-down box and the check box options. Click the "Validate this document" button. Your page will be analyzed and a Results page that shows a report of violations of the DTD that is used by your web page. The error messages are shown with a light gray background and a

"pointer" to the offending portion of the code. Experiment with the options and notice the additional displays that are created. Don't worry if your web page does not pass the validations the first time you try. Many well-known web sites have pages that do not validate—even http://yahoo.com had validation errors at the time this was written. Modify your web page document and revalidate it until you see a message that states "Congratulations, this document validates as XHTML 1.0 Transitional!" See Figure 8.5.

Below are the results of checking this document for XML well-formedness and validity.

  No errors found! *

Congratulations, this document validates as XHTML 1.0 Transitional!

Figure 8.5 This indicates the web page has passed the validation.

This page also provides you with some code and an image to display to tell the world that your page validated. Print the browser view of this page.

You can also validate pages directly from the web. Try validating the W3C's home page at http://w3.org, Yahoo! at http://yahoo.com, and your school's home page. Visit http://validator.w3.org and enter the URL of the web page you would like to validate in the URI (Uniform Resource Indicator) text box. Set the character encoding and document type drop-down boxes to "detect automatically". Click on the "Validate this page" button. View the results. Experiment with the character encoding and doctype options. The W3C's page should pass the validation. Don't worry if the other pages do not validate. Validation is not required for web pages. However, web pages that pass the validation should display well in most browsers. (*Note:* If you have published pages to the web, try validating one of them instead of your school's home page.)

2. Web authoring applications such as Macromedia Dreamweaver and Microsoft FrontPage both provide functions such as spelling checks, link checks, and load time calculation. They each also have unique features. Dreamweaver's reporting includes link checking, accessibility, and code validation. FrontPage will display many different reports, including orphaned pages (pages with no links to them), old pages (pages that have not been recently updated), and high bandwidth pages. Automated testing is provided by other applications besides web authoring tools. This exercise will give you practice using two testing tools that offer free demonstrations on the Web: NetMechanic and Dr. Watson.

   a. NetMechanic offers a free trial of their HTML Toolbox Application at http://www.netmechanic.com/toolbox/html-code.htm. Visit this site and test the home page of your school. At the time this was written there were a number of options, allowing up to five pages to be checked. After the test is run, a results page will be displayed with ratings related to Link Check, Bad Links Report, HTML Check, Browser Compatibility, Load Time, and Spell Check. Each category has a link to a detailed display that describes the types of errors found. Print out the browser view of this results page to hand in to your instructor. (*Note:* If you have published pages to the web, try validating one of them instead of your school's home page.)

b. The Dr. Watson site offers free web page validation at http://watson.addy.com/. Visit this site and test the home page of your school. After the test is run, a report is displayed with categories including Server response, Estimated download speed, Syntax and style analysis, Spelling check, Link verifications, Images, Search engine compatibility (see Chapter 11), Site link popularity (see Chapter 11), and Source code. Print out the browser view of this report page to hand in to your instructor. (*Note:* If you have published pages to the Web, try validating one of them instead of your school's home page.)

Web Research

A. This chapter discussed options for hosting web sites. In this research exercise you will search for web host providers and report on three that meet the following criteria:

- Support Microsoft FrontPage Server Extensions
- Offer e-commerce capabilities
- Provide at least 50MB hard disk space

Either use your favorite search engine to find web host providers or visit web host directories such as http://webhosts.thelist.com/business and http://www.hostindex.com/. Create a web page that presents your findings. Include links to your three web host providers. Your web page should include a table of information such as: set-up fees, monthly fees, domain name registration costs, amount of hard disk space, type of e-commerce package, and cost of e-commerce package. Use color and graphics appropriately on your web page. Place your name in the e-mail address at the bottom of the web page. Print both the source code (from Notepad) and the browser view of your web page.

B. This chapter discussed the different job functions that are needed to develop large web sites. Choose a job role that interests you. Search for information about available jobs in your geographical area. Try searching for technology jobs with your favorite search engine or visit a job site such as http://monster.com, http://dice.com, http://techies.com, or http://brassring.com and search for your desired location and job type. Find three possible job positions that interest you and report on them. Create a web page that includes a brief description of the job role you have chosen, a description of the three available positions, a description of the types of experience required and/or educational background required for the job positions, and the salary range (if available). Organize your findings in a table. Use color and graphics appropriately on your web page. Place your name in the e-mail address at the bottom of the web page. Print both the source code (from Notepad) and the browser view of your web page.

Chapter Review Answers

1. d

2. a

3. a

4. b

5. d

6. a

7. d

8. c

9. a

10. c

11. usability testing

12. graphic designer

13. UNIX and Linux

14. A careful review of your competitor's web presence will help you design a site that will stand out from the rest and be more appealing to your shared customer-base. Note both the good and bad components of their sites.

15. Trying to contact technical support can give you a general idea of the responsiveness of the web host provider to issues and problems. If the technical support staff is slow getting back to you at this point, don't be surprised if you get the same type of service when you have a problem and need help immediately. While not fail-safe, a quick response to a simple question at least gives the appearance of a well-organized, professional, and responsive technical support staff.

Chapter
9

Cascading Style Sheets

Now that you've had an introduction to XHTML, graphics, web design and web site development concepts, you are ready to study a more advanced technique of formatting web pages—Cascading Style Sheets (CSS). CSS is not new—it was first proposed as a standard by the W3C in 1996. However, CSS has just recently begun to be supported by browsers and other user agents in a more standard manner. CSS is a useful technology for separating the presentation style of the web page from the information on the web page itself.

You may recall that the `<font>` tag is deprecated. This means that while it is still part of the W3C recommendation, it will be dropped from the recommendation in the future. CSS fulfills the function of the `<font>` tag in addition to providing many other web page formatting and positioning capabilities. This chapter introduces you to the use of CSS on the Web.

Learning Outcomes

In this chapter, you will learn how to:

▶ **Describe the evolution of style sheets from print media to the web**

▶ **List advantages of using Cascading Style Sheets**

▶ **Create style sheets that configure common page and text properties**

▶ **Apply inline styles**

▶ **Use embedded style sheets**

▶ **Use external style sheets**

Overview of Cascading Style Sheets

Style sheets have been used in desktop publishing for years to apply typographical styles and spacing instructions to printed media. CSS provides this functionality (and much more) for web developers. It allows web developers to apply typographic styles (typeface, font size, etc.) and spacing instructions to a web page.

CSS is a flexible, cross-platform, standards-based language developed by the W3C. Its description of CSS can be found at http://www.w3.org/Style/. Be aware that CSS, even though years old, is still considered an emerging technology and the two most popular browsers still do not support it in exactly the same way. There is a CSS reference page at http://webreview.com/style/css1/charts/mastergrid.shtml that depicts the way styles are supported by various browsers and platforms. This chapter concentrates on those aspects of CSS that are supported well by popular browsers.

Advantages of Cascading Style Sheets

There are a number of advantages to using CSS:

- **Greater typography and page layout control,** including font size, line spacing, letter spacing, indents, margins, and element positioning.
- **Style is separate from structure.** The format of the text and colors used on the page can be configured and stored separate from the body section of the web page document.
- **Styles can be stored** in a separate document and linked to from the web page. When the styles are modified, the XHTML remains intact. This means that if your client decides to change the background color from red to white you only need change *one* file that contains the styles, instead of *each* web page document.
- **Potentially smaller documents.** Since the formatting is separate from the document, the actual documents should be smaller.
- **No need for <font> tags.** This will result in more concise and easily understood web page documents.
- **Easier site maintenance.** Again, if the styles need to be changed it is possible to complete the modifications by changing only the style sheet.

Are you beginning to see there might be an advantage to using CSS? You may be wondering if there are any disadvantages to using CSS. In fact, there is one large disadvantage—CSS technology is not yet uniformly supported by browsers. This disadvantage will be less of an issue in the future as the browsers comply with standards.

Types of Cascading Style Sheets

There are a number of different methods used to incorporate CSS technology in a web site: inline, embedded, external, and imported.

- **Inline styles.** Inline styles are coded in the body of the web page as an attribute of an XHTML tag. The style only applies to the specific element that contains it as an attribute
- **Embedded styles.** Embedded styles are defined in the header of a web page. These style instructions apply to the entire web page document.

- **External styles.** External Styles are coded in a separate text file. This text file is linked to the web page by using a `<link>` tag in the header section.
- **Imported styles.** Imported styles are similar to external styles in that they are coded in a separate text file. They are not widely supported by browsers at this time. This chapter concentrates on the other three types of CSS.

Introduction to CSS Syntax

Style sheets are composed of rules that describe the styling to be applied. Each rule contains a selector and a declaration. The selector can be an XHTML element, a class name (that you create yourself), or an id name (that you create yourself). This example concentrates on applying styles to XHTML elements. The declaration is the property you are setting (such as color or typeface) and the value you are assigning to it.

For example, the following CSS rule shown in Figure 9.1 would set the color of the text used on a web page to the color blue.

Figure 9.1 *Using CSS to set the text color to blue*

In the example above, the selector is the XHTML body tag and the declaration sets the color property to the value of blue. If you wanted the background color of the web page to be yellow, the CSS rule could be expanded as follows:

```
body { color: blue;
       background-color: yellow; }
```

This could also be written using hexadecimal color values

```
body { color: #0000FF;
       background-color: #FFFF00; }
```

Notice that both the background-color and text properties were configured in the example above. To avoid surprising results caused by default browser colors, the W3C recommends that the background-color property be set when the text color is configured.

Have you ever wondered why some text-based links are not underlined? This can be accomplished with a style applied to the anchor tag. The following style rule selects the anchor tag (denoted by the "a") and sets the property of text-decoration (the underline) to none.

```
a { text-decoration:none }
```

You might be asking yourself how you would know what properties and values are allowed to be used. While this chapter introduces you to some commonly used properties, as you continue to work with CSS, you will find the master compatibility chart at http://webreview.com/style/css1/charts/mastergrid.shtml helpful because you can click on any property and get an explanation and example of its use. The CSS Recommendations from the W3C are at http://www.w3.org/TR/REC-CSS1 and http://www.w3.org/TR/REC-CSS2/. Table 9.1 presents a summary of the CSS properties used in this chapter.

Table 9.1 *Common CSS Properties*

Property	Description	Values
background-color	Background color on the web page	Any valid color
color	Text color	Any valid color
font-family	Name of a font or font family	Any valid font or a font family such as "serif", "sans-serif", "fantasy", "monospaced", or "cursive"
font-size	The size of the text font	This varies. It is most common to use pt (standard font point sizes) or px (pixels).
font-weight	The "boldness" or weight of the font	This varies. The text values normal, bold, bolder, and lighter can be used. The numeric values 100, 200, 300, 400, 500, 600, 700, 800, and 900 can be used.
font-style	The style of the font	normal, italic, oblique
text-decoration	Determines whether text is underlined. This style is most often applied to hyperlinks.	The value "none" will cause a hyperlink not to be underlined in a browser that normally processes in this manner.
line-height	The spacing allowed for the line of text	It is most common to use a percentage for this value. For example, a value of 200% would double-space.
text-align	The alignment of text	center, justify, left, right
background-image	Background image on web page	url(imagename.gif) or url(imagename.jpg)

At this point, you should have a very general idea of how styles work. The next section provides practice as you try examples of creating inline, embedded, and external styles.

Using Cascading Style Sheets

This section focuses on the three common types of CSS: inline, embedded, and external. You will create practice web pages utilizing each type. Finally, some strategies for using CSS are discussed. As you work, you may want to refer to Table 9.1.

Inline Styles

Inline styles are coded as attributes on XHTML tags. The style attribute is used with a value of the properties you need to set. Each property is separated from its value with a colon (:). The following code will set the text color of a **\<h1\>** tag to a shade of red:

```
<h1 style="color:#CC0000">This is displayed as a red heading</h1>
```

If there is more than one property, they are separated by a semicolon (;). The following code sets the text in the heading to red and italic.

```
<h1 style="color:#CC0000;font-style:italic">This is displayed as a red heading in
  italic style</h1>
```

The following code example uses an inline style to set the background color to green, text color to white, text font to Arial, and text size to 14px (pixels) for the paragraph.

```
<p style="background-
color:green;color:white;
  font-face:Arial;font-size:14px">This
  paragraph is using an inline style.</p>
```

Are there different ways to configure colors using CSS?

CSS syntax allows you to configure colors in a number of ways, including hexadecimal color values, color names, and decimal color values. For example, Table 9.2 shows the syntax for setting the color of the text for a paragraph to the color red.

Table 9.2

CSS Syntax	Color Type
`p { color:red }`	Color name
`p { color:#FF0000 }`	Hexadecimal color value
`p { color:#F00 }`	Shorthand hexadecimal (one character for each hexadecimal pair)
`p { color:255, 0 0 }`	Decimal color value

The examples in this book use either Hexadecimal color value or Color name to configure colors using CSS. The color chart on the inside leaf of the back cover provides examples of the color created by hexadecimal values in the Web Color Palette.

By now you are aware that the best way to learn new coding technologies is to practice them. In this Hands-On Practice you will configure a paragraph using inline styles. The styles will specify a green background with white text using Arial font that is 24 pixels in size. A sample is shown in Figure 9.2.

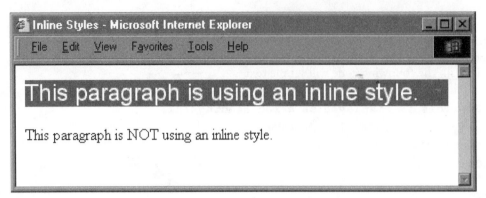

Figure 9.2 *Web page using inline styles*

Launch Notepad and type in the following XHTML:

```
<?xml version="1.0" encoding="UTF-8"?>
<!DOCTYPE html PUBLIC "-//W3C//DTD XHTML 1.0 Transitional//EN"
   "http://www.w3.org/TR/xhtml1/DTD/xhtml1-transitional.dtd">
<html xmlns="http://www.w3.org/1999/xhtml">
<head>
<title>Inline Styles</title>
</head>
<body>
<p style="background-color:#00FF00;color:#FFFFFF;font-family:Arial;
  font-size:24px">This paragraph is using an inline style.</p>
<p>This paragraph is NOT using an inline style.</p>
</body>
</html>
```

Save your file as inline.htm. Test your page in a browser and compare it with Figure 9.2. The student disk contains a sample solution at Chapter9/inline.htm. Note that the paragraph that used a style has the green background, white text, Arial font, and larger font size. The paragraph that does not use a style is displayed using default browser settings.

XHTML Elements Used with Styles. The **<div>** and **<span>** block-level tags are often used with styles to format page areas. In the next two examples you will experiment with these tags. The **<div>** tag is used to create a specially formatted division or area of a web page. It can be used to format that area and places a line break before and after the division. Use the **<div>** tag when you need to format an area that is separated from the rest of the web page by line breaks. The **<div>** tag is also useful to define an area that will contain other block-level tags (such as paragraphs or spans) within it. The **<span>** tag will format an area on the page that is *not* physically separated from others by line breaks. Use the **<span>** tag if you need to format an area that is contained within another, such as within a paragraph.

You will work with **<div>** *and* **<span>** *tags in this Hands-On Practice. Open a new file in Notepad and type in the following code to experiment with the* **<div>** *tag. This contains a sentence before the* **<div>**, *a sentence inside the* **<div>**, *and a sentence after the* **<div>**.

```
<?xml version="1.0" encoding="UTF-8"?>
<!DOCTYPE html PUBLIC "-//W3C//DTD XHTML 1.0 Transitional//EN"
   "http://www.w3.org/TR/xhtml1/DTD/xhtml1-transitional.dtd">
<html xmlns="http://www.w3.org/1999/xhtml">
<head>
<title>Inline Styles Using a Div</title>
</head>
<body>
  <div>  This sentence is NOT using an inline style.
    <div style="background-color:#00FF00;color:#FFFFFF;font-family:Arial;
     font-size:24px">This sentence is in a div using an inline style.
    </div>This sentence is NOT using an inline style.
  </div>
</body>
</html>
```

Save your page as divexp.htm and test it in a browser. Your page should look similar to the one shown in Figure 9.3. The student disk contains a sample solution at Chapter9/divexp.htm. The sentences may wrap differently, depending on your browser window size.

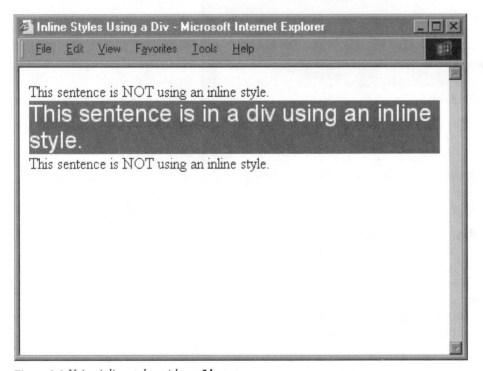

Figure 9.3 *Using inline styles with a* **<div>** *tag*

Next, you will experiment with the **<span>** *tag. Open a new file in Notepad. This web page will contain a sentence before the* **<span>**, *a sentence inside the* **<span>**, *and a sentence after the* **<span>**. *Type the following code:*

```
<?xml version="1.0" encoding="UTF-8"?>
<!DOCTYPE html PUBLIC "-//W3C//DTD XHTML 1.0 Transitional//EN"
   "http://www.w3.org/TR/xhtml1/DTD/xhtml1-transitional.dtd">
<html xmlns="http://www.w3.org/1999/xhtml">
<head>
<title>Inline Styles Using a Span</title>
</head>
<body>
  <div>This sentence is NOT using an inline style.
    <span style="background-color:#00FF00;color:#FFFFFF;
    font-family:Arial;font-size:24px">
    This sentence is in a span using an inline style.
    </span>
    This sentence is NOT using an inline style.
  </div>
</body>
</html>
```

Save your page as spanexp.htm and test it in a browser. Your page should look similar to the one shown in Figure 9.4.

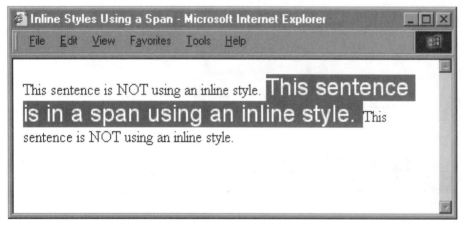

Figure 9.4 *Using Inline Styles with a* **<span>** *tag*

Compare your page to Figure 9.3, which uses the **<div>** *tag to apply the style. Note the difference in the line breaks when you use* **<span>** *and* **<div>**.

It is important to remember that inline styles apply only to the specific XHTML tag with which they are associated. Very often it is necessary to apply a style to all *instances of an XHTML tag or to a specific category or class of items on a page. This is when embedded styles can be very helpful.*

Embedded Style Sheets

Embedded styles apply to an entire web page. Embedded styles are placed within a **<style>** tag located in the header section of a web page. The opening **<style>** tag begins the embedded style rules and the closing **</style>** tag ends the area containing embedded style rules. When using the **<style>** tag, you do not need the style attribute. However, the **<style>** tag does use a type attribute that should have the value of "text/css".

The following code is an example of a **<style>** tag that uses embedded styles to set the text color, text font, and background color of the page.

```
<style type="text/css">
body { background-color: #000000;
       color: #FFFFFF;
       font-family:Arial,sans-serif;
}
</style>
```

The indentation is not required for the styles to work, but it makes the styles more readable and easier to maintain than one long row of text. The styles are in effect for the entire web page document because they were applied to the **<body>** tag using the "body" selector. Do you notice something new about the font-family property? The value of "Arial,sans-serif" will cause the browser to look for the Arial font first and use it to display the text. If the browser doesn't find Arial, whatever sans-serif font family is on the computer will be used to display the text.

Hands-On Practice 9.3

Now let's place the style in a web page and see a working example. Launch Notepad and type in the following code:

```
<?xml version="1.0" encoding="UTF-8"?>
<!DOCTYPE html PUBLIC "-//W3C//DTD XHTML 1.0 Transitional//EN"
   "http://www.w3.org/TR/xhtml1/DTD/xhtml1-transitional.dtd">
<html xmlns="http://www.w3.org/1999/xhtml">
<head>
<title>Embedded Styles</title>
<style type="text/css">
body { background-color: #000000;
       color: #FFFFFF;
       font-family:Arial,sans-serif;
}
</style>
</head>
<body>
  <h1>Hello World—Using an embedded style!</h1>
  <p>Even this sentence picks up the embedded style.</p>
</body>
</html>
```

Save your page as embedded.htm and test it in a browser. Your page should look similar to the one shown in Figure 9.5.

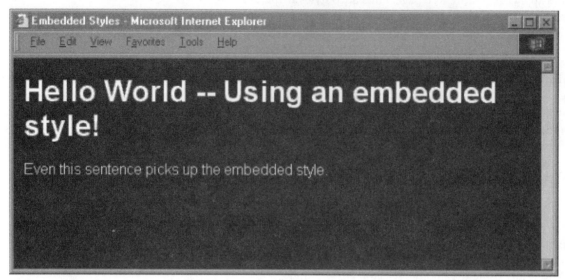

Figure 9.5 *Using embedded styles*

Let's make a small change to the style in embedded.htm. Add a new "h1" selector and set the font-style to italic and the color to red. The code is as follows.

```
<style type="text/css">
body { background-color: #000000;
       color: #FFFFFF;
       font-family:Arial,sans-serif;
}
h1     { font-style:italic;
         color: #FF0000;
}
</style>
```

Save your page as embedded2.htm and test it in a browser. Your page should look similar to the screen shot in Figure 9.6. The student disk contains a sample solution at Chapter9/embedded2.htm.

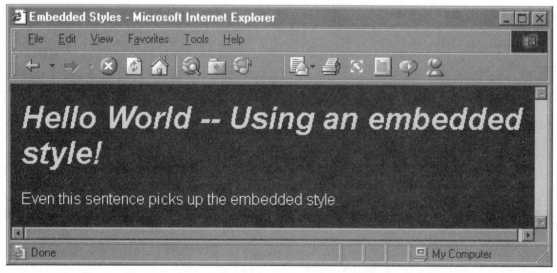

Figure 9.6 *The* **<body>** *and* **<h1>** *tags are configured with embedded styles.*

Using CSS with the class Selector. There are times when you'd like to apply a CSS rule to a certain class of elements on a web page and not necessarily tie the style to a particular XHTML tag. This is when you use the class selector. Let's create a new version of the page with a class named "new". All elements that should be treated as "new" will have red text and italic style. When setting a style for a class, a dot or period (.) in front of the class name in the style sheet. The following code contains the same body styles as the earlier example, but will create a class called "new" in a style sheet.

```
<style type="text/css">
body { background-color: #000000;
        color: #FFFFFF;
        font-family:Arial,sans-serif;
}
.new { text: #FF0000;
        font-style:italic;
}
</style>
```

The styles set in the "new" class can be applied to any XHTML element you wish. You do this by using the class attribute, such as **class="new"**. Do not write the dot in front of the class value in the XHTML tag where the class is being applied. The following code will apply the "new" class styles to an **<h1>** tag:

```
<h1 class="new">This heading is part of the new class</h1>
```

The following code will apply the "new" class styles to a **<p>** tag:

```
<p class="new">This paragraph is part of the new class</p>
```

Hands-On Practice 9.4

In this Hands-On Practice you will create a web page that uses the "new" class. Launch Notepad and type in the following code:

```
<?xml version="1.0" encoding="UTF-8"?>
<!DOCTYPE html PUBLIC "-//W3C//DTD XHTML 1.0 Transitional//EN"
    "http://www.w3.org/TR/xhtml1/DTD/xhtml1-transitional.dtd">
<html xmlns="http://www.w3.org/1999/xhtml">
<head>
<title>Embedded Styles with Class</title>
<style type="text/css">
body { background-color: #000000;
        color: #FFFFFF;
        font-family:Arial,sans-serif;
}
.new { color: #FF0000;
        font-style:italic;
}
</style>
</head>
<body>
  <h1 class="new">This heading is important.</h1>
  <h1>This heading is not important.</h1>
  <p>This paragraph is not important.</p>
  <p class="new">This paragraph is important.</p>
</body>
</html>
```

Save your file as embeddedclass.htm and test it in a browser. Your page should look similar to the image shown in Figure 9.7. The student disk contains a sample solution at Chapter9/embeddedclass.htm. Notice how the class styles are applied to the tags that are part of the class.

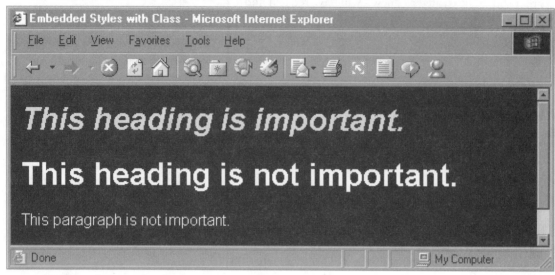

Figure 9.7 *Using classes and styles*

Using CSS with the id Selector. There are times when you'd like to apply a certain style to a particular XHTML element but not to all occurrences of that element. The id selector can be useful in this instance. For example, you can create a style for an id named "new" to differentiate any "new" areas on the web page and display those using red text. When setting a style for an id, place a hash mark (#) in front of the id name in the style sheet. The following code below will configure an id called "new" in a style sheet:

```
<style type="text/css">
#new { color: #FF0000;
}
</style>
```

The styles set in the "new" id can be applied to any XHTML element you wish by using the id attribute, **id="new"**. Do not write the "#" in front of the class value in the XHTML tag. The following code will apply the "new" class style to an **<h1>** tag:

```
<h1 id="new">Frequently Asked Questions</h1>
```

The following code will apply the "new" class styles to a **<p>** tag:

```
<p id="new">This paragraph will be displayed using styles configured in the new id</p>
```

Using CSS with an id selector is similar to using CSS with a class selector. It is common practice to use an id selector to refer to a single XHTML element and a class to refer to multiple XHTML elements.

The next type of CSS to be discussed, external style sheets, are the most versatile. They can be used to create styles that apply to an entire web site.

External Style Sheets

External style sheets are contained in a text file separate from the XHTML documents. The **<link>** tag is a self-contained tag used in the header section of an XHTML document to link the style sheet with the web page. This allows multiple web pages to link to the same external style sheet file. The external style sheet text file is saved with the file extension .css and contains only style rules—it does not contain any XHTML tags.

The advantage of this technique is that styles are configured in a single file. This means that when styles need to be modified only one file needs to be changed, instead of multiple web pages. On large sites this can save a web developer much time and increase productivity. Let's get some practice with this useful technique.

Hands-On Practice 9.5

Launch Notepad and type in the style rules to set the background-color of a page to blue and the text to white. Save it as color.css. The code is

```
body { background-color: #0000FF;
       color: #FFFFFF;
}
```

Next, link that style to a web page using the **<link>** *tag in the header section of the page. Three attributes are used with the* **<link>** *tag to associate a web page with an external style sheet: rel, href, and type. The value of the rel attribute is stylesheet. The value of the href attribute is the name of the style sheet file. The value of the type attribute is text/css, which is the MIME type for a style sheet. The XHTML code to link color.css to a web page is as follows:*

```
<link rel="stylesheet" href="color.css" type="text/css" />
```

Ready to try it out? Launch Notepad and type in the following XHTML:

```
<?xml version="1.0" encoding="UTF-8"?>
<!DOCTYPE html PUBLIC "-//W3C//DTD XHTML 1.0 Transitional//EN"
   "http://www.w3.org/TR/xhtml11/DTD/xhtml11-transitional.dtd">
<html xmlns="http://www.w3.org/1999/xhtml">
<head>
<title>External Styles</title>
  <link rel="stylesheet" href="color.css" type="text/css" />
</head>
<body>
  <p>This web page uses an external style sheet.</p>
</body>
</html>
```

Save the file as external.htm in the same folder as color.css. Test your page in a browser. Your file should look similar to the screen shot shown in Figure 9.8.

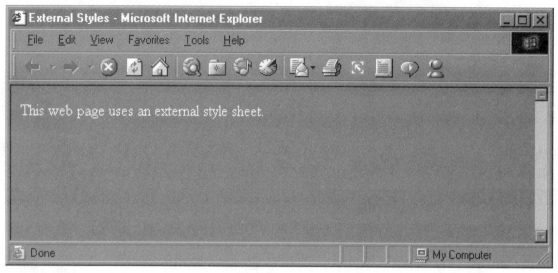

Figure 9.8 *This page links to an external style sheet.*

The color.css style sheet can be linked to any number of web pages. If you ever need to change the style of formatting, you only need to change a single file (color.css) instead of multiple files (all the web pages). As mentioned earlier, this technique can boost productivity on a large site.

Take a moment now and modify color.css so that the font-family is Arial. Be sure to save color.css. Redisplay your external.htm page in a browser. It should look similar to the page shown in Figure 9.9. The student disk contains a sample solution in the Chapter9/9.5/part2 folder.

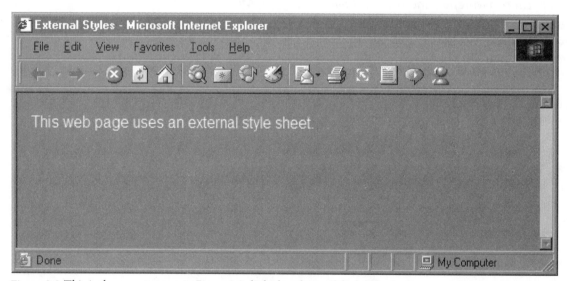

Figure 9.9 *This is the same page as in Figure 9.8, linked to the modified style sheet*

These are simple examples, but the advantage of having only a single file to update is significant for both small and large web sites.

You may have been wondering about the "cascade" in Cascading Style Sheets. The next section introduces how the external, embedded, and inline styles work together.

The "Cascade"

Figure 9.10 shows the "cascade" that applies the styles in order from outermost (external styles) to innermost (actual XHTML coded on the page). This way site-wide styles can be configured but overridden when needed by more granular (or page-specific) styles.

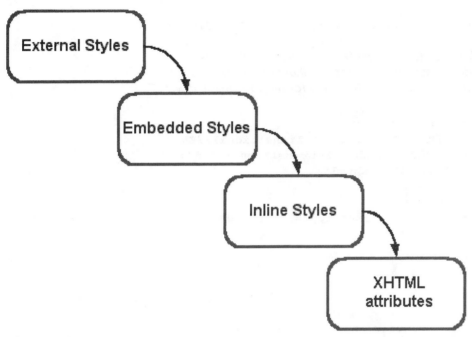

The "Cascade"

Figure 9.10 *The "cascade" of Cascading Style Sheets*

External styles can apply to multiple pages. If a web page contains both a link to an external style sheet and embedded styles, the external styles will be applied first, then the embedded styles will be applied. This allows a web developer to override global external styles on selected pages.

If a web page contains both embedded styles and inline styles, the embedded styles will be applied first, then the inline styles are applied. This allows a web developer to override page-wide styles for particular XHTML tags or classes.

Any XHTML tags will override embedded and external styles. For example, a **`<font>`** tag will override corresponding font-related styles configured for the page.

You will experiment with the "cascade" in this Hands-On Practice as you work with a web page that uses external, embedded, and inline styles. Begin by creating an external style sheet called site.css that sets the background-color of the web pages to a shade of yellow (#FFFF66) and the font-size to 24px. The code is shown below.

```
body { background-color:#FFFF66;
      font-size: 24px;
}
```

Next, create a web page called page1.htm that links to the file site.css and has an embedded style that sets the text color to blue. The file page1.htm will contain two paragraphs of text. The XHTML used to code the first paragraph will not use any styles. The XHTML used to code the second paragraph will use inline styles to set the text color to red and the font-size to 14 px. The code for page1.htm is shown as follows

```
<?xml version="1.0" encoding="UTF-8"?>
<!DOCTYPE html PUBLIC "-//W3C//DTD XHTML 1.0 Transitional//EN"
   "http://www.w3.org/TR/xhtml1/DTD/xhtml1-transitional.dtd">
<html xmlns="http://www.w3.org/1999/xhtml">
<head>
<title>External Styles</title>
   <link rel="stylesheet" href="site.css" type="text/css" />
<style>
body { color: #0000FF;
}
</style>
</head>
<body>
   <p>This paragraph does not contain inline styles.</p>
   <p style="color:#FF0000;font-size:14px">
   This paragraph contains inline styles and should be red with 14 px font</p>
</body>
</html>
```

Save both site.css and page1.htm in the same folder. Display page1.htm in a browser. Your page should look similar to the sample shown in Figure 9.11. The student disk contains a sample solution at Chapter9/page1.htm.

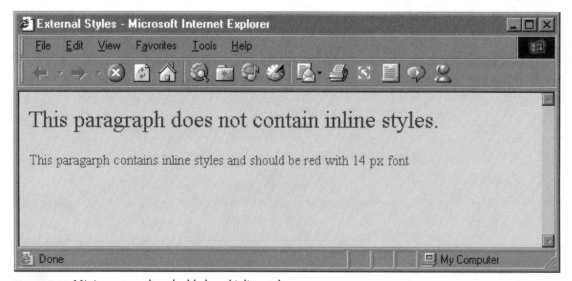

Figure 9.11 *Mixing external, embedded, and inline styles*

Take a moment to examine the page1.htm web page and compare it with its source code. The web page picked up the yellow background and 24px font size from the external style. The embedded style configured the text to be the color blue. The first paragraph in the web page does not contain any inline styles, so it inherits the style rules in the external and embedded style sheets. The second paragraph contains an inline style of red text color and 14 px font size—these settings override the corresponding external and embedded styles.

Just to prove that you can link to a single external style sheet from multiple web pages, let's try it. Launch Notepad and create a new web page called page2.htm. This page should link to the site.css file but not contain any embedded or inline styles. The code for page2.htm is as follows:

```
<?xml version="1.0" encoding="UTF-8"?>
<!DOCTYPE html PUBLIC "-//W3C//DTD XHTML 1.0 Transitional//EN"
   "http://www.w3.org/TR/xhtml1/DTD/xhtml1-transitional.dtd">
<html xmlns="http://www.w3.org/1999/xhtml">
<head>
<title>External Styles Page 2</title>
  <link rel="stylesheet" href="site.css" type="text/css" />
</head>
<body>
  <p>This is page 2</p>
</body>
</html>
```

Save your page2.htm file in the same folder as site.css and test it in a browser. Your page should look similar to the screen shot in Figure 9.12. The student disk contains a sample solution at Chapter9/ page2.htm. Notice that it picked up the background color and font size from the external style sheet, site.css.

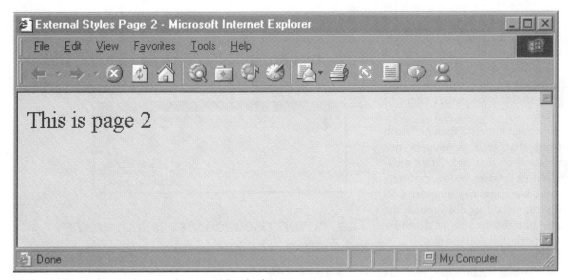

Figure 9.12 *Another page using the external style sheet*

CSS Pseudo-classes and Links

Have you ever visited a web site and found that the text hyperlinks changed color when you moved the mouse pointer over them? This is often accomplished using a special technique in CSS called a pseudo-class. The four pseudo-classes that can be applied to the anchor tag are shown in Table 9.3.

Table 9.3

Pseudo-class	When Applied
link	Default state for a link that has not been visited.
visited	Default state for a visited link.
hover	Triggered when the mouse moves over the link.
active	Triggered when the link is actually clicked.

The syntax of pseudo-classes uses a colon (:) to apply the pseudo-class to the anchor tag. The following code sample will configure text hyperlinks to initially be red. The sample also uses the a:hover to configure the links to change their appearance when the visitor places the mouse pointer over them so that the underline disappears and the color changes.

```
<style type="text/css">
a:link { color:#FF0000;
}
a:hover { text-decoration:none;
        color:#000066;
}
</style>
```

Figure 9.13 shows part of a web page at http://akiva.com that uses this technique. Note the position of the mouse pointer over the "Printable Version" link—the link color has changed and has no underline.

While some web design experts, such as Jakob Nielsen, recommend that web developers not change the default look of text links, this technique is often used. Most modern browsers (Internet Explorer 4+ and Netscape 6+) support CSS pseudo-classes. Netscape 4.x does not support the hover pseudo-class, but the technique degrades gracefully and the hyperlink is still usable.

While **<font>** tags are still used on the web, CSS and other formatting techniques such as Extensible Style Sheet Language (XSL) will be important as you increase your technical expertise. The next section discusses some strategies for using CSS right now, even before browsers uniformly support this technology.

Text links are initially configured to be red. They are underlined by default.

The "hover" pseudo-class is triggered by the mouse. The link is now blue with no underline.

Figure 9.13 *Using the hover pseudo-class*

CSS Strategies

The following are a few hints and strategies for using style sheets now—before they are universally supported.

- Always include end tags (even though browsers usually display the page, anyway) for all XHTML container tags.
- Design and code the page to look acceptable, then use style sheets for extra-special effects and formatting.
- Use style sheet components that will degrade gracefully. Check the compatibility charts and test, test, test, test, test.
- Use **<div>** and **<span>** tags to create logical page sections. Be aware that Netscape 4.x handles the **<div>** tag better than it handles the **<span>** tag.
- Use style sheets in intranet environments—you know exactly what browsers your visitors will be using.
- Consider using a browser detection script (discussed in Chapter 12) to test for a specific browser and link to the style sheet coded specifically for that browser. Think about the applications of this for user agents other than browsers, such as cell phones and PDAs. To change the presentation, check the access device (user agent) and apply the appropriate style sheet! See Figure 9.14 for a screen shot of Nokia's Demo at http://www.nokia.com/xhtmldemo/.

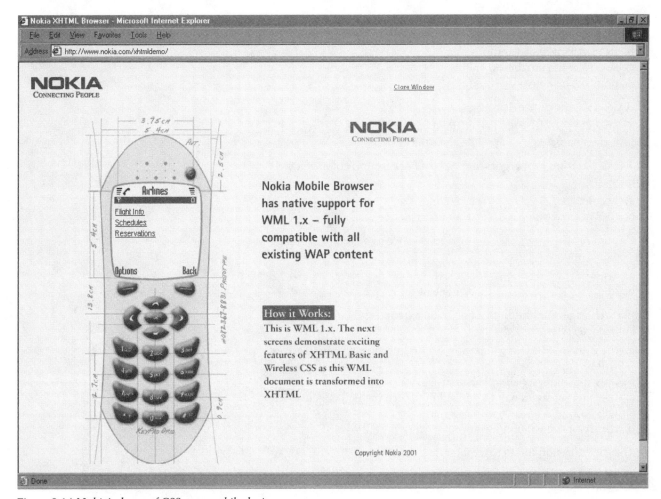

Figure 9.14 *Nokia's demo of CSS on a mobile device*

Chapter 9 Review

Summary

This chapter introduced Cascading Style Sheet rules associated with color and text on web pages. There is much more that you can do with CSS: positioning, hiding and showing page areas, formatting margins, formatting borders. As you continue your study of web development you will learn about these additional uses. To learn more now about CSS check out the tutorials at http://echoecho.com/css.htm, http://www.mako4css.com, or visit the W3C site for official specifications.

Visit the text web site at http://www.webdevfoundations.net for examples, updated information, and the links listed in this chapter.

Review Questions

Multiple Choice

1. Which type of CSS is coded in the body of the web page as an attribute of an XHTML tag?
   - a. embedded
   - b. inline
   - c. external
   - d. imported

2. CSS rules are comprised of
   - a. selectors and declarations
   - b. properties and declarations
   - c. selectors and attributes
   - d. none of the above

3. A CSS selector can be
   - a. an XHTML element
   - b. a class name
   - c. an id name
   - d. all of the above

4. The declaration property used to set the background color of a web page is
   - a. bgcolor
   - b. background-color
   - c. color
   - d. none of the above

5. Configure a(n) _____ to apply a style to a certain group of elements on a web page.
   - a. group
   - b. id
   - c. class
   - d. none of the above

6. If a web page contains both a link to an external style sheet and embedded styles,
   - a. the embedded styles will be applied first, then the external styles will be applied
   - b. only the inline styles will be used
   - c. the external styles will be applied first, then the embedded styles will be applied
   - d. the web page will not display

7. The file extension for an external style sheet is
   - a. ess
   - b. css
   - c. htm
   - d. No file extension is necessary.

8. The _____ tag is used to associate a web page with an external style sheet.

   a. `<target>`   c. `<include>`

   b. `<a>`   d. `<link>`

9. Which of the following configures a background image called sand.gif for a web page using CSS?

   a. `body {background-image:url(sand.gif); }`

   b. `document {background:sand.gif; }`

   c. `body {background:sand.gif'}`

   d. none of the above

10. Which of the following configures a class called special with red text, 24px and Arial or sans-serif font using CSS?

   a. `special { color: red; font-size:24px;`
       `font-family:Arial,sans-serif;}`

   b. `.special { color: red; font-size:24px;`
       `font-family:Arial,sans-serif;}`

   c. `.special { text:red;font-size:24px;`
       `font-family:Arial,sans-serif;}`

   d. `.#special { text:red;font-size:24px;`
       `font-family:Arial,sans-serif;}`

Fill in the Blank

11. The _____ tag is useful for creating logical areas on a web page that are embedded within paragraphs or other block formatting elements.

12. CSS is a technology that is _____ supported by browsers.

13. CSS eliminates the need for the _____ tag.

14. The _____ tag is useful for creating areas on a web page that are physically separated from other areas.

15. CSS was first proposed as a standard by the W3C in _____.

Apply Your Knowledge

1. **Predict the Result.** Draw and write a brief description of the web page that will be created with the following XHTML code:

```
<?xml version="1.0" encoding="UTF-8"?>
<!DOCTYPE html PUBLIC "-//W3C//DTD XHTML 1.0 Transitional//EN"
   "http://www.w3.org/TR/xhtml1/DTD/xhtml1-transitional.dtd">
<html xmlns="http://www.w3.org/1999/xhtml" >
<head>
<title>Predict the Result</title>
<style type="text/css">
body { background-color:#000066;
       color:#CCCCCC;
       font-family:Arial,sans-serif;
       font-size:12px;
}
h1 { background-color:#FFFFFF;
     color:#000066;
     font-size:20px;
}
```

continues

```
a:link { color:#FFFF66;
}
.footer { font-size:10px;
              font-style:italic;
}
</style>
</head>
<body>
  <div align="center">
    <h1>Trillium Technologies</h1>
    <br />
    <p>Home <a href="about.htm">About</a> <a href="services.htm">Services</a>
    </p>
  </div>
    <p>Our professional staff takes pride in its working relationship with our
    clients by offering personalized services that listen to their needs, develop
    their target areas, and incorporate these items into a well presented web site
    that works.</p>
    <p> </p>
    <p> </p>
  <div align="center">
    <p class="footer">Contact <a href="mailto:web@trilliumtechnologies.biz">
      web@trilliumtechnologies.biz</a>
    <br />
    Copyright &copy; 2003 Trillium Technologies</p>
  </div>
</body>
</html>
```

2. **Fill in the Missing Code.** This web page should be configured so that
   the background and text colors have good contrast. The **<h2>** tag
   should use Arial font. Some CSS properties and values, indicated by
   "_", are missing. Some XHTML tags, indicated by "<_>", are missing.
   Fill in the missing code.

```
<?xml version="1.0" encoding="UTF-8"?>
<!DOCTYPE html PUBLIC "-//W3C//DTD XHTML 1.0 Transitional//EN"
   "http://www.w3.org/TR/xhtml1/DTD/xhtml1-transitional.dtd">
<html xmlns="http://www.w3.org/1999/xhtml" >
<head>
<title>Trillium Technologies</title>
<style type="text/css">
body { background-color: #0066CC;
      color: "_";
}
h2 { "_":"_"
}
<_>
<_>
<body>
  <h2>Trillium Technologies</h2>
  <p> Our professional staff takes pride in its working relationship with our clients
      by offering personalized services that listen to their needs, develop their
      target areas, and incorporate these items into a well presented web site that
      works.
  </p>
</body>
</html>
```

3. **Find the Error.** Why won't this page display?

```
<?xml version="1.0" encoding="UTF-8"?>
<!DOCTYPE html PUBLIC "-//W3C//DTD XHTML 1.0 Transitional//EN"
    "http://www.w3.org/TR/xhtml1/DTD/xhtml1-transitional.dtd">
<html xmlns="http://www.w3.org/1999/xhtml" >
<head>
<title>Trillium Technologies</title>
<style type="text/css">
body { background-color:#000066;
       color:#CCCCCC;
       font-family:Arial,san-serif;
       font-size:12px
}
<style>
</head>
<body>
  <h2>Trillium Technologies</h2>
  <p> Our professional staff takes pride in its working relationship with our clients
      by offering personalized services that listen to their needs, develop their
      target areas, and incorporate these items into a well presented web site that
      works.
  </p>
</body>
</html>
```

Hands-On Exercises

1. **Practice writing CSS.**
   a. Write the XHTML for a large heading that uses inline styles to configure the background color of red and the text color of white.
   b. Write the XHTML and CSS code for an embedded style sheet that configures a background color of white and a text color of green.
   c. Write the CSS code for an external style sheet that configures the text to be brown, 14px in size, and in the Arial, Verdana or a sans-serif font.
   d. Write the XHTML and CSS code for an embedded style sheet that configures a class called "new" that is bold and shown in italics.
   e. Write the XHTML and CSS code for an embedded style sheet that configures links without underlines; background color of white; text color of black; is in the Arial, Helvetica, or sans-serif font; and has a class called "new" that is bold and italic.
   f. Write the CSS code for an external style sheet that configures a page background image of parchment.gif; text color of #000099; is in the Arial, Helvetica, or sans-serif font; and an id called "new" that is bold and italic.

2. **Experiment with external style sheets.** In this exercise you will create two external style sheet files and a web page. You will experiment with linking the web page to the external style sheets and note how the display of the page is changed.
   a. Create an External Style Sheet (call it format1.css) to format as follows: document background color of white, document text color of #000099, and document font family of Arial, Helvetica, or sans-serif. Hyperlinks should have a background color of grey (#CCCCCC). **<h1>** elements should use Times New Roman font with red text color.

b. Create an external style sheet (call it format2.css) to format as follows: document background color of yellow, document text color of green. Hyperlinks should have a background color of white. **<h1>** elements should use Times New Roman font with white background color and green text color.

c. Create a web page about your favorite movie that displays the movie name in a **<h1>** tag, a description of the movie in a paragraph, and an unordered (bulleted) list of the main actors and actresses in the movie. The page should also have a hyperlink to a web site about the movie. Place an e-mail link to yourself on the web page. Do not use any **<font>** tags in the web page. This page should link to the format1.css file. Save the page as moviecss1.htm. Be sure to test your page in more than one browser. Hand in printouts of format1.css, the movie.htm source code (print in Notepad) and the browser display of your moviecss1.htm.

d. Modify the moviecss1.htm page to link to the format2.css external style sheet instead of the format1.css file. Save the page as moviecss2.htm and test it in a browser. Notice how different the page looks! Hand in printouts of format2.css, the moviecss2.htm source code (print in Notepad), and the browser display of your moviecss2.htm.

3. **Practice with external style sheets.** In this exercise you will create two web pages that link to the same external style sheet. After modifying the configuration in the external style sheet, you will test your pages again and find that they automatically pick up the new style configuration. Finally, you will add an inline style to one of the pages and find that it takes effect and overrides the external style.

a. Create a web page that includes a table listing at least three advantages of utilizing CSS. The text "CSS Advantages" should be contained within **<h1>** tags. This page should include a hyperlink to the W3C web site. Write the XHTML code so that one of the advantages is configured to be a class called "important". Place an e-mail link to yourself on the web page. Do not use any **<font>** tags in the web page. The web page should use the external style sheet called ex3.css. Save the page as advantage.htm.

b. Create a web page that includes a table listing at least three disadvantages of utilizing Cascading Style Sheets. The text "CSS Disadvantages" should be contained within **<h1>** tags. This page should include a hyperlink to the W3C web site. Write the XHTML code so that one of the disadvantages is configured to be a class called "important". Place an e-mail link to yourself on the web page. Do not use any **<font>** tags in the web page. The web page should use the external style sheet called ex3.css. Save the page as disadvantage.htm

c. Create an external style sheet (call it ex3.css) to format as follows: document background color of white, document text color of "#000099" and document font family of Arial, Helvetica, or sans-serif. Hyperlinks should have a background color of gray (#CCCCCC). **<h1>** elements should use Times New Roman font with black text color. The "important" class should use red italic text.

d. Launch a browser and test your work. Display the advantage.htm page. It should have used the formatting configured in ex3.css. If it did not, verify the syntax used in ex3.css and see the note below about Netscape and the **\<td>** element. Modify the web page and/or the css file until your page displays as requested. Display the disadvantage.htm page. It should have also used the formatting configured in the ex3.css file. Create printouts of ex3.css, advantage.htm, and disadvantage.htm source code (print in Notepad), the browser display of advantage.htm, and the browser display of disadvantage.htm. Label these printouts Exercise 3d.

Note: With some versions of Netscape, the **\<td>** tag does not properly inherit the styles set for a **\<body>** tag. One work-around is to apply the same styles to the **\<td>** tag as to the **\<body>** tag.

```
body,td {background-color: white;
… additional styles here …
}
```

e. Change the configuration of the external style sheet (ex3.css) to use a document background color of black, document text color of white, and **\<h1>** text color of gray (#CCCCCC). Save the file. Launch a browser and test the advantage.htm and disadvantage.htm pages. Notice how they each pick up the styles from the external style sheet. Create printouts of the advantage.htm and disadvantage.htm browser display and label them as Exercise 3e.

f. Modify the advantage.htm file to use an inline style. The inline style should be applied to the **\<h1>** tag and configure it to have red text. Save the advantage.htm page and test in a browser. Notice how the **\<h1>** text color specified in the style sheet is overridden by the inline style. Print the browser display of advantage.htm and label it as Exercise 3f.

Each of these case studies will continue throughout most of the text. In this chapter CSS is implemented in the web sites.

A. JavaJam Coffee House

See Chapter 2 for an introduction to the JavaJam Coffee House case. Figure 2.20 shows a site map for the JavaJam web site. The pages were created in earlier chapters. You will use the existing web site as a start while you create a new version that uses an external style sheet.

Hands-On Practice Case

1. Create a folder called javajamcss. Copy all the files from your javajam folder into the javajamcss folder.

2. Open each web page (index.htm, menu.htm, performances.htm, and jobs.htm) using Notepad and perform the following edits: Remove the attributes from the **<body>** tag; delete **<font>** and **</font>** tags; and add a link to an external style sheet called java.css. Save each file in the javajamcss folder.

3. The goal of this case study is to recreate the look of your page using styles (not using any **<font>** tags). Take a few moments to examine the XHTML of the original JavaJam pages (in your javajam folder) and jot down the formatting used on the pages, such as background color and font attributes. Notice that different font sizes are used for the text that displays the address and the text that displays the footer. Look for other configuration differences. Here are some hints: The document background color is #999966; the document text color is black; and the document font-family is set to Arial, Helvetica, and sans-serif. Note that if your pages use tables you may also have to apply these styles to the **<td>** tag (see Hands-On Exercise 3d). You may need to create classes (such as "address" or "footer") to apply font sizes. You may also need to apply styles to tags such as **<h1>** or **<li>**. Use Notepad to create an external style sheet called java.css that performs these configurations and any others that you may have noticed as you analyzed your pages. You may be thinking—it would have been better to do this before the pages were created. That's the advantage of doing analysis and design before the production of web pages. Save the java.css file in the javajamcss folder.

4. Launch a browser and test the pages in the javajamcss folder. Compare them to the original pages in the javajam folder. Modify your java.css file as needed to configure your pages. Be sure to test in more than one browser.

5. Experiment with modifying the java.css file. Change the page background color, the font family, and so on. Test your pages in a browser. Isn't it amazing how a change in a single file can affect multiple files when external style sheets are used?

B. Fish Creek Animal Hospital

See Chapter 2 for an introduction to the Fish Creek Animal Hospital case. Figure 2.23 shows a site map for the Fish Creek web site. The pages were created in earlier chapters. You will use the existing web site as a start while you create a new version that uses an external style sheet.

Hands-On Practice Case

1. Create a folder called fishcreekcss. Copy all the files from your fishcreek folder into the fishcreekcss folder.

2. Open each web page file in the fishcreekcss folder (index.htm, menu.htm, performances.htm, and jobs.htm) using Notepad and perform the following edits: remove the attributes from the **<body>** tag; delete **<font>** and **</font>** tags; and add a link to an external style sheet called fishcreek.css. Save each file in the fishcreekcss folder.

3. The goal of this case study is to recreate the look of your page using styles (not using any **<font>** tags). Take a few moments to examine the XHTML of the original Fish Creek pages (in your fishcreek folder) and jot down the formatting used on the pages such as background color and font attributes. Notice that different font sizes are used for the text that displays the hyperlinks and the page footer. Look for other configuration differences. Here are some hints: The document background color #6699FF; the document text is white; and the document font-family is set to Arial, Helvetica, sans-serif. Note that if your pages use tables you may also have to apply these styles to the **<td>** tag (see Hands-On Exercise 3d). You may need to create classes ("footer") to apply font sizes or other formatting. You may also need to apply styles to tags such as **<dt>**. Use Notepad to create an external style sheet called fishcreek.css that performs these configurations and any others that you may have noticed as you analyzed your pages. You are probably thinking—it would have been better to do this before the pages were created. That's the advantage of doing analysis and design before the production of web pages. Save the fishcreek.css file in the fishcreekcss folder.

4. Launch a browser and test the pages in the fishcreekcss folder. Compare them to the original pages in the fishcreek folder. Modify your fishcreek.css file as needed to configure your pages. Be sure to test in more than one browser.

5. Experiment with modifying the fishcreek.css file. Change the page background color, the font family, font color, and so on. Test your pages in a browser. Notice that multiple pages display differently because they link to the single file (fishcreek.css) that configures their formatting.

C. Pete the Painter

See Chapter 2 for an introduction to the Pete the Painter Case. Figure 2.26 shows a site map for the Pete the Painter web site. The pages were created in earlier chapters. You will use the existing web site as a start while you create a new version of this web site that uses an external style sheet.

Hands-On Practice Case

1. Create a folder called paintercss. Copy all the files from your painter folder into the paintercss folder.

2. Open each web page file in the paintercss folder (index.htm, services.htm, estimate.htm, and testimonials.htm) using Notepad and perform the following edits: Remove the attributes from the **<body>** tag; remove the bgcolor attribute from the **<td>** tags; delete **<font>** and **</font>** tags; and add a link to an external style sheet called painter.css. Save each file in the paintercss folder.

3. The goal of this case study is to recreate the look of your page using styles (not using any **<font>** tags). Take a few moments to examine the XHTML of the original Pete the Painter pages (in your painter folder) and jot down the formatting used on the pages such as document background color, table cell background color, and font attributes. Notice that different font sizes are used for the text that displays the footer. Note that different font faces are used for the table cells that have a background color configured. Look for other configuration differences. Here are some hints: The document background color is white; the document text color is black; and document font-family is set to Arial, Helvetica, sans-serif. Note that if your pages use tables you may also have to apply these styles to the **<td>** tag (see Hands-On Exercise 3d). You may need to create classes (such as "footer" or "heading") to configure a special font size, font family, or background color for certain page areas. Use Notepad to create an external style sheet called painter.css that performs these configurations and any others that you may have noticed as you analyzed your pages. Again, you may be thinking it would have been better to do this before the pages were created. That's the advantage of doing analysis and design before the production of web pages. The painter.css file should be saved in the paintercss folder.

4. Launch a browser and test the pages in the paintercss folder. Compare them to the original pages in the painter folder. Modify your painter.css file as needed to configure your pages. Be sure to test in more than one browser.

5. Experiment with modifying the painter.css file. Change the page background color, the font family, and so on. Test your pages in a browser. Notice how a change in a single file can affect multiple files when external style sheets are used.

Web Research

A. This chapter introduced using CSS to configure web pages. Use a search engine to search for CSS resources. Here are two resources to help you get started:

- http://www.w3.org/Style/CSS/
- http://www.webreview.com/style/css1/charts/mastergrid.shtml

Create a web page that provides a list of at least five CSS resources on the web. For each CSS resource provide the URL, web site name, and a brief description. Your web page should contain a table and use color. Place your name in the e-mail address at the bottom of the web page. Print both the source code (from Notepad) and the browser view of your web page.

B. There is still much for you to learn about CSS. A great place to learn about web technology is on the Web itself. Use a search engine to search for CSS tutorials. Here are a few resources to get you started:

- http://www.echoecho.com/css.htm
- http://www.mako4css.com
- http://www.htmlgoodies.com/beyond/css.html

Choose a tutorial that is easy to read. Select a section that discusses a CSS technique that was not covered in this chapter. Create a web page that uses this new technique. The web page should provide the URL of your tutorial, the name of the web site, and a description of the new technique you discovered. Place your name in the e-mail address at the bottom of the web page. Print the external style sheet (if you used one), the web page source code (from Notepad), and the browser view of your web page.

Chapter Review Answers

1. b

2. a

3. d

4. b

5. c

6. c

7. b

8. d

9. a

10. b

11. `<span>`

12. not uniformly

13. `<font>`

14. `<div>`

15. 1996

Chapter 10

Web Media

*T*he saying goes, "A picture is worth a thousand words." You already are aware that graphics help to make web pages compelling. This chapter introduces other types of media, including audio, video, and streaming media. Appropriate movies and sounds on your web pages can make them more interesting and informative. Sources of these media types, the XHTML code needed to place the media on a web page, and suggested uses of the media are discussed.

Learning Outcomes

In this chapter, you will learn about:

▶ **Helper applications and plug-ins**

▶ **Audio file types and how to obtain them**

▶ **Adding sound to a web page**

▶ **Video file types and how to obtain them**

▶ **Adding video to a web page**

▶ **Streaming media**

Helper Applications and Plug-ins

Web browsers are designed to display web pages and GIF, JPG, and PNG images, among others. When the media is not one of these types, the browser searches for a **plug-in** or **helper application** configured to display the file type. If it cannot find a plug-in or helper application on the visitor's computer, the web browser offers the visitor the option saving the file to their computer. The visitor may have a program that can open the file or the visitor will simply not be able to experience the media file. This could be disappointing or frustrating to a web page visitor. In order to provide your web page visitors with a good experience at your site, use media files that are supported by the most common helper applications and plug-ins (more on this later).

A helper application is a program that can handle a particular file type (such as .wav or.mpg) to allow the user to open the special file. The helper application runs in a window separate from the browser. A newer and more common method is for the browser to invoke a plug-in application. The plug-in can run directly in the browser window so that the visitor can open media objects directly into the web page.

The most commonly used plug-ins for video and audio media include:

- RealOne Player (http://real.com)
- Windows Media Player (http://www.microsoft.com/windows/windows media/download/default.asp) or visit http://microsoft.com and search for "Media Player"
- Apple QuickTime (http://www.apple.com/quicktime/download/) or visit http://www.apple.com and search for QuickTime

You may be surprised at the number of plug-ins that exist. Netscape provides a list of plug-ins used with its browser at http://home.netscape.com/plugins/index.html. Most plug-ins are free and can be easily downloaded and installed. As a web developer one of your goals should be usability. Some visitors will simply leave your page if you require them to download and install a new plug-in. Try sticking with audio and video files that use the most popular plug-ins—your visitors probably already have them.

Sounds can be used to set a mood for a web site. They can also be used to provide additional information—an explanation of an image, a message from the company's chief executive officer, the pronunciation of a word, and so on. The next section discusses types of audio files used on the Web.

What about the Adobe Acrobat and Macromedia Flash Player plug-ins?

The Adobe Acrobat plug-in displays PDF document files. This is a very common plug-in for documents and white papers on the Web. The Macromedia Flash Player plug-in displays .swf (Flash) format files. These can contain audio and animation along with interactivity and are discussed in Chapter 12.

Audio File Types

The following file extensions are commonly used to designate audio files.

- **.WAV (Wave file).** This format was originally created by Microsoft. It is a standard on the PC platform but is also supported by Macs.
- **.AIFF (Audio Interchange File Format).** This is one of the most popular audio file formats on the Mac platform. It is also supported on the PC platform (use the extension .aif).
- **.MID (Musical Instrument Digital Interface—MIDI).** These files contain instructions to recreate a musical sound rather than a digital recording of the sound itself. The advantage of this concise format is small file size, but the disadvantage is the limited number of types of sounds that can be reproduced.

- **.AU (Sun UNIX sound file).** This is an older type of sound file that generally has poorer sound quality than the newer audio file formats. It only uses 8-bit samples instead of the 16-bit samples used by some of the newer audio file types.
- **.MP3 (MPEG-1 Audio Layer-3).** This sound file uses an advanced compression algorithm that results in the MP3 file being about one twelfth the size of the original audio file. The MP3 technology standards were developed under the sponsorship of the Motion Picture Experts Group (MPEG), http://www.mpeg.org/MPEG/index.html.

Obtaining Audio Files

There are a number of ways that you can obtain audio files. You could record your own sounds, download sounds or music from a free site, record music from a CD, or purchase a CD of sounds. There are some ethical issues related to using sounds and music created by others.

 You may only publish sounds or music that you have created yourself or that you have obtained the rights (sometimes called a *license)* to publish.

The Windows and Mac operating systems contain audio recording utilities. You need a sound card and microphone. If you are using Windows, launch the Sound Recorder application by selecting Start, Programs, Accessories, Entertainment, Sound Recorder. This will allow you to create and edit sound files. As you can see in Figure 10.1, the controls are similar to those on a tape recorder.

Figure 10.1 *Windows Sound Recorder*

The recording process will be similar for other operating systems. If the built-in application is too tame for you, consider investigating the commercial software that is available to edit media. Sonic Foundry (http://www.sonicfoundry.com) provides the software tools needed for the entire digital media production process, from content creation through final delivery. Other products can be found by searching for audio and video editing software on the Web.

If you are wondering how to create an MP3 sound file, the process is a little more complex. First, you use a program called a **ripper** to copy a selection from a CD onto your hard drive in a .wav file format. Then you use another program called an **encoder** to convert the .wav file to an MP3 file. There are applications such as Media Box (http://www.e-soft.co.uk/) or Audio MP3 Maker (http://www.share2.com/mp3maker/) that combine the ripper and encoder into a single program. Copyright and licensing are discussed later in this section.

A commercial CD can only be copied for personal use and not for publishing to the Web. Contact the owner of the copyright to request permission to use the music.

There are many sources of audio files on the web. Some offer free files, such as Design Gallery Live (http://dgl.microsoft.com/) or FreeAudioClips.com (http://www.freeaudioclips.com/). Others, like SoundRangers (http://www.soundrangers.com/), may offer one or two free sounds but are ultimately in the business of selling sound tracks and CDs. An interesting resource for free sound is at the Flash Kit site (http://www.flashkit.com); click on the "Sound Loops" link. While this site is intended for Macromedia Flash developers, the sound files can be used without Flash. The AltaVista search engine (http://altavista.com), offers specific searches for both audio and video files.

Before you publish a media file on the Web, be sure to obtain the rights to use it from the creator or the copyright owner.

Audio files can be quite large and it is important to be aware of the amount of time required to download them for play. If you decide to use an audio file on a web page, make it as brief as possible. If you are recording your own audio files, be aware that the sampling rate and bit depth will affect the file size. A **sampling rate** is a value related to the number of digital sound samples taken per second when the sound is recorded. It is measured in kilohertz (KHz). Common sampling rates vary from 8 KHz (AM radio quality sound or sound effects) to 11.025 KHz (most music) to 55.1 KHz (music CD quality sound). As you would expect, a sound recorded at 55.1 KHz has a much larger file size than a sound recorded at 8 Khz. Bit depth or resolution is another factor in audio file size. A sound recorded with 8-bit resolution (useful for a voice or other simple sounds) will have a smaller file size than a sound recorded using 16-bit resolution (music CD quality).

Now that you've got a sound or music file, what can you do with it? You could play an audio file as a background sound when the page loads. Or you could allow your web page visitors to choose whether they want to listen to a sound. The XHTML code used to work with audio files is discussed in the next few sections.

Using Sound on a Web Page

One method to give your web page visitors access to a sound is to create a simple hyperlink that references the sound file. The XHTML code to link to a sound file called ringing.wav is

```
<a href="ringing.wav" title="Hear a telephone ring.">telephone ringing</a>
```

If your web site visitor clicks on the link, the plug-in for .wav files that is installed on his or her computer (probably RealOne Player, Windows Media Player, or QuickTime) will display. Your web page visitor can then use the plug-in to play the sound.

A more sophisticated way to include sound on your page is to embed the sound in the page and optionally display a control panel for the sound. The **<embed>** tag is usually used for this even though it is not part of the W3C XHTML 1.0 specification. The W3C XHTML 1.0 specification provides the **<object>** tag as a means to embed audio and other file types in a web page. Examples of both tags are provided in this section. Because browser support of the **<embed>** tag is non-standard, you should test embedded files on the browsers and platforms your target audience will be using.

The <embed> Tag

The **<embed>** tag can be used to place sound and other media in a web page. It is a self-contained tag and does not have a corresponding closing tag. Table 10.1 lists the attributes of the **<embed>** tag when it applies to media files.

Table 10.1 *Attributes of Media* **<embed>** *Tags*

Attribute	Value	Usage
src	Valid file name, name of media file	Required. Provides the name of the file to be played.
controls	"console", "smallconsole", "playbutton", "pausebutton", "stopbutton", "volumelever"	Optional. Configures the appearance of the media control console.
width	Numeric, number of pixels	Optional. Configures the width of media control console.
height	Numeric, number of pixels	Optional. Configures the height of media control console.
autostart	"true", "false"	Optional. Determines if the media will play automatically when the page is loaded. If omitted, media does not automatically play.
loop	Numeric value or "true" for continuous play (may not be uniformly supported)	Optional. Repeats the media file.
align	"baseline" (default), "left", "right", "center", "top"	Optional. Aligns the media control console.
hidden	"true"	Optional. Hides the default media console.

In the following XHTML code, the **<embed>** tag configures the web page to show a small console that can be used to control the sound. Because autostart is set to false, the sound does not play immediately when the page is loaded, it plays only when the web page visitor uses the console to start the sound.

```
<embed src="catch.wav" autostart="false" controls="smallconsole" height="25"
  width="100" />
```

Where did you get the sound file?

The sound file was found at http://flashkit.com and is used by permission of the author, Mikkel Meldgaard (mamp7@hotmail.com) who has recorded Mikkel Metal on the Echocord recording label (http://www.echocord.com/).

A web page using the example **<embed>** tag can be found on the student disk at Chapter10/audio1.htm. A screen shot is shown in Figure 10.2.

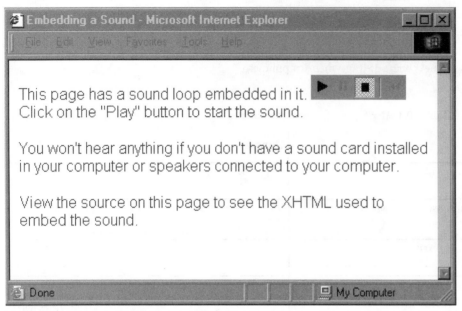

Figure 10.2 *Sample audio1.htm*

Hands-On Practice 10.1

In this Hands-On Practice you will create a web page that contains a control to let a web page visitor play a sound. Copy the catch.wav sound file from the Chapter10 folder on the student disk and save it to your floppy disk or hard drive. Launch Notepad or another text editor. Create a web page with the heading **"Playing Sounds with the Embed Tag"** *and an* <embed> *tag to play the sound file when the page loads. Use the sample code and list of* <embed> *tag attributes in Table 10.1 as a guide. Save your page as ch10page1.htm and test it in a browser. Experiment with the console, autostart, height, width, and loop attributes. Try to test your page in different browsers and browser versions.*

The <object> Tag

Another technique that can be used to place sound and other media on a web page is the **<object>** tag. It is a container tag and should be closed with an **</object>** tag. The **<object>** tag is part of the W3C standard and you should become familiar with its use. However, it is not as well supported by browsers as the **<embed>** tag. The attributes of the **<embed>** tag and the attributes of the **<object>** tag are quite similar. Table 10.2 lists the attributes of the **<object>** tag when used with media files.

Table 10.2 *Attributes of Media* **<object>** *Tags*

Attribute	Value	Usage
data	Valid file name, name of audio file	Required. Provides the name of the file to be played.
type	A valid MIME type such as audio/midi, audio/wav, etc.	Optional. Specifies the MIME type of the media file.
width	Numeric, number of pixels	Optional. Configures the width of media control console.
height	Numeric, number of pixels	Optional. Configures the height of media control console.
autostart	"true", "false". If omitted, media does not automatically play.	Optional. Determines if the media will play automatically when the page is loaded. If omitted, media does not automatically play.
loop	Numeric value, or "true" for continuous play (not uniformly supported)	Optional. Determines how many times the media file will repeat.
hidden	"true" (not uniformly supported)	Optional. Hides the default media console.

The XHTML code to use the **<object>** tag to embed a sound loop in a web page is

```
<object data="catch.wav" autostart="false" height="50" width="100"
  type="audio/wav" ></object>
```

A sample page using this **<object>** tag can be found on the textbook's student disk at Chapter10/audio2.htm. See Figure 10.3 for a screen shot.

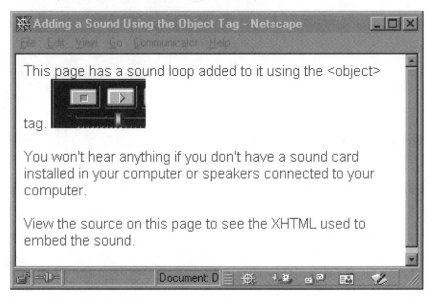

Figure 10.3 *Sample audio2.htm*

*In this Hands-On Practice you will create a web page that plays a sound when it is loaded by a browser. If you have not done so already, copy the catch.wav sound file from the Chapter10 folder on the student disk and save it to your floppy disk or hard drive. Launch Notepad or another text editor and create a web page that contains the heading **"Playing Sounds with the Object Tag"** and uses the `<object>` tag to display a console that lets the web page visitor play the sound. Use the sample code and list of `<object>` tag attributes in Table 10.2 as a guide. Save your page as ch10page2.htm and test it in a browser. Experiment with the autostart, height, width, and loop attributes. Try to test your page in different browsers and browser versions.*

Background Sounds

Sometimes web developers and clients would like a sound to play when a page loads. Use this technique with caution. If someone is listening to their favorite CD while they surf the Web, do they *really* want to hear the theme music from Gilligan's Island while your page loads? With that said, here's the lowdown on how to embed a sound in a web page.

One common technique is to use an `<embed>` tag. Although not part of the W3C XHTML 1.0 specification, `<embed>` tags are widely used. Future versions of browsers should support the use of the `<object>` tag for the purpose of the background sound. At the time this was written, the most commonly used browsers still did not support the use of the `<object>` tag to play a background sound.

The XHTML code for a background sound loop in a web page is

```
<embed src="catch.wav" autostart="true" hidden="true"
  loop="true" />
```

A sample page that uses the `<embed>` tag to hide the media console and play a background sound when the web page loads can be found on the student disk at Chapter10/audio3.htm.

What about the `<bgsound>` tag?

As you surf the Web, you may find pages that use the `<bgsound>` tag. Earlier versions of Internet Explorer did not support the `<embed>` tag and instead supported a proprietary `<bgsound>` tag that was placed in the header section of the web page. This tag is only supported by Internet Explorer and is not part of the W3C standard. The `<bgsound>` tag is no longer needed for a number of reasons. Current versions of Internet Explorer now support the `<embed>` tag and offer improved support of the `<object>` tag.

*In this Hands-On Practice you will create a web page that plays a sound when it is loaded by a browser. If you have not done so already, copy the catch.wav sound file from the Chapter10 folder in the student disk and save it to your floppy disk or hard drive. Create a web page that contains the heading **"Playing Sounds in the Background"** (configure with `<h1>` or `<h2>` tags) and uses the `<embed>` tag to start the sound when the page is loaded without displaying a console. Use the sample code and list of `<embed>` tag attributes in Table 10.1 as a guide. Save your page as ch10page3.htm and test it in a browser. Experiment with the loop attribute. Try to test your page in different browsers and browser versions.*

By now you should have a feel for some of the issues involved with adding media to a web page. If different browsers (and browser versions) offered uniform support for XHTML tags and attributes, a web developer's job would be much easier.

Another consideration is accessibility for *all* your web page visitors. Be aware that some of your visitors will not be able to hear your sounds or music. Include appropriate text descriptions of these items.

The next section introduces the use of video on web pages. Download time issues become even more important when video is included because both images and sounds are stored in the video file.

Video File Types

The following file extensions are commonly used to designate video files:

- **.MOV (QuickTime).** This format was originally created by Apple and used on the Macintosh platform. The QuickTime for Windows plug-in supports this file format on the Windows platform. Because it has universal support, this format is widely used on the Web. While other video file formats must download the entire video file before playback, QuickTime is smart enough to begin to play before the entire file is downloaded, giving the effect of streaming video.
- **.AVI (Microsoft Audio Video Interleaved file for Windows).** This was the original standard video format for PC platforms and is still widely used.
- **.MPG (MPEG).** The MPG technology standards were developed under the sponsorship of the MotionPicture Experts Group (MPEG), http:// www.mpeg.org/MPEG/index.html. This format is supported on both Windows and Mac platforms.

Obtaining Video Files

Just as with audio files, there are a number of ways that you can obtain video files, including recording your own, downloading videos, purchasing a CD that contains videos, or searching for video files on the Web (see http://altavista.com).

Be aware that there are ethical issues related to using videos that you did not create yourself. You must obtain the rights or license to publish videos created by other individuals before publishing them on your web site.

Digital cameras such as the Sony Mavica and others have the capability to take still photographs as well as short MPG movies. This can be an easy way to obtain short video clips. Digital camcorders and webcams record digital videos. Use a video capture card to access analog VHS videos. Once you have created your video, software such as Adobe Premiere (http:// www.adobe.com/products/premiere/main.html), Apple QuickTime (http:// www.apple.com/quicktime/), or Sonic Foundry Video Factory (http:// www.sonicfoundry.com/products) can be used to edit and configure your video masterpiece.

Using Video on a Web Page

The simplest method to give your web page visitors access to a video is to create a hyperlink that references the video file. The XHTML code to link to an MPG video about my dog, Sparky, is

```
<a href="sparky.mpg" title="Video of dog barking">Sparky!
  (Caution: long video download)</a>
```

If your web site visitor clicks on the link, the plug-in associated with .mpg files installed on his or her computer (probably QuickTime, Windows Media Player, or Real Player) will display. He or she will have the option of playing the video. There are other methods available for including videos directly on your web page: the **<embed>** tag, the **<object>** tag, and using the dynsrc attribute on an **<img>** tag (Internet Explorer only). All three methods are discussed next. Just as with audio files, testing in your target audience's environment is crucial to successful use of video on the web.

 Also remember to supply text descriptions of videos in order to provide accessible pages for your web site visitors.

The <embed> Tag

The **<embed>** tag can be used to place a video control just as it can be used to place a sound control on a web page. The attributes used by the **<embed>** tag were provided in the section on audio files. A sample page that uses the **<embed>** tag to display a video file is shown in Figure 10.4.

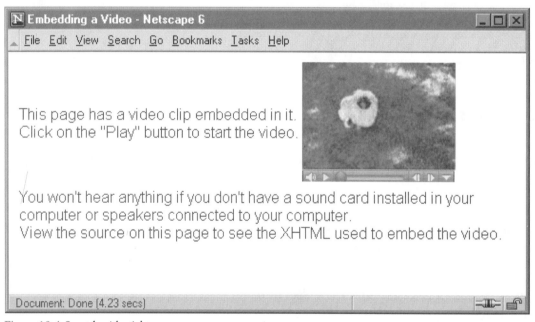

Figure 10.4 *Sample video1.htm*

The XHTML code to embed this video is

```
<embed src="sparky.mpg" autostart="false" width="160"
  height="120" />
```

A sample page using the code shown above can be found on the student disk at Chapter10/video1.htm. The values you use for the height and width should be as close to the actual size of the recorded video as possible. Don't try to stretch the video to make it larger—you won't be pleased with the results.

*In this Hands-On Practice you will create a web page that allows a visitor to play a video. Copy the sparky.mpg file from the Chapter10 folder on the student disk and save it to your floppy disk or hard drive. Launch Notepad or another text editor and create a web page that contains the heading **"Playing a Video"** and uses the* **<embed>** *tag. Use the sample code and list of* **<embed>** *tag attributes in Table 10.1 as a guide. Save your page as ch10page4.htm and test it in a browser. Try to test your page in different browsers and browser versions.*

The <object> Tag

The **<object>** tag can also be used to embed video files in web pages. It is a container tag and should be closed with an **</object>** tag. The attributes used by the **<object>** tag are listed in Table 10.2.

A sample page using the **<object>** tag to display a video can be found on the student disk at Chapter10/video2.htm. Depending on your browser plug-ins, the video may not display on this page using the **<object>** tag. (*Hint:* The sample pages were tested using the QuickTime plug-in for mpg files.) This plug-in issue can be a problem for video components. Testing with your target audience in mind as well as giving your visitors hints on the most appropriate plug-ins will help. Most videos on the Web are placed on pages using the **<embed>** tag or are streamed (more on this in the following section). The XHTML code to use the **<object>** tag to embed this video file in a web page is

```
<object data="sparky.mpg" type="video/mpeg" autostart="false" width="160"
  height="120" >A video displaying a cute Pekingese dog barking.</object>
```

Note that the text contained between the **<object>** and **</object>** tags is used to provide a text description of the video. This area will be read by some assistive technologies such as screen readers.

In this Hands-On Practice you will create a web page that uses the **<object>** *tag to play a video clip for a web page visitor. If you have not already done so, copy the sparky.mpg file from the Chapter10 folder in the student disk and save it to your floppy disk or hard drive. Launch Notepad or another text editor and create a web page that contains the heading **"Using the Object Tag to Play a Video"** and that uses the* **<object>** *tag. Use the sample code and list of* **<object>** *tag attributes in Table 10.2. Save your page as ch10page5.htm and test in a browser. Try to test your page in different browsers and browser versions.*

Internet Explorer Only Options

If you are doing web development for an intranet, you may have the luxury of knowing that all of the users will be using a certain browser, such as Internet Explorer. When this is the case, why not take advantage of a browser-specific feature? The dynsrc (dynamic source) attribute can be added to an **<img>** tag to indicate a video. A screen shot of a sample page using this technique is shown in Figure 10.5.

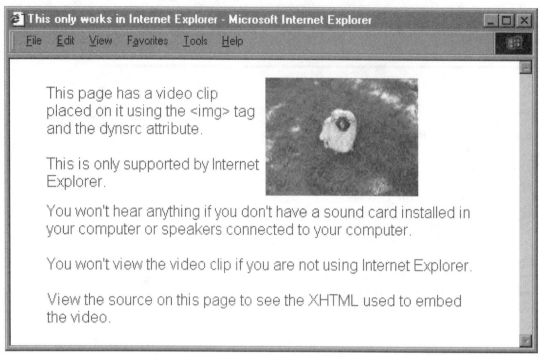

Figure 10.5 *This page uses the dynsrc attribute on the* **<img>** *tag and is only supported by Internet Explorer.*

The XHTML code for the **<img>** tag is

```
<img dynsrc="sparky.mpg" autostart="true" width="160" height="120"
   alt="Sparky Video 1.2 MB" />
```

A sample page using the code shown above can be found on the student disk at Chapter10/dynsrc.htm. While this is an interesting way to add video to your web pages, it only works with Internet Explorer, so use it with caution.

Browser Compatibility and Accessibility

At this point, you should be familiar with adding standard audio and video to a web page. The fact that both the **<object>** and the **<embed>** tags can be used to play media files is confusing for many web developers. Keep in mind that while the **<embed>** tag seems to be well supported by current browser versions, the **<object>** tag is the W3C standard. It is important to be comfortable with both. Further, not all the attributes are uniformly supported by current browser versions. This makes it critical that you test your page in the browsers (and browser versions) you expect your web page visitors to use.

Also, in order to provide a positive experience for all your web page visitors, you should provide alternate content or text descriptions of the media files you use on your web site. Applications such as Media Access Generator (MAGpie) can add captioning to videos. See the National Center for Accessible Media's web site at http://ncam.wgbh.org/webaccess/magpie/ for the most up-to-date information on the application.

Remember that with most traditional audio and video the entire file usually has to be downloaded before it can be played. The resulting lag time forces the web site visitor to wait—not the best user experience. The next section introduces streaming media, which finds a way around this issue.

Streaming Media

As previously mentioned, one disadvantage of a regular audio or video file is that the web site visitor must wait for the entire file to download before beginning to experience it. Streaming media corrects this problem—it begins to play almost immediately and uses **buffering** to capture the next portion of the file download. If the Internet is not congested, the result is a continuous playback of the audio or video file. In addition to the buffering, there can be communication between the web browser and web server—the stream is adjusted to the bandwidth available. There are three major components to the use of streaming media:

- **Authoring.** Streaming media is usually created with an authoring tool, such as RealNetworks RealProducer. This software enables you to format video and audio into a streaming format ready to be distributed by RealNetworks media servers.
- **Distribution.** The web server needs software to handle the streaming media—such as checking connection speed and adjusting the stream to the available bandwidth. One application that does this is RealNetworks RealSystem Server 8. It is available in a free version that delivers choreographed multimedia presentations—RealAudio 8, RealVideo 8, Flash animation, images, slides, and streaming text—over the Internet or corporate intranets for up to 25 simultaneous users. Certain streaming media can be created to work without a special streaming web server—in this case it streams at a preset, constant rate.

- **Playback.** Your web site visitors need a streaming media player to view streaming media. Three common players are Windows Media Player, RealNetworks RealPlayer, and QuickTime Player. For an example of streaming media, visit the CNN video news site at http://cnn.com/video. A screen shot is shown in Figure 10.6.

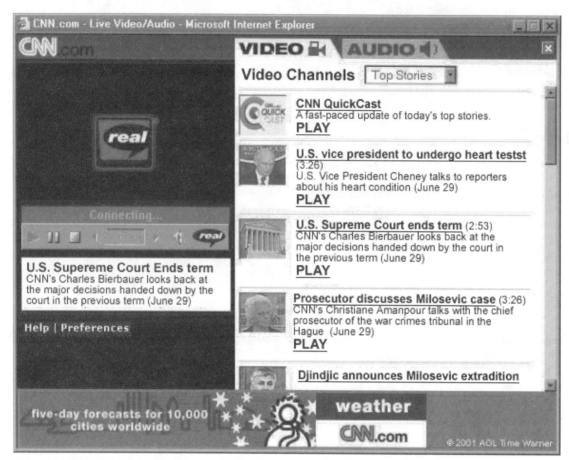

Figure 10.6 *The CNN web page about to display a streaming video*

Introduction to RealNetworks Streaming Media

The previous section discussed three components needed with streaming media: authoring, distribution, and playback. This section examines these components as they relate to RealNetworks streaming media.

Authoring

There are a number of applications created by RealNetworks that can be used to create streaming media, including RealSlideshow and RealProducer. RealSlideshow can be used to create streaming presentations of graphics, text, and audio—similar to an "in-person" slide show. RealProducer (see the screen shot in Figure 10.7) can be used to create both streaming audio and video.

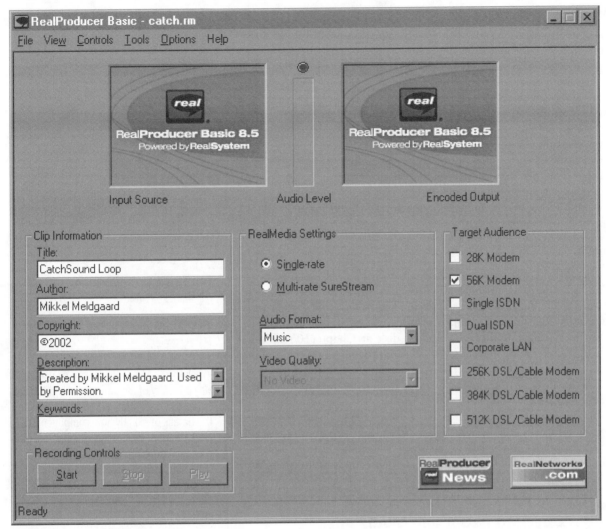

Figure 10.7 *The RealProducer Basic main window*

There are two components to every streaming media production: the media file itself (.rm file extension) and the metafile (.ram file extension). The metafile (which means "file about a file") is a text file that contains a link to the streaming media file. Web developers who want to use streaming media code a link to the metafile (not the media file). Streaming media files cannot be directly referenced by web pages because this would cause them to be downloaded in their entirety instead of being streamed. An example of the metafile is shown in Figure 10.8.

Figure 10.8 *The catch.ram metafile*

Distribution

To use a streaming media file with a web page, you must upload three files to the web server: the media file (.rm extension), the metafile (.ram extension), and the web page. There are two ways to distribute RealNetworks streaming media. The first method requires your web host provider to purchase and install RealServer from RealNetworks. RealServer can handle multiple users and monitor streaming rates of the client computers. This is needed for a commercial, heavy traffic site. Be aware that RealServer is not inexpensive and your web host provider may not want to install it.

A second option (which is free) is to stream the content using HTTP (the protocol that web browsers and web servers use to communicate). In this case, the media is transmitted at a preset, constant speed and the stream is not monitored. However, the underlying advantage of streaming media—faster playback—still exists.

Playback

Web page visitors whose browser is equipped with the RealOne Player or RealPlayer (older version) plug-in will experience streaming media. If the web site is using the RealServer, the stream will be adjusted to the bandwidth available; otherwise a constant stream will be sent. Use a browser to display the web page found on the student disk at Chapter10/real.htm. This page uses a streaming audio file, called catch.rm. Click on the "sound loop" link and the RealOne Player should launch to play the audio file. Figure 10.8 shows screen shot of the metafile (called catch.ram; the media file itself is catch.rm) in Notepad.

Now that you are more knowledgeable about media and web pages you may be wondering about copyright issues. What rights do you have as an author? What options do you have as a student? The next section discusses copyright as it applies to web pages and media files. The concept of fair use of copyrighted materials is introduced.

 Copyright Issues and Media Files

It is very easy to copy and download an image, audio, or video file from a web site. It may be very tempting to place someone else's file in one of your own projects, but that may not be ethical or lawful. Only publish web pages, images, and other media that you have personally created or have obtained the rights or license to use. If another individual has created an image, sound, video, or document that you believe would be useful on your own web site, ask permission to use the material instead of simply grabbing it. All work (web pages, images, sounds, videos, etc.) is copyrighted—even if there is no copyright symbol and date on the material.

Be aware that there are times when students and educators can use *portions* of each other's work and not be in violation of copyright law. This is called **fair use**. Fair use is use of a copyrighted work for purposes such as criticism, reporting, teaching, scholarship, or research. Criteria used to determine fair use are as follows

- The use must be educational and not commercial.
- The nature of the work copied should be factual rather than creative.
- The amount copied must be as small of a portion of the work as possible.
- The copy does not impede the marketability of the original work.

Visit http://gigalaw.com and http://www.copyrightwebsite.com for some additional insights on copyright.

FAQ

What is Windows Media Player?

Windows Media Player can be used to play a variety of media files but is designed to work with Windows Media Technologies. The details of exactly how components work together (authoring, distribution, and playback) differ from RealNetworks streaming media. However, the basic concepts remain the same—Microsoft Windows Media Technologies use both a metafile (.asx—Advanced Stream Redirector) and a media file (.asf—Active Streaming Format). There are also a number of authoring and distribution tools available to create media in Windows Media Player format. For an overview of Windows Media visit http://www.microsoft.com/windows/windowsmedia/overview/default.asp or search Microsoft's site for "streaming media".

Chapter 10 Review

Summary

This chapter introduced the XHTML techniques used to place sound, video, and streaming media files on web pages. It also discussed accessibility, usability, and copyright as they relate to media use on the Web. Visit the text web site at http://www.webdevfoundations.net for examples, updated information, and the links listed in this chapter.

Review Questions

Multiple Choice

1. .wav, .aiff, .mid, and .au are types of
   a. audio files
   b. video files
   c. both audio and video files
   d. none of the above

2. Tags that can be used to add media to a web page are
   a. the **<media>** tag
   b. only the **<object>** tag
   c. the **<audio>** and **<video>** tags
   d. the **<embed>** and **<object>** tags

3. When the **<embed>** tag is used to add media to a web page,
   a. the control console is always shown
   b. the file always plays automatically
   c. only the Windows operating system can play the file
   d. none of the above

4. The code to add a video called "welcome.mpg" to a web page is
   a. `<embed src="welcome.mpg" height="100" width="100"></embed>`
   b. `<embed src="welcome.mpg" height="100" width="100" />`
   c. `<video src="welcome.mpg" height="100" width="100" />`
   d. none of the above

5. The code to play an audio file called hello.wav as a background sound as soon as the page loads is
   a. `<embed src="hello.wav" background="true" hidden="true" loop="true"></embed>`
   b. `<embed src="hello.wav" autostart="true" hidden="true" loop="true" />`
   c. `<embed src="hello.wav" autostart="true" hidden="true" loop="true"></embed>`
   d. `<embed src="hello.wav" background="true" hidden="true" loop="true" />`

6. To provide for usability and accessibility,
   a. use video and sound whenever possible
   b. supply text descriptions of audio and video files that appear in your web pages
   c. never use audio and video files
   d. none of the above

7. Keeping in mind that it is easy to copy files from other's web sites, select the true phrase from the following:

   a. There is no copyright on the web.
   b. It is OK to use files created by others if you give them credit.
   c. You should obtain permission before using files created by others.
   d. None of the above

8. Streaming media has three components:

   a. streaming, media, web page
   b. authoring, distribution, playback
   c. bandwidth, buffer, playback
   d. none of the above

9. What does a browser use to play media such as audio and video files?

   a. stream   c. plug-in
   b. program   d. none of the above

10. What attribute is used to specify the console type for an **<embed>** tag?

   a. console   c. config
   b. controls   d. settings

Fill in the Blank

11. When recording human speech in an audio file, _____ resolution is sufficient.

12. _____ is use of a copyrighted work for purposes such as criticism, reporting, teaching, scholarship, or research.

13. When using streaming media the web page refers to the _____ which refers to the _____.

Short Answer

14. List at least two reasons not to use audio or video on a web page.

15. Describe an advantage of streaming media over standard (non-streaming) media.

Apply Your Knowledge

1. **Predict the Result.** Draw and write a brief description of the web page that will be created with the following XHTML code:

```
<?xml version="1.0" encoding="UTF-8"?>
<!DOCTYPE html PUBLIC "-//W3C//DTD XHTML 1.0 Transitional//EN"
   "http://www.w3.org/TR/xhtml1/DTD/xhtml1-transitional.dtd">
<html xmlns="http://www.w3.org/1999/xhtml" >
<head>
<title>Predict the Result</title>
<style type="text/css">
body { background-color:#000066;
       color:#CCCCCC;
       font-family:Arial,sans-serif;
       font-size:12px}
h1 { background-color:#FFFFFF;
     color:#000066;
     font-size:20px;}
```

continues

```
  </style>
  </head>
  <body>
    <div align="center">
      <h1>Sound Example</h1>
      <br />
      <embed src="bark.wav" autostart="false"
        controls="smallconsole" height="25" width="100" />
    </div>
  </body>
  </html>
```

2. **Fill in the Missing Code.** This web page should allow a visitor to play a video file called services.mpg that is 200 pixels wide and 175 pixels high. Some XHTML tags, indicated by "<_>", are missing. Some XHTML attributes, indicated by "_" are missing. Fill in the missing code.

```
<?xml version="1.0" encoding="UTF-8"?>
<!DOCTYPE html PUBLIC "-//W3C//DTD XHTML 1.0 Transitional//EN"
  "http://www.w3.org/TR/xhtml1/DTD/xhtml1-transitional.dtd">
<html xmlns="http://www.w3.org/1999/xhtml" >
<head>
<title>Trillium Technologies</title>
</head>
<body>
  <h2>Trillium Technologies</h2>
  <div>
    <p> Video Tour of Our Services</p><br />
    <object data="_" type="video/mpeg" autostart="_" width="_"
      height="_" >Video Tour of Trillium Technologies Services</object>  </p>
</body>
</html>
```

3. **Find the Error.** The sound file bark.wav has been saved in the same folder as this web page. Why doesn't this sound play when the page is loaded?

```
 <?xml version="1.0" encoding="UTF-8"?>
<!DOCTYPE html PUBLIC "-//W3C//DTD XHTML 1.0 Transitional//EN"
  "http://www.w3.org/TR/xhtml1/DTD/xhtml1-transitional.dtd">
<html xmlns="http://www.w3.org/1999/xhtml" >
<head>
<title>Sound Sample</title>
</head>
<body>
<body>
  <h1>Sparky!</h1>
  <p>
    <embed src="bark.wav" autostart="false"  hidden="true" />
  </p>
</body>
</html>
```

Hands-On Exercises

1. Practice working with media:

   a. Write the XHTML to add a video called "demo1.mpg" to a web page.

   b. Write the XHTML to add a background sound called "message.wav" to a web site. It should only play once.

   c. Write the XHTML to add a background sound called "theme.mid" to a web page that will loop repeatedly.

   d. Write the XHTML to add an audio file to a web page that can be controlled by the visitor. The audio file is called "lesson1.wav".

2. Create a web page about your favorite movie that contains one of the following: an audio file containing your review of the movie (use Windows Sound Recorder or a similar program to record your voice), an audio clip from the movie, a video clip from the movie, or an audio clip from the movie soundtrack. Place an e-mail link to yourself on the web page. Save the page as movie10.htm. Hand in printouts of both the source code (print in Notepad) and the browser display of your page.

3. Create a web page about your favorite music CD that contains either a brief audio file containing your review of the CD (use Windows Sound Recorder or a similar program to record your voice) or an audio clip from the CD. Place an e-mail link to yourself on the web page. Save the page as cd10.htm. Hand in printouts of both the source code (print in Notepad) and the browser display of your page.

4. Create a web page about a current political figure who you admire that contains one of the following: an audio file containing your thoughts about the political figure (use Windows Sound Recorder or a similar program to record your voice), an audio clip of an interview with the individual that you selected, or a brief video clip of the individual you selected. Place an e-mail link to yourself on the web page. Save the page as political10.htm. Hand in printouts of both the source code (print in Notepad) and the browser display of your page.

Web Site Case Study

Each of these case studies will continue throughout most of the text. In this chapter, you will add media to the web sites.

A. JavaJam Coffee House

See Chapter 2 for an introduction to the JavaJam Coffee House case. Figure 2.20 shows a site map for the JavaJam web site. The pages were created in earlier chapters. Use the javajamcss folder created in the Chapter 9 case study. Your task is to add a background sound to the Home page (index.htm).

Hands-On Practice Case

Copy the catch.wav sound file from the student disk in the Chapter10 folder and save it to your floppy disk in the javajamcss folder.

Launch Notepad and open the Home page (index.htm) in the javajamcss folder. Modify index.htm so that the sound file plays continuously when the page is loaded. (*Hint:* use an **<embed>** tag.) Save your page. Test your page using several browsers. You should hear the sound clip.

B. Fish Creek Animal Hospital

See Chapter 2 for an introduction to the Fish Creek Animal Hospital case. Figure 2.23 shows a site map for the Fish Creek web site. The pages were created in earlier chapters. Use the fishcreekcss folder created in the Chapter 9 case study.

You have two tasks:

1. Add a background sound to the Home page (index.htm).

2. Add a video to the Ask the Vet page (askvet.htm). See Figure 10.9 for a sample screen shot.

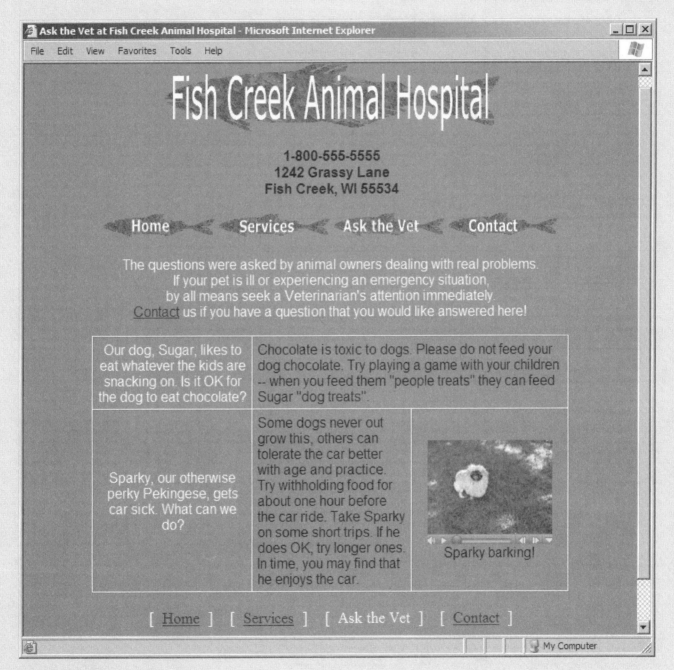

Figure 10.9 *Fish Creek Ask the Vet page*

Hands-On Practice Case

1. Add a background sound to the Home page (index.htm).

   - Copy the bark.wav sound file from the student disk in the Chapter10 folder and save it to your floppy disk in the fishcreekcss folder.

   - Launch Notepad and open the index.htm file in the fishcreekcss folder. Modify index.htm so that the sound file plays once when the page is loaded. (*Hint:* Use an **<embed>** tag.) Save your page. Test your page using several browsers. You should hear the sound.

2. Add a video to the Ask the Vet page (askvet.htm).

   - Copy the sparky.mpg video file from the student disk in the Chapter10 folder and save it to your floppy disk in the fishcreekcss folder.

   - Launch Notepad and open the askthevet.htm file in the fishcreekcss folder. Modify the questions and answers on the askthevet.htm page to display a video. in the last row of the questions and answers table. See the screen shot in Figure 10.9 for a guide. (*Hint:* You may need to adjust the columns of the table.) Use the **<embed>** tag to configure the video for display. Use the attributes and values listed in Table 10.3 on the **<embed>** tag:

Table 10.3

Attribute	Value
src	sparky.mpg
height	120
width	150
autostart	false
controls	smallconsole
align	center

   - Save your page. Test your page using several browsers.

C. Pete the Painter

See Chapter 2 for an introduction to the Pete the Painter case. Figure 2.26 shows a site map for the Pete the Painter web site. The pages were created in earlier chapters. Use the paintercss folder created in the Chapter 9 case study. Your task is to add a background sound to the Services page (services.htm).

Hands-On Practice Case

Copy the painter.wav or painter2.wav sound file from the student disk in the Chapter10 folder and save it to your floppy disk in the paintercss folder.

Launch Notepad and open the Services page (services.htm) in the paintercss folder. Modify services.htm so that the sound file plays once when the page is loaded. (*Hint:* Use an **<embed>** tag.) Save your page. Test your page using several browsers. You should hear the sound.

Web Research

A. This chapter mentioned some software applications that can be used to create and edit media files. With those as a starting point, search for more applications on the Web. Create a web page that lists at least five media authoring applications. Organize your page with a table that provides the name of the software application, the URL, a brief description, and the price. Place your name in an e-mail link on the web page. Your page should play some background music. Include the sound loop (catch.wav) from this chapter, record your own, or find an appropriate sound file on the Web. Print both the source code (from Notepad) and the browser view of your web page.

B. Issues related to copyright were discussed in this chapter. With the resources provided as a starting point, search for additional information related to copyrights and the Web. Create a web page that provides five helpful facts about copyright and the Web. Provide the URLs of the web sites you used as resources. Place a media console on the page to allow the visitors to play an audio file while they read your page. Include the sound loop (catch.wav) from this chapter, record your own, or find an appropriate sound file on the Web. Print both the source code (from Notepad) and the browser view of your web page.

Chapter Review Answers

1. a

2. d

3. d

4. b

5. b

6. b

7. c

8. b

9. c

10. b

11. 8-bit

12. Fair use

13. metafile, media file

14. Reasons not to use audio or video on web pages:
    a. Audio and video files can get quite large. A web page visitor with a dial-up connection to the Internet may not want to wait minutes for media to download.
    b. Not all web page visitors will be able to hear the audio or see the video. Some type of text description must be provided to describe the media.
    c. Adding media to web pages requires much testing to ensure cross-browser compatibility.

15. Streaming media provides a more immediate experience for the web page visitor. Instead of waiting for a long download, the audio or video can begin to play after only a small portion of it is downloaded.

Chapter 11

Promotion for Web Developers

Y ou've built it—now what can you do to attract visitors to your web site? Once you get visitors, how do you interest them in returning? Getting listed on search engines, site affiliations, and ad banners are some of the topics that are discussed in this chapter.

Learning Outcomes

In this chapter, you will learn how to:

▶ **Tell the difference between search engines and search indexes**

▶ **Describe the components of a search engine**

▶ **Design web pages that are friendly to search engines**

▶ **Request that a web site be added to a search engine**

▶ **Monitor a search engine listing**

▶ **List other web site promotion activities**

Search Engines and Search Indexes Overview

What do you do when you need to find a web site? Most people launch their favorite search engine. A recent Nielsen/NetRatings survey found that nine out of ten web users visit a search engine, portal or community site every month. These web users also revisit the sites frequently, almost five times per month.

Search engines and search indexes are a very popular way of navigating the web and finding web sites. A Consumer Daily Question Study conducted for keen.com found that when web users need an answer to a question, search engines are their top information resource. The findings indicated that search engines were used over 31 percent of the time; more than any other option (such as asking friends, reading a newspaper, etc.) to research and answer questions by participants.

Appearance in a search engine lends an aura of legitimacy to a web site. A study by NPD Group showed that consumers are five times more likely to purchase goods or services as a result of finding a site through a search engine listing than through a banner advertisement.

Getting listed in a search engine can both help customers to find your site and increase the chances that they will purchase from you. Search engine listings can be an excellent marketing tool for your business. To harness the power of search engines and search indexes (sometimes called search directories), it helps to know how they work.

Popular Search Engines and Search Indexes

According to a survey by Nielsen/NetRatings (reported at http://searchenginewatch.com/reports/netratings.html), Yahoo! (http://yahoo.com) and MSN (http://msn.com) were the two most popular sites used for searching the Web during March 2002. Of those surveyed, 29.4% used Yahoo! and 28.1% used MSN during this time. Other popular search engines include Google, AOL, Ask Jeeves, InfoSpace, AltaVista, Overture, LookSmart, Netscape, and Dogpile. Figure 11.1 contains a chart of the top five search sites reported in this survey.

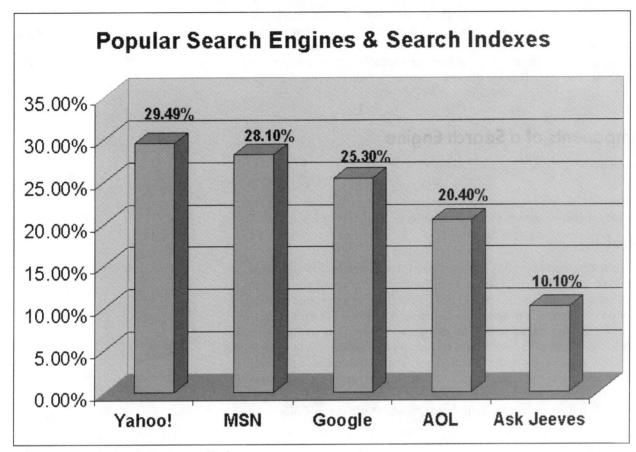

Figure 11.1 *Popular Search Engines and Indexes*

Let's take a closer look at Yahoo! (http://yahoo.com). Even though Yahoo! is usually referred to as a search engine, it is actually a search index (sometimes called a search directory). That is because each site is reviewed by an editor at Yahoo! Yahoo! maintains a hierarchical category of topics and places web site listings into these categories. When visitors use Yahoo! they have the option of immediately typing in a search term or drilling down into the hierarchy for relevant sites. When Yahoo! shows results from a search, the results are grouped as follows:

- Inside Yahoo! matches (Yahoo!'s own content)
- Category matches (Yahoo's index categories)
- Sponsor matches (paid advertisements)
- Web site matches (from Yahoo!'s index)
- Web page matches (from the Google (http://google.com) search engine database)

It is not easy to get a commercial web site listed in the Yahoo! directory. The first task is to submit your site for review. Commercial sites need to pay a fee (currently several hundred dollars) just to be reviewed by a Yahoo! editor. If the editor at Yahoo! decides that a web site has content of value and should be listed, the site is then **indexed** or placed into a category, and information on that site is stored in Yahoo!'s database. Suggestions on getting your site ready for this review appear later in this chapter. Sometimes web site owners need to improve and submit their sites multiple times before the site is listed in Yahoo!

Another search index is the Open Directory Project at http://www.dmoz.org. It contains a hierarchy of topics and sites related to each topic. In this project anyone can volunteer to be an editor and review sites. There is no cost to submit your site to the Open Directory Project. An added benefit to being listed in the Open Directory Project is that the database containing the approved sites is used by a number of search engines, including Google, Netscape and AOL.

Components of a Search Engine

Search engines have three components:

- Robot
- Database (also used by search directories)
- Search form (also used by search directories)

Robot

A **robot** (sometimes called a spider or bot) is a program that automatically traverses the hypertext structure of the Web by retrieving a web page document and following any hyperlinks on the page. It moves like a robot spider on the Web, accessing and documenting web pages. The robot categorizes the pages and stores information about the web site and the web pages in a database. While various robots may work differently, in general they access and may store the following sections of web pages: title, meta tag keywords, meta tag description, and some of the text on the page (usually either the first few sentences or the text contained in heading tags). Visit the Web Robots Pages at http://www.robotstxt.org if you'd like more details about web robots.

Database

A **database** is a collection of information organized so that its contents can easily be accessed, managed, and updated. Database management systems (DBMSs) such as Oracle, Microsoft SQL Server, or IBM DB2 are used to configure and manage the database. The web page that displays the results of your search has information from the database used by the search engine site. Some search engines, such as AOL (http://www.aol.com), iWon (http://www.iwon.com), and MSN (http://www.msn.com) use a database provided by Inktomi (http://www.inktomi.com).

Search Form

The **search form** is the component of a search engine that you are most familiar with. You have probably used a search engine many times but not thought about what goes on "under the hood." The search form is the graphical user interface that allows a user to type in a word or phrase to search for. It is usually just a text box and a submit button. The visitor to the search engine types words (called keywords) related to his or her search into the text box. When the form is submitted, the data typed into the text box is sent to a server-side script that searches the database using the keywords entered. The **search results** (also called a *result set*) is a list of information, such as the URLs for web pages, that meet your criteria. This result set is formatted in a web with a link to each page along with additional information that might include the page title, a brief description, the first few lines of text, or the size of the page. The type of additional information varies by search engine. Next, the web server at the search engine site sends the search results page to your browser for display.

The order in which the pages are displayed may depend on paid advertisements, alphabetical order, and link popularity (more on this later). Each search engine has its own policy for ordering the search results. Be aware that these policies can change over time.

The components of a search engine (robot, database, and search form) work together to obtain information about web pages, store information about web pages, and provide a graphical user interface to facilitate searching for and displaying a list of web pages relevant to given keywords. Now that you are aware of the components of search engines, let's get to the most important part—how to design your pages to promote your web site.

Designing Your Pages for Promotion

If you have followed recommended web design practices you've already designed your web site so that the pages are appealing and compelling to your target audience. How can you also make your site work with search engines? This section provides some suggestions and hints on designing your pages for search engines—a process called **search engine optimization**.

Keywords

Spend some time brainstorming about terms and phrases that people may use when searching for your site. They should be words or phrases that describe your web site or business. These terms and phrases are your keywords. Create a list of them and don't forget to add common misspellings of your keywords to the list.

Double-check the page titles (text contained between the **<title>** tags) and page headings (text contained between heading tags such as **<h1>**, **<h2>**, etc.) on your web site. Make sure the text used for your title is descriptive, includes your organization name, and also contains one or more keywords, if possible. If it is appropriate for the web page content, also include some keywords in the text contained between heading tags. Some search engines will give a higher list position if keywords are also included in a page title or headings. Do not spam keywords—that is, do not list them over and over again. The programs behind search engines become more sophisticated all the time and you can actually be *prevented* from being listed if it is perceived that you are not being honest or are trying to cheat the system.

Description

What is special about your web site that would make someone want to visit? With this in mind, write a few sentences about your web site and/or business. This description should be inviting and interesting so that a person searching the Web will choose your site from the list provided by a search engine or search directory. Some search engines will display your description in their search engine results.

At this point you have created a description of your site and a list of appropriate keywords. You might be wondering how these apply to the actual web pages. The keywords and description are placed on a web page by adding XHTML meta tags to the page header area.

Meta Tags

Meta tags are self-contained tags that are placed in the header section of a web page. They should follow the **<title>** tag. There are a number of uses for meta tags. This concentrates on their use to provide a description of the site and list of keywords for use by search engines.

The syntax of meta tags is as follows:

```
<meta name="value" content="value" />
```

The name attribute indicates the use of the meta tag. The content attribute indicates values needed for that specific use. The keywords value for the name attribute indicates that the use of the meta tag is to list keywords. The description value for the name attribute indicates that the use of the meta tag is to provide a description. For example, the keywords and description meta tags for a web site about a web development consulting firm called Acme Design could be configured as follows:

```
<meta name="keywords" content="Acme Design web
    development e-commerce ecommerce consulting
    consultation maintenance redesign Akme" />
<meta name="description" content="Acme Design,
    a premier web consulting group that specializes
    in e-commerce, web site design, web site
    development, and web site redesign." />
```

Listing in a Search Engine and Search Index

According to a recent study by The Direct Marketing Association (http://www.the-dma.org), 66% of web marketers surveyed rated search engines as the top method used to drive traffic to their sites. While very effective, it is not always easy to get listed in a search engine or search directory. Table 11.1 below shows the steps involved in submitting your site to a search engine or search directory.

What if I do not want a search engine to index a page?

Sometimes there will be pages that you do not want indexed, perhaps test pages or pages only meant for a small group of individuals (such as family or coworkers). Meta tags can be used for this purpose, also. To indicate to a search engine robot that a page should not be indexed and the links should not be followed, do not place keywords and description meta tags in the page. Instead, add a "robots" meta tag to the page:

```
<meta name="robots"
content="noindex,nofollow" />
```

Table 11.1 *Submission to a Search Engine or Search Directory*

Search Engine (such as Lycos or MSN)	Search Directory (such as Yahoo! or the Open Directory Project)
Step 1: Visit search engine site and look for the "Add site" or "List URL" link. This is usually on the home page (or about page) of the search engine. Be patient—these links are sometimes not obvious.	Step 1: Visit the search directory and follow the hierarchical listings until the page that is most suited for your site appears. Take some time choosing the most appropriate category. Look for the "Suggest a Site" or "add URL" link on the page.
Step 2: Follow the directions listed on the page and submit the form to request that your site is added to the search engine. (Sometimes there is a fee for an automatic listing, called paid inclusion—more on this later.)	Step 2. Follow the directions listed on the page and submit the form to request that your site be reviewed for inclusion in the directory. (Commercial sites must pay Yahoo! to review their web site. This does not guarantee inclusion.)
Step 3: The spider from the search engine will index your site. This may take several weeks. (Sometimes there is a fee for an express submit option that will speed this process.)	Step 3: An editor (a real person) will visit your site. This may take several weeks. Search directories such as Yahoo! and the Open Directory (http://dmoz.org) review the content of the site—only sites with worthwhile content are included.
Step 4: Several weeks after you submit your web site, check the search engine or search directory to see if your site is listed. If you are not listed, review your pages and check whether they are "friendly" to robots and display in common browsers.	

There is a trend away from free listing in search engines. The current trends are toward paying for being considered to be listed in a search engine or directory (often referred to as an *express submit* or *express inclusion*) and paying for preferential listing in search engine displays (called *sponsoring* or *advertising*). Some search engines, such as Teoma (http://ww.teoma.com), will only accept submissions from their paid subscribers. Many businesses regard payment for an express treatment or a preferential listing as another marketing expense, such as paying for a newspaper ad or a listing in the Yellow Pages.

Express Inclusion

Some search engines such as AltaVista (http://altavista.com) and LookSmart (http://looksmart.com), offer an express service for web site submission and possible inclusion. The cost for this service varies, but is $299 as of this writing. These express services guarantee quick results, some within 48 hours. However, they reserve the right not to list your submission. For example, a page that is machine-generated, contains minimal or no content, and whose sole purpose is to persuade a visitor to click on another page would not be listed. On some search engine sites, additional benefits of the express program include more frequent updates of your pages in the search engine database and the opportunity to add enhancements such as logos, icons, and custom links to your listing for a small fee. Figure 11.2 shows an example from AltaVista of a sample web site listing that has taken advantage of this service.

Welcome to LetsTravelOnline.com!

Save on all of your travel needs right now! From airline tickets to hotel reservations to entertainment and more, we have the best prices on the web!
Fare Specials: LA-Hawaii $349; New York-Paris $779 First Class
On Sale   Price Finder   Online Reservations   Contact Us   Help
URL: http://www.letstravelonline.com/ • Related pages • Translate

Figure 11.2 *Altavista.com display using custom icon and links*

Preferential Listing

Google is one search engine that recently began offering two methods of preferential listing: Premium Sponsorships, which are shown at the top of the search results, and the AdWords Program, which are listed on the right-side column of the search results. Figure 11.3 depicts a screen shot of a search for "pet supplies" that shows these preferential listings. Expect to see search engines and search directories change their preferential listing programs over time.

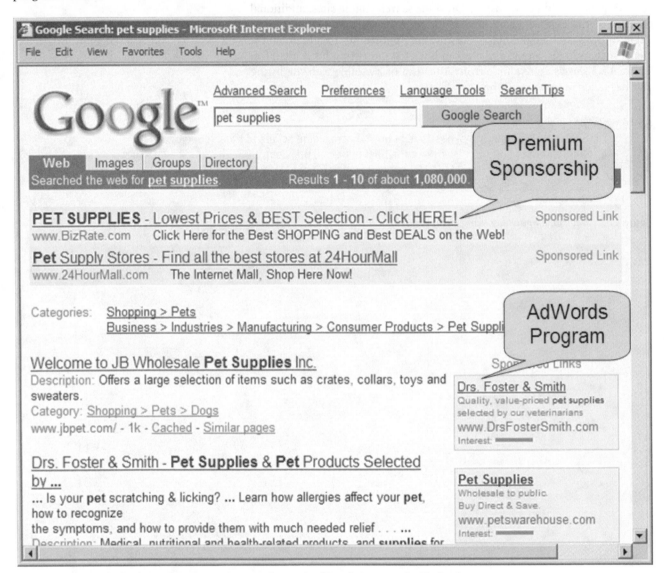

Figure 11.3 *Google display with Premium Sponsorship and AdWords Program highlighted*

There are a number of alliances between certain search engines and search directories. As mentioned earlier, Inktomi powers a number of sites (including AOL, MSN, HotBot, and NBCi). If you submit and are listed in one of these sites, your information should eventually turn up in the other search engine sites powered by Inktomi. Google powers the secondary listings (web page matches) at Yahoo!. The Open Directory Project (http://www.dmoz.org) provides directory services for a number of search engines, including Google, AOL, Lycos, and HotBot. Be warned that these alliances can change over time. However, by being aware of them, you can maximize the chances of your web site turning up when a search is performed.

Your clients will want the web site to appear instantaneously in search engines and search directories. However, it can take some time between the submission and day that the site appears in a search engine or search directory list. According to NetMechanic, it can take between four and six weeks for a web site to be listed on Lycos (http://lycos.com) or Google (http://google.com). Since four weeks on the Web is "longer than forever," a small charge for express submission or express inclusion may seem to be a justifiable business expense.

Monitoring Search Engine and Search Index Listings

As your sites get listed, it becomes important to determine which keywords are working for you. Usually you need to fine-tune and modify your keywords over time. Here are a few methods to determine which keywords work:

- **Manual checking.** Visit search engines and type in the keywords. Assess the results. You might consider keeping a record of the search engine, keyword, and page ranking.
- **Web site log file analysis.** Every visitor to your web site, including those who were referred by search engines, is recorded in your web site log. You can discover whether your keywords are successful by analyzing your log. The log is a rather cryptic text file. See Figure 11.4 for a partial log.

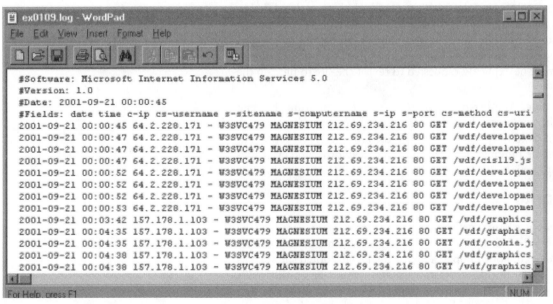

Figure 11.4 *A web site log file contains useful information but can be difficult to read.*

Web analysis software can analyze your log file and create easy-to-use charts and reports. If you have your own web site and domain name, many web host providers allow free access to the log and may even run web analysis reports as part of your monthly web hosting fee. By checking information in the log, you can determine not only what keywords are working, but which search engines your visitors are using. See Figure 11.5 for part of a log analysis report showing keywords actually used at Yahoo! to find a particular web site.

Top Search Engines with Keywords Detail			
Engines	Keywords	Keywords Found	% of Total
Yahoo	quotations	280	37.68%
	educational	182	24.49%
	education	144	19.38%
	web	83	11.17%
	background	73	9.82%
	javascript	59	7.94%
	pictures	54	7.26%
	on	36	4.84%
	quotation	31	4.17%
	java	28	3.76%

Figure 11.5 *Partial log file analysis report*

Web log analysis is a powerful marketing tool because you can determine exactly how visitors are finding your site. This lets you know which keywords are working and which are not. Perhaps with additional thought, you can add new variations of the productive keywords to your list. If you examine Figure 11.5 you will notice that "quotations" and "educational" are the most popular keywords on Yahoo! for this particular web site. The developers of this web site could add keywords related to these keywords or common misspellings of the most popular keywords. Improving the keywords may increase the number of visitors to the site. Some search engines routinely revisit sites that they have listed. Other search engines must be explicitly requested to revisit the site to pick up the new keywords.

• **Automated tools.** Another option is to purchase a program that can help you monitor your search engine positioning. Automated tools, such as WebPosition Gold (http://webpositiongold.com), can create reports of your search engine rankings, analyze and track keywords, and even submit your sites to search engines.

Link Popularity

Link popularity is a rating determined by a search engine based on the number of sites that link to a particular web site and the quality of the sites that the links are from. For example, a link from a well-known site such as Martha Stewart's site, http://marthastewart.com, would be considered a higher quality link than one from your friend's home page on a free web server somewhere. The link popularity of your web site can determine its order in the search engine results page. One way to check which sites link to yours is to analyze your log file. Another method is to visit a web site that offers a link popularity checking service (options include http://linkpopularity.com and http://linkpopularitycheck.com). These sites will run a report that checks link popularity on a number of search engines. A third method is to visit particular search engines and check for yourself. At Google and AltaVista, type "link:yourdomainname.com" into the search box and the sites that link to yourdomainname.com will be listed.

Search engines and search directories are not the only tools you can use to bring visitors to your web site. The next section takes a look at some of the other options.

Other Site Promotion Activities

There are a number of other ways you can promote your web site, including affiliate programs, banner ads, banner exchanges, reciprocal link agreements, newsletters, personal recommendations, traditional media advertising, and including your URL on all promotional materials.

Affiliate Programs

The essence of **affiliate programs** is that one web site (the affiliate) promotes another web site's products or services (the merchant) in exchange for a commission. Both web sites benefit from this association. Amazon.com reportedly began the first affiliate marketing program—and its Amazon Associate program is still going strong. By joining this program your web site can feature books with a link to the Amazon web site. If one of your visitors purchases a book, you get a commission. Amazon benefits because you have delivered an interested visitor who may purchase items now or in the future. Your site benefits from both the prestige of being affiliated with a known site such as Amazon and the potential for income from the program.

View the Commission Junction web site (http://www.commissionjunction.com) for a program that matches web sites with potential affiliate programs. Their service allows publishers (web site owners and developers) to choose from a wide range of advertisers and affiliate programs. Benefits to web developers include the opportunity to partner with leading advertisers, earn additional revenue from web site visitors or ad space, and view real-time tracking and reporting.

Banner Ads

A **banner ad** is typically a graphic image that is used to announce and advertise the name or identity of a site. Banner ads are image hyperlinks and display the site they are advertising if clicked on. You have probably seen them many times as you surfed the Web. They've been around quite some time—hotwired.com (now http://hotwired.lycos.com) introduced the first banner ad in 1994 to promote AT&T.

There is no official size for a banner ad. However, research performed by the Interactive Advertising Bureau (http://www.iab.net) reports that the standard size for a full banner ad is 468 x 60 pixels. Visit its web site for a full listing of types of ads and common sizes (http://www.iab.net/iab_banner_standards/bannersource.html). Costs charged by web sites to display your banner ad can vary. Some web sites charge by the impression (usually in terms of cost per thousand, or CPM). Others charge only for click-throughs—when the banner ad is clicked on. Some search engines sell banner ads and will display your ad on a results page for a keyword that relates to your site (for a fee, of course!). See Figure 11.6 for some timely marketing by a web site that specializes in flowers.

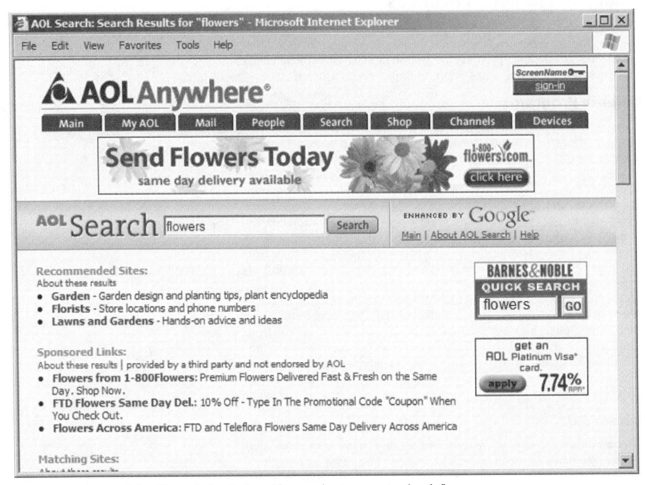

Figure 11.6 *AOL search for "flowers" also display ad banners for sites associated with flowers*

The effectiveness of banner ads has been a topic of study. If you are like most web site visitors, you do not click on ad banners. This means that ad banners do not necessarily generate more immediate visitors to a site. The Interactive Advertising Bureau researched the relationship between ad banners and brand awareness in 1998. A summary of their research can be found at http://www.mbinteractive.com/site/iab/exec.html. The study showed that brand awareness increased 30% after only one viewing of a banner ad (called an *exposure* or *impression*). The study concluded that the lack of click-throughs doesn't matter: "Banner exposure itself was responsible for 96% of the brand enhancement, while a click-through only contributed 4%." Of course, the thinking is that increased brand awareness will increase the likelihood of an actual web site visit in the future.

If the costs associated with banner ads seem to outweigh their benefits, consider a "free" option, a banner exchange.

Banner Exchange

While the details of **banner exchange programs** vary, the essence is that you agree to show banners from other sites and they will show your banner. Information on banner exchanges may be found at http://www.bcentral.com/products/bn/default.asp (or visit http://bcentral.com/ and search for "banner exchange") and at http://www.impressionz.com/. Banner exchanges can be beneficial to all sites involved because of the free advertising.

Reciprocal Link Agreements

A **reciprocal link agreement** is usually between two sites with related or complementary content. You both agree to link to each other. The result should be more visitors for each site. If you find a site that you'd like to set up a reciprocal link agreement with, contact its webmaster (usually by e-mail) and ask! Since some search engines partially determine rankings on the number of links to a web site, well-placed reciprocal link agreements can help both sites.

Newsletters

A newsletter can bring return visitors to your site. The first step is to collect e-mail addresses. Allow web site visitors to opt in to your newsletter by filling out a form. See Figure 11.7 for a partial screen shot from the ASP 101 web site (http://asp101.com).

Figure 11.7 *Sample newsletter subscription request*

Offer your visitors some perceived value—timely information on a topic, discounts, and so on. Send out the newsletter with fresh, compelling content at regular intervals. This helps to remind your previous visitors about your site. They may even forward the newsletter to a colleague and bring a new visitor to your site.

"Sticky" Site Features

Updating your web site often and keeping your content fresh will encourage visitors to return to your site. How to keep them there? Make your web site sticky. **Stickiness** is to the ability to keep visitors at your site. Display your interesting and compelling content along with features that encourage stickiness such as news updates, polls and surveys, and chats or message boards.

Personal Recommendations

While forwarding a newsletter is a form of **personal recommendation**, some sites make it even easier to tell a friend about them. They offer a link that is used with a phrase such as "E-mail This Article", "Send this page to a friend" or "Tell a colleague about this site." See Figure 11.8 for a partial screen shot of the Business 2.0 web site (http://www.business2.com).

Figure 11.8 *This site makes it easy to tell friends about interesting articles.*

This personal recommendation brings a new visitor who is likely to be interested in the content of your site.

Web Rings

Web rings are more appropriate for non-commercial sites than for businesses. However, a web ring can bring quite a few visitors. Join a ring of sites on a similar topic. Visitors can surf from site to site and know that the content should interest them. You could even create your own web ring. See Yahoo! (http://dir.webring.yahoo.com/rw) or RingSurf (http://www.ring-surf.com/) for more information.

Newsgroup and Listserv Postings

Subscribe to relevant Usenet newsgroups, listservs, or forums related to your web site content. Do not reply to postings with an advertisement of your site. Instead, reply to postings when your response can offer assistance or advice. Include a signature line with your web site URL. Be subtle —you can get banned from some listservs if the moderator perceives you are merely advertising. However, by offering friendly, helpful advice in a newsgroup or listserv you can market your web site in a subtle, positive manner at no cost other than your Internet connection.

Your Internet service provider may provide access to Usenet newsgroups. Google also provides access at http://groups.google.com/. Listservs can be run by individuals or by organizations.

Traditional Media Ads and Existing Marketing Materials

Don't forget to mention your web site in any print, TV, or radio ads your organization may be running. Include the URL of your web site on all brochures, stationery, and business cards. This will help make your web site easily found by your current and potential customers.

Chapter 11 Review

Summary

This chapter introduced concepts related to promoting your web site. The activities involved in submitting web sites to search engines and search directories were discussed along with techniques for making your web site more useful to search engines. Other web site promotion activities such as banner ads and newsletters were also examined. At this point, you should have an idea of what is involved in the other side of web site development—marketing and promotion. You can help the marketing staff by creating web sites that work with search engines and directories by following the suggestions in this chapter.

Visit the text web site at http://www.webdevfoundations.net for examples, updated information, and the links listed in this chapter.

Review Questions

Multiple Choice

1. The components of _____ are the robot, database, and search form.
   - a. a search directory
   - b. a search engine
   - c. both search directories and search engines
   - d. none of the above

2. Meta tags should be placed in the _____ section of a web page.
   - a. header
   - b. body
   - c. comment
   - d. none of the above

3. The first step in submitting your web site to search engines and search directories is to
   - a. join an affiliate program
   - b. visit the search engine and submit your web site
   - c. prepare your pages for search engines by adding keyword and description meta tags to your pages
   - d. none of the above

4. It can often take _____ between the time you submit your site and the time it is listed in a search engine.
   - a. several hours
   - b. several days
   - c. several weeks
   - d. several months

5. The _____ contains information about which keywords are bringing visitors to your web site.
   - a. web position log
   - b. web site log
   - c. search engine file
   - d. none of the above

6. A rating determined by a search engine based on the number of links to a particular site and the qualities of those links is called
   - a. link checking
   - b. reciprocal linking
   - c. link popularity
   - d. none of the above

7. The most popular method used by visitors to find web sites is
   a. banner ads
   b. hearing about web sites on television
   c. search engines and search directories
   d. personal recommendations

8. A promotion method whose main purpose is to bring return visitors to your web site is
   a. newsletters   c. TV ads
   b. banner exchanges   d. none of the above

9. The main benefit of banner ads is
   a. bringing many new visitors to your site
   b. increasing awareness of the web site
   c. both bringing many new visitors and increasing awareness of the site
   d. none of the above

10. An impression is created when
    a. a search form is completed
    b. a visitor recommends your site to a friend
    c. your site is listed in a search engine
    d. your ad is viewed by a web site visitor

Fill in the Blank

11. _____ refers to the ability to keep web page visitors at your site.

12. Use _____ to indicate that you do not want a web page to be indexed.

13. _____ are a frequently used information research resource.

14. Besides listing in a search engine, a web site can be promoted by _____.

15. Paying to be included or listed preferentially in a search engine is considered by many organizations to be _____.

Hands-On Exercises

1. Practice writing keyword and description meta tags. For each scenario described here, write the XHTML to create appropriate meta tags and justify your choice of keywords.
   a. Lanwell Publishing is a small independent publisher of English as a second language (ESL) books used for secondary school and adult continuing education learners. The web site offers textbooks and teacher manuals.
   b. RevGear is a small specialty truck and auto repair shop in Schaumburg, Illinois. They also sponsor a local drag racing team.
   c. Morris Accounting is a small accounting firm that specializes in tax return preparation and accounting for small businesses. The owner, Greg Morris, is a CPA and Certified Financial Planner.

2. Choose one of the company scenarios listed in exercise 1 (Lanwell Publishing, RevGear, or Morris Accounting). Create a home page for the site that includes the meta tags, appropriate page titles, and keywords used appropriately in headings. Place an e-mail link to yourself on the web page. Save the page as scenario.htm. Hand in printouts of both the source code (print in Notepad) and the browser display of your page.

3. Choose one of the company scenarios listed in exercise 1 (Lanwell Publishing, RevGear, or Morris Accounting). Create a web page that lists at least three possible activities that could be used to promote the site in addition to search engine submission. For each activity explain why it could be helpful for the web site. Place an e-mail link to yourself on the web page. Save the page as promotion.htm. Hand in printouts of both the source code (print in Notepad) and the browser display of your page.

Web Site Case Study

Each of these case studies will continue throughout most of the text. In this chapter, you will focus on meta tags needed to promote the web sites.

A. JavaJam Coffee House

See Chapter 2 for an introduction to the JavaJam Coffee House case. Figure 2.20 shows a site map for the JavaJam web site. The pages were created in earlier chapters. Use the javajamcss folder created in the Chapter 9 case study. Your task is to add appropriate keywords and description meta tags to each page in the web site.

Hands-On Practice Case

Review the JavaJam case introduction in Chapter 2. Take a moment to view the pages you have created in earlier chapters. While you are touring the site, jot down keywords that might be appropriate for the entire web site. Also write down keywords that would be appropriate for specific pages, such as the Jobs page or Performances page. Don't forget to add common misspellings of words to your keyword list. Next, write a brief paragraph that describes the JavaJam site.

Launch Notepad and edit the web pages in the javajamcss folder. Add keywords and description meta tags to each page. Save each page. Test your pages in a browser. They shouldn't look any different, but they are much more friendly to search engines!

B. Fish Creek Animal Hospital

See Chapter 2 for an introduction to the Fish Creek Animal Hospital case. Figure 2.23 shows a site map for the Fish Creek web site. The pages were created in earlier chapters. Use the fishcreekcss folder created in the Chapter 9 case study. Your task is to add appropriate keywords and description meta tags to each page in the web site.

Hands-On Practice Case

Review the Fish Creek case introduction in Chapter 2. Take a moment to view the pages you have created in earlier chapters. While you are touring the site, jot down keywords that might be appropriate for the entire web site. Also write down keywords that would be appropriate for specific pages, such as the Services page or Contact page. Don't forget to add common misspellings of words to your keyword list. Next, write a brief paragraph that describes the Fish Creek site.

Launch Notepad and edit the web pages in the fishcreekcss folder. Add keywords and description meta tags to each page. Save each page. Test your pages in a browser. They will not look different, but they are much more friendly to search engines!

C. Pete the Painter

See Chapter 2 for an introduction to the Pete the Painter case. Figure 2.26 shows a site map for the Pete the Painter web site. The pages were created in earlier chapters. Use the paintercss folder created in the Chapter 9 case study. Your task is to add appropriate keywords and description meta tags to each page in the web site.

Hands-On Practice Case

Review the Pete the Painter case introduction in Chapter 2. Take a moment to view the pages you have created in earlier chapters. While you are touring the site, jot down keywords that might be appropriate for the web site. Also write down keywords that would be appropriate for specific pages, such as the Testimonials page or Services page. Don't forget to add common misspellings of words to your keyword list. Next, write a brief paragraph that describes the Pete the Painter site.

Launch Notepad and edit the web pages in the paintercss folder. Add keywords and description meta tags to each page. Save each page. Test your pages in a browser. They shouldn't look any different, but they are much more friendly to search engines!

Web Research

A. This chapter discussed a number of web site promotion techniques. Choose one method (search engine submission, affiliate programs, banner ads, etc.) to research. Obtain information from at least three different web sites about the promotion technique you chose. Create a web page that lists at least five hints or facts about the promotion method along with helpful links that provide additional information on the hint or fact. Provide the URLs of the web sites that you used as resources. Organize your page with a table. Place your name in an e-mail link on the web page. Print both the source code (from Notepad) and the browser view of your web page.

B. Search engine and search directory submission rules seem to be constantly changing. Research three search engines and/or search directories and determine the following:

- Are free submissions accepted? If so, are they restricted to noncommercial sites?

- What types of paid submissions are accepted? How do they work—what is the fee structure, listing guarantee, and so on?

- What types of paid advertisements are available? How do they work—what is the fee structure, for example?

- Is there any information about the usual time frame for the submission to be listed?

  Create a web page that uses a table to describe your findings. Provide URLs of the web sites you used as resources. Place your name in an e-mail link on the web page. Print both the source code (from Notepad) and the browser view of your web page.

Chapter Review Answers

1. b

2. a

3. c

4. c

5. b

6. c

7. c

8. a

9. b

10. d

11. stickiness

12. `<meta name="robots" description="noindex,nofollow" />`

13. search engines and search indexes

14. Any of the following: affiliate programs, banner ads, banner exchanges, reciprocal link agreements, newsletters, personal recommendations, traditional media advertising, and including your URL on all promotional materials.

15. a reasonable expense related to advertising and marketing their organization

Chapter 12

Introduction to Web Page Interactivity

Y ou have probably experienced interactivity on web pages many times—moving the mouse to cause a new image to appear, clicking on radio buttons to take a survey, or clicking on a product while you watch and listen to a Flash movie about a company. These are all examples of web page interactivity. Adding the right touch of interactivity to a web page can make it engaging and compelling for your web site visitors.

Technologies commonly used to add interactivity to web pages include JavaScript, Java applets, DHTML, CGI and server-side processing, and Flash. This chapter will introduce you to adding interactive components to web pages.

The purpose of this chapter is to introduce you to these techniques and provide sample uses. Learning to write JavaScript, Java applets, DHTML, CGI scripts, and Flash animations are more fully explored in other books. As you read this chapter and try the examples, concentrate on the features and capabilities of each technology, rather than on trying to master the details.

Learning Outcomes

In this chapter, you will learn how to:

▶ Describe the features and common uses of JavaScript

▶ Add JavaScript code to a web page

▶ Describe the features and common uses of Java applets

▶ Add a Java applet to a web page

▶ Describe the features and common uses of DHTML

▶ Add a DHTML effect to a web page

▶ Describe the features and common uses of CGI

▶ Invoke CGI from a web page

▶ Describe the features and common uses of Macromedia Flash

▶ Add a Flash animation to a web page

▶ Find free JavaScript, Java applets, DHTML, CGI, and Flash resources on the Web

▶ Describe other technologies that can be used to add web page interactivity

353

JavaScript

JavaScript is an object-based scripting language. In JavaScript you work with the objects associated with a web page document: the window, the document, and the elements such as forms, images, and links. JavaScript, developed by Netscape, was originally called LiveScript. When Netscape collaborated with Sun Microsystems on modifications to the language, it was renamed JavaScript. JavaScript is *not* the same as the Java programming language. Unlike Java, JavaScript cannot be used to write stand-alone programs that can run outside of a web browser. JavaScript statements can be placed in a separate file (with a .js extension) accessed by a web browser, but JavaScript statements are more commonly embedded directly in the web page along with the XHTML. In either case, the web browser interprets the JavaScript statements. JavaScript is considered to be a client-side scripting language—it runs on the web client (the browser) and not the web server. (*Note:* While Netscape does offer server-side JavaScript for its web servers, JavaScript is commonly used as a client-side scripting language.)

Common Uses of JavaScript

JavaScript is often used to respond to events such as moving the mouse, clicking a button, and loading a web page. It is also often used to edit and verify information on XHTML form elements such as text boxes, check boxes, and radio buttons. Common uses of JavaScript are described here.

Displaying a Message Box. A **message box** is user interface that displays a message and an OK button. When the user clicks the OK button, the message box disappears. See Figure 12. 1 for an example of a web page that displays a message box.

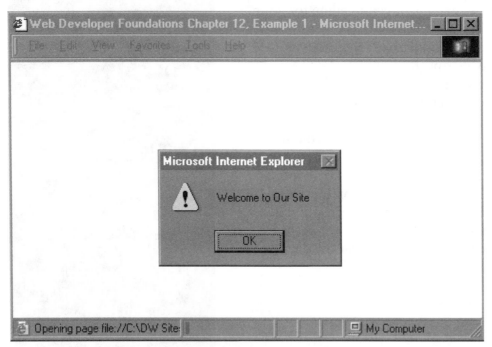

Figure 12.1 *JavaScript used to display a welcome message*

JavaScript uses a feature called the **alert method** to display message boxes. You can try out the sample page on the student disk at Chapter12/ex1.htm. View the source to take a look at the JavaScript used to display a message box.

Select list navigation. A sample page using the **jump menu** shown in Figure 12.2 can be found on the student disk at Chapter12ex2.htm.

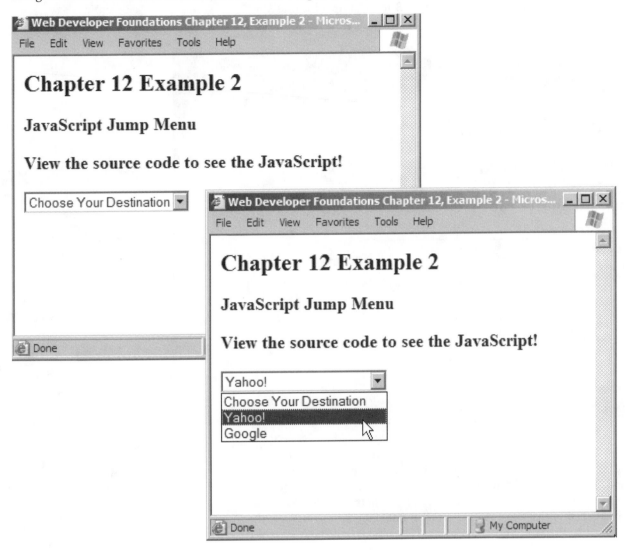

Figure 12.2 *JavaScript jump menu*

In the jump menu, a form with a select element lets the visitor choose the next web page to display. The options in the select element each contain a URL. When the button is clicked, JavaScript is invoked to identify which item was selected and then link to that site.

Editing and Validating Form Information. JavaScript can also be used with XHTML forms to verify the information being submitted before a CGI script is invoked. See Figure 12.3 for a sample form used to collect e-mail addresses.

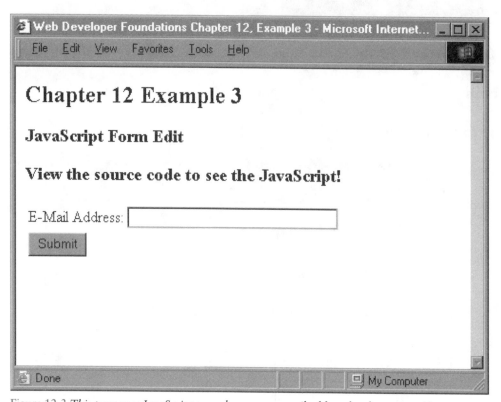

Figure 12.3 *This page uses JavaScript to make sure an e-mail address has been entered.*

The sample form can be found on the student disk at Chapter12/ex3.htm. JavaScript has been placed on the page to edit the e-mail address on the form each time the visitor clicks the Submit button. In this example, JavaScript verifies that the e-mail text box is not empty, does not have the value of a blank space, and contains an @ symbol. If all these edits are passed, JavaScript will submit the form information to the web server. If any of the edits fail, a message box will be displayed to the visitor.

Creating a Pop-up Window. Now you know what can be used to create all those annoying pop-up windows—it's JavaScript! The **window.open method** is used to open a specially configured browser window, called a pop-up window.

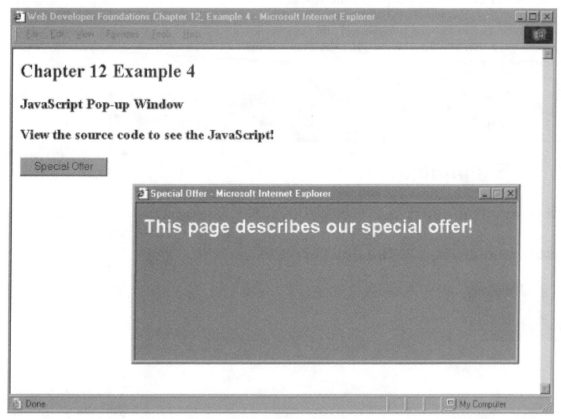

Figure 12.4 *JavaScript is used to display a pop-up window*

A web page that displays a "Special Offer" pop-up window, shown in Figure 12.4, can be found on the student disk at Chapter12/ex4.htm.

Triggering Image Rollovers. An **image rollover** (sometimes called *image swapping*) is the effect of an image changing when the mouse pointer is placed over a hyperlink. An **event** can be described as an action taken by the user. When the user places the mouse pointer over an object such as a hyperlink, the **onmouseover event** is triggered. When the user moves the mouse pointer off an object such as a hyperlink, the **onmouseout event** is triggered. JavaScript can be used to respond to these and other events. See Figure 12.5 for a web page that contains JavaScript to respond to the onmouseover and onmouseout events.

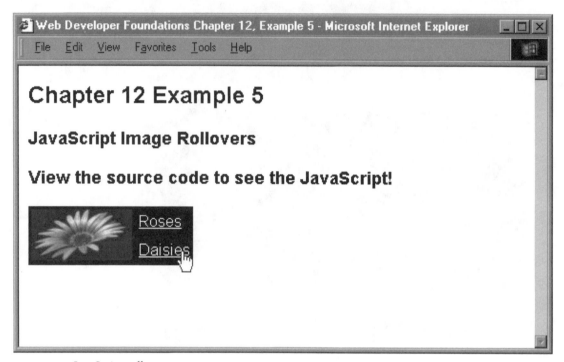

Figure 12.5 *JavaScript rollovers*

The sample page shown in Figure 12.5 can be found on the student disk at Chapter12/ex5.htm. JavaScript is used to change the src attribute of a named image each time an onmouseover or onmouseout event is triggered.

Changing Status Messages. Have you ever noticed the text in the status bar changing as you move the mouse pointer over hyperlinks? This effect also uses JavaScript triggered by onmouseover and onmouseout events. A web page that displays this feature is shown in Figure 12.6 and can be found on the student disk at Chapter12/ex6.htm. The **window.status property** is used by JavaScript to set the value of the browser's status bar.

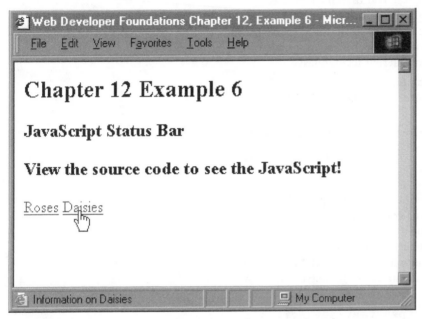

Figure 12.6 *JavaScript is used to change the window's status bar.*

Displaying the Current Date. You may notice that some web pages display the day of the week and the current date. Figure 12.7 shows a web page with this feature (see the student disk, Chapter12/ex7.htm).

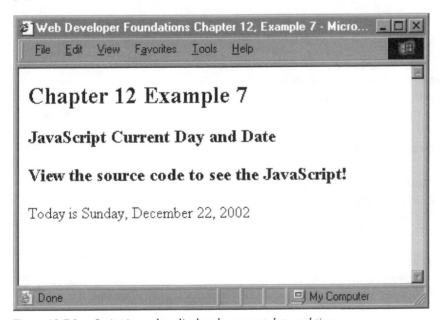

Figure 12.7 *JavaScript is used to display the current date and time.*

In this case, JavaScript is placed directly in the body of the web page wherever the current date should be displayed. The **document.write() method** is used to write the information on the web page document.

Performing Calculations. JavaScript is often used to perform calculations, including those used in mortgage calculators and e-commerce shopping carts. A web page with a mortgage calculator can be found on the student disk at Chapter12/calc.htm.

Versatility. As you viewed the examples, you may have noticed the versatility of JavaScript. It is a workhorse on the Web—editing form information, handling image rollovers, opening specialized windows, and so on. You may be wondering how these effects are created. JavaScript code can be added to a web page using either of two different techniques:

- Place JavaScript code between **<script>** tags.
- Place JavaScript code as part of an event attached to an XHTML element.

The following sections provide examples and hands-on practice using these techniques.

The <script> Tag

The **<script>** tag indicates the beginning JavaScript code in an XHTML document. The **<script>** tag is a container tag. Two attributes are commonly used: language and type. The value of the language attribute indicates the name of the scripting language being used—in our case "JavaScript". The value of the type attribute indicates the MIME type of the text between the **<script>** tags—in our case "text/javascript". A sample is shown here

```
<script language="JavaScript" type="text/javascript">
...JavaScript code goes here...
</script>
```

The **<script>** tag can be used in either the header or body section of a web page. The placement of the **<script>** tag depends on what the JavaScript is supposed to do.

Hands-On Practice 12.1

*It was previously mentioned that JavaScript code can be used to display a message box (called an **alert** in JavaScript) on a web page. Now let's look more carefully at how this is done. The JavaScript statements to display an alert when a page loads are placed between **<script>** tags.*

Launch Notepad and create a web page that displays an alert by typing in this code:

```
<?xml version="1.0" encoding="UTF-8"?>
<!DOCTYPE html PUBLIC "-//W3C//DTD XHTML 1.0 Transitional//EN"
   "http://www.w3.org/TR/xhtml1/DTD/xhtml1-transitional.dtd">
<html xmlns="http://www.w3.org/1999/xhtml">
<head>
<title>Hands-On Practice 12.1</title>
<script language="JavaScript" type="text/javascript">
<!-- this comment will hide the JavaScript from browsers that don't support it
alert("Welcome to Our Site")
// -->
</script>
```

continues

```
</head>
<body>
<h1>You've just used JavaScript!</h1>
</body>
</html>
```

As you examine this code you will notice the opening `<script>` *tag followed by an XHTML comment. The purpose of the comment is to hide the script from browsers that do not support JavaScript. If this XHTML comment were omitted, a browser that did not support JavaScript would display the JavaScript code statements right on the web page! There is only one line of JavaScript statement in this example:*

```
alert("Welcome to Our Site")
```

This is the JavaScript alert method that displays a message to a user. The text of the message is placed within quotation marks. The line preceeding the `</script>` *tag contains* `// -->`*. The // indicates a comment to JavaScript and the* `-->` *indicates the closing of the XHTML comment. Save your page as js1.htm and test it in a browser. See Figure 12.1 for an image of the alert box on the screen. You can compare your work with the solution on the student disk at Chapter12/js1.htm.*

Using JavaScript Events

As mentioned earlier, when a web page visitor places the mouse over an element on a web page, the onmouseover event is triggered. When the mouse is moved off an element the onmouseout event is triggered. Java-Script can be configured to perform actions when these and other events occur including clicking (**onclick**), loading a page (**onload**), and unloading a page (**onunload**). The JavaScript is added directly to the XHTML tag with the type of event as an attribute. The value of the event attribute will contain one or more JavaScript statements.

To add onmouseover and onmouseout events to a hyperlink, you write the events and their script in the anchor (`<a>`) tag. The screen shot in Figure 12.6 (also found on the student disk Chapter12/ex6.htm) shows a page that uses JavaScript to change the text in the browser window status bar when a visitor places the mouse pointer over a hyperlink. The browser window is an object that can be accessed by JavaScript. The **window.status property** is used to refer to the browser window status bar.

Hands-On Practice 12.2

In this Hands-On Practice you will launch Notepad and create a web page that changes the text in the status bar of the browser window when the visitor triggers the onmouseover and onmouseout events. The code is shown here.

```
<?xml version="1.0" encoding="UTF-8"?>
<!DOCTYPE html PUBLIC "-//W3C//DTD XHTML 1.0 Transitional//EN"
   "http://www.w3.org/TR/xhtml1/DTD/xhtml1-transitional.dtd">
<html xmlns="http://www.w3.org/1999/xhtml">
<head>
<title>Hands-On Practice 12.2</title>
</head>
<body>
<a href="js1.htm"
onmouseover="window.status='JavaScript Hands-On Practice 1';return true"
onmouseout="window.status='Working with JavaScript';return true">Exercise 1</a>
</body>
</html>
```

Notice how the onmouseover and onmouseout events were coded as attributes directly in the XHTML anchor tag. The values associated with the events are JavaScript statements that modify the contents of the status bar on the browser window (called window.status).

Save the page as js2.htm and test it in a browser. Compare your results with Figure 12.8. Watch the text in the status bar change as you move the mouse over the hyperlinks.

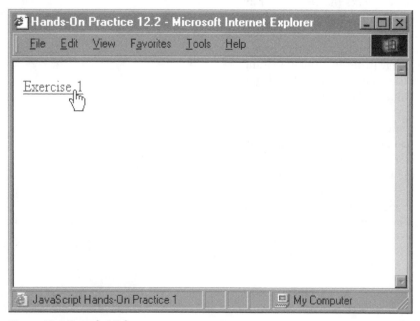

Figure 12.8 *Sample js2.htm*

Why doesn't my JavaScript work?

If you are experiencing errors as you test your JavaScript try the following:

- Check the syntax of the statements that you typed. Pay very close attention to upper- and lowercase letters, spaces, and quotations.
- Verify that you have saved the page with your most recent changes.
- Verify that you are testing the most recent version of the page (refresh or reload the page).
- If you get an error, use the error messages that are displayed by the browser. Internet Explorer will try to tell you the line number that had the problem. Count each line from the top (including blank lines) to find the line the error message refers to. Some web authoring tools such as Microsoft FrontPage and Macromedia Dreamweaver provide line numbers for the XHTML/JavaScript source code. Netscape will try to point to the exact spot where it began having problems. Type "javascript:" into the address text box of the browser to display the JavaScript console (shown in Figure 12.9).

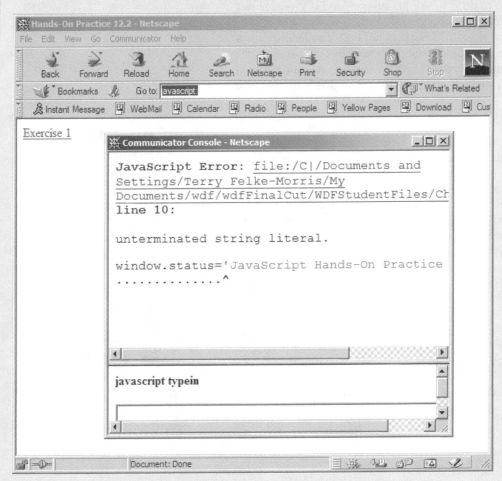

Figure 12.9 *Netscape has a built-in JavaScript debugger.*

Some web authoring tools, such as Macromedia Dreamweaver include a JavaScript debugging feature that can help you test your code.

- Verify that your browser settings support JavaScript. The browser menu selections that you use for this vary for each browser. In Interrnet Explorer, select Tools, Options, Advanced, and view the chosen settings. In Netscape 4.x, select Edit, Preferences, Advanced, and examine the settings.

Free JavaScript Resources

There is a lot to learn about JavaScript, but there are many free resources for JavaScript code and JavaScript tutorials on the Web. There is even online documentation for JavaScript at http://docs.iplanet.com/docs/manuals/javascript.html.

Here are a few sites that offer free tutorials or free scripts:

- JavaScript Tutorials (http://echoecho.com/javascript.htm)
- JavaScript Tutorials (http://www.pageresource.com/jscript/index4.htm)
- The JavaScript Source at Internet.com (http://javascript.internet.com/)

As you visit these and other web sites, be aware that it is not ethical simply to copy and paste JavaScript that another person has written. Many web sites that offer free JavaScript require you link to them or place comments in the JavaScript to indicate who the author is. While it is unlikely that you would be sued for borrowing someone's JavaScript, the right thing to do is to ask permission, and if given, honor any request for links or identification.

Once you are comfortable with XHTML, the JavaScript language is a good technology to learn as you continue your studies. Try some of the resources listed and get your feet wet. The next section introduces a programming language, Java, which is often confused with JavaScript because the names are similar.

Java

Java is an object-oriented programming (OOP) language developed by Sun Microsystems. An object-oriented program consists of a group of cooperating objects that exchange messages for the purpose of achieving a common objective. Java is not the same language as JavaScript. It is more powerful and much more flexible than JavaScript. Java can be used to develop both stand-alone executable applications and applets that are invoked by web pages. Java applets are platform independent; that means they can be written and run on any platform—Mac, UNIX, Linux, Windows. Java applets are compiled (translated from the English-like Java statements to an encoded form) and saved as **.class files** which contain byte code. The byte code is interpreted by the Java Virtual Machine (JVM) in the web browser. The JVM interprets the byte code into the proper machine language for the operating system. The applet is then executed and appears on the web page. See Figure 12.10 for a diagram that shows this process.

When a Java applet loads, the area reserved for it on the web page displays a gray box until the applet begins to execute.

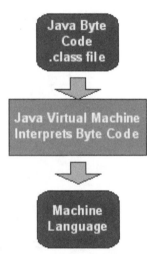

Figure 12.10 *The Java Virtual Machine interprets the byte code into machine language.*

Common Uses of Java Applets

Processing Navigation Bars and Buttons. Java applets are frequently used to process interactive navigation bars on web pages. JavaPowered.com offers many navigation applets. A free navigation applet can be found at http://www.pressit.de/menu/navbar/navbar.htm. The Plutonium Software (http://www.plutoniumsoftware.com) site uses an interesting Java applet for navigation.

Manipulating Images. Java can be used to manipulate images in a number of ways. Visit http://www.codebrain.com/java/codebrainslider/index.html for a sample slide show. Perhaps one of the best known Java applet images is the "Lake Applet" from http://javaboutique.internet.com/Lake, shown in Figure 12.11.

This applet not only manipulates the lower portion of an image to make it look like a lake, it also functions as a hyperlink.

Creating Text Effects. Java applets can also be used to create text effects such as the sample applet shown in Figure 12.12 (see the student disk Chapter12/ex8.htm).

Figure 12.11 *The classic Lake Applet*

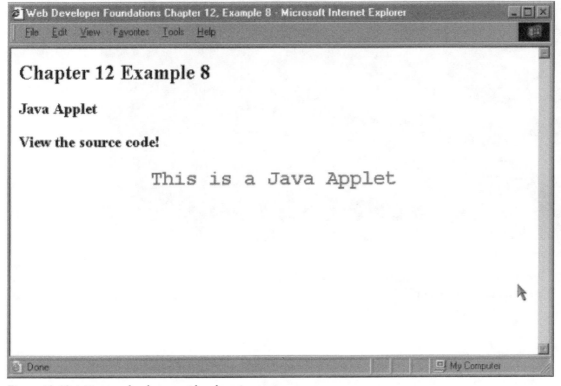

Figure 12.12 *A Java applet that provides changing text*

Other text effects can be found at web sites such as http://www.javapowered.com/text.html.

Creating Games. Another popular use of Java applets is to create games for web pages. Figure 12.13 shows Drop Zone, from Plutonium Software's http://www.minatrix.com game site.

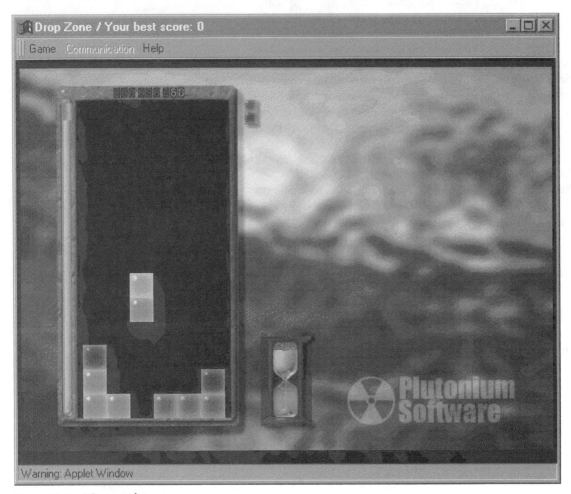

Figure 12.13 *A Java applet game*

Try Java on the Brain (http://www.javaonthebrain.com/brain.html) for other examples of classic games as Java applets.

Using Web and Business Applications. While image effects and games are fun, the use of Java applets in business applications has been increasing for functions such as financial calculations and visualization. The jars.com (http://www.jars.com) site provides a Java applet review service and has many applets that are useful in a business environment. One example is NetCharts from http://visualmining.com, shown in Figure 12.14.

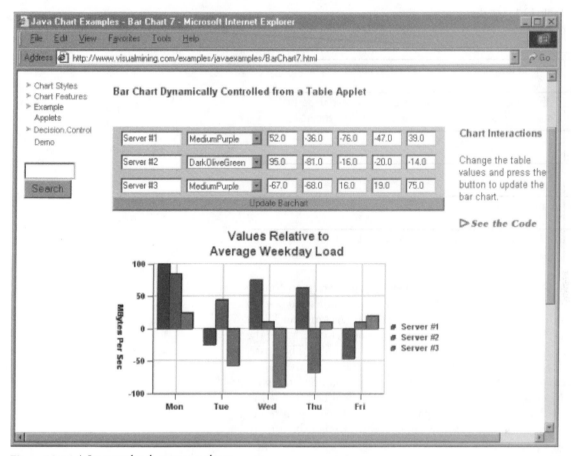

Figure 12.14 *A Java applet that creates charts*

Quote.com (http://quote.com) offers a LiveCharts Java applet with real time stock quotes. These types of applets often connect to databases on the web server and can be very powerful tools if you need to display live data in a visual manner.

You can see that Java applets can perform a variety of functions on web pages. As a web developer your usual role will not be that of a Java programmer—that is, you should not be expected to write Java applets. However, you could be asked to work with a Java programmer to place his or her applets on your web site. Whether you obtain an applet from a coworker or find one on a free site, you need to code XHTML to display the applet.

Adding a Java Applet to a Web Page

The **<applet>** tag specifies the beginning of an applet area in the body of a web page. Its closing tag, **</applet>**, specifies the ending of an applet area in the body of a web page. The **<applet>** tag has a number of attributes described in Table 12.1.

Table 12.1 *Attributes of the* **<applet>** *Tag*

Attribute	Value
code	Name of the applet file. This has a .class file extension.
codebase	If the applet is not in the same folder as the web page, the codebase indicates the folder that contains the applet.
height	Specifies the height of the applet area in pixels.
width	Specifies the width of the applet area in pixels.
alt	A text description of the applet.
id	Alphanumeric, no spaces. The value must be unique and not used for other id values on the same XHTML document.

In addition, most applets need special values, or parameters, to configure their processing. An applet that shows images and handles navigation would need parameters to accept the file names of the images and the URLs for the hyperlinks. The programmer who creates an applet determines the parameter values and names required by a specific Java applet. Therefore, expect each applet to require different parameters. Parameters are configured with **<param>** tags. The **<param>** tag is a self-contained tag with two attributes: name and value. The parameter name will be provided to you in the applet documentation. The parameter value will be different depending on the function of the applet. One parameter might be used to set a background color; another parameter could be used contain a person's name. A description of the type of value expected should be contained in the applet documentation.

Hands-On Practice 12.3

In this Hands-On Practice you will launch Notepad and create a web page that contains a Java applet. This example will use the Fader26 applet (provided by Johannes Schellen). This applet displays text messages one at a time. The list of text messages is obtained from a text file (.txt file extension) that you will create. An example of this applet at work can be found on the student disk at Chapter12/ex8.htm.

Let's get started. Create a folder called testapplet on your disk. Copy the applet file (fader26.class) from the student disk at Chapter12/fader26.class and place it in the same folder as the web page. Do not change the name of the applet.

Whether you obtain an applet from a free web site or from a coworker, each applet should have some accompanying documentation that indicates what parameter it expects. Documentation for the Fader26 applet appears in Table 12.2.

Table 12.2 *Documentation for Fader26 Applet*

Parameter Name	Parameter Value
AppletHome	http://www.crosswinds.net/~fader
Data	The name of the text file containing the message to be displayed *Note:* Each line in the text file should begin with text=.
bgColor	This is the background color of the Java applet area. Use a hexadecimal color value.

Launch Notepad and create a web page that invokes this applet. The beginning XHTML is as follows:

```
<?xml version="1.0" encoding="UTF-8"?>
<!DOCTYPE html PUBLIC "-//W3C//DTD XHTML 1.0 Transitional//EN"
   "http://www.w3.org/TR/xhtml1/DTD/xhtml1-transitional.dtd">
<html xmlns="http://www.w3.org/1999/xhtml">
<head>
<title>Hands-On Practice 12.3</title>
</head>
<body>
```

Now you are ready to add the XHTML to place the Java applet on your web page. First, write the `<applet>` *tag to reserve an area of the web page that is 30 pixels high and 610 pixels wide for the fader26.class applet. The code is*

```
<applet code="fader26.class" height="30" width="610">
```

Next, create the parameter tags. The code for the parameter tags is

```
<param name="AppletHome" value="http://www.crosswinds.net/~fader/" />
<param name="Data" value="mymessage.txt" />
<param name="bgColor" value="#FFFFFF" />
```

Finally, an ending applet tag `</applet>`*, ending body tag* `</body>`*, and ending* `</html>` *tag are needed. The code shown in Notepad is displayed in Figure 12.15.*

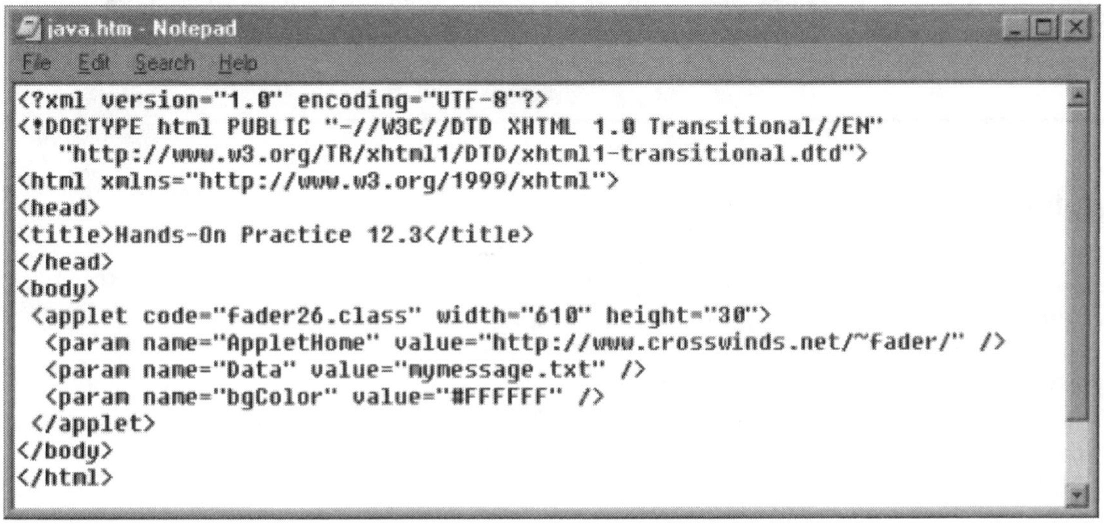

```
java.htm - Notepad
File  Edit  Search  Help
<?xml version="1.0" encoding="UTF-8"?>
<!DOCTYPE html PUBLIC "-//W3C//DTD XHTML 1.0 Transitional//EN"
   "http://www.w3.org/TR/xhtml1/DTD/xhtml1-transitional.dtd">
<html xmlns="http://www.w3.org/1999/xhtml">
<head>
<title>Hands-On Practice 12.3</title>
</head>
<body>
 <applet code="fader26.class" width="610" height="30">
  <param name="AppletHome" value="http://www.crosswinds.net/~fader/" />
  <param name="Data" value="mymessage.txt" />
  <param name="bgColor" value="#FFFFFF" />
 </applet>
</body>
</html>
```

Figure 12.15 *Sample web page code using the fader26 Java applet*

Save the file in the testapplet folder with the file name of java.htm. You are not yet ready to test the page—you need to create and format the text file that the applet expects. This applet expects each line of text to begin with `text=`. *Figure 12.16 shows a sample text file created using Notepad.*

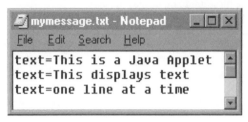

Figure 12.16 *The text file needed by the Fader26 Java applet*

Use this as a guide to create your text file. Save your text file as mymessage.txt in the testapplet folder. The name of the text file must match the value of the "Data" parameter in the XHTML code. Now launch your page in a browser. The applet should display your text one line at a time.

FAQ

Why doesn't my Java applet work?

If your applet does not function as expected, verify the following:

- Are Java applets enabled in your browser?
- Is the applet saved in the testapplet folder?
- Is the applet saved with the name fader26.class (all letters must be in lowercase)?
- Are the java.htm and mymessage.txt files saved in the testapplet folder?
- Does the code attribute on the `<applet>` tag have the value of fader26.class?

Be aware the disadvantage of using Java applets is the lag between the time the web page is initially loaded and the time the applet actually begins to execute. Your web page visitor will see a gray box in the area reserved for the applet until it begins executing.

To provide accessibility for all your web page visitors, regardless of whether their browser or user-agent can process a Java applet, the `<applet>` *tag should be modified to use an alt attribute and include a text description of the Java applet. A sample of the modified code is shown here with the additions in green.*

```
<applet code="fader26.class" height="30"
width="610"
alt="Java applet: displays a promotional message one
line at a time">
<param name="AppletHome" value="http://www.crosswinds.net/~fader/" />
<param name="Data" value="mymessage.txt" />
<param name="bgColor" value="#FFFFFF" />
This Java applet displays a message one line at a time. Message: This is a Java
applet. This displays text one line at a time.
</applet>
```

Free Java Applet Resources

Now that you are familiar with applets, you may be wondering how to write them. The organization that developed the Java programming language, Sun Microsystems, offers documentation and other resources on their web site at http://java.sun.com. Be aware that the Java programming language is very powerful, but quite complex. There are many resources for free and commercial Java applets on the Web. Here are a few helpful sites:

- http://www.javapowered.com
- http://www.javaonthebrain.com
- http://www.jars.com
- http://www.gamelan.com

As you visit these and other Java resource sites, keep in mind that some Java applets are copyrighted. Be sure to obtain permission from the creator of the applet before using it on your site. There may be some requirements for giving credit to the creator either by name or by linking to their web site. Follow the instructions provided with the applet. Some applets are free to use in personal web sites but require licenses for use in commercial web sites.

The next section continues our look at web page interactivity with an introduction to Dynamic Hypertext Markup Language (DHTML).

Dynamic HTML (DHTML)

Dynamic HTML is not a single technology; it is a group of technologies that work together to change a web page after it has been downloaded. These technologies allow the web page to respond to user actions. The following three technologies are used:

- **Document Object Model (DOM).** The DOM defines every object and element on a web page. Its hierarchical structure can be used to access page elements and apply styles to page elements. A portion of a basic DOM is shown in Figure 12.17.

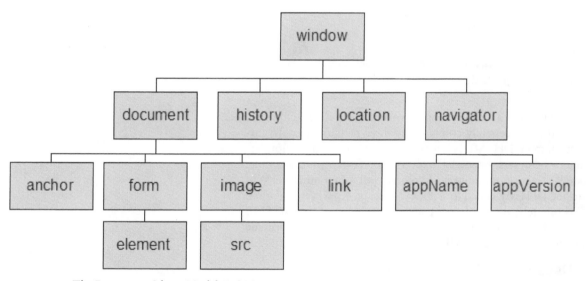

Figure 12.17 *The Document Object Model (DOM)*

- **Cascading Style Sheets (CSS).** From Chapter 9 you already know that CSS can be used to apply formatting styles to web page elements. CSS can also be used to position elements on a web page and even to modify their visibility.
- **Client-side Scripting.** Scripting languages such as JavaScript, VBScript, or JScript are used to access the DOM and manipulate the elements.

Figure 12.18 shows a web page that uses DHTML to show a specific text message when the visitor places the mouse pointer over a hyperlink (see the student disk Chapter12/ex9.htm).

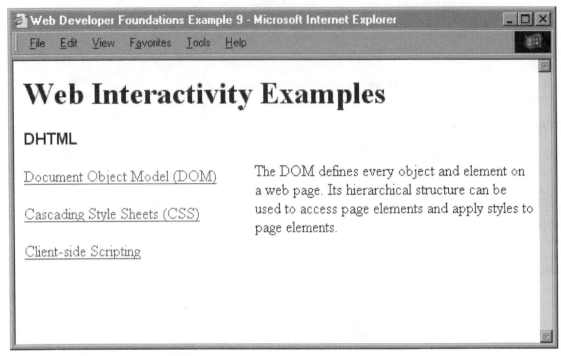

Figure 12.18 *Web page with DHTML*

DHTML frequently has a long learning curve because of the extent of the knowledge needed to successfully combine the three technologies. To further complicate matters, DHTML is implemented differently by major versions of the major browsers, Internet Explorer and Netscape. For example, DHTML coded to work in Internet Explorer will often not work in Netscape. Further, DHTML coded to work in Netscape 4.x will not work in Netscape 6. Fortunately, there is better convergence between the DHTML implementations of Internet Explorer 5 and Netscape 6, it should become easier to write cross-browser DHTML in the future.

Common Uses of DHTML

Hiding and Showing Text. The appearance of text that describes anchor tags or images is another common effect that uses DHMTL. The DHTML sample in Figure 12.18 used this effect. For a slightly different application of the same effect, visit http://wizardingworld.com and explore its map to see this effect in action.

Navigation. The horizontal navigation shown in Figure 12.19 utilizes DHTML. This navigation type has become quite popular and is seen in both horizontal and vertical versions.

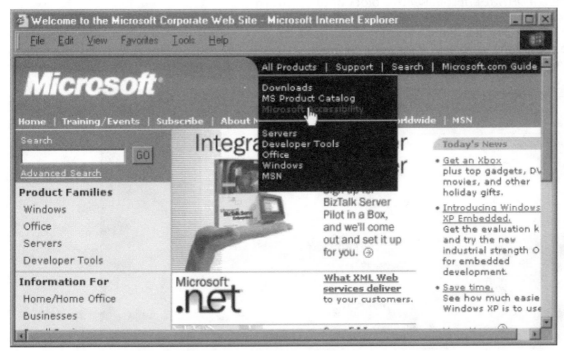

Figure 12.19 *Microsoft's web site uses DHTML navigation.*

The lists of choices under each category (All Products, Support, Search, etc.) appear and disappear as you move your mouse pointer over the category heading. A good source of DHTML code, including navigation menus, is the Dynamic Drive web site at http://www.dynamicdrive.com.

Image Effects. Various image effects ranging from mouse trails to altering images to slide shows can be applied with DHTML. See http://terryfelke.com for a mouse trail example. For an example of using DHTML to create a slide show, see the DHTML Shock site at http://dhtmlshock.com/scripts.asp?CategoryID=9 or visit http://dhtmlshock.com and search for "slide show".

Adding DHTML to a Web Page

The code needed to add a DHTML effect to a web page varies depending on the desired effect. The JavaScript tends to get complex because of the differences in the syntax required for different browsers and browser versions. It is a good idea to become comfortable with CSS and JavaScript before tackling DHTML.

In this Hands-On Practice you will launch Notepad and create a web page that contains a DHTML effect in which a block of text moves from the upper left-hand corner of the browser window to a specified point on the page. See the screen shot in Figure 12.20 for an example and try the sample on the student disk at Chapter12/dhtml.htm.

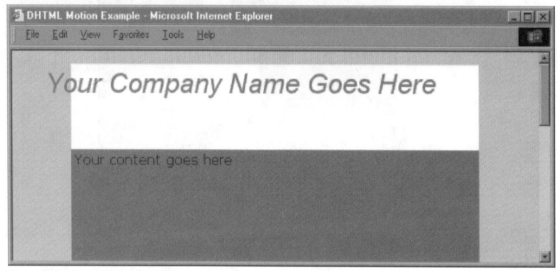

Figure 12.20 *Sample dhtml.htm page*

Notice how the text, "Your Company Name Goes Here", moves in from the upper left-hand side of the browser window. You are provided with the code to create this effect. DHTML—the combination of scripting, CSS, and the document object model—is complex and requires much study. The purpose of this Hands-On Practice is to give you with experience using a DHTML effect on a web page.

Let's get started. Create a folder called testdhtml on your disk. Copy the dhtml.css and dhtml.js files from the student disk Chapter12 folder. Save the files in your testdhtml folder. The dhtml.css file contains configurations for the portion of the page that moves, the **id="animate"**. *The dhtml.js contains the JavaScript statements that cause the animate id to move.*

Next, launch Notepad and create the web page to produce the effect of moving text and to format the page with a table. The code is as follows.

```
<?xml version="1.0" encoding="UTF-8"?>
<!DOCTYPE html PUBLIC "-//W3C//DTD XHTML 1.0 Transitional//EN"
   "http://www.w3.org/TR/xhtml1/DTD/xhtml1-transitional.dtd">
<html xmlns="http://www.w3.org/1999/xhtml">
<head>
<title>DHTML Motion Example</title>
<link rel="stylesheet" href="dhtml.css" type="text/css" />
<script src="dhtml.js" language="JavaScript" type="text/javascript"></script>
</head>
<body onload="motion()">
```

continues

```
<div id="animate">Your Company Name Goes Here</div>
<table border="0" width="80%" align="center" cellspacing="0" cellpadding="3">
 <tr>
   <td bgcolor="#FFFFFF" height="100"> </td>
 </tr>
 <tr>
   <td bgcolor="#996600" height="600" valign="top">Your content goes here</td>
 </tr>
</table>
</body>
</html>
```

*Save your page as dhtml.htm in the testdhtml folder and test it in a
browser. Did your text move? If so—great! If not, check your code
for typographical errors and use the tips for debugging JavaScript
mentioned earlier in the chapter.*

How does the text move on dhtml.htm?

The key is that JavaScript (located in file dhtml.js) works with CSS to change the position of the web page "animate" id and its contents. Notice how the Cascading Style Sheet was referenced with the **<link>** tag and the external JavaScript was referenced with the **<script>** tag.

The text that should be animated is placed between **<div>** tags and assigned to the "animate" id. The code for dhtml.css is shown here.

```
body { background-color:#CCCC99; }
body,td { font-family:Verdana,sans-serif; }
#animate { position: absolute;
           left: -90px;
           top: -20px;
           font-family: Arial,sans-serif;
           font-size: 30px;
           font-style: italic;
           color: #996600; }
```

The configuration for **"#animate"** sets the color, size, font-family, and initial top and left positions for this id. As the top and left position of the id is changed by JavaScript code (contained in the the dhtml.js file), the text appears to move. The **<body>** tag contains an onload event that invokes JavaScript when the page is loaded by a browser. The Javascript manipulates the **<div>** with the "animate" id on the web page and changes its position until it is 80 pixels in from the left. At that point the JavaScript stops moving the **<div>**. The JavaScript must handle the multiple document object models of Netscape 4.x, Internet Explorer 4, and Netscape 6. Yes, it's a little complicated. Hopefully, this helps you to see how CSS, JavaScript, and the DOM of a web page are related.

Don't worry if DHTML seems very complex and cryptic to you—it *is* complex and very demanding to code because of the different document object models supported by various browsers and browser versions. The good news is that recent releases of web authoring tools such as Macromedia Dreamweaver and Microsoft FrontPage can be used to select and configure a number of "canned" DHTML effects, such as navigation menus, text movement, and page transitions. You may also be surprised at the sources of free DHTML code on the Web.

Sources of Free DHTML

There are many available resources for DHTML on the Web. Here are some helpful sites:

- http://dynamicdrive.com
- http://dhtmlcentral.com
- http://www.opencube.com
- http://brainjar.com
- http://www.dhtmlshock.com

As you visit these and other DHTML resource sites, keep in mind that some may be copyrighted. Be sure to obtain permission from the creator of the DHTML before using it on your site and follow any instructions for giving credit to the source. Some sites allow personal use of their DHTML for free but require licenses for commercial use.

If you choose to use free DHTML, be very careful about which browsers it is meant to work with. Some sites clearly indicate the browsers supported by each DHTML effect, such as dynamicdrive.com. Other sites, such as brainjar.com, contain code that is meant to only work in the newer releases of browsers and is not backward compatible to Netscape 4.x. Testing is crucial when you are using DHTML.

Also, always offer your visitors an alternate method in case the DHTML does not work. For example, if you use DHTML for a navigation bar, offer plain text navigation at the bottom of the page.

As you have seen, DHTML can be used to create interesting movement and effects on web pages. Another technology that can be used to create similar types of effects as well as complex interactions and product demonstrations is Macromedia Flash. The Flash format (.swf file extension) is becoming ubiquitous on the Web. Microsoft even used a Flash file to showcase a demonstration of the features of FrontPage 2002! The next section introduces you to using this technology on web pages.

Macromedia Flash

Flash is a popular multimedia application developed by Macromedia. It is often used to create animation and multimedia effects on web pages. The animations can be as simple as the Flash effect shown in Figure 12.21 (see the student disk at Chapter12/ex10.htm). Flash can also be used to create many more complex effects, including full-screen animations, banner ads, and interactive site navigation using integrated audio clips.

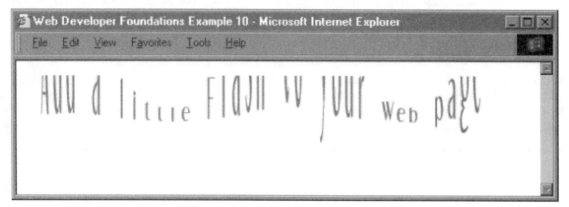

Figure 12.21 *Sample Flash web page*

Flash animations are stored in a file with a .swf file extension. Unlike other media, .swf files play as they download and give the perception of speedy display of complex graphic animations. Flash animations can be interactive; they can be scripted, with a language called ActionScript, to respond to mouse clicks, accept information in text boxes, and invoke CGI or other server-side scripting.

Flash requires a browser plug-in, which is free and readily available for download from Macromedia. According to Macromedia, over 96% of web browsers have a Flash plug-in installed.

Macromedia licenses the Macromedia Flash file format to third-party developers. This means that you can use applications other than Macromedia Flash to create a Flash (.swf) effect. Adobe's LiveMotion (http://www.adobe.com/products/livemotion/main.html) and Swish (http://www.swishzone.com/), a low-cost application, are just two of the third-party tools that can be used to create media in the .swf format. Even Macromedia Dreamweaver can be used to create Flash text and Flash button effects, which are stored in .swf files.

Common Uses of Flash

Navigation. Flash is often used to create an interactive navigation area on a web page. See Figure 12.22 for the home page of the city of Denver, http://www.denvergov.org/default.asp. It uses Flash to offer and describe main navigation choices.

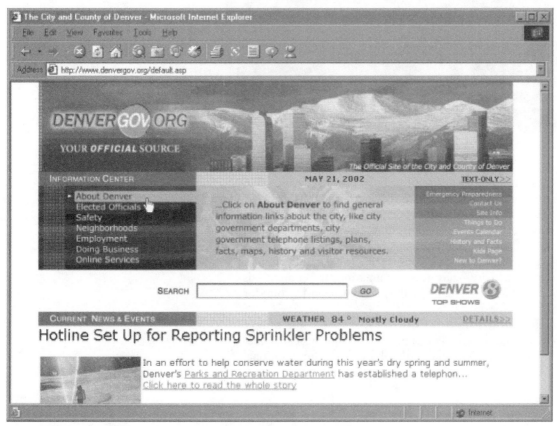

Figure 12.22 *Flash is used to provide navigation and interactive descriptions.*

Visit the Healing Earth Holistic Center at http://www.healingearth holisticcenter.com/he_set.html and experience a navigation bar that reads the choices aloud to you. Another example navigation using Flash can be found Utah State University's home page at http://www.usu.edu.

Splash Screen. The term *splash screen* is from client-server applications that display an introductory, or splash, screen while the program loads. Splash screens can set the tone or introduce a web site. Check out John's Cycles, shown in Figure 12.23, for a splash screen that gets you in the mood for motorcycles.

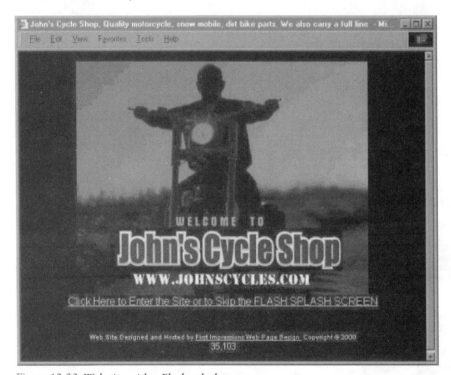

Figure 12.23 *Web site with a Flash splash screen*

A design note for splash screens: give your web site visitors a way to skip the animation by placing a simple text link to the main page of your site.

Entire Web Site. Flash can be used to create entire web sites, including navigation, content, and forms. A compelling example is 2advanced Studios (http://www.2advanced.com/flashindex.htm). At the time this was written, the source code of the web page consists of a table that contains a Flash object. All the interactivity—navigation, animation, and content—is coded in the Flash .swf file. Visit Neon Sky (http://www.neonsky.com) for another example of this type of web site.

Flash Innovation and Imagination. As you viewed the sample sites you may have noticed the creativity, innovation, and sheer imagination that some of them exhibit. Visit the textbook's web site for additional links to Flash web sites.

Web Design and Flash

Some of the Flash examples above are quite compelling. However, not everyone is an advocate of Flash. While some web developers and web visitors love Flash effects, Jakob Nielsen—the noted web design guru—has some serious concerns about Flash and usability. In his Alertbox article on Flash (http://www.useit.com/alertbox/20001029.html) Nielsen states, "Although multimedia has its role on the Web, current Flash technology tends to discourage usability for three reasons: it makes bad design more likely, it breaks with the Web's fundamental interaction style, and it consumes resources that would be better spent enhancing a site's core value." Macromedia has responded to these concerns and has formed a strategic relationship with the Nielsen Norman Group to focus on improving the usability and accessibility of Flash media.

Today's web developer needs to know how to add a Flash .swf file to a web page. If you are working on a large project, a graphic designer may create the effect and pass it to you for placement on a page. If you are working on a small project, you may be expected to create Flash .swf files yourself. Macromedia offers a free trial download of the Flash application, including a few tutorials and lessons on using Flash.

Adding a Flash Animation to a Web Page

You've seen some examples of Flash and are aware of issues related to Flash and web usability. Now let's take a look at the XHTML that is needed to use Flash media on a web page.

Both the **<object>** tag and the **<embed>** tag are used to place Flash media on a page because some versions of currently popular browsers such as Netscape support the **<embed>** tag and do not fully support the **<object>** tag. Use the **<noembed>** tag to contain a text description of the Flash media to improve accessibility.

The **<object>** tag specifies the beginning of Flash media on a web page. Its closing tag, **</object>**, specifies the ending of Flash media. As discussed in Chapter 10, the **<object>** tag is a multipurpose tag for adding various types of objects to a web page. The **<object>** tag's attributes vary, depending on the type of object being referenced. The attributes required when working with Flash media are described in Table 12.3.

Table 12.3 *Flash Media Attributes*

<object> Attribute	**Description and Value**
classid	The class ID for the Flash plug-in. The current value is **"clsid:D27CDB6E-AE6D-11cf-96B8-444553540000"**.
codebase	The URL of the Flash plug-in. (It allows for easy download if the web page visitor does not have the Flash plug-in installed.) The current value is **"http://download.macromedia.com/pub/shockwave/cabs/flash/ swflash.cab#version=4,0,2,0"**.
height	Specifies the height of the object area in pixels.
width	Specifies the width of the object area in pixels.

The Flash object needs special values, called parameters, to configure the name of the .swf file, quality of the media, and background color of the page areas. These are configured with **<param>** or parameter tags. Parameters used with Flash media are shown in Table 12.4.

Table 12.4 *Flash Media Parameters*

Parameter Name	Parameter Value
movie	File name of the Flash media (.swf file)
quality	Describes the quality of the media. Usually the value "high" is used.
bgcolor	Background color of the Flash media area. Use a hexadecimal color value.

All the **<param>** tags for the object appear before the ending **</object>** tag. An example will be given later in this section. The **<embed>** tag is also used to provide for web browsers that do not support the **<object>** tag. The **<embed>** tag is coded after the **<param>** tags, but before the ending **</object>** tag. An overview of this tag placement is listed here:

```
<object … object attributes go here….
    <param name="movie" …value attribute goes here… />
     <param name="quality" …value attribute goes here… />
      <param name="bgcolor" …value attribute goes here… />
<embed … object attributes go here…. />
<noembed> … a brief description of the Flash media can go here along with a link to
alternate text content if appropriate… </noembed>
</object>
```

The required **<embed>** tag attributes for Flash media are described in Table 12.5.

Table 12.5 *Flash Media* **<embed>** *Tag Attributes*

<embed> Attribute	Description and Value
src	Name of the Flash media (.swf) file
quality	Describes the quality of the media. Usually the value "high" is used.
pluginspage	URL of the Flash plug-in. (It allows for easy download if the web page visitor does not have the Flash plug-in installed.) The current value is **"http://www.macromedia.com/shockwave/download/ index.cgi?P1_Prod_Version=ShockwaveFlash"**
type	MIME type of the Flash media. The value is **"application/x-shockwave-flash"**.
bgcolor	Background color of the Flash media area. Use a hexadecimal color value.
height	Specifies the height of the object area in pixels.
width	Specifies the width of the object area in pixels.

The **<noembed>** tag is a container tag. Use it to provide a brief text description of the Flash media. Include a link to a web page containing alternate text content if needed. While the developers of assistive technologies such as screen readers are working toward the support of Flash media, it is not yet the norm.

If this seems like a lot of tags and parameters to remember, it is! Most web developers obtain an example of adding Flash media to a web page and copy and edit it slightly on new pages. Some web authoring applications, such as Macromedia Dreamweaver, will automatically generate this code when you select to insert a Flash object on your page.

Hands-On Practice 12.5

In this Hands-On Practice you will launch Notepad and create a web page that displays a Flash button. Your page will look like the one shown in Figure 12.24, which can be found on the student disk at Chapter12/flash.htm.

Figure 12.24 *Flash example*

The Flash button on the page will animate when the mouse is placed on it and will link to the Macromedia web site when clicked (if you are connected to the Internet while viewing this page).

Let's get started. Create a folder called testflash on your disk. Copy the flashbutton.swf file from the student disk Chapter12 folder and save it in your testflash folder.

Next, launch Notepad and create the page that will display this Flash button. The XHTML code is shown here:

```
<?xml version="1.0" encoding="UTF-8"?>
<!DOCTYPE html PUBLIC "-//W3C//DTD XHTML 1.0 Transitional//EN"
   "http://www.w3.org/TR/xhtml1/DTD/xhtml1-transitional.dtd">
<html xmlns="http://www.w3.org/1999/xhtml">
<head>
<title>Hands-On Practice 12.5</title>
```

continues

```
</head>
<body bgcolor="#FFFFFF" text="#000000">
<h1>Flash Sample</h1>
<object classid="clsid:D27CDB6E-AE6D-11cf-96B8-444553540000" codebase=
"http://download.macromedia.com/pub/shockwave/cabs/flash/swflash.cab#version=4,0,2,0"
width="147" height="34">
<param name="movie" value="flashbutton.swf" />
<param name="quality" value="high" />
<param name="bgcolor" value="#FFFFFF" />
<embed src="flashbutton.swf" quality="high" pluginspage=
"http://www.macromedia.com/shockwave/download/index.cgi?P1_Prod_Version=ShockwaveFlash"
type="application/x-shockwave-flash" width="147" height="34" bgcolor="#FFFFFF" />
<noembed>This is a Flash button that links to <a href="http://macromedia.com">Macromedia's
web site</a>
</noembed>
</object>
</body>
</html>
```

*Save your file in the testflash folder as flash.htm and test it in a
browser. If this seemed to be very tedious XHTML, don't worry—
many web authoring tools automate the process of writing code to
place Flash effects on a web page. All you would do is point and
click to the .swf file you are using. Macromedia Dreamweaver also
offers the option of creating Flash buttons and Flash text effects in
this point-and-click manner.*

Flash Resources

There are many sources of free Flash animations and Flash tutorials
on the web. In addition to resources at the Macromedia site, http://
macromedia.com, the following sites contain tutorials and news about Flash:

- http://flashkit.com
- http://www.actionscript.org
- http://www.ultrashock.com

As you visit these and other Flash resource sites, keep in mind
that some Flash media is copyrighted. Obtain permission
from the creator of the media before using it on your site and follow any
instructions for giving credit to the source. Some sites allow personal use of
their Flash media for free but require licenses for commercial use.

Macromedia has been working toward increasing the accessibility of Flash objects and has released Flash MX, which uses
the Flash Player 6. This newer version of Flash is accessible by assistive
technologies such as screen readers, enabling rich content for a wider audience of web page visitors.

Flash MX and the Flash Player 6 support Microsoft Active Accessibility,
which provides both a standard way for client technology to communicate
with assistive technologies and a way for developers to ensure that the
client software they create to this standard can include Macromedia Flash
support. Visit Macromedia's web site (http://www.macromedia.com) for
the most up-to-date information on the issue of Flash and accessibility.

Keep in mind that while strides have been taken in providing accessible Flash media, not all of your web page visitors using assistive technology will have the most recent applications—the `<noembed>` tag will provide alternate content for these visitors.

You should now be familiar with a number of technologies that can add interactivity to web pages. While interactivity makes web pages more interesting and compelling for web page visitors, the processing power of the Web is the connection between client and server. CGI handles the passing of information between web page visitors, the clients, and the web server databases and text files. This topic was discussed in Chapter 6, but it is so important that we revisit it in the next section.

Common Gateway Interface (CGI)

In the world of information technology, a *gateway* describes a connection point between two networks or systems. Common Gateway Interface (CGI), is a standard method for web pages to request special processing on the web server, such as database queries, sending e-mails, or handling form data. CGI provides a standard way for a web server to pass a web visitor's request to a program or script stored on the server, receive a response from the program or script, and send that response to the web browser for display.

Steps in Utilizing CGI

1. Web page invokes CGI by a form or hyperlink.
2. CGI script on web server is executed.
3. CGI script accesses requested database, file, or process.
4. Web server returns web page with requested information or confirmation of action.

CGI programs and scripts can be written in many languages, including Perl, C, C++, and Shell. The most common language for CGI scripts is Perl. CGI scripts and programs are often stored on the web server in a folder called cgi-bin or bin.

Common Uses of CGI

CGI is most often used to
- Search a database
- Place an order at an online store
- Send a web page to a friend
- Subscribe to a newsletter
- Any type of server-side file or e-mail processing is a candidate for CGI.

Using CGI

CGI scripts and programs are invoked by their URL. This URL can be typed in the address bar of a browser window, coded in XHTML as the href on an anchor tag, or coded in XHTML as the action on a form tag.

Browser Window Address Bar. The easiest way to invoke a CGI script is to type its URL in the browser window. This means that you must know the URL of the script. The Perl script, date.pl, prints the date and time from the web server. If you are connected to the Internet, try typing http://terryfelke.com/cgi-bin/date.pl the address bar of a browser window. Your display should be similar to the one shown in Figure 12.25.

Figure 12.25 *This page was created by the Perl script date.pl.*

The actual Perl script to create this very simple page is shown in Figure 12.26.

```
date.pl - Notepad
File   Edit   Search   Help
print "Content-type:text/html\n\n";
print "<html><head><title>Test Page</title></head>\n";
print "<body>\n";
$date=localtime(time);
($day, $month, $num, $time, $year) = split(/\s+/,$date);
($hour, $min, $sec)=split(/:/,$time);
if ($hour > 12) {$hour-=12;$am="pm"}
else {$am="am"};
$date="$day, $month $num, $year, $hour:$min $am (CST)";
print $date;
print "</body></html>\n";
```

Figure 12.26 *The source code of the Perl script date.pl*

Don't worry, you won't be writing Perl scripts just yet. However, if you are curious, visit http://perl.com for more information.

Invoke a CGI from an Anchor Tag. The same script could be invoked from an anchor tag as follows:

```
<a href="http://terryfelke.com/cgi-bin/date.pl">Server Date and Time</a>
```

Invoke a CGI from a Form. When a web page visitor clicks the Submit button on a form, the form data is sent to the URL in the form tag's action attribute. This URL should be a CGI script or other server-side processing technique. Figure 12.27 shows a screen shot of a sample form that invokes a CGI script, which can be found on the student disk at Chapter12/form.htm.

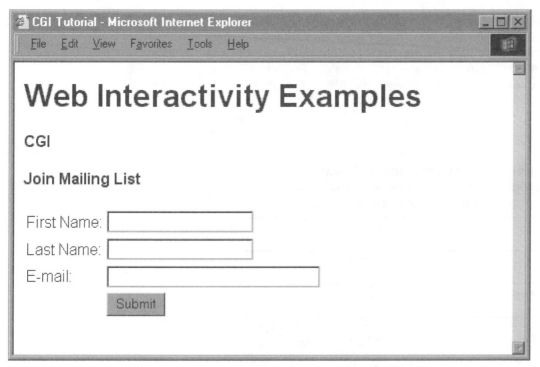

Figure 12.27 *A web page with a form that invokes CGI*

This form accepts information for a mailing list that is saved to a text file on a web server. The example invokes a CGI script called emaillist.pl located at the domain name terryfelke.com in the cgi-bin folder. The form tag needs to be configured as follows:

```
<form action="http://terryfelke.com/cgi-bin/maillist.pl" method="post">
```

When the user fills out the form and clicks the Submit button, the form data is sent to the URL of the action attribute. The method attribute (See Table 12.6) determines how the form data will be sent to the web server.

Table 12.6

Method Attribute	Status of Form Data
get (default)	The form data is appended to the URL in the format of name-value pairs.
post (recommended by the W3C)	This is more secure because the name-value pairs are not placed in the URL but are placed in the body (entity-body) of the HTTP request.

In this Hands-On Practice you will create a web page that contains a form and invokes a Perl script to process the form information. Your computer must be connected to the Internet for this exercise. If you have not done so already, take a moment to try out the sample form found on your student disk at Chapter12/form.htm.

Each server-side script that you use will provide some documentation about its input (the form elements that it expects to receive) and its output (the web page, text file, database update, or e-mail message that it produces). Sample documentation for the Perl script used in this exercise, called mailist.pl, is shown in Table 12.7. As you code the XHTML, notice how the form elements correspond to this documentation.

Table 12.7 *Documentation for Script maillist.pl*

Script URL: http://terryfelke.com/cgi-bin/maillist.pl
Processing: This script accepts a first name, last name, and email address. It then displays the values in a web page.

Input Elements	first	First Name
	last	Last Name
	email	E-mail Address
Output	This creates a confirmation web page that displays a message including the first name, last name and e-mail address.	

Launch Notepad and enter the code shown below:

```
<?xml version="1.0" encoding="UTF-8"?>
<!DOCTYPE html PUBLIC "-//W3C//DTD XHTML 1.0 Transitional//EN"
    "http://www.w3.org/TR/xhtml1/DTD/xhtml1-transitional.dtd">
<html xmlns="http://www.w3.org/1999/xhtml">
<head>
<title>Hands-On Practice 12.6</title>
<style type="text/css">
body,td {font-family:Arial,sans-serif; }
</style>
</head>
<body>
  <h2>Join Mailing List</h2>
    <form name="myForm" method="post"
      action="http://terryfelke.com/cgi-bin/maillist.pl">
    <table border="0">
      <tr>
        <td>First Name:</td>
        <td> <input type="text" name="first" size="20" /></td>
      </tr>
      <tr>
        <td>Last Name:</td>
        <td><input type="text" name="last" size="20" /></td>
      </tr>
      <tr>
```

continues

```
      <td>E-mail:</td>
      <td><input type="text" name="email" size="30" /></td>
    </tr>
    <tr>
    <td> </td>
    <input type="hidden" name="nameit" value="results.txt" />
    <td><input type="submit" value="Submit" /></td>
    </tr>
  </table>
  </form>
</body>
</html>
```

*Save your file as form.htm. Make sure your computer is connected
to the Internet and test your page in a browser. Once you submit
your form, the CGI Perl script should display a confirmation page
similar to the one shown in Figure 12.28.*

Figure 12.28 *The web page created by the CGI script*

*You may have noticed that the script is invoked whenever you click
the Submit button on the web page, even if you do not enter any
information for the name or e-email address. Often client-side
scripting such as JavaScript edits the form fields before sending the
information to the Web server. Try out another version of the form,
which can be found on the student disk at Chapter12/
formwithedits.htm.*

*Many companies and web host providers have a stock set of CGI
scripts that they use over and over. These have documentation and
will indicate the URL of the script and any form field names that the
script expects.*

CGI Resources

There are many CGI resources on the Web. If you'd like the official overview try http://hoohoo.ncsa.uiuc.edu/cgi/overview.html. The W3C has a resource page at http://www.w3.org/CGI/.

Sources of Free CGI Scripts. To use free CGI Scripts you need to have access to a web server that supports the CGI language used by the script. Most free scripts use Perl. Contact your web host provider to determine what is supported. Be aware that many free web host providers do not support CGI (you get what you pay for!). Here are a few sites that offer free CGI scripts and other resources:

- http://www.worldwidemart.com/scripts/
- http://cgi.resourceindex.com/Programs_and_Scripts/Perl/
- http://www.extropia.com/

Sources of Free Remote-Hosted CGI Scripts. If your web host provider does not support CGI, free remotely-hosted scripts may be an option. The script is not hosted on your server so you don't need to worry about installing it or whether your web host provider will support it. The disadvantage is that there usually is some advertising displayed. Here are a few sites that offer this service:

- http://formbuddy.com
- http://hostedscripts.com
- http://response-o-matic.com

Other Technologies Used for Server-Side Processing

Other types of technologies can be used for server-side scripting, form processing, and information sharing:

- JavaServer Pages (http://java.sun.com/products/jsp/)
- Active Server Pages (Visit http://msdn.microsoft.com/ and search for "Active Server Pages".)
- ColdFusion (http://www.macromedia.com/software/coldfusion/)
- PHP (http://www.php.net)
- Microsoft's .NET Framework (http://www.microsoft.com/net/)
- Web Services (http://webservicesarchitect.com, http://webservices.org, and http://www.uddi.org/)

Any of these technologies would be a good choice for future study. Web developers often learn the client-side first (HTML and JavaScript), and then progress to learning a server-side scripting or programming language.

Chapter 12 Review

Summary

The purpose of this chapter was to introduce you to a number of technologies used to add interactivity to web pages. As you continue your studies, you may choose to specialize in one or more of these technologies. Visit the text web site at http://www.webdevfoundations.net for examples, updated information, and the links listed in this chapter.

Review Questions

Multiple Choice

1. JavaScript can be described as
   a. an object-based scripting language
   b. an easy form of Java
   c. a language created by Microsoft
   d. none of the above

2. `<script>` tags can
   a. be used to contain JavaScript statements
   b. be placed in both the header and the body section of a web page
   c. both a and b
   d. none of the above

3. Java can be described as
   a. a more sophisticated form of JavaScript
   b. an object-oriented programming language
   c. a language created by Netscape
   d. none of the above

4. Java applets
   a. are contained in files with the .class extension
   b. are not copyrighted
   c. must be saved in a different folder than web pages
   d. none of the above

5. DHTML uses a combination of three technologies to create interactive web pages. The technologies are
   a. client-side scripting, Document Object Model, web browser
   b. client-side Scripting, CSS, Java
   c. Document Object Model, CSS, web browser
   d. Document Object Model, CSS, client-side scripting

6. Animations in Flash format (.swf) can be created
   a. only by Macromedia Flash
   b. by a number of applications, including Adobe LiveMotion
   c. with Microsoft FrontPage
   d. none of the above

7. Which is a standard method for web pages to request special processing on the web server, such as database queries, sending e-mails, or handling form data?

    a. DHTML   c. JavaScript

    b. CGI   d. none of the above

8. The parameters needed by a Java applet are configured using

    a. DHTML   c. parameter tags

    b. the applet tag   d. none of the above

9. The _____ tag(s) are used to place a .swf file on a web page.

    a. **`<script>`**

    b. **`<object>`** and **`<embed>`**

    c. **`<script>`** and **`<object>`**

    d. **`<applet>`**

10. The technology best used to process a jump menu on a web page is

    a. DHTML   c. JavaScript

    b. Flash   d. none of the above

Fill in the Blank

11. In the context of web page interactivity, a(n) _____ can be described as an action taken by the user.

12. To provide for _____ when creating interactive web pages using DHTML navigation, place a row of text navigation links on the page.

13. When displaying a Java applet, the browser invokes the _____ to interpret the bytecode into the appropriate machine language.

14. _____ was developed by a joint effort between Netscape and Sun Microsystems.

15. The _____ defines every object and element on a web page.

Apply Your Knowledge

1. **Predict the Result.** Draw and write a brief description of the web page that will be created with the following XHTML code.

```
<?xml version="1.0" encoding="UTF-8"?>
<!DOCTYPE html PUBLIC "-//W3C//DTD XHTML 1.0 Transitional//EN"
   "http://www.w3.org/TR/xhtml1/DTD/xhtml1-transitional.dtd">
<html xmlns="http://www.w3.org/1999/xhtml">
<head>
<title>Trillium Technologies</title>
</head>
<body>
  <h1>Trillium Technologies</h1>
<p>
  Home
  | <a href="about.htm"
onmouseover="window.status='All About Trillium Technologies';return true"
onmouseout="window.status='Trillium Technologies';return true"
title="All About Trillium Technologies">About</a>
  | <a href="services.htm"
onmouseover="window.status='Services at Trillium Technologies';return true"
onmouseout="window.status='Trillium Technologies';return true"
```

continues

```
title="Services at Trillium Technologies">About</a>
  </p>
  <p><img="workplace.jpg" alt="Trillium Technologies Professionals at work"
height="400" width="500" /></p>
  <p align="center" style="font-size:10px">
  Copyright &copy; 2002 Trillium Technologies</p>
</body>
</html>
```

2. **Fill in the Missing Code.** This web page should display a form that will invoke the server-side script addlist.asp using the post method. Some XHTML tags, indicated by <_>, are missing. Some XHTML attributes, indicated by "_", are missing. Fill in the missing code.

```
<?xml version="1.0" encoding="UTF-8"?>
<!DOCTYPE html PUBLIC "-//W3C//DTD XHTML 1.0 Transitional//EN"
    "http://www.w3.org/TR/xhtml1/DTD/xhtml1-transitional.dtd">
<html xmlns="http://www.w3.org/1999/xhtml" >
<head>
<title>Trillium Technologies</title>
</head>
<body>
  <h2>Join Mailing List</h2>
  <form name="myForm" method="_" action="_">
  <table border="0">
    <tr>
      <td> Name:</td>
      <td> <input type="text" name="name" size="40" /></td>
    </tr>
    <tr>
      <td>E-mail:</td>
      <td><input type="text" name="email" size="30" /></td>
    </tr>
    <tr>
    <td> </td>
    <td><_></td>
    </tr>
  </table>
  <_>
</body>
</html>
```

3. **Find the Error.** The purpose of the following web page is to display an applet stored in the applets folder called demo.class. The applet requires no parameters. Why doesn't the applet display?

```
<?xml version="1.0" encoding="UTF-8"?>
<!DOCTYPE html PUBLIC "-//W3C//DTD XHTML 1.0 Transitional//EN"
    "http://www.w3.org/TR/xhtml1/DTD/xhtml1-transitional.dtd">
<html xmlns="http://www.w3.org/1999/xhtml" >
<head>
<title>Find the Error<title>
</head>
<body>
  <div align="center">
```

continues

```
<applet codebase="applet" code="demo.class" height="50" width="600"
alt="Java applet: Preview demonstration of new version of DemoWare">
This Java applet displays a demonstration of the latest version of DemoWare —
 the software that will take your online product demonstrations to a new level.
</applet>
</div>
</body>
</html>
```

Hands-On Exercises

1. Practice writing XHTML.

   a. Write the XHTML to place a Java applet called mylink.class on a
      web page. This applet needs an area that is 300 pixels wide and 40
      pixels high. Its parameters are documented below:

Parameter Name	Parameter Value
LinkURL	Any URL
LinkDescription	Text describing the link

   b. Write the XHTML to add a Flash file called intro.swf to a web
      page. The effect needs an area that is 500 pixels wide and 200
      pixels high. Center the effect horizontally in the page.

2. Create a web page about your favorite movie that contains links to three
   web pages. These links can connect to your choice of sites related to the
   movie. Possibilities are reviews and web sites about the actors in the
   movie. Add JavaScript to the page to change the text in the status bar
   when the web page visitor places their mouse pointer over each link. Use
   Hands-On Practice 12.1 as a guide. Place an e-mail link to yourself on
   the web page. Save the page as movie12.htm. Hand in printouts of both
   the source code (print in Notepad) and the browser display of your page.

3. Create a web page about your favorite music group that uses either the
   Java applet described in Hands-On 12.3 or a Java applet of your choice.
   The applet should display the names of songs performed by the group.
   Place an e-mail link to yourself on the Web page. Save the page as
   cd12.htm. Hand in printouts of both the source code (print in Notepad)
   and the browser display of your page.

Each of these case studies will continue throughout most of the text. In this chapter, you add interactive effects to the web sites.

A. JavaJam Coffee House

See Chapter 2 for an introduction to the JavaJam Coffee House case. Figure 2.20 shows a site map for the JavaJam web site. The pages were created in earlier chapters. Use the javajamcss folder created in the Chapter 9 case study.

Your task is to add a moving logo DHTML effect to the home page. This logo will move in from left to right across the top of the web page.

Hands-On Practice Case

Obtain the dhtml.css and the javajam.js files used in this case study from the student disk. The image files are located in the Chapter12 folder. Save them to your floppy disk in the javajamcss folder.

Launch Notepad and open the home page (index.htm) in the javajamcss folder. Modify index.htm to link to the dhtml.css file and to treat the javajam.js file as a script. See the Hands-On Practice exercises in this chapter for help.

Continue to modify index.htm and create a division (use **<div>** tags) that contains the JavaJam logo (javalogo.gif). Assign an id with the value "animate" to the **<div>**. Add an event to the body tag to so that the motion() function will begin each time the page is loaded. (*Hint:* **<body onload="motion()">**). Save your page. Test your page using several browsers. You should see the logo move.

B. Fish Creek Animal Hospital

See Chapter 2 for an introduction to the Fish Creek Animal Hospital case. Figure 2.23 shows a site map for the Fish Creek web site. The pages were created in earlier chapters. Use the fishcreekcss folder created in the Chapter 9 case study.

Your task is to add image rollovers to the navigation area. When the web page visitor places the mouse pointer over one of the navigation images, the image will change (called *image swapping* or *image rollovers*). You will add this feature to the Home page of the site, as shown in Figure 12.29.

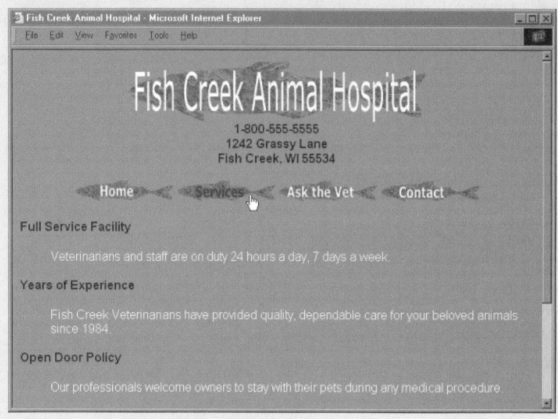

Figure 12.29 *New Fish Creek Home page with image rollovers*

Hands-On Practice Case

1. Your home page (index.htm in the fishcreekcss folder) should already display the logo (fishcreeklogo.gif) and navigation images (home.gif, services.gif, askthevet.gif, contact.gif). If it does not, obtain the logo and navigation images from the student disk (Chapter4/CaseStudyStarters folder), save them to your floppy disk in the fishcreekcss folder, and modify the index.htm page as follows. Use Figure 12.29 as a guide and place the logo.gif near the top of the page. Use the rest of the images to create a graphic navigation bar. The Services (services.gif), Ask the Vet (askthevet.gif) and Contact (contact.gif) images should each link to their corresponding pages (services.htm, askthevet.htm, and contact.htm).

2. Copy the new images for this case from the student disk (Chapter12 folder) and save them to the fishcreekcss folder. These are the images that will display when your web page visitor places the mouse pointer

over one of the image links: serviceson.gif, asktheveton.gif, contacton.gif, and homeon.gif (note the homeon.gif image is not used on the index.htm page but is included for completeness).

3. Modify the index.htm page to use JavaScript to handle mouseovers.

- Add the name attribute to each image used for navigation. For example, the **<img>** tag for the Services image should be modified as follows:

```
<img border="0" src="services.gif" alt="Fish Creek Services" width="132" height="27" name="services" />
```

Modify the Ask the Vet and Contact **<img>** tags in a similar manner. The value of the name attribute should not contain any spaces.

- Add onmouseover and onmouseout events to each image hyperlink. The events will change the src attribute on the image to a new value. For example, the hyperlink for the services.htm page should be modified as follows:

```
<a href="services.htm" onmouseover="document.services.src='serviceson.gif'" onmouseout="document.services.src='services.gif'">
```

Note the following:

  ○ **document.services.src** corresponds to the src attribute on the **<img>** tag with the name attribute value of "services". (You are using the DOM!) When the visitor places the mouse over the image link, document.services.src is set to the new image file (serviceson.gif). When the visitor moves the mouse off of the image link, **document.services.src** is set to the old image file (services.gif).

  ○ Be very careful with single and double quotes—they always travel in pairs!

- The image links for the Ask the Vet and Contact pages should be modified in a similar manner similar to the Services image link. Save your page. Test your page in several browsers. You should see the images swap.

C. Pete the Painter

See Chapter 2 for an introduction to the Pete the Painter case. Figure 2.26 shows a site map for the Pete the Painter web site. The pages were created in earlier chapters. Use the paintercss folder created in the Chapter 9 case study.

Your task is to modify the Testimonials page (testimonials.htm). The thumbnail links currently open images in the same window as the web site. Add JavaScript to the page so that the links to the images open in a new window that is only 420 pixels wide and 420 pixels high. You will be given the JavaScript code to add to the page.

Hands-On Practice Case

1. Launch Notepad and open the Testimonials page (testimonials.htm) in the paintercss folder. Modify all the thumbnail image links to open in the same window that is only 420 pixels x 420 pixels. Use the following example as a guide.

   • The first thumbnail on the page links to the "paintroom.jpg" file. The XHTML for the anchor tag is currently
   ```
   <a href="paintroom.jpg">
   ```
   When the link is clicked, the image should open in a new window of the requested size. The anchor tag should be changed as shown here:

   ```
   <a href="javascript:myWindow=window.open('paintroom.jpg','myWindow',
   'top=200, left=200,width=420,height=420');myWindow.focus()">
   ```

   This JavaScript opens a new window named myWindow, places the image paintroom.jpg in the window, configures the window to be 200 pixels from the top of the document, 200 pixels in from the left side of the document, 420 pixels wide, 420 pixels high, and has focus (meaning that it is shown on top of the window that contains the testimonials page).

   • Modify the image links for the undecorated.jpg and the foyer.jpg to show those images in the window named myWindow. Save your page. Test your page using several browsers. You should see the images open in the same window. See the screen shot in Figure 12.30 for a sample.

Figure 12.30 *Pete the Painter Testimonials page with pop-up window*

Web Research

A. Choose one method of web interactivity discussed in this chapter: JavaScript, Java applets, DHTML, Flash, or CGI. Use the resources listed in the chapter as a starting point, but also search the Web for additional resources on the interactivity method you have chosen. Create a web page that lists at least five useful resources along with a brief description of each. Organize your page with a table that provides the name of the site, the URL, a brief description of what is offered, and a recommended page (such as a tutorial, free script, etc.) for each resource. Place your name in an e-mail link on the web page. Print both the source code (from Notepad) and the browser view of your web page.

B. Choose one method of web interactivity discussed in this chapter: JavaScript, Java applets, DHTML, Flash, or CGI. Use the resources listed in the chapter as a starting point, but also search the Web for additional resources on the interactivity method you have chosen. Find either a tutorial or free download that uses the method of web interactivity that you have chosen. Create a web page that uses the code or download that you found. Describe the effect and list the URL of the resource on the web page. Place your name in an e-mail link on the web page. Print both the source code (from Notepad) and the browser view of your web page.

Chapter Review Answers

1. a
2. c
3. b
4. a
5. d
6. b
7. b
8. c
9. b
10. c
11. event
12. accessibility
13. Java Virtual Machine
14. JavaScript
15. Document Object Model (DOM)

Chapter 13

E-Commerce Overview

E-commerce is the buying and selling of
goods and services on the Internet. Whether
business-to-business, business-to-consumer, or
consumer-to-consumer, web sites that support
e-commerce seem to be everywhere. This chapter
provides an overview of this topic.

What Is E-Commerce?

A formal definition of e-commerce is the integration of communications, data management, and security technologies that allows individuals and organizations to exchange information related to the sale of goods and services. Major functions of e-commerce include the buying of goods, the selling of goods, and the performance of financial transactions on the Internet.

Advantages of E-Commerce

There are a number of advantages to both businesses and consumers when engaging in e-commerce. For businesses the many advantages include the following.

- **Reduced Costs.** Online businesses can stay open 24 hours a day without the overhead of a brick-and-mortar facility. Many businesses establish a web site before attempting to do e-commerce. When they add e-commerce functions to their web site, the site becomes a source of revenue and, in many cases, pays for itself.

- **Increased Customer Satisfaction.** Businesses can use their web sites to improve communication with customers and increase customer satisfaction. E-commerce sites often contain a FAQs page. The availability of customer service representatives by e-mail, a discussion forum, or even online chat (see http://humanclick.com) can also improve customer relations.

- **More Effective Data Management.** Depending on the level of automation, e-commerce sites can perform credit card verification and authorization, update inventory levels, and interface with order fulfillment systems. This manages the organization's data in a more efficient manner.

- **Potentially Higher Sales.** An e-commerce store that is open 24 hours a day, seven days a week and is available to everyone on the planet has a potential for higher sales than the traditional brick-and-mortar storefront.

Businesses aren't the only beneficiaries of e-commerce; consumers see some advantages as well, including the following.

- **Convenience.** Consumers can shop at any time of the day. There is no travel time to get to the store. Some consumers prefer web site shopping over traditional catalog shopping because they can view additional images and join discussion forums about the products.

- **Easier Comparison Shopping.** There is no driving from store to store to check the price on an item. Customers can easily surf the web and compare prices and value.

- **Wider Selection of Goods.** Since it is so convenient to shop and compare, consumers have a wider selection of goods available for purchase.

As you can see, e-commerce provides a number of advantages for both businesses and consumers.

Risks of E-Commerce

There are risks involved in any business transaction, and e-commerce is no exception. Possible issues for businesses include the following.

- **Loss of Sales If Technology Fails.** If your web site isn't available or your e-commerce form processing does not work, customers may not return to your site. It is always important to have a user-friendly, reliable web site, but when you engage in e-commerce, reliability and ease of use become critical factors in the success in your business.

- **Fraudulent Transactions.** The possibility of fraudulent credit card purchases or crank orders placed by vandals (or thirteen-year old kids with time on their hands) are risks that businesses need to deal with.

- **Customer Reluctance.** Although more and more consumers are willing to purchase over the Web, the target market of your business may not be. By offering incentives such as free shipping or a "no questions asked" returns policy, your business may be able to attract these consumers.

- **Increased Competition.** Because the overhead for an e-commerce site can be much lower than that of a traditional brick-and-mortar store, a company operating out of someone's basement can be just as impressive as a long-standing organization if its web site looks professional. Because it is much easier to enter the marketplace with an e-commerce store there will be increased competition for your business.

Businesses are not alone in needing to deal with risks associated with e-commerce Consumers may perceive the following risks:

- **Security Issues.** Later in this chapter you will learn how to determine whether a web site has Secure Sockets Layer (SSL) for encryption and security of information. The general public may not know how to determine whether a web site is using this encryption method and be wary of placing a credit card order. Another, possibly the more important issue, is what the site does with your information *after* it is transmitted on the Internet. Is the database secure? Are the database backups secure? These questions are difficult to answer. It's a good idea only to purchase from sites that you consider to be reputable.

- **Privacy Issues.** Many sites post privacy policy statements. These describe what the site will do (or not do) with the information given to them. Some sites only use the data for internal marketing purposes. Other sites sell the data to outside companies. Web sites can and do change their privacy policies over time. Consumers may be leery of purchasing online because of the potential lack of privacy.

- **Purchasing Based on Photos and Descriptions.** There is nothing like holding and touching an item before you purchase it. Consumers run the risk of purchasing a product they will not be happy with because they are using photographs and written descriptions to make their decision. If an e-commerce site has a generous return policy, consumers will feel more confident about purchasing.

- **Returns.** It is often more difficult to return an item to an e-commerce store than to a brick-and-mortar store. Consumers may not want to risk this inconvenience.

E-Commerce Business Models

Both businesses and consumers are riding the e-commerce wave. There are four common e-commerce business models: business-to-consumer, business-to-business, consumer-to-consumer, and business-to-government.

- **Business-to-Consumer (B2C).** Most of the business-to-consumer selling takes place in online stores. Some, like Amazon.com (http://amazon.com) are online only. Others are click-and-mortar—electronic storefronts for well-known brick-and-mortar stores such as Sears (http://sears.com).

- **Business-to-Business (B2B).** E-commerce between two businesses often takes the form of exchanging business supply chain information among vendors, partners, and business customers. Electronic Data Interchange (EDI) is also in this category.

- **Consumer-to-Consumer (C2C).** Individuals are selling to each other on the Internet. The most common format is that of the auction. The most well-known auction site is eBay, http://ebay.com, which was founded in 1995.

- **Business-to-Government (B2G).** Businesses are selling to the government on the Internet. There are very strict usability standards for businesses targeting governmental agencies. Section 508 of the Rehabilitation Act requires that electronic and information technology (including web pages) used by federal agencies be accessible to people with disabilities. See http://www.section508.gov for more information.

Businesses began exchanging information electronically many years before the Web came into existence, using Electronic Data Interchange.

Electronic Data Interchange (EDI)

Electronic Data Interchange (EDI) is the transfer of data between companies over a network. This facilitates the exchange of standard business documents, including purchase orders and invoices. EDI is not new; it has been in existence since the 1960s. Organizations that exchange EDI transmissions are called trading partners.

The Accredited Standards Committee X12 (ASC X12), is chartered by the American National Standards Institute (ANSI), to develop and maintain EDI standards. These standards include transaction sets for common business forms, such as requisitions and invoices. This allows businesses to reduce paperwork and communicate electronically.

EDI messages are placed in transaction sets. A transaction set consists of a header, one or more data segments which are strings of data elements separated by delimiters, and a trailer. Newer technologies such as XML and web services are allowing trading partners virtually unlimited opportunities to customize their information exchange over the Internet.

Now that you are aware of possibilities of e-commerce and the types of business models, are you wondering where the most money is being made? The next section takes a look at some statistics related to e-commerce.

E-Commerce Statistics

You may be surprised to discover that the most money is being made in B2B e-commerce—businesses selling to other businesses. According to Forrester Research, in 1998 business-to-business revenue in the United States amounted to $43 billion and total business-to-consumer revenue was only $8 billion. Forrester projects that by 2003 estimated B2B revenue will be $1,131 billion and estimated B2C revenue will be $108 billion. As illustrated in Figure 13.1, both these increases are quite large. However, the most money is being made in B2B e-commerce.

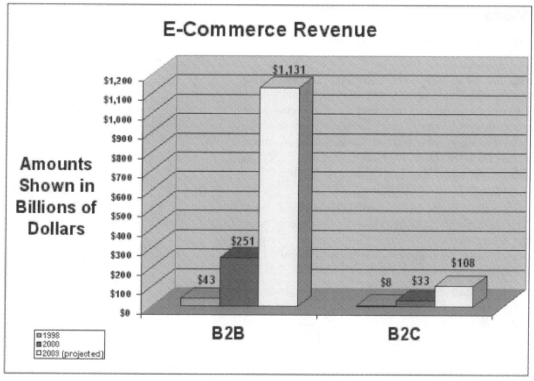

Figure 13.1 *The greatest increases are projected for B2B e-commerce.*

Who are your potential online consumers? A study by Harris Interactive discussed on CyberAtlas (http://cyberatlas.internet.com/big_picture/geographics/article/0,,5911_1011491,00.html) indicates that Internet users in the United States generally mirror the U.S. population but are slightly younger, more educated and more affluent. Table 13.1 shows an excerpt of this research.

Table 13.1 *Online Population*

Online Population Compared with U.S. Popluation		
	2002 Online Population	**U.S. Population (2000 Census)**
Male	49%	48%
Female	51%	52%
Household Income Less than $25K	19%	25%
Household Income $25K to $50K	23%	29%
Household Income Higher than $50K	45%	32%
Adults 18-49	74%	64%

E-Commerce Issues

Doing business on the Internet is not without its problems. Here are some common issues.

- **Intellectual Property**. There has been some recent controversy regarding intellectual property rights and domain names. Cybersquatting is the practice of registering a domain name that is a trademark of another entity in the hopes of profiting by selling the domain name to the entity. The Internet Corporation for Assigned Names and Numbers (ICANN) sponsors the Uniform Domain Name Dispute Policy at http://www.icann.org/udrp/udrp.htm that can be used to combat cybersquatters.

- **Security.** Security is a constant issue on the Internet. Distributed denial of service (DDoS) attacks have shut down popular e-commerce sites. Some of these attacks are carried out by *script kiddies* (teenagers with technical knowledge and sometimes malicious intent) who literally have nothing better to do than cause havoc on the Web.

- **Fraud.** Fraudulent web sites that ask for credit card numbers without any intent of delivering products or with fraudulent intent are an understandable source of concern for consumers.

- **Taxation.** State governments and local municipalities need sales taxes to fund education, public safety, health, and many other essential services. When an item is purchased at a retail store, the sales tax is collected from the purchaser by the seller at the time of sale and periodically remitted by the seller to the state in which the sale occurred.

  When an item is purchased on the Internet, the seller usually does not collect and remit the sales tax. In this situation, many states require that the consumer file a use tax and pay the amount that would have been collected. In reality, few consumers do this and very few states attempt to enforce it. Our local governments are losing revenue that would have funded worthwhile programs.

  There have been some movements to require that sales tax be collected on all Internet purchases. At the time this was written, the moratorium on Internet sales tax was still in effect. However, state and local governments are losing sources of revenue as more consumers turn to online shopping. Look for the topic of Internet sales tax to continue to be controversial in the future.

- **International Commerce.** Web sites that target a global audience have additional concerns. If it is decided to offer the site in multiple languages there is an option of automatic translation programs (http://www.systranlinks.com) and companies that offer customized web site translation services (http://www.worldlingo.com). Be aware that the graphical user interface (GUI) that works with English may not work with other languages. For example, comparable words and phrases often take quite a few more letters in German than in English. If your GUI doesn't have enough white space in the English version of the site, how will it look in the German version?

  How will your international customers pay you? If you accept credit cards, the credit card company will perform the currency conversion. What about the culture of your target international audience? Have you studied the target countries and made certain that your site is appealing and not offensive? Another issue related to international commerce is the cost of shipping and the availability of delivery to remote destinations.

Now that you are familiar with the concept of e-commerce, let's take a closer look at encryption methods and security for e-commerce. The next section introduces encryption methods, SSL, and digital certificates.

E-Commerce Security

Encryption

Encryption is used to ensure privacy within an organization and on the Internet. Encryption is the conversion of data into an unreadable form, called a **ciphertext**. Ciphertext cannot be easily understood by unauthorized individuals. **Decryption** is the process of converting the ciphertext back into its original form, called plain text or **clear text**, so it can be understood. The process of encryption and decryption requires an algorithm and a key.

Encryption is important on the Internet because information in a packet can be intercepted as it travels the communications media. If a hacker or business competitor intercepts an encrypted packet, he or she will not be able to use the information (such as a credit card number or business strategy) because it cannot be read.

A number of types of encryption are commonly used on the Internet, including symmetric-key encryption and asymmetric-key encryption. These are introduced below.

Figure 13.2 *Symmetric-key encryption uses a single key*

Symmetric-Key Encryption. Symmetric-key encryption, shown in Figure 13.2, is also called *single-key encryption* because both the encryption and decryption use the same key. Since the key must be kept secret from others, both the sender and receiver must know the key before communicating using encryption. An advantage of symmetric-key encryption is speed.

Asymmetric-Key Encryption. Asymmetric-key encryption is also called *public-key encryption* because there is no shared secret. Instead, two keys are created at the same time. This key pair contains a public key and a private key. The public key and the private key are mathematically related in such a way that it is unlikely anyone would guess one of the pair even with knowledge of the other. Only the public key can decrypt a message encrypted with the private key and only the private key can decrypt a message encrypted with the public key (see Figure 13.3). The public key is available via a digital certificate (more on that later). The private key should be kept secure and secret. It is stored on the web server (or other computer) of the key owner. Asymmetric-key encryption is much slower than symmetric-key encryption.

Figure 13.3 *Asymmetric-key encryption uses a key pair*

Integrity

The encryption methods described above help to keep the contents of a message secret. However, e-commerce security is also concerned with making sure that messages have not been altered or damaged during transmission. A message is said to have **integrity** if it can be proven that is has not been altered. **Hash functions** provide a way to ensure the integrity of messages. A hash function, or *hash algorithm*, transforms a string of characters into a usually shorter fixed-length value or key, called a **digest**, which represents the original string.

The security methods discussed above, especially the techniques of symmetric-key and symmetric-key encryption, are used as part of SSL, the technology that helps to make commerce on the Internet secure. The next section introduces this technology.

Secure Sockets Layer (SSL)

Secure Sockets Layer (SSL) is a protocol that allows data to be privately exchanged over public networks. It was developed by Netscape and is used to encrypt data sent between a client (usually a web browser) and a web server. SSL utilizes both symmetric and asymmetric keys.

SSL provides secure communication between a client and server by using:

- Server and (optionally) client digital certificates for authentication
- Symmetric-key cryptography with a "session key" for bulk encryption
- Public-key cryptography for transfer of the session key
- Message digests (hash function) to verify the integrity of the transmission

You can tell that a web site is using SSL by the protocol in the web browser address text box—it shows "https" instead of "http". Also, Internet Explorer and Netscape browsers display a lock icon when SSL is used as shown in Figure 13.4.

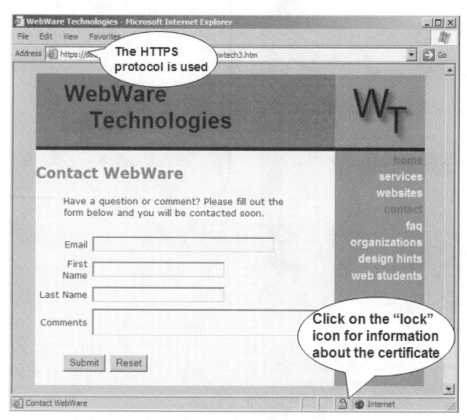

Figure 13.4 *The browser indicates that SSL is being used.*

Digital Certificate

SSL enables two computers to communicate securely by posting a digital certificate for authentication. A **digital certificate** is a form of an asymmetric key that also contains information about the certificate, the holder of the certificate, and the issuer of the certificate. The contents of a digital certificate include

- The public key
- Effective date of the certificate
- Expiration date of the certificate

- Details about the certificate authority—the issuer of the certificate
- Details about the certificate holder
- A digest of the certificate content

VeriSign (http://verisign.com) is a well-known certificate authority (CA). A recent version of their certificate is shown in Figure 13.5.

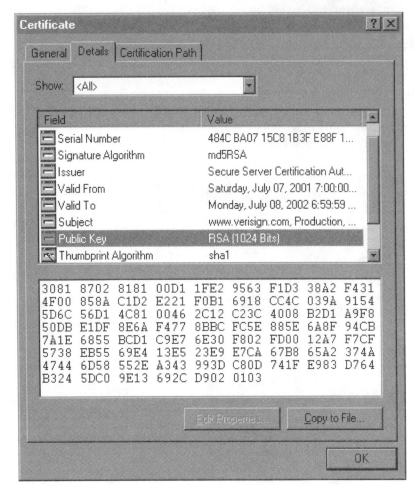

Figure 13.5 *VeriSign Digital Certificate*

Do I have to apply for a certificate?

If you are accepting any personal information on your web site such as credit card numbers you should be using SSL. One option is to visit a certificate authority (such as VeriSign or Thawte (http://www.thawte.com) and apply for your own certificate. There may be a waiting period and you will need to pay an annual fee.

As an alternative, your web host provider may let you piggyback on its certificate. There is normally a setup and/or monthly fee for this service. Usually, it assigns a folder to you on its secure server. You would place the web pages (and associated files such as images) that need to be processed in a secure manner in the folder. When linking to the web pages use "https" instead of "http" on your absolute links. Contact your web host provider for details.

To obtain a certificate, you request a certificate from a certificate authority and pay the application fee. The certificate authority verifies your identity, issues your certificate, and supplies you with a public/private key pair. Store the certificate in your software—such as a web server, web browser, or e-mail application. The certificate authority makes your certificate publicly known.

SSL and Digital Certificates

A number of steps are involved in the SSL authentication process. The web browser and web server go through initial handshaking steps, exchanging information about the server certificate and keys. Once trust is established, the web browser encrypts the single secret key (symmetric key) that will be used for the rest of the communication. From this point on, all data is encrypted through the secret key. Table 13.2 depicts this process.

Table 13.2 *SSL Encryption Process Overview*

Browser		"hello"		Server
Browser	←	"hello" + server certificate	←	Server
Browser	←	The server's private key is used to encrypt a message. Only the public key can decrypt this message.	←	Server

The browser now verifies the identity of the web server. It obtains the certificate of certificate authority (CA) that signed the server's certificate. Then the browser decrypts the certificate digest using the CA's public key (held in a root CA certificate). Next, it takes a digest of the server's certificate. The browser compares the digests and checks the expiration date of the certificate. If all is valid, the next step occurs.

Browser		The browser generates a session key and encrypts with the server public key.		Server
Browser	←	The server sends a message encrypted with the session key.	←	Server

All future transmissions between the browser and server are encrypted with the session key.

At this point you have a general idea of how SSL works to protect the integrity of information on the Internet, including the information exchanged in e-commerce transactions. The next section takes a closer look order and payment processing in e-commerce.

Order and Payment Processing

In B2C e-commerce, the products for sale are displayed in an online catalog. On large sites, these catalog pages are dynamically created using server-side scripts to access databases. Each item usually has a button or image that invites the visitor to "Buy Me" or "Add to Cart". Items selected are placed in a virtual shopping cart. When visitors are finished shopping, they click on a button or image link indicating they want to "Check Out" or "Place Order". At this point, the items in their shopping cart are usually displayed on a web page with an order form.

Secure ordering is facilitated through the use of SSL. Once the order is placed, there are a number of methods to pay for the merchandise or service; the payment methods, called payment models, are cash, check, credit, and smart card.

Cash Model

The **cash model** is the most difficult to implement—how do you send cash through a computer? You don't. You use e-cash. You purchase **digital money** from a bank and deposit it in a digital wallet. The transfer of funds is immediate. Vendors who provide this service include InternetCash (http://www.internetcash.com/) and eCoin (http://www.ecoin.net).

Check Model

In the **check model** consumer writes a digital check to make the purchase. As with real-world checks, the availability of funds must be verified and the funds are not transferred immediately. One vendor that provides this service is CheckFree (http://www.checkfree.com).

How do I find out about the most recent security issues?

The CERT Coordination Center at http://www.cert.org is a federally funded research and development center operated by Carnegie Mellon University. The CERT name is derived from an acronym for "Computer Emergency Response Team". One of its functions is to act as a clearinghouse of information related to security issues and incidents. CERT issues advisories that describe security problems and offers suggestions for preventing or correcting them.

Security issues are a real and growing problem. In 1989 CERT handled 132 incident reports. That number has grown each year. There were 21,756 incidents reported in 2000 and over 52,000 incidents reported in 2001.

Credit Model

Credit card payment processing is a very important component of an e-commerce web site. Funds from the customer need to be transferred to the merchants' bank. In order to accept credit cards, the site owner must apply for a merchant account and be approved. A merchant account is an agreement between the business and the bank that allows you to take credit card orders. You may also need real-time credit card verification using a merchant gateway or third party such as Authorize.Net (http://www.authorizenet.com). A diagram of the process is shown in Figure 13.6.

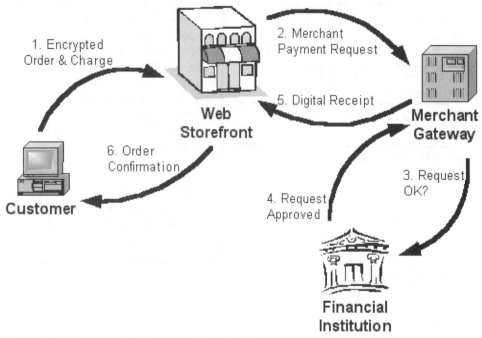

Figure 13.6 *The processing flow in credit card orders*

Secure Electronic Transactions (SET), is a standard protocol that enables secure credit card transactions on the Internet. It provides security for credit card payments as they travel the Internet between merchant sites and processing banks. SET uses public key cryptography and digital certificates.

While merchant accounts can be expensive, there are low-cost solutions such as PayPal (http://www.paypal.com). Originally intended for consumer-to-consumer credit card sales, PayPal now offers credit card and shopping cart services for business web site owners.

Smart Card

The **smart card** model is widely used in Europe, Australia, and Japan. A smart card is similar to a credit card, but it has an integrated circuit instead of a magnetic strip embedded in it. The smart card is inserted into a smart card reader. Expect to see more smart card applications in the United States in the coming years.

You have probably shopped at online stores and found some easy to work with and others difficult. A large problem for e-commerce sites is abandoned shopping carts—visitors who begin to shop but never place an order. The next section explores types of storefront solutions and shopping carts.

E-Commerce Storefront Solutions

A number of different e-commerce storefront options are available to business owners and web developers. They range from as simple as an instant online storefront supplied by another web site to building your own shopping cart system. This section examines some of the options.

Instant Online Storefront

You supply the products—the **instant online storefront** does the rest. There is no need to install software. All you do is use your web browser to point and click your way to a virtual store. You use a template provided by the online storefront and choose features, configure settings, and add your products—upload images, descriptions, prices, and captions.

There are some disadvantages to this approach. You are limited by the templates offered by the online storefront provider. The number of products you can sell may also be limited. Your store may have a "look and feel" similar to the other instant stores hosted at the provider. However, this approach provides a low-overhead, low-risk approach for a small business owner with limited technical expertise. The storefront provider will often also provide merchant account and payment automation.

Some instant storefront solutions are free with limited service or a limited number of products. Other are fee-based and may charge a hosting fee, processing fees, and monthly fees. A few popular instant storefront solutions are Yahoo! (http://store.yahoo.com), Bigstep (http://www.bigstep.com), and FreeMerchant (http://www.freemerchant.com). Figure 13.7 shows screen shots from a trial store on Yahoo!

This Yahoo! store took 5 minutes to create!

Figure 13.7 *Yahoo! makes it easy to create a instant storefront.*

Off-the-Shelf Shopping Cart Software

With this approach, software that provides a standardized set of e-commerce features is purchased, installed on your web server, and customized. Many web host providers offer this storefront software, which usually includes a shopping cart, order processing, and optional credit card payment processing. **Shopping cart software** provides an online catalog where your visitors can browse, add items to their virtual shopping cart, and check out through an order form when they are ready to purchase. Two popular shopping carts offered by web host providers are Miva Merchant (http://www.miva.com) and Mercantec SoftCart (http://www.mercantec.com). Figure 13.8 shows a typical shopping cart page on a web site. It provides the options to place an order, continue shopping, or cancel the order.

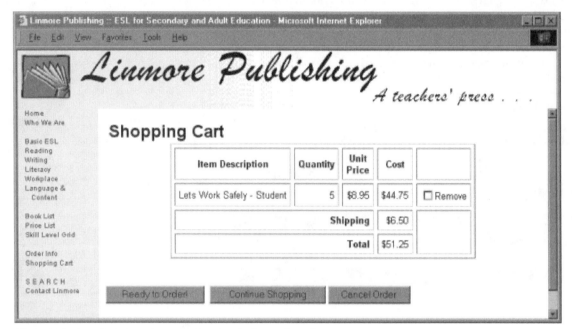

Figure 13.8 *A typical shopping cart showing the item selected*

Custom-Built Solution

Custom building a large-scale e-commerce web site entirely from scratch usually requires expertise, time, and a sizeable budget! The advantage is that you get exactly what you need. Software development tools for a custom-built site may include Macromedia Dreamweaver, Microsoft Visual Studio .NET, Macromedia ColdFusion, IBM's WebSphere Commerce Studio, a database management system (DBMS), and CGI or other server-side scripting. Custom-built solutions may also require a **commerce server**, which is a web server enhanced with support for certain commerce activities. IBM's WebSphere Commerce Suite and Microsoft's Commerce Server are two choices.

Semi-Custom-Built Solutions on a Budget

If the scope of your e-commerce endeavor is small and you want to avoid the cookie-cutter look of an instant storefront, some other options may be worth considering. These include getting pre-written shopping cart and order processing scripts, hiring a company such as PayPal, and buying e-commerce add-ons to popular web authoring tools.

There are a number of free shopping cart scripts available on the Web. Try searching http://aspcode.net, http://www.perlshop.org, http://www.mals-e.com, or http://www.extropia.com for some alternate solutions. The difficulty level and exact processing of these solutions vary. Each web site has instructions and documentation about its product. Some may require you to register and provide you with specific XHTML code. Others may require you to download and install the scripts on your own web server.

PayPal offers shopping cart and payment verification for businesses at a very low cost. PayPal writes the code you need to place on your web pages to interface with them. You only need to copy and paste it in.

A number of Microsoft FrontPage and Macromedia Dreamweaver add-ins, or extensions, provide shopping cart functionality. One easy solution is JustAddCommerce (http://www.richmediatech.com), which allows you to configure and add shopping cart and order buttons to your pages just as easily as you can add images and tables. Screen shots of the point-and-click interface are shown in Figures 13.9 and 13.10.

Figure 13.9 *The Microsoft FrontPage user interface for JustAddCommerce*

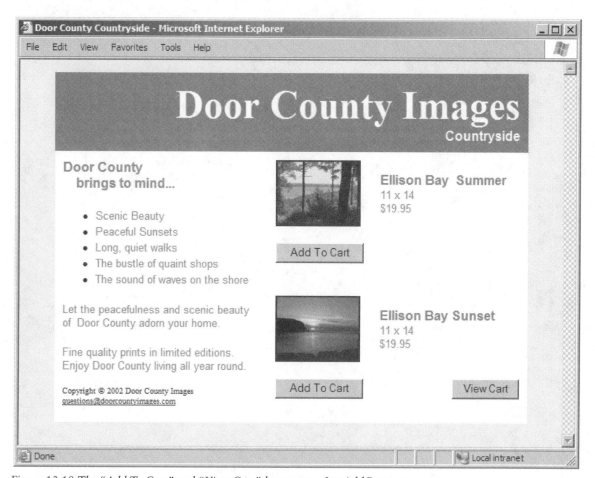

Figure 13.10 *The "Add To Cart" and "View Cart" buttons use JustAddCommerce*

This add-in is available for both Microsoft FrontPage and Macromedia Dreamweaver. Other shopping cart solutions for Microsoft FrontPage can be found by visiting http://microsoft.com/frontpage and looking for links to e-commerce applications. A selection of extensions for Macromedia Dreamweaver can be found at http://www.macromedia.com/exchange/dreamweaver/. These budget-wise solutions work best for businesses that fit the standard business model and do not require special processing needs.

Chapter 13 Review

Summary

This chapter introduced basic e-commerce concepts and implementations. Consider taking an e-commerce course to continue your study of this dynamic and growing area of web development.

Visit the text web site at http://www.webdevfoundations.net for examples, updated information, and the links listed in this chapter.

Review Questions

Multiple Choice

1. Which is a major function of e-commerce?
   a. using SSL to encrypt orders
   b. adding items to a shopping cart
   c. the buying and selling of goods
   d. none of the above

2. For businesses, which is an advantage of using e-commerce?
   a. reduced costs
   b. ability to comparison shop
   c. using shopping carts
   d. none of the above

3. For businesses, which is a potential risk when using e-commerce?
   a. increased customer satisfaction
   b. the possibility of fraudulent transactions
   c. inconvenience of returns
   d. none of the above

4. The most money is being generated in which type of e-commerce?
   a. B2G
   b. B2C
   c. B2B
   d. C2C

5. Choose the option that best describes how a web site owner can obtain a digital certificate.
   a. Digital certificates are automatically created when you register for a domain name.
   b. Visit a certificate authority and apply for a digital certificate.
   c. Digital certificates are automatically created when you are listed in a search engine.
   d. None of the above is true.

6. Issues uniquely related to international e-commerce include
   a. language, currency conversion
   b. browser version, screen resolution
   c. bandwidth, Internet service provider
   d. none of the above

7. Which is a standard protocol used to enable secure credit card transactions on the Internet?

    a. SSL   c. SSI

    b. SET   d. none of the above

8. A disadvantage of an instant online storefront is that

    a. the store is based on a template and may look very similar to other online stores

    b. the store can be ready in minutes

    c. the store cannot accept credit cards

    d. none of the above

9. Most commercial _____ include(s) an online catalog, a shopping cart, and a secure order form.

    a. web host providers

    b. shopping cart software

    c. web server software

    d. e-commerce hosting packages

10. Which of the following is true?

    a. A merchant account allows you to use SSL on your web site.

    b. Shopping cart add-ins or extensions are available for popular web authoring tools such as Microsoft FrontPage and Macromedia Dreamweaver.

    c. Instant storefronts are what most large-scale e-commerce sites use.

    d. None of the above is true.

Fill in the Blank

11. _____ is an encryption method that uses a single shared, private key.

12. _____ can be described as the transfer of data between different companies using networks.

13. A digital certificate is a form of a(n) _____ that also contains additional information about the entity holding the certificate.

14. _____ is a protocol that allows data to be privately exchanged over public networks.

Short Answer

15. List one option for a web site that needs to reach audiences that speak different languages.

Hands-On Exercises

1. In this Hands-On Exercise you will create an instant storefront. Choose one of the following web sites that offer free trial online stores: http://store.yahoo.com, http://www.miva.com (choose "Miva Now"), or http://www.earthstores.com. Web sites are constantly changing their policies, so these sites may no longer offer free trials when you do this assignment. If this is the case, check the text's web site for updated information, ask your instructor for assistance, or search the Web for free online storefronts or trial stores. If you are certain you have found a web site that offers a free trial store, continue with this exercise and create a store that meets the following criteria:

   - Name: Door County Images
   - Purpose: To sell fine quality prints of Door County scenery
   - Target Audience: Adults age 40+ who have visited Door County, are middle to upper-class, and enjoy nature, boating, hiking, cycling, and fishing
   - Item 1: Print of Ellison Bay at Sunset, Size 11" by 14", Price $19.95
   - Item 2: Print of Ellison Bay in Summer, Size 11" by 14", Price $19.95

   Figure 13.11 shows a page from a sample store using Earthstores instant storefront.

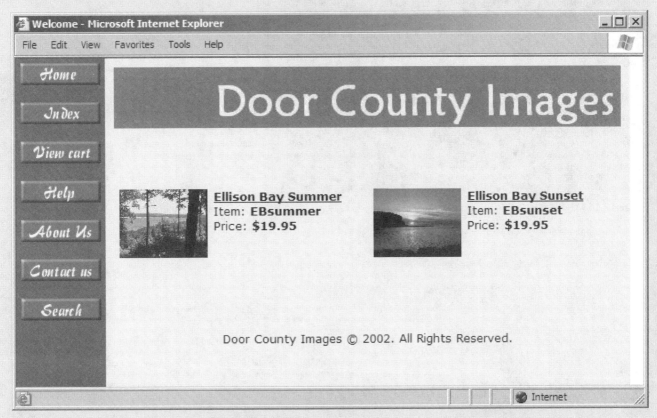

Figure 13.11 *An instant store created at http://www.earthstores.com*

Create a folder called doorcounty. The images shown in Figures 13.12, 13.13, 13.14, 13.15, and 13.16 can be found on the student disk in the Chapter13 folder. Copy them into your doorcounty folder.

Door County Images

Figure 13.12 *Door County Images logo (logo.jpg)*

Figure 13.13 *Ellison Bay in Summer thumbnail (summer_small.jpg)*

Figure 13.14 *Ellison Bay at Sunset thumbnail (sunset_small.jpg)*

Figure 13.15 *Ellison Bay in Summer (summer.jpg)*

Figure 13.16 *Ellison Bay at Sunset (sunset.jpg)*

Once you are all organized, visit the web site you have chosen to host your free store. You will have to log in, choose options, and upload your images. Follow the instructions provided. Most free online store sites have a FAQ section or technical support available to help if you get stuck. After you have completed your store, print out the browser view of the home page and catalog page.

Each of these case studies has continued throughout most of the text. In this chapter, you will add a catalog page for an online store to the web sites. This catalog page will connect to sample shopping cart and order pages at the textbook's web site.

A. JavaJam Coffee House

See Chapter 2 for an introduction to the JavaJam Coffee House case. Figure 2.20 shows the initial site map for the JavaJam web site. The pages were created in earlier chapters. Use the javajamcss folder created in the Chapter 9 case study.

As frequently happens with web sites, the client, Julio Perez, is pleased with the response to the site and has an idea about a new use for it—selling JavaJam gear, such as T-shirts and coffee mugs. This new page, gear.htm, will be part of the main navigation of the site. All pages should link to it. A revised site map is shown in Figure 13.17.

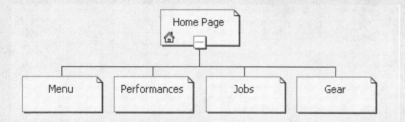

Figure 13.17 *Revised JavaJam site map*

The Gear page should contain the description, image, and price of each product. It should link to a shopping cart system when the visitor wants to purchase an item. You may access a demonstration shopping cart/ordering system provided by the textbook's web site. If you have access to a different shopping cart system, check with your instructor and ask if you can use it instead.

Hands-On Practice Case

Copy the javamug.gif,. javatshirt.gif, and viewtrans.gif image files from the Chapter13 folder on the student disk and save them to your floppy disk in the javajamcss folder.

Launch Notepad and modify each existing web page (index.htm, jobs.htm, performances.htm, menu.htm) in the javajamcss folder to link to the Gear page (gear.htm) in the main navigation. See Figure 13.18 for a sample change on the Performances page.

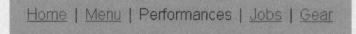

Figure 13.18 *Revised JavaJam text navigation*

Now you are ready to create the Gear page. Figure 13.19 shows a sample of the completed Gear page.

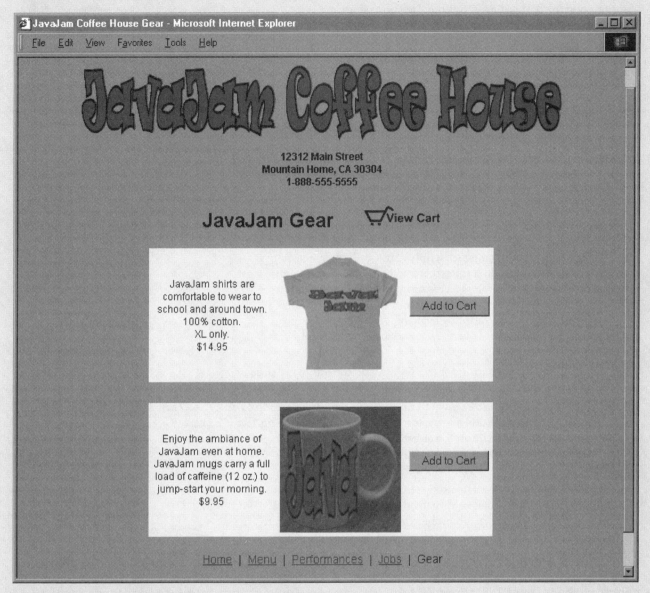

Figure 13.19 *JavaJam gear.htm*

One way to be productive is to create pages based on earlier work. Launch Notepad and open the Performances page (performances.htm). Save the file as gear.htm. This will give you a head start and ensure that the pages on the web site are similar. Perform the following modifications:

1. Change the page title to an appropriate phrase.

2. Modify the links appropriately. Remove the link to the Gear page and add a link to the Performances page (performances.htm).

3. Replace the introductory text with the words "JavaJam Gear" and the viewtrans.gif image contained within **<h2>** tags. The image should have no border. Use an appropriate value for the alt attribute. Place five blank spaces between the text "JavaJam Gear" and the image (use ** ** for each space).

4. Set the width of the table to 425 pixels.

5. Replace the contents of the first row of the table. Place the following description in the first cell: Description: "JavaJam shirts are comfortable to wear to school and around town. 100% cotton. XL only. $14.95". Place the following image in the second cell: javashirt.gif height="150" width="150". Delete the contents of the third cell (we will work on this later).

6. Replace the contents of each cell in the second row with the nonbreaking space ( ).

7. Replace the contents of the third row of the table. Place the following description in the first cell: Description: "Enjoy the ambiance of JavaJam even at home. JavaJam mugs carry a full load of caffeine (12 oz.) to jump-start your morning. $9.95". Place the following image in the second cell: javamug.gif height="150" width="150". Delete the contents of the third cell (we will work on this later).

8. Next, you will add a shopping cart button to each item for sale. This is placed in a form. The action on the form is the ASP script called http://www.webdevfoundations.net/scripts/cart.asp. Remember that whenever you use server-side scripts, there will be some documentation or specifications for you to follow. This script processes a limited shopping cart that only works with two items. The gear.htm web page will pass information to the script by using hidden fields in the form that contains the button to invoke the script. Please pay careful attention to detail when working on this.

To place the shopping cart button for the T-shirt, add the following code to the third cell of the first row:

```
<form method="post" action="http://www.webdevfoundations.net/scripts/cart.asp">
     <input type="hidden" name="desc1" value="JavaJam Shirt" />
     <input type="hidden" name="cost1" value="14.95" />
     <input type="submit" value="Add to Cart" />
</form>
```

This XHTML invokes a server-side script that processes a demonstration shopping cart. The hidden fields named **"desc1"** and **"cost1"** are sent to the script when the Submit button is clicked. These indicate the name and cost of the item.

The process for adding the shopping cart button for the mug is similar, using hidden form fields named "desc2" and "cost2". The XHTML is

```
<form method="post" action="http://www.webdevfoundations.net/scripts/cart.asp">
     <input type="hidden" name="desc2" value="JavaJam Mug" />
     <input type="hidden" name="cost2" value="9.95" />
     <input type="submit" value="Add to Cart" />
</form>
```

9. You earlier placed the viewtrans.gif image on the page on the same line as the "JavaJam Gear" text. Visitors will click on this image to view the contents of the shopping cart. Recall that when you use server-side scripts there are sometimes special configuration needs. Add anchor tags around the image to indicate that it is a special link to the cart. The XHTML is

```
<a href="http://www.webdevfoundations.net/scripts/cart.asp?view=yes">
image tag goes here</a>
```

Save your page and test it in a browser. It should look similar to the one shown in Figure 13.19. Click on the "Add to Cart" button for the JavaJam shirt. The demonstration shopping cart will display and your screen should be similar to the one pictured in Figure 13.20.

Figure 13.20 *A Shopping Cart page created by the server-side script that processes the shopping cart and order*

Experiment with the cart and try to purchase both items. You simulate placing an order, as shown in Figure 13.21. The shopping cart and order pages are for demonstration purposes only.

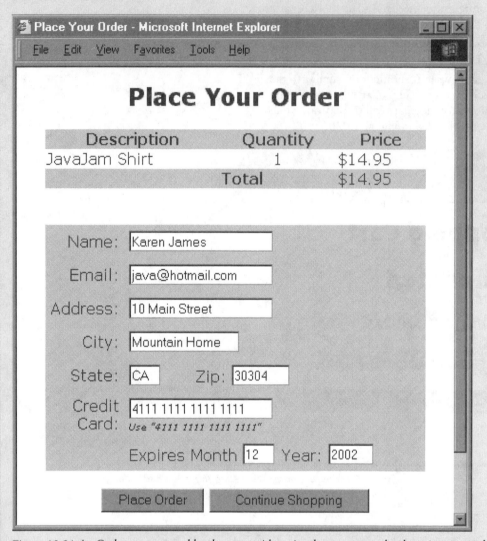

Figure 13.21 *An Order page created by the server-side script that processes the shopping cart order*

How does the cart.asp server-side script work?

The cart.asp file is an ASP script. It is coded to accept a number of form fields and process them. It creates a web page based on the values and fields that were passed to it. Table 13.3 shows the form fields and values used by the cart.asp file.

Table 13.3

Script URL: http://www.webdevfoundations.net/scripts/cart.asp
Processing: This script accepts product and price information, displays a shopping cart, and finally displays an order page.
Limitation: This script can only handle two products.

Input Elements	desc1	Contains the description of the first product. It is displayed on the shopping cart page.
	cost1	Contains the per item cost of the first product. It is displayed on the shopping cart page
	desc2	Contains the description of the second product. It is displayed on the shopping cart page.
	cost2	Contains the per item cost of the second product. It is displayed on the shopping cart page.
	view	If the value is "yes", the shopping cart is displayed.
Output	Shopping Cart web page	Displays the shopping cart. The web page visitor is given the option to continue shopping or to display the order page to place an order.
	Order web page	Displays an order form. The web page visitor is given the option to place the order or to continue shopping.
	Order Confirmation page	Displays a message to confirm that an order was placed. If this were an actual web site, the order would also be saved on a server-side file or database.

B. Fish Creek Animal Hospital

See Chapter 2 for an introduction to the Fish Creek Animal Hospital case. Figure 2.23 shows the initial site map for the Fish Creek web site. The pages were created in earlier chapters. Use the fishcreekcss folder created in the Chapter 9 case study.

Often once a web site is created, your client will think of additional ways to use it. The owner of Fish Creek, Magda Patel, is pleased with the response to the site and has a new use for it—selling sweatshirts and tote-bags with the Fish Creek logo. She already has these materials for sale at her front desk in the animal hospital and her customers seem to like them. This new "Shop" page, shop.htm, will be part of the main navigation of the site. All pages should link to it. A revised site map is shown in Figure 13.22.

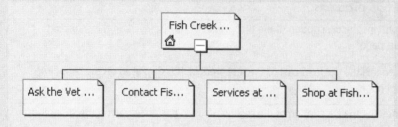

Figure 13.22 *Revised Fish Creek site map*

The Shop page should contain the description, image, and price of each product. It should link to a shopping cart system when the visitor wants to purchase an item. You may access a demonstration shopping cart/ordering system provided by the textbook's web site. If you have access to a different shopping cart system, check with your instructor and ask if you can use it instead.

Copy the fishtote.gif, fishsweat.gif, viewtrans.gif, shop.gif, and shopon.gif image files from the Chapter13 folder on the student disk and save them to your fishcreekcss folder.

Launch Notepad and modify each existing web page (index.htm, services.htm, askthevet.htm, contact.htm) in the fishcreekcss folder to link to the Shop page (shop.htm) in the main navigation. Add the shop.gif to the top navigation bar as shown in Figure 13.23 on the Home page (index.htm).

Figure 13.23 *Revised Fish Creek navigation*

Now you are ready to create the Shop page. Figure 13.24 shows a sample of the completed page.

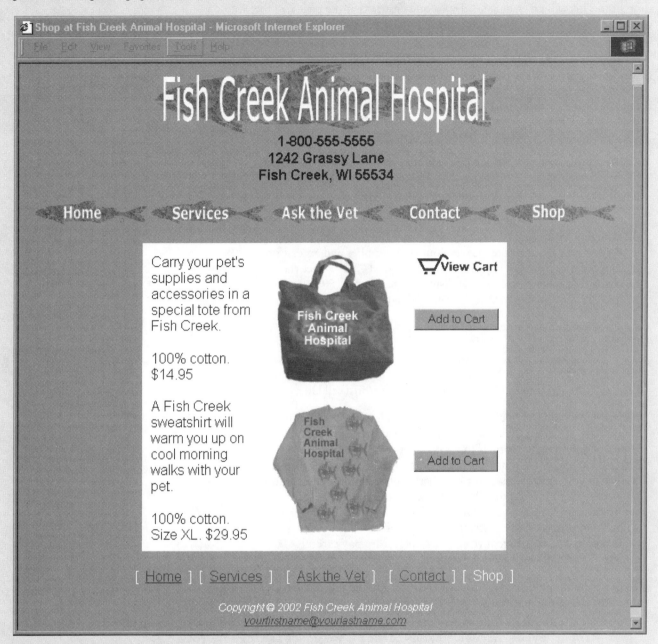

Figure 13.24 *Fish Creek shop.htm*

One way to be productive is to create pages based on earlier work. Launch Notepad and open the Home page (index.htm). Save the file as shop.htm. This will give you a head start and ensure that the pages on the web site are similar. Perform the following modifications:

1. Change the page title to an appropriate phrase.

2. Modify the links on the page as appropriate. Remove the link from the "Shop" image and text link. Place a link on the "Home" image and text link.

3. Delete the definition list on the page.

4. Create a table with two rows, three columns, and a width of 425 pixels, a white background, cellspacing set to 5 pixels, and cellpadding set to 5 pixels. Format the text in the table to be the color #000000 and in the Arial font.

5. Add content to the first row of the table. Place the following description in the first cell: Description: "Carry your pet's supplies and accessories in a special tote from Fish Creek. 100% cotton. $14.95". Place the following image in the second cell: fishtote.gif height="150" width="150". You will format the third cell later.

6. Add content to the second row of the table. Place the following description in the first cell: Description: "A Fish Creek sweatshirt will warm you up on cool morning walks with your pet. 100% cotton. Size XL. $29.95". Place the following image in the second cell: fishsweat.gif height="150" width="150". You will format the third cell later.

7. Next, we will add a shopping cart button to each item for sale. This shopping cart button is placed in a form in the third cell of each table row. The action on the form is the ASP script called http://www.webdevfoundations.net/scripts/cart.asp. Remember that whenever you use server-side scripts, there will be some documentation or specifications for you to follow. This script processes a limited shopping cart that only works with two items. The shop.htm web page will pass information to the script by using hidden fields in the form that contains the button to invoke the script. Please pay careful attention to detail when working on this.

To place the shopping cart button for the tote, add the following code to the third cell of the first row:

```
<form method="post" action="http://www.webdevfoundations.net/scripts/cart.asp">
     <input type="hidden" name="desc1" value="Fish Creek Tote" />
     <input type="hidden" name="cost1" value="14.95" />
     <input type="submit" value="Add to Cart" />
</form>
```

This XHTML invokes a server-side script that processes a demonstration shopping cart. The hidden fields named "desc1" and "cost1" are sent to the script when the Submit button is clicked. These indicate the name and cost of the item.

The process for adding the shopping cart button for the sweatshirt is similar, using hidden form fields named "desc2" and "cost2". The XHTML is

```
<form method="post" action="http://www.webdevfoundations.net/scripts/cart.asp">
     <input type="hidden" name="desc2" value="Fish Creek Sweatshirt" />
     <input type="hidden" name="cost2" value="29.95" />
     <input type="submit" value="Add to Cart" />
</form>
```

8. Add the viewtrans.gif to the page, below Fish Creek's address but above the navigation bar. Place the image in a division (use the `<div>` tag) that has right alignment. The image should have no border. Use an appropriate value for the alt attribute. Visitors will click on this image to view the contents of the shopping cart. Recall that when you use server-side scripts there are sometimes special configuration needs. Add anchor tags around the image to indicate that it is a special link to the cart. The XHTML is

```
<a href="http://www.webdevfoundations.net/scripts/cart.asp?view=yes">
image tag goes here</a>
```

Save your page and test it in a browser. It should look similar to the one shown in Figure 13.24. Click on the "Add to Cart" button for the Fish Creek Sweat Shirt. The demonstration shopping cart will display and your screen should be similar to the one pictured in Figure 13.20. Experiment with the cart and try to purchase both items. You can go ahead and simulate placing an order as shown in Figure 13.21. The shopping cart and order pages are for demonstration purposes only.

C. Pete the Painter

See Chapter 2 for an introduction to the Pete the Painter case. Figure 2.26 shows a site map for the Pete the Painter web site. The pages were created in earlier chapters. Use the paintercss folder created in the Chapter 9 case study.

Pete Johnson is the owner of Pete the Painter. He has begun to write some how-to books for his clients and would like to offer them on the web site. He would like a new Store page that will offer two of his books. This new Store page, store.htm, will be part of the main navigation of the site. All pages should link to it. A revised site map is shown in Figure 13.25.

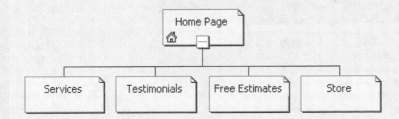

Figure 13.25 *Revised Pete the Painter site map*

The Store page should contain the description, image, and price of each product. It should link to a shopping cart system when the visitor wants to purchase an item. You may access a demonstration shopping cart/ordering system provided by the textbook's web site. If you have access to a different shopping cart system, check with your instructor and ask if you can use it instead.

Copy the primer.jpg, decorate.jpg, and view.jpg image files from the Chapter13 folder on the student disk and save them to your paintercss folder.

Launch Notepad and modify each existing web page (index.htm, services.htm, testimonials.htm, estimate.htm) in the paintercss folder to link to the Store page (store.htm) in the main navigation. See Figure13.26 for sample navigation.

Home | Services | Testimonials | Free Estimate | Store

Figure 13.26 *Revised Pete the Painter navigation*

Now you are ready to create the Store page. Figure 13.27 shows a sample of the completed page.

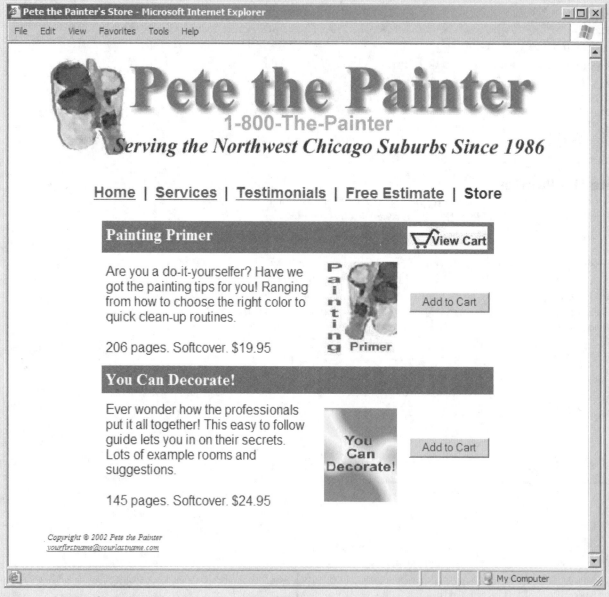

Figure 13.27 *Pete the Painter store.htm*

One way to be productive is to create pages based on earlier work. Launch Notepad and open the Testimonials page (testimonials.htm). Save the file as store.htm. This will give you a head start and ensure that the pages on the web site are similar. Perform the following modifications:

1. Change the page title to an appropriate phrase.

2. Modify the links on the page as appropriate. Remove the "Store" text link. Add a "Testimonials" link.

3. Delete the last two rows of the table on the page. Add a column to the table. The first and third rows should contain one cell that spans three columns.

4. Modify the content of the first row in the table. Replace the text with "Painting Primer". Add the view.jpg image to the cell. The image should be aligned right, vertically aligned in the absolute middle of the cell, and have no border. Be sure to place an appropriate value for the alt attribute on the image tag. You will make this image into a hyperlink later in the exercise.

5. Modify the content of the second row of the table. Replace the content of the first cell with:

   "Are you a do-it-yourselfer? Have we got the painting tips for you! Ranging from how to choose the right color to quick clean-up routines. 206 pages. Softcover."

   Replace the content of the second cell with the primer.jpg (width="90", height="112") image.

6. Add content to the third cell. The visitor will click a button to indicate that they wish to purchase an item. This shopping cart button is placed in a form. For this exercise, the action on the form is the ASP script called http://www.webdevfoundations.net/scripts/cart.asp. Remember that whenever you use server-side scripts, there will be some documentation or specifications for you to follow. This script processes a limited shopping cart that only works with two items. The store.htm web page will pass information to the script by using hidden fields in the form that contains the button to invoke the script. Please pay careful attention to detail when working on this. To add the shopping cart button for the Painting Primer book to the third cell, write the following code.

```
<form method="post" action="http://www.webdevfoundations.net/scripts/cart.asp">
    <input type="hidden" name="desc1" value="Painting Primer" />
    <input type="hidden" name="cost1" value="19.95" />
    <input type="submit" value="Add to Cart" />
</form>
```

   This XHTML invokes a server-side script that processes a demonstration shopping cart. The hidden fields named "desc1" and "cost1" are sent to the script when the Submit button is clicked. These indicate the name and cost of the item.

7. Modify the content of the third table row. Replace the text with "You Can Decorate!"

8. Modify the content of the fourth row of the table. Replace the content of the first cell with: "Ever wonder how the professionals put it all together? This easy to follow guide lets you in on their secrets. Lots of example rooms and suggestions. 145 pages. Softcover." Replace the content of the second cell with the decorate.jpg image (width="90", height="112"). Add content to the third cell by writing the XHTML for the form with the shopping cart button:

```
<form method="post" action="http://www.webdevfoundations.net/scripts/cart.asp">
    <input type="hidden" name="desc2" value="You Can Decorate!" />
    <input type="hidden" name="cost2" value="19.95" />
    <input type="submit" value="Add to Cart" />
</form>
```

This XHTML invokes a server-side script that processes a demonstration shopping cart. The hidden fields named "desc2"and "cost2" are sent to the script when the Submit button is clicked. These indicate the name and cost of the item.

9. Add a special hyperlink to the view.jpg image in the first row of the table. This will link to the server-side script described above in a very special way. When a visitor clicks on the image, the server-side script will display the contents of his or her shopping cart. Recall that when you work with server-side scripts, they often have special configuration needs. Place anchor tags around the image tag to create the special hyperlink shown below:

```
<a href="http://www.webdevfoundations.net/scripts/cart.asp?view=yes">
image tag goes here</a>
```

Save your page and test in a browser. It should look similar to the one shown in Figure 13.27. Click on the "Add to Cart" button for the Painting Primer. The demonstration shopping cart will display and your screen should be similar to the one pictured in Figure 13.20. Experiment with the cart and try to purchase both items. You can go ahead and simulate placing an order as shown in Figure 13.21. The shopping cart and order pages are for demonstration purposes only.

Web Research

A. Just how popular is e-commerce? How many of your friends, family members, coworkers, and classmates purchase on the Web? Survey at least 20 people. Determine the following:

- How many have purchased an item online
- How many have shopped but not purchased online
- How many purchase online once a year, once a month, or once a week
- What their age range is (18 to 25, 26 to 39, 40 to 50, over 50)
- Their gender
- Their level of education (high school, some college, college graduate, graduate school)
- Their favorite online shopping site

Create a web page that uses multiple tables that illustrate your findings. Also comment on the results and draw some conclusions. Search the Web for statistics that support your conclusions. Use http://www.nua.net/surveys/, http://cyberatlas.internet.com, and http://www.ecommercetimes.com as starting points for your research. Place your name in an e-mail link on the web page. Print both the source code (from Notepad) and the browser view of your web page.

B. This chapter provided a number of resources for e-commerce shopping cart and ordering systems. Use them as a starting point. Search the Web for additional resources. Find at least three shopping cart systems that you feel would be easy to use. Create a web page that reports on your findings. Organize your page with a table that lists the information along with the URLs of the web sites you used as resources. Include information such as the product name, brief description, cost, and web server requirements (if any). Place your name in an e-mail link on the web page. Print both the source code (from Notepad) and the browser view of your web page.

Chapter Review Answers

1. c

2. a

3. b

4. c

5. b

6. a

7. b

8. a

9. d

10. b

11. symmetric encryption

12. EDI

13. asymmetric key

14. SSL

15. The web site developers may use an automatic translation program or other customized web translation service.

Notes

Notes

Web Developer's
Handbook

Web Developer's Handbook

Introduction

In this handbook you will find additional information and tutorials. The XHTML Reference contains detailed information on XHTML along with an introduction to XML syntax. The Special Characters section contains a handy list of the codes needed to display symbols and other special characters on a web page. The CSS Property Reference provides a list of Cascading Style Sheet properties used for text formatting and color selection. Using FTP will be helpful if you'd like an introduction or a refresher on publishing a web site. The Comparison of HTML and XHTML discusses the differences in syntax between the two markup languages and provides side-by-side examples.

XHTML Reference

The newest version of HTML is XHTML, which uses the tags and attributes of HTML along with the syntax of XML. For the most part you will use the same tags and attributes in HTML and XHTML; the major change is the syntax and additional restrictions in XHTML. This section provides an introduction to XML syntax and a detailed list of XHTML tags and attributes. It should be helpful as a reference as you write web pages. This section is comprised of five major areas:

- XML Syntax
- General XHTML Syntax Guidelines
- Basic Tags
- Header Section Tags
- Body Section Tags

XML Syntax

An XML document must be well-formed. A **well-formed document** is a document that adheres to the syntax rules of the language. Here are the key syntax rules of XML:

- XML is case sensitive.
- An XML document must contain one or more elements.
- All XML elements must have an opening tag and a closing tag. All tags are enclosed in angle brackets.
- All XML elements must be properly nested. **Nesting** is the use of one or more elements inside other elements. The most recently opened element must be the next one closed.
- All attribute values in XML must be contained in quotes.
- All XML documents must begin with a statement declaring it to be an XML document.
- All XML documents must have an opening and closing tag that form the root element within which all other elements in the document must be contained. The **<html>** and **</html>** tags serve this purpose for web page documents.

General XHTML Syntax Guidelines

Since XHTML uses the syntax of XML, it must follow the XML syntax rules. The following guidelines specify examples of how this is accomplished when using XHTML.

1. All XHTML elements (the tags and their attributes) should be lowercase.
2. The **\<head\>** and **\<body\>** tags are required.
3. The **\<title\>** tag is the first tag in the header section.
4. All container tags must use their opening and closing tags.
5. All self-contained tags (sometimes called empty elements) must be properly closed. For example, use **\<hr /\>** instead of **\<hr\>**.
6. All attribute values should be contained in quotation marks.
7. All attributes should have values. For example, use
   ```
   <input type="checkbox" checked="checked" name="IE" value="yes" />
   ```
   instead of
   ```
   <input type="checkbox" checked name="IE" value="yes" >.
   ```
8. There should be no line breaks or extra blank spaces between attributes.
9. Tags should not overlap, they should be properly nested. For example, use
   ```
   <b><em>This is important</em></b>
   ```
   instead of
   ```
   <b><em>This is important</b></em>.
   ```
10. These tag-specific nesting restrictions apply:
    - A **\<form\>** tag cannot contain another **\<form\>** tag.
    - An **\<a\>** tag cannot contain another **\<a\>** tag.
    - A **\<pre\>** tag cannot contain any of the following tags: **\<img\>**, **\<object\>**, **\<big\>**, **\<small\>**, **\<sub\>**, or **\<sup\>**.
11. Formatting should be configured with style sheets and **\<font\>** tag should be avoided.
12. The name attribute is deprecated in XHTML 1.0 as applied to bookmarks and named fragment identifiers. This has the greatest affect on **\<a\>** and **\<map\>** tags. XHTML uses the id attribute to configure bookmarks and named fragment identifiers.
13. The web page document should begin with an XML declaration:
    ```
    <?xml version="1.0" encoding="UTF-8"?>
    ```
14. The XML declaration should be followed with a Document Type Definition (DTD). There are three DTDs: Strict, Transitional, and Frameset. The Strict DTD is not usually used by commercial web sites because it requires the exclusive use of CSS and does not allow any deprecated elements. Use the Transitional DTD for most XHTML web page documents. Use the Frameset DTD for web page documents that describe a frameset.

Strict DTD
```
<!DOCTYPE html PUBLIC "-//W3C//DTD XHTML 1.0 Strict//EN"
   "http://www.w3.org/TR/xhtml1/DTD/xhtml1-strict.dtd">
```

Transitional DTD
```
<!DOCTYE html PUBLIC "-//W3C//DTD XHMTL 1.0 Transitional//EN"
  "http://www.w3.org/TR/xhtml1/DTD/xhmtl1-transitional.dtd">
```

Frameset DTD

```
<!DOCTYE html PUBLIC "-//W3C//DTD XHMTL 1.0 Frameset//EN"
  "http://www.w3.org/TR/xhtml1/DTD/xhmtl1-frameset.dtd">
```

15. The root element (immediately after the DTD) must be an **<html>** tag that refers to the XML namespace, as shown in this example:

    <html xmlns="http://www.w3.org/1999/xhtml" >

Basic Tags

The XML Directive

<?xml version="1.0" encoding="UTF-8"?>

This XML directive indicates that the document is based on the XML 1.0 standard. It also indicates that the character encoding (the internal representation of letters, numbers, and symbols) used by this document is UTF-8, a form of Unicode. This XML directive will be the first line in each web page that you write.

The DOCTYPE (DTD) Tag

The DOCTYPE or DTD tag identifies the markup language used in a document. Three DTDs are valid in XHTML. They are listed in the Table 1.

Table 1 XHTML Document Type Definitions

DTD	Description

XHTML 1.0 Transitional	`<!DOCTYPE html PUBLIC "-//W3C//DTD XHTML 1.0 Transitional//EN"`
	`    "http://www.w3.org/TR/xhtml1/DTD/xhtml1-transitional.dtd">`
	
	This is the least strict specification for XHTML 1.0. It allows the use of both CSS and traditional formatting instructions such as fonts. This DTD is used for most of the coding in this text.

XHTML 1.0 Strict	`<!DOCTYPE html PUBLIC "-//W3C//DTD XHTML 1.0 Strict//EN"`
	`    "http://www.w3.org/TR/xhtml1/DTD/xhtml1-strict.dtd">`
	
	Requires exclusive use of CSS. Does not allow any deprecated elements.

XHTML 1.0 Frameset	`<!DOCTYPE html PUBLIC "-//W3C//DTD XHTML 1.0 Frameset//EN"`
	`    "http://www.w3.org/TR/xhtml1/DTD/xhtml1-frameset.dtd">`
	
	Required for pages using XHTML frames. This DTD is used on the frameset pages coded in this text.

The HTML Tag

<html></html>

The **<html>** tag contains the code that describes the web page document. The tag also describes the location of the documentation for the elements being used (called the XML namespace or xmlns). This additional information is added to the **<html>** tag in the form of an xmlns attribute. The xmlns attribute points to the URL of the XHTML namespace used in the document, the standard "http://www.w3.org/1999/xhtml". The **<html>** tag is the first tag in a web page after the DOCTYPE tag. For example:

```
<?xml version="1.0" encoding="UTF-8"?>
<!DOCTYPE html PUBLIC "-//W3C//DTD XHTML 1.0 Transitional//EN"
   "http://www.w3.org/TR/xhtml1/DTD/xhtml1-transitional.dtd">
<html xmlns="http://www.w3.org/1999/xhtml" >
… the rest of your web page goes here….
</html>
```

The Head Tag

`<head></head>`

The head tag is required and contains the header area of a web page document. The main purpose of the header area is to describe the document. The header usually contains title and meta tags. It may also contain JavaScript code and CSS.

The Body Tag

`<body></body>`

The body tag is required and contains the body area of a web page document—the part of the document that is displayed in the browser window. It can contain many different types of XHTML tags along with text and JavaScript.

Header Section Tags

The Title Tag

`<title></title>`

The title contains the title of the page, which displays in the browser's title bar. This tag must be the first tag in the header section.

The Meta Tag

`<meta name="keywords" content="a list of words that describe your site" />`
`<meta name="description" content="a brief description of your site" />`

Meta tags have various purposes. Some, such as the keywords and description meta tags, are used by search engines. This is a self-contained tag.

The Link Tag

`<link />`

The self-contained link tag configures a web page to use an external style sheet. Link tag attributes and their values are shown in Table 2.

Table 2 Link Tag Attributes

Attribute	Values	Usage
href	URL of the external stylesheet (.css file)	Identifies which stylesheet is being used.
rel	"stylesheet"	Indicates the link is a stylesheet.
type	"text/css"	Indicates the MIME type of the stylesheet file.

The Base Tag

`<base />`

The self-contained base tag is most often used with pages displayed within a frameset. It sets a default target frame for the hyperlinks on the page. The attribute of target is set to the name of the window or frame in which all the hyperlinks should display.

The Script Tag

`<script></script>`

This script tag configures a web page to use client-side scripting. Table 3 shows script tag attributes and their values.

Table 3 Script Tag Attributes

Attribute	Value	Usage
language	The scripting language, usually "JavaScript"	Indicates the scripting language being used.
src	URL of the external script file (usually a .js file)	Identifies the external file containing scripting commands. If this attribute is omitted, the script is contained between the `<script>` tags.
type	"text/js"	Indicates the MIME type of the JavaScript file.

An example follows:

```
<script language="JavaScript" type="text/js">
JavaScript statements go here….
</script>
```

When strict XML syntax is applied, any JavaScript statements should be surrounded by character data (CDATA) statements. This tells the XML parser to ignore the JavaScript statements as arbitrary character data and not to process them. The syntax is

```
<script language="JavaScript" type="text/js">
<![CDATA[
JavaScript statements go here….
]]>
</script>
```

Unfortunately this generates a JavaScript error in most current browsers and so is not used. This problem can be circumvented by accessing external JavaScript files, as shown here.

```
<script language="Javascript" type="text/javascript" src="script.js">
</script>
```

In this case all the JavaScript statements are located in the external file called script.js and no CDATA statement is needed.

The Style Tag

`<style></style>`

The style tag configures a web page to use an embedded style sheet. The attribute of type is set to "text/css" and indicates the MIME type of the stylesheet.

Body Section Tags

The Body Tag

`<body></body>`

The body tag contains the body area of a web page document. Body tag attributes configure properties for the web page. Table 4 shows body tag attributes and values.

Table 4 Body Tag Attributes

Attribute	Value	Usage
alink	A valid color. The W3C recommends hexadecimal colors.	Configures the color of the active hyperlinks on the web page.
background	The name of an image file	Places a background image on the web page. If the image is smaller than the page, it will be repeated, or tiled, on the browser window.
bgcolor	A valid color. The W3C recommends hexadecimal colors.	Configure the background color of the web page.
bgproperties	"fixed"	When combined with a background image, this property will fix the background image, simulating the effect of a watermark as the web page visitor scrolls down the page. Only used by Internet Explorer.
leftmargin	Number of pixels	Configures the left margin of the web page. Only used by Internet Explorer.
link	A valid color. The W3C recommends hexadecimal colors.	Configures the color of the hyperlinks on the web page.
marginheight	Number of pixels	Configures the top margin of the web page. Only used by Netscape.
marginwidth	Number of pixels	Configures the left margin of the web page. Only used by Netscape.
text	A valid color. The W3C recommends hexadecimal colors.	Configures the color of the text on the web page.
topmargin	Number of pixels	Configures the top margin of the web page. Only used by Internet Explorer.
vlink	A valid color. The W3C recommends hexadecimal colors.	Configures the color of the visited hyperlinks on the web page.

Block-Level Elements

The Preformatted or Preserved Text Tag

`<pre></pre>`

The preformatted tag handles text in a special way. Any text contained between preformatted tags is considered to be preformatted text and any line breaks or spacing will be preserved.

The Paragraph Tag
`<p></p>`

This paragraph tag creates a paragraph of text. The browser displays the paragraph with a blank line before and after the paragraph. The align attribute specifies the horizontal placement of the paragraph. The values for the align attribute are "left" (default), "right", and "center".

The Heading Tag
`<h1></h1>`

The heading tag contains headings and important points. The text contained between the heading tags is placed on its own line. There are six levels of heading tags: **`<h1>`** (the largest), **`<h2>`**, **`<h3>`**, **`<h4>`**, **`<h5>`**, **`<h6>`** (the smallest).

The align attribute specifies the horizontal placement of the heading. The values for the align attribute are "left" (default), "right", and "center".

The Blockquote Tag
`<blockquote></blockquote>`

The blockquote tag indents text. The text contained between blockquote tags is indented from both the left and right margins.

The Division Tag
`<div></div>`

The division tag creates a separate division, or logical area, on a web page. A line break occurs before and after the division. The division tag is often used for alignment. For example, in

```
<div align="center">
Web page content goes here
</div>
```

all content between **`<div>`** tags will be centered. The align attribute specifies the horizontal placement of the division. The values for the align attribute are "left" (default), "right", and "center".

The Span Tag
`<span></span>`

The span tag creates a separate logical area on a web page without any line breaks before or after. It is often used to apply styles.

List Tags

The Definition List
`<dl></dl>`

The definition list tag creates a definition list. It is used with the **`<dt>`** and **`<dd>`** tags.

`<dt></dt>`

The defined term tag identifies a defined term in a definition list.

`<dd></dd>`

The definition tag identifies a definition in a definition list.

The Ordered List
`<ol></ol>`

The ordered list tag creates an ordered, or numbered, list. It is used together with line item (`<li>`) tags. The type attribute on the ordered list tag configures the type of ordering. See Table 5.

Table 5 Ordered List Tag Attributes

Attribute	Value	Symbol
type	1	Numerals (the default)
	A	Uppercase letters
	a	Lowercase letters
	I	Roman numerals
	i	Lowercase roman numerals

The Line Item Tag
`<li></li>`

The line item tag identifies a line item in ordered and unordered lists.

The Unordered List
`<ul></ul>`

The unordered list tag creates an unordered, or bulleted, list. It is used together with line item (`<li>`) tags. The type attribute on the unordered list tag configures the bullet displayed. Attributes are shown in Table 6.

Table 6 Unordered List Tag Attributes

Attribute	Value
type	disc (default)
	circle
	square

Text-Level Elements

The Font Tag
`<font></font>`

The font tag formats text. This tag is deprecated. Table 7 describes the attributes of the font tag.

Table 7 Font Tag Attributes

Attribute	Value	Usage
color	A valid color. The W3C recommends hexadecimal colors.	Used to configure the color of the text.
face	A valid font name such as "Arial" or "Times New Roman"	Configures the font type of the text. If the font specified is not installed, the text will display in the browser's default font.
size	Absolute size: Integers ranging from "1" to "7". The default is "3".	Configures the size of the text. "1" is the smallest, "7" is the largest.

Logical Style Tags

Logical style tags are a group of tags that specify both the logical use and format of the text. Table 8 shows logical style tags and examples of their use.

Table 8 Logical Style Tags

Element	Example	Usage
`<strong>`	**strong** text	Causes text to be emphasized or to stand out from surrounding text. Usually displays in bold.
`<em>`	*emphasized* text	Causes text to be emphasized in relation to other text on the page. Usually displayed in italic.
`<cite>`	*cite* text	Identifies a citation or reference.
`<code>`	`code` text	Identifies program code samples. Usually a fixed-space font.
`<dfn>`	*dfn* text	Identifies a definition of a word or term.
`<kbd>`	`kbd` text	Identifies user text to be typed. Usually a fixed-space font.
`<samp>`	`samp` text	Shows program sample output.
`<var>`	*var* text	Identifies and displays a variable or program output.

Physical Style Tags

Physical style tags configure the physical display of the text. Table 9 depicts physical style tags and examples of their use.

Table 9 Physical Style Tags

Element	Example	Usage
`<b>`	**bold** text	Displays as bold text
`<i>`	*emphasized* text	Displays text in italic
`<big>`	big text	Displays text larger than normal size
`<small>`	small text	Displays text smaller than normal size
`<sub>`	subscript text	Displays in smaller text, below the baseline
`<sup>`	superscript text	Displays in smaller text, above the baseline
`<strike>`	~~strikethrough~~ text	Displays text with a line through it
`<tt>`	`teletype` text	Displays text in teletype or fixed-space font
`<u>`	underlined text	Displays text underlined. Avoid using this because underlined text can be confused with hyperlinks.

The Break Tag
`<br />`

The self-contained break tag creates a line break. The next XHTML element is displayed on a new line.

The Horizontal Rule Tag
`<hr />`

The self-contained horizontal rule tag creates a horizontal line on the web page. Only the width attribute is consistently recognized by Netscape Navigator 4.x browsers. All attributes are shown in Table 10.

Table 10 Horizontal Rule Tag Attributes

Attribute	Value	Usage
align	"left" "center" (default) "right"	Aligns the horizontal line on the web page.
border	Number of pixels	Configure the size of the border of the line.
color	A valid color. The W3C recommends hexadecimal colors.	Configure the color of the horizontal line.
noshade	"noshade"	Prevents a shadow from being displayed under the line.
size	Number of pixels	Configure the height of the line.
width	Numeric percentage	Configures a line that takes up a percentage of the width of the browser window. `<hr width="50%">`
	Number of pixels	Configures a line that takes up an exact number of pixels in the browser window. `<hr width="60">`

The Anchor Tag

`<a></a>`

The anchor tag creates a hyperlink. The text or image contained between the anchor tags is displayed by the browser as a hyperlink, as in these examples:

`<a href="http://mycompany.com">My Company</a>`

This creates an absolute hyperlink to the URL specified, in this case mycompany.com.

`<a href="mypage.htm">My Page</a>`

This creates a relative link to the named file, in this case mypage.htm.

`<a href="mypage.htm" title="My Page">My Page</a>`

This creates a relative link to the named file, in this case mypage.htm. It will also display the text associated with the title attribute in a tool tip alongside the link when the visitor places the mouse pointer on the link.

`<a href="mailto:me@me.com">Send e-mail to me@me.com</a>`

This creates a link to an e-mail address. If a default mail program is configured for the browser, the mail program will launch and get ready to send a message with the e-mail address provided, in this case me@me.com.

`<a href="#top">Back to Top</a>`

This creates an internal link to a bookmark or named fragment on the same web page, in this case to the named fragment called "top".

`<a id="top" name="top"></a>`

This identifies a portion of a web page as a bookmark or named fragment, in this case, the named fragment called "top". Older browsers such as Netscape 4 do not support the id attribute. The name attribute is used in addition to the id attribute to provide backward compatibility.

`<a target="parent" href="mypage.htm">My Page</a>`

This configures the window that the hyperlinked page will display in. The target attribute is most often used with frames. Table 11 lists the anchor tag attributes.

Table 11 Anchor Tag Attributes

Attribute	Value	Usage
accesskey	A character on the keyboard that appears in the hyperlink description	Configures a hot key to activate the link without using the mouse pointer.
href	A valid URL or web page file name	Creates a link to the named page or named element.
id	Text name, alphanumeric, beginning with a letter, no spaces	Uniquely identifies the element. This value can be used by a corresponding hyperlink.
name	Text name, alphanumeric, beginning with a letter, no spaces	Identifies the element. This value is used by a corresponding anchor tag with a href attribute. This is deprecated in XHTML but is included for backward compatibility.
tabindex	Numeric	Changes the order of the links accessed by pressing the Tab key. Default order is the order the links are placed on the page.
target	See Table 12 below.	Configures the window that displays the link. The default is the current window. See Table 12.
title	A brief text description	Configures a brief text description that will display in some browsers when a mouse pointer is placed over the link.

Values for the target attribute are shown in Table 12.

Table 12 Target Attribute Values

Target Attribute Value	Result
"_top"	Busts out of a frameset and displays the hyperlinked page in the entire browser window.
"_blank"	Opens a new browser window to display the hyperlinked page.
"_parent"	Displays the hyperlinked page in the frame that contains the current frameset.
"_self"	Displays the hyperlinked page in the same window.
A valid frame name value configured in a frameset page.	Displays the hyperlinked page in the named window.

Graphic Tags

The Image Tag

```
<img src="image.gif" />
```

The self-contained image tag displays an image file. Attributes for the image tag are shown in Table 13.

Table 13 Image Tag Attributes

Attribute	Value	Usage
align	"left" (default), "center", "right", "top", "texttop", "middle", "absmiddle", "bottom"	Aligns the image relative to the text on the page.
alt	A brief text description of the image	Provides accessibility to visitors unable to view the image.
border	Number of pixels for image border. "0" will prevent the border from being displayed.	Configures the border area on the image.
height	Number of pixels	Configures the height of the image.
hspace	Number of pixels	Configures space to the left and right of the image.
id	Text name, alphanumeric, beginning with a letter, no spaces	Identifies the image. The value must be unique and not used for other id values on the same XHTML document.
longdesc	URL of web page with detailed description of the image	Used by some assistive technologies to provide accessibility to the information in the image.
name	Text name, alphanumeric, beginning with a letter, no spaces	Names the image so that it can be easily accessed by client-side scripting languages such as JavaScript. This attribute is deprecated in XHTML but is used to provide backward compatibility with browsers that support HTML.
src	Name of the image file (required)	Configures the image file to be displayed.
title	A brief text description	Configures a text description that will display when the visitor moves the mouse pointer over the image.
usemap	The text name of an image map.	This corresponds to the name value on the associated map tag.
vspace	Number of pixels	Configures space above and below the image.
width	Number of pixels	Configures the width of the image.

The Map Tag
`<map></map>`

The map tag is a container tag that identifies the beginning and the end of an image map. The name attribute is used to associate the map tag with its corresponding image tag. The `<img>` tag is configured with the usemap attribute to indicate which map to use. Attributes for the map tag are shown in Table 14.

Table 14 Map Tag Attributes

Attribute	Value	Usage
id	Text name, alphanumeric, beginning with a letter, no spaces	Identifies the map. This value is used by the corresponding image tag. The value must be unique and not used for other id values on the same XHTML document.
name	Text name, alphanumeric, beginning with a letter, no spaces	Identifies the map. This value is used by the corresponding image tag. This is deprecated in XHTML but is included for backward compatibility.

The Area Tag
`<area />`

The self-contained area tag configures a hyperlink on an image map. Attributes for the area tag are in Table 15.

Table 15 Area Tag Attributes

Attribute	Value	Usage
alt	A brief text description of the portion of the image	Provides accessibility to visitors unable to view the image.
coords	Numeric pixels See Table 16.	Configures the coordinates of the clickable image area.
href	URL or web page document name.	Configures the web page that will display when the area is clicked.
shape	"rect" indicates rectangle "circle" indicates circle "poly" indicates polygon	Configures the shape of the area.

Each shape has a different syntax used to list the coordinates (coords) of the hyperlink area. See Table 16.

Table 16. Area Tag Shapes and Coords Attribute Values

Shape	Coords	Meaning
circle	"x,y,r"	The coordinates at point (x,y) indicate the center of the circle. The value of r is the radius of the circle.
polygon	"x1, y1, x2, y2, x3, y3", etc.	The values of each (x,y) pair represent the coordinates of a corner point of the polygon.
rectangle	"x1,y1, x2, y2"	The coordinates at point (x1,y1) represent the upper-left corner of the rectangle. The coordinates at point (x2,y2) represent the lower-right corner of the rectangle.

Table Tags

The Table Tag
`<table></table>`

This tag creates a table. Attributes of the table tag are listed in Table 17.

The Table Row Tag
`<tr></tr>`

This tag creates a table row. Attributes of the table row tag are listed in Table 18.

The Table Cell Tag
`<td></td>`

This tag creates a table cell. Attributes of the table cell tag are listed in Table 19.

The Table Header Tag
`<th></th>`

This tag creates a table header cell. Table header cells display text in bold font face and centered.

Common Table Attributes

Table 17 Table Tag Attributes

Attribute	Value	Usage
align	"left" (default), "center", "right"	Specifies the horizontal alignment of the table. A `<div>` tag is recommended for alignment instead of this attribute.
background	File name of an image	Specifies the image to display in the table background. This attribute can also be used with `<td background="image.gif">`
bgcolor	A valid color. The W3C recommends hexadecimal colors.	Specifies the color of the background. This attribute can also be used with `<tr>` and `<td>`.
border	Number of pixels. "0" indicates no border.	Specify the size of the border around the cells.
cellpadding	Number of pixels	Specifies the amount of space between the cell's borders and its contents.
cellspacing	Number of pixels	Specifies the amount of space between cells.
rules	"rows" indicates the interior border displays between rows only. "groups" indicates the interior border displays around groups (see `<tbody>`) only. "all" indicates the default border display.	Configures the interior border in a table.
width	Number of pixels or a percentage	Specifies the width of the table.

Table 18 Attributes for the <tr> Tag

Attribute	Value	Usage
align	"left" (default), "center", "right"	Specifies the horizontal alignment of the cells.
bgcolor	A valid color. The W3C recommends hexadecimal colors.	Specifies the color of the background. (Not supported by Netscape.)
valign	"top", "middle" (default), "bottom"	Specifies the vertical alignment of the cells.

Table 19 Attributes for the <td> Tag

Attribute	Value	Usage
align	"left" (default), "center", "right"	Specifies the horizontal alignment of the cell.
background	File name of an image	Specifies the image to display in the table cell background.
bgcolor	A valid color. The W3C recommends hexadecimal colors.	Specifies the color of the background.
colspan	Numeric	Specifies the number of columns spanned by a cell.
rowspan	Numeric	Specifies the number of rows spanned by a cell.
valign	"top", "middle" (default), "bottom"	Specifies the vertical alignment of the cell.
width	Number of pixels or a percentage	Specifies the width of the cell.
height	Number of pixels	Specifies the height of the cell.

Table Section Tags

<thead></thead>

The table head tag defines a block of one or more table header rows.

<tbody></tbody>

The table body tag divides a table into sections. It delineates one or more rows as a group. Use the rules attribute on the **<table>** tag to visually indicate the group.

<tfoot></tfoot>

The table foot tag defines a block of one or more table footer rows.

Frames Tags

The Frameset Tag

<frameset></frameset>

The frameset tag configures a web page that uses frames. The browser window is divided into multiple smaller windows so that multiple web pages can be displayed and individually scrolled at the same time. Attributes for the frameset tag are shown in Table 20. Examples of the rows and cols attributes are shown here.

Rows Attribute. The rows attribute specifies how the window will be divided vertically into rows of pixels (think of it as forming one row under another across the screen). The value can be a percentage of the browser window, a number of pixels or the special asterisk value (*). The special asterisk value tells the browser to calculate the appropriate space for the window. A value is given for each frame row. There can be multiple frames. For example, to create a frameset with two horizontal frames—one using 25% of the window and the other using what is left of the window—the code is `<frameset rows="25%,*">`.

Cols Attribute. The cols attribute specifies how the window will be divided horizontally into columns of pixels (think of it as forming one column next to another across the screen). The value can be a percentage of the browser window, a number of pixels, or the special asterisk value (*). The special asterisk value tells the browser to calculate the appropriate space for the window. A value is given for each frame column. There can be multiple frames. For example, to create a frameset with two vertical frames—one using 200 pixels of the window and the other using what is left of the window—the code is `<frameset cols="200,*">`.

Table 20 Frameset Tag Attributes

Attribute	Value	Usage
border	Number of pixels	Specifies the width of the frame borders in the frameset.
bordercolor	A valid color. The W3C recommends hexadecimal colors.	Specifies the color of the frame borders in the frameset. Default color is gray.
cols	Number of pixels, percentage, or "*" to indicate remaining window area	Reserves vertical areas (columns) of the browser window
frameborder	"0" or "1" (default)	"0" indicates that no frame borders will be visible in the frameset. "1" indicates that frame borders will display in the frameset (default).
framespacing	Number of pixels	Specifies the width of the frameborders in the frameset. Use this instead of the border attribute.
rows	Number of pixels, percentage or "*" to indicate remaining window area	Reserves horizontal areas (rows) of the browser window.
title	A brief text description	Provides a text description of the frameset that can be used by assistive technologies.

The Frame Tag
`<frame />`

The self-contained frame tag specifies a single frame or area of the window contained within a frameset. Attributes for the frame tag are shown in Table 21.

Table 21 Frame Tag Attributes

Attribute	Value	Usage
bordercolor	A valid color. The W3C recommends hexadecimal colors.	Configures the color of the frame border.
frameborder	"0" or "1" (default)	"0" indicates that no frame borders will be visible for this frame. "1" indicates that frame borders will display for this frame (default).
id	Alphanumeric, no spaces. The value must be unique and not used for other id values on the same XHTML document.	This attribute is optional. It provides a unique identifier for the frame.
longdesc	URL of web page with detailed description of the frame	Provides a detailed text description of the frame. This may be accessed by assistive technologies.
marginheight	Number of pixels	Configures the top and bottom margins for the frame.
marginwidth	Number of pixels	Configures the width of the right and left margins for the frame.
name	Text name, beginning with a letter, no spaces	Names the frame, so that it may be targeted by other frames. This is deprecated in XHTML but is used to provide backward compatibility with browsers that support HTML.
noresize	"noresize"	Does not allow a web page visitor to resize a frame by dragging the frame border with the mouse.
scrolling	"yes", "no", "auto" (default)	Configures whether the frame has a scroll bar. The default is "auto", which configures the browser to add a scroll bar automatically when needed.
src	URL or file name	Configures what web page will be displayed in the frame (required).
target	"_top", "_blank", "_self" (default), valid frame name, valid window name	Sets the default window for all links in the frame to use. See the description of the target attribute (Table 12) for more information.
title	Text phrase that describes the frame	Configures the title of the frame. This can be accessed by screen readers and is recommended by the W3C to improve accessibility.

The Noframes Tag
`<noframes></noframes>`

The noframes tag configures what will display on browsers and other user agents that don't support frames.

The Inline Frame Tag

`<iframe></iframe>`

The inline frame tag configures a special scrolling area that displays a different web page document. This does not need to be associated with a frameset and can be placed on the body of any web page. Some older browsers, such as Netscape 4, do not support inline frames. Place content that should be displayed if the inline frame is not supported between the opening and closing inline frame tags. The inline frame tag is not part of the W3C Recommendation.

Attributes for the inline frame tag are shown in Table 22.

Table 22 Inline Frame Tag Attributes

Attribute	Value	Usage
align	"left" (default), "right", "center"	Specifies the horizontal alignment of the iframe.
frameborder	"0" or "1" (default)	"0" indicates that no frame borders will be visible for this inline frame. "1" indicates that frame borders will display for this inline frame (default).
height	Number of pixels	Height of the inline frame in pixels
id	Alphanumeric, no spaces. The value must be unique and not used for other id values on the same XHTML document.	This attribute provides a unique identifier for the inline frame.
longdesc	URL of web page with detailed description of the contents of the inline frame	Provides a detailed text description of the frame. This may be accessed by assistive technologies.
marginheight	Number of pixels	Configures the top and bottom margins of the inline frame.
marginwidth	Number of pixels	Configures the width of the right and left margins of an inline frame.
name	Text name, beginning with a letter, no spaces	Configures the name of the inline frame. This is required when using the target attribute to configure hyperlinks. This attribute is deprecated in XHTML but is used to provide backward compatibility with browsers that support HTML.
scrolling	"yes", "no", "auto" (default)	Determines whether scrollbars will appear if the document displayed is larger than the size of the inline frame.
src	Valid file name of a web page document (required)	Configures the name of the file to be displayed in the inline frame.
title	Text phrase that describes the inline frame	Configures the title of the inline frame. This can be accessed by screen readers and is recommended by the W3C to improve accessibility.
width	Number of pixels	Configures the width of the inline frame in pixels.

Form Tags

The Form Tag

`<form></form>`

The form tag configures a form that can accept information from a web site visitor. The form information may be processed using a server-side script or executable program. Attributes for the form tag are shown in Table 23.

Table 23 Form Tag Attributes

Attribute	Value	Usage
action	File name or URL of the program or script that will handle the form data	Specifies the name of the server-side program or script that will handle the form data.
id	Alphanumeric, no spaces. The value must be unique and not used for other id values.	Provides a unique identifier for the form.
method	"post"	Preferred by the W3C. Sends the form data to the web server as a part of the entity body of the HTTP response. Form data is not visible in the URL.
	"get" (default)	Sends the form data to the web server as part of the URL
name	Text name, beginning with a letter, no spaces	This attribute is optional. It names the form so that it can be easily accessed by client-side scripting languages such as JavaScript to edit and verify the form information before the server-side processing is invoked. This attribute is deprecated in XHTML but is used to provide backward compatibility with browsers that support HTML.
target	See Table 12.	Specifies the window used to display the form response. The default is the current window. See Table 12.

Form Element Tags

The Input Tag

`<input />`

The stand-alone input tag configures an input element for a form. The attributes and their values determine the type of input element displayed on the web page. Attributes for the input tag are listed in Table 24.

Table 24 Input Tag Attributes

Attribute	Value	Usage
type	"text", "checkbox", "radio", "hidden", "submit", "reset", "button", "image", "password"	Configures a specific form element (required).
accesskey	A character on the keyboard	Configures a hot key that immediately places the cursor on the form element.
checked	"checked"	Used with type="checkbox" or type="radio". Indicates that the form element is selected.
disabled	"disabled"	Prevents the cursor from being placed in the form element.
id	Text name, beginning with a letter, no spaces	Provides a unique identifier for the form element that can be used to associate the element with a label tag or act as a named fragment identifier.
maxlength	Numeric	Configures the maximum number of characters allowed in a text input area.
name	Text name, beinning with a letter, no spaces	Names the form element. The name value is used by JavaScript, CGI, and other server-side processing.
size	Numeric	Configures the width in characters of a text input area on screen.
src	File name of an image	Used with type="image"
tabindex	Numeric	Changes the order of the form element accessed by pressing the Tab key. Default order is the order the form elements are placed on the page.
title	A brief text description	Configures a brief text description that will display in some browsers when a mouse pointer is placed over the element.
value	Text or numeric characters	Provides the value given to a form element which is passed to the form handler.

The Textarea Tag

`<textarea></textarea>`

The textarea tag configures a multi-line text input area on a form, sometimes called a scrolling text box. Text contained within the textarea tags will be initially displayed in the scrolling text box. Attributes for the textarea tag are shown in Table 25.

Table 25 Textarea Tag Attributes

Attribute	Value	Usage
accesskey	A character on the keyboard	Configures a hot key that immediately places the cursor on the form element.
cols	Numeric	Configures the number of columns in the textarea.
id	Text name, beginning with a letter, no spaces	Provides a unique identifier for the form element that can be used to associate the element with a label tag or act as a named fragment identifier.
disabled	"disabled"	Prevents the cursor from being placed in the textarea.
name	Text name, beginning with a letter, no spaces	Names the form element.
rows	Numeric	Configures the number of rows displayed on the screen in the textarea.
tabindex	Numeric	Changes the order of the form element accessed by pressing the tab key. Default order is the order the form elements are placed on the page.
title	A brief text description	Configures a brief text description that will display in some browsers when a mouse pointer is placed over the element.
wrap	"virtual"	As the text is entered, the cursor automatically drops to the next line at the end of each line. When the text is sent to the server, there are no line breaks except where the Enter key has been pressed.
	"physical"	When the text is sent to the server, line breaks are placed where the text wraps to the next line in the scrolling text box.
	"off" (default)	The text is entered all on one line, and the Enter key must be pressed to drop to the next line. One line of text is transmitted to the server.

The Select Tag

`<select></select>`

The select tag configures a select box to display a menu of items, sometimes called a list box or drop-down list box. The individual menu items are configured with option tags. Attributes for the select tag are shown in Table 26.

Table 26 Select Tag Attributes

Attribute	Value	Usage
accesskey	A character on the keyboard	Configures a hot key that immediately places the cursor on the form element.
disabled	"disabled"	Prevents the cursor from being placed in the select list
id	Text name, beginning with a letter, no spaces	Provides a unique identifier for the form element that can be used to associate the element with a label tag or act as a named fragment identifier.
multiple	"multiple"	Allows multiple selections from the list.
name	Text name, beginning with a letter, no spaces	Names the form element.
size	Numeric	Provides the number of elements to be displayed. If size is configured, the select list is displayed as a scrolling list. If size is omitted, the select list is a drop-down list.
tabindex	Numeric	Changes the order of the form element accessed by pressing the Tab key. Default order is the order the form elements are placed on the page.
title	A brief text description	Configures a brief text description that will display in some browsers when a mouse pointer is placed over the element.

The Option Tag

`<option></option>`

The option tag configures an item within a select element. The text contained between the option tags is displayed in the select box. Attributes for the option tag are displayed in Table 27.

Table 27 Option Tag Attributes

Attribute	Value	Usage
selected	"selected"	Configures an option selected by default.
value	Text or numeric characters	A value given to a form element that is passed to the form handler if the item is selected.

The Label Tag
`<label></label>`

The label tag configures a text label that is associated with a form element. Attributes are shown in Table 28.

Table 28 Label Tag Attributes

Attribute	Value	Usage
accesskey	A character on the keyboard	Configures a hot key that immediately places the cursor on the form element.
for	Corresponds to the value of an id attribute on a form element.	Associates a text label with a form element.
title	A brief text description	Configures a brief text description that will display in some browsers when a mouse is placed over the label.

The Fieldset Tag
`<fieldset></fieldset>`

The fieldset tag configures a group of form elements. It is used together with the legend (`<legend>`) tag.

The Legend Tag
`<legend></legend>`

The legend tag is only used within the fieldset tag. It configures a text description for the fieldset grouping. Attributes are listed in Table 29.

Table 29 Legend Tag Attributes

Attribute	Value	Usage
accesskey	A character on the keyboard	Configures a hot-key that immediately places the cursor on the first form element in the legend area.
align	"top", "bottom". "left", "right"	Configures the alignment of the text legend.
title	A brief text description	Configures a brief text description that will display in some browsers when a mouse pointer is placed over the text legend.

The Button Tag
`<button></button>`

The button tag creates an area on the web page that will act like a standard form button. Configures web page content that is coded between the `<button>` and `</button>` tags as the form button. Attributes are listed in Table 30.

Table 30 Button Tag Attributes

Attributes	Value	Usage
accesskey	A character on the keyboard	Configures a hot-key that immediately places the cursor on the area.
id	Text name, beginning with a letter, no spaces	Provides a unique identifier for the form element that can be used to associate the element with a label tag or act as a named fragment identifier.
name	Text name, beginning with a letter, no spaces	Names the form element so that it can be easily accessed by client-side scripting languages (such as JavaScript) or by server-side processing. The name should be unique.
title	A brief text description	Configures a brief text description that will display in some browsers when a mouse pointer is placed over the area.
type	submit	Functions as a submit button.
	reset	Functions as a reset button.
	button	Functions as a button.
value	Text or numeric characters	A value given to a form element that is passed to the form handler.

Miscellaneous Tags

The Applet Tag
`<applet></applet>`

The `<applet>` tag is used to specify the beginning of an applet area in the body of a web page. The closing tag, `</applet>`, specifies the ending of an applet area in the body of a web page. Attributes for the applet tag are shown in Table 31.

Table 31 Applet Tag Attributes

Attribute	Value	Usage
alt	A text description of the applet.	Provides alternate content for visitors unable to access the applet.
code	The file name of a Java applet (.class extension). Required.	Configures the name of the applet file.
codebase	A folder name.	Configures the name of the folder that contains the applet. This is needed if the applet is not in the same folder as the web page.
height	Number of pixels	Configures the height of the applet area.
id	Alphanumeric, no spaces. The value must be unique and not used for other id values on the same XHTML document.	Provides a unique identifier for the applet.
width	Number of pixels	Configures the width of the applet area.

The Parameter Tag
`<param />`

The parameter tag is used to pass values or parameters to an object or Java applet. This tag is always used with either an `<applet>` or `<object>` tag.

The No Break Tag
`<nobr></nobr>`

The `<nobr>` tag is used to contain areas on a web page, such as groups of images, that should remain on the same line regardless of the size of the browser window.

The Object Tag
`<object></object>`

The object tag can be used to place sound and other media on a web page. It is a container tag and should be closed with an `</object>` tag. The object tag is part of the W3C standard; you should become familiar with its use. However, it is not as well supported by browsers as the `<embed>` tag. Table 32 lists the attributes of the object tag when used with media files.

Table 32 Object Tag Attributes

Attribute	Value	Usage
autostart	"true", "false"	Determines if the media will play automatically when the page is loaded. If omitted, media does not automatically play.
data	Valid file name, name of media file (required)	Provides the name of the file to be played.
height	Number of pixels	Specifies the height of media control console.
hidden	"true" (not uniformly supported)	Hides the default media console.
loop	Numeric value, or "true" for continuous play (not uniformly supported)	Determines how many times the media file will repeat.
type	A valid MIME type such as audio/midi, audio/wav, etc.	Specifies the MIME type of the media file.
width	Number of pixels	Configures the width of media control console.

The Embed Tag
`<embed />`

This tag is not part of the W3C XHTML 1.0 specification but is included here because it is commonly used. The W3C recommends using the object tag instead. The embed tag can be used to place sound and other media in a web page. It is a self-contained tag and does not have a corresponding closing tag. Table 33 lists the attributes of the embed tag when it is used with media files.

Table 33 Attributes of the Embed Tag

Attribute	Value	Usage
align	"baseline" (default), "left", "right", "center", "top"	Aligns the media control console.
autostart	"true", "false"	Determines whether the media will play automatically when the page is loaded. If omitted, media does not automatically play.
controls	"console", "smallconsole", "playbutton", "pausebutton", "stopbutton", "volumelever"	Configures the appearance of the media control console.
height	Number of pixels	Configures the height of media control console.
hidden	"true"	Hides the default media console.
loop	Numeric value or "true" for continuous play (may not be uniformly supported)	Repeats the media file.
src	Valid file name, name of media file (required)	Provides the name of the file to be played.
width	Number of pixels	Configures the width of media control console.

The Noembed Tag
`<noembed></noembed>`

The noembed tag is not part of the W3C XHTML 1.0 specification but is included here because it is often used. The noembed tag is a container tag. It can appear after an embed tag to provide alternate content that may be used by browsers or assistive technologies such as screen readers.

The Comment Tag
`<!-- your comment goes here -->`

The comment tag is special in that anything between the opening "<!--" and the closing "-->" is considered to be a comment and is ignored by the browser. This tag can be used to document and describe XHTML.

The Marquee Tag
`<marquee></marquee>`

The marquee tag is not part of the W3C XHTML 1.0 specification and only works in Internet Explorer. It displays text contained between the marquee tags in a scrolling fashion, like a movie marquee.

The Blink Tag
`<blink></blink>`

The blink tag is not part of the W3C XHTML 1.0 specification and is only supported by Netscape. It causes the text contained between the blink tags to flash on and off—blinking. This is very annoying and should be avoided.

Special Characters

Special characters, or entity characters, such as the copyright symbol and nonbreaking spaces, often appear on web pages. Table 34 lists a selection of special characters in order of their numeric code. The most commonly used special characters are shown in bold. The W3C's list of special characters can be found at http://www.w3.org/MarkUp/html-spec/html-spec_13.html.

Table 34 Special Characters

Entity Name	Numeric Code	Descriptive Code	Character
quotation mark	&#34;	&quot;	"
ampersand	&#38;	&amp;	&
less-than sign	&#60;	&lt;	<
greater-than sign	&#62;	&gt;	>
nonbreaking space			a blank space
inverted exclamation	&#161;	&iexcl;	¡
cent sign	&#162;	&cent;	¢
pound sterling	&#163;	&pound;	£
general currency sign	&#164;	&curren;	¤
yen sign	&#165;	&yen;	¥
broken vertical bar	&#166;	&brvba;r	¦
section sign	&#167;	&sect;	§
umlaut	&#168;	&uml;	¨
copyright	&#169;	&copy;	©
feminine ordinal	&#170;	&ordf;	ª
left angle quote	&#171;	&laquo;	«
not sign	&#172;	&not;	¬
soft hyphen	&#173;	&shy;	-
registered trademark	&#174;	&reg;	®
macron accent	&#175;	&macr;	¯
degree sign	&#176;	&deg;	°
plus or minus	&#177;	&plusmn;	±
superscript two	&#178;	&sup2;	²
superscript three	&#179;	&sup3;	³
acute accent	&#180;	&acute;	´
micro sign (Mu)	&#181;	&micro;	µ
paragraph sign	&#182;	&para;	¶
middle dot	&#183;	&middot;	·
cedilla	&#184;	&cedil;	¸
superscript one	&#185;	&sup1;	¹
masculine ordinal	&#186;	&ordm;	º
right angle quote	&#187;	&raquo;	»
fraction one fourth	&#188;	&frac14;	¼
fraction one half	&#189;	&frac12;	½
fraction three fourths	&#190;	&frac34;	¾
inverted question mark	&#191;	&iquest;	¿
small e, grave accent	&#232;	&egrave;	è
small e, acute accent	&#233;	&eacute;	é

CSS Property Reference

Cascading Style Sheet properties that are commonly used to format font, text, and color are listed in this section. Unless otherwise noted, each property applies to all XHTML elements.

Table 35 Cascading Style Sheet Properties

Property	Values	Usage
background-color	Valid hexadecimal color value or color name	Configures the background color of element. `background-color:#CCCCCC;` Default background color is determined by the browser.
background-image	url keyword with valid image file name	Configures an image file as the background for an element. `background-image:url(parchment.gif);`
color	Valid hexadecimal color value or color name	Configures the foreground (text) color `color:#0000FF;` The default is determined by the browser.
font-family	Valid font name or a font family such as "serif", "sans-serif", "fantasy", "monospaced", "cursive"	Configures the type of font used to display the element. `font-family:Arial,Verdana,sans-serif;` Default font is determined by the browser.
font-size	Numeric point (pt) or pixel (px) size, absolute size ("xx-small", "x-small", "small", "medium", "large", "x-large", "xx-large"), relative size ("smaller", "larger")	Configures the size of the font used to display the element. `font-size:smaller;` The default font size is medium.
font-style	"normal" (default), "italic", "oblique"	Configures the style of the text. `font-style:italic;`
font-variant	"normal" (default), "small-caps"	Configures display as regular text or in small capital letters. `font-variant:small-caps;`
font-weight	Numeric values ("100", "200", "300", "400", "500", "600", "700", "800") Relative values ("normal" (default), "bold", "bolder", "lighter")	Configures the boldness of the text. `font-weight:bolder;`
text-align	"left", "right", "center", "justify"	Configures the alignment of text in an element. This applies to block-level elements. `text-align:center;` Default depends on browser.
text-decoration	"none","underline", "overline", "line-through", "blink"	Configures the text, usually the placement of a line above, under, or through the text. The example below is commonly used to remove the default underline from hyperlinked text. `text-decoration:none;`
vertical-align	"baseline", "sub", "super", "top", "text-top", "middle", "bottom", "text-bottom"	Configures the vertical alignment of an inline element or table cell element. `vertical-align:middle;`

Table 36 Pseudo-Classes

Pseudo-Classes Used with the Anchor Element

link	Configures the state for the link before it is visited. `a:link { color:#00FF00; text-decoration: none;}`
visited	Configures the state for a visited link. `a:visited { color:#CCCCCC; text-decoration: none;}`
hover	Triggered when the mouse pointer is placed on the link. `a:hover { color:#FF0000; text-decoration: none;}`
active	Triggered when the link is clicked. `a:active { color:#FF0000; text-decoration: none;}`

There are many more CSS properties—positioning elements on web pages, selecting media types, and so on. Visit the W3C's web site, http://www.w3.org/TR/REC-CSS2/propidx.html, for a complete list of CSS properties.

Using FTP

FTP stands for File Transfer Protocol. A protocol is a convention or standard that enables computers to speak to one another. FTP is used copy files and folders over the Internet.

The Windows operating system includes a command-line FTP program. However, you will find it easier to transfer files if you install an FTP program that allows you to point and click to transfer your files. WS_FTP is a popular FTP application for computers running Microsoft Windows. Fetch is a popular FTP application for Macintosh computers.

If you don't already have an FTP application installed on your computer, visit http://download.com or http://shareware.com and search for "FTP Client" or "FTP Program". A common shareware version of WS_FTP is WS_FTP LE. The screen shots in this handbook use WS_FTP LE. Other FTP applications work in a similar manner and should have some type of help or tutorial.

After you download your FTP application, install the program on your computer using the instructions provided. Check the readme file, usually named readme.txt, for information. Once the program is installed, launch it. If you are using WS_FTP LE, a Session Properties dialog box similar to the one shown in Figure 1 will display.

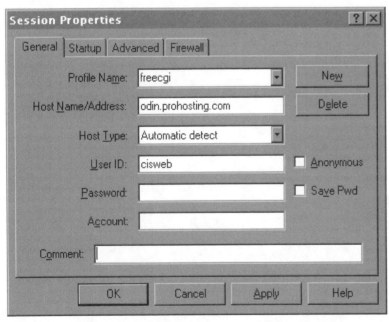

Figure 1 *FTP Session Properties dialog box*

If you don't see this Session Properties dialog box on your screen, look in the bottom left corner of the WS_FTP LE program window for a Connect button and click it. The Session Properties dialog box should now be displayed. The Session Properties dialog box is used to configure your FTP session. The values shown in the Figure 1 Session Properties dialog box are just samples—your web host will provide you with the correct information for your web site.

Connect to Your Web Host

Your first task is to set up the program so it can connect to your web host. As mentioned, your web host will provide you with the following information: Host Name/Address, User ID, and Password. In the Session Properties dialog box, click on the New button and fill in the text box fields.

Table 37 shows the WS_FTP LE configuration. If you are using a different shareware FTP program, your configuration may be slightly different.

Table 37 Fields used by WS_FTP LE

Profile Name	Think of a brief name that describes the site or web server and type it here. For example, you could use your own name for the profile of your personal web site and the client's name for the profiles of websites you create for your clients.
Host Name/Address	Normally your web host will tell you the address you need to use to connect to their server using FTP. Most often the address is in the form ftp.servername.com. Contact your web host to get the proper FTP
Host Type	This can almost always be left on Auto Detect, which will let the program determine the host type and configure it automatically. If you have difficulty connecting, you will need to find out from your web host what host type it is using.
User ID	This is the user name the web host assigned to you for its system.
Password	This is the password the web host assigned to you for use on its system. When you type your password, asterisks will display in this field.
Account	This is almost always left blank. Your web host will inform you if you need to use this field.
Comment	This is an optional field. You can add your own comments and descriptions here.
Anonymous	You will only need to check this box if you are connecting to a host that allows anonymous FTP. In most cases, you will leave this box unchecked. It is usually checked if you connect to a site that allows you access to download files only.
Save Pwd	Check this box if you want the program to save your password, so you do not need to retype it each time you connect. It is recommended that you uncheck the box so that if someone else uses your computer they would have to type the correct password to connect to the server.

Once you have entered the appropriate information in the text boxes, click OK. If all values are correct, you will connect to the web host and view a dialog box similar to the one shown in Figure 2. It is normal for the connection to take several seconds or as much as a minute to establish. If you get an error message, verify your information and contact your web host if necessary.

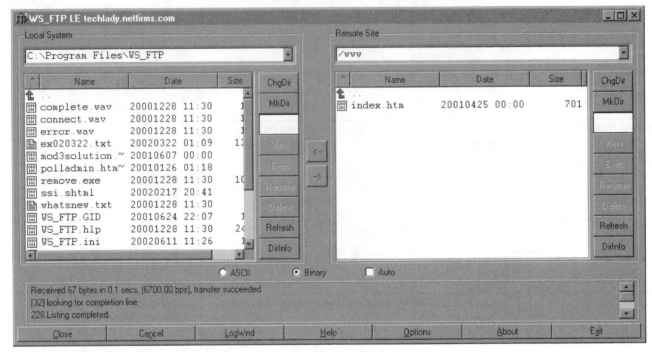

Figure 2 *Sample FTP application showing the local system and the remote site.*

Take a moment to view the FTP window. Your computer, the Local System, is shown on the left and the web server, the Remote Site, is shown on the right. The type of display is slightly similar to Windows Explorer. The current drive and folder are shown at the top of each side. The scrolling list box displays the files in the folder. You can locate files on your computer by changing drives and moving up and down in the folder list. To change to a different folder, select it (or the up arrow at the top of the list) and click on the ChgDir button.

It's very easy to transfer files from your computer to your web sever. Follow these steps:

1. Select the file you need to transfer by clicking on it. It will be highlighted.
2. Click the right arrow button in the middle section of the display to send the file to the web server.
3. Watch as messages appear in the lower portion of the dialog box. In a few seconds or a few minutes (depending on the size of the file) you should see your file appear in the list on the right side of the dialog box. Your file is now on the web server—the file transfer is complete!
4. To view your page, launch a browser and type in the URL followed by your file name.

The FTP application also allows you to rename files, delete files, create and remove directories (folders), and transfer files from web servers to your local system. As you work with FTP experiment with some of these features—it is an easy-to-use, yet powerful application.

Additional FTP Resources

- http://www.ipswitch.com/Support/WS_FTP/tutorial_66/index.html. This tutorial can get you started with WS_FTP (the non-shareware version).
- http://www.eurekais.com/brock/ftp_tutorial/. This tutorial discusses a popular shareware FTP program.
- http://support.t3west.com/tutorials/mac.html. This tutorial can get you started with Fetch, a popular Mac FTP application.

Comparison of HTML and XHTML

As you have traversed the Web and viewed the source code of pages created by others, you may have noticed that the style and syntax of the coding is different than the XHTML syntax that you have been studying. Those pages were most likely written following HTML syntax. If you view the source code of web pages generated by web authoring tools such as Microsoft FrontPage or Macromedia Dreamweaver, you will also notice some syntax differences because in versions as recent as FrontPage 2002 and Dreamweaver 4, these applications still generated HTML instead of XHTML. Hope is in sight, however—the newer Dreamweaver MX can be easily configured to generate XHTML code.

The newest version of HTML is actually XHTML—e**X**tensible **H**yper-**T**ext **M**arkup **L**anguage. XHTML uses the tags and attributes of HTML along with the syntax of XML (e**X**tensible **M**arkup **L**anguage). For the most part you will use the same tags and attributes in HTML and XHTML; the major change is the syntax and additional restrictions in XHTML. These restrictions were added so that more efficient programs could be written to process web pages automatically. Let's take a look at specific examples of differences between HTML and XHTML.

XML Directive

Since XHTML follows XML syntax, each document should begin with an XML directive. HTML has no such requirement.

HTML
Not required

XHTML
```
<?xml version="1.0" encoding="UTF-8"?>
```

Document Type Definition

Both XHTML and HTML have three distinct document type definitions: strict, transitional, and frameset. They are listed here.

HTML Strict DTD
```
<!DOCTYPE HTML PUBLIC "-//W3C//DTD HTML 4.01//EN"
  "http://www.w3.org/TR/html4/strict.dtd">
```

HTML Transitional DTD
```
<!DOCTYPE HTML PUBLIC "-//W3C//DTD HTML 4.01 Transitional//EN"
  "http://www.w3.org/TR/html4/loose.dtd">
```

HTML Frameset DTD
```
<!DOCTYPE HTML PUBLIC "-//W3C//DTD HTML 4.01 Frameset//EN"
  "http://www.w3.org/TR/html4/frameset.dtd">
```

XHTML Strict DTD
```
<!DOCTYPE html PUBLIC "-//W3C//DTD XHTML 1.0 Strict//EN"
  "http://www.w3.org/TR/xhtml1/DTD/xhtml1-strict.dtd">
```

XHTML Transitional DTD
```
<!DOCTYE html PUBLIC "-//W3C//DTD XHMTL 1.0 Transitional//EN"
  "http://www.w3.org/TR/xhtml1/DTD/xhmtl1-transitional.dtd">
```

XHTML Frameset DTD

```
<!DOCTYE html PUBLIC "-//W3C//DTD XHMTL 1.0 Frameset//EN"
  "http://www.w3.org/TR/xhtml1/DTD/xhmtl1-frameset.dtd">
```

The HTML Tag

XHTML requires that the root element (immediately after the DTD) be an **<html>** tag that refers to the XML namespace. HTML has no such requirement.

HTML
```
<HTML>
```

XHTML
```
<html xmlns="http://www.w3.org/1999/xhtml" >
```

Uppercase Versus Lowercase

The HTML standard recommended that tags and attributes use upper-case. The XHTML standard follows XML syntax, which requires lowercase.

HTML
```
<TABLE>
```

XHTML
```
<table>
```

Use of Quotation Marks with Attributes

The XHTML standard requires that the values for all attributes be enclosed in quotation marks. This was valid in HTML but was not always done.

HTML
```
<TABLE BORDER=0>
```

XHTML
```
<table border="0">
```

Container Tags

The XHTML standard requires that both the opening and closing tags for all container tags be used. HTML does not require this.

HTML
```
This is the first paragraph.<p>
This is the second paragraph.<p>
```

XHTML
```
<p>This is the first paragraph.</p>
<p>This is the second paragraph.</p>
```

Self-Contained Tags

The XHTML standard requires that all self-contained tags be properly closed using " **/>**". HTML does not require this.

HTML

```
This is the first line.<br>
This is the second line.
```

XHTML

```
This is the first line.<br />
This is the second line.
```

Use of Attribute Values

The XHTML standard requires that all attributes be assigned values. HTML allows some attributes, such as noresize or checked, to be minimized. Since these attributes only have a single value, HTML does not require that the value be provided.

HTML

```
<INPUT TYPE=RADIO CHECKED NAME=GENDER>
```

XHTML

```
<input type="radio" checked="checked" name="gender" />
```

Source Code Line Breaks

The XHTML standard requires that there be no line breaks or extra blank spaces between attributes. HTML has no such requirements.

HTML

```
<INPUT TYPE=RADIO
CHECKED          NAME=GENDER>
```

XHTML

```
<input type="radio" checked="checked" name="gender" />
```

Required Tags

XHTML requires the **<head>** and **<body>** tags. This restriction does not apply to HTML.

Header Section Tag Order

XHTML requires that the **<title>** tag be the first tag in the header section. HTML does not have this restriction.

Nesting Tags

XHTML requires appropriate nesting of tags. The opening and closing container tags must nest and not overlap each other. This restriction does not apply to HTML.

HTML
```
<B><EM>This is important</B></EM>
```

XHTML
```
<b><em>This is important</em></b>
```

The <font> Tag

The **<font>** tag is deprecated in XHTML. It is recommended that web developers use CSS to configure formatting instructions instead of the **<font>** tag. While CSS can be used with HTML, it is more common to see **<font>** tags.

HTML
```
<P><FONT FACE=ARIAL>This is a sentence.</FONT></P>
```

XHTML
```
<p style="font-family:arial,verdana">This is a sentence.</p>
```

Bookmarks

The "name" attribute is deprecated in XHTML as applied to bookmarks and named fragment identifiers. This has the greatest affect on **<a>** and **<map>** tags. HTML requires the name attribute. It's a good idea for XHTML web developers to include both attributes in order to be backward compatible with web browsers that do not support XHTML.

HTML
```
<A NAME=TOP>
```

XHTML
```
<a name="top" id="top"></a>
```

JavaScript and the <script> Tag

XHTML considers JavaScript statements to be arbitrary character data (CDATA). The XML parser should not process them. The CDATA statement tells the XML parser to ignore the JavaScript. This is not part of HTML and not supported by many current browsers. A comparison of the XHTML and HTML syntax is listed here.

HTML
```
<SCRIPT LANGUAGE="JavaScript" TYPE="text/js">

JavaScript statements go here
</SCRIPT>
```

XHTML
```
<script language="JavaScript" type="text/js">
<![CDATA[
JavaScript statements go here
]]>
</script>
```

An alternative way to use JavaScript on a web page that is supported by XHTML standards is to place JavaScript statements in their own separate (.js) file. This file can be configured by the **<script>** tag. HTML also supports this syntax.

HTML

```
<SCRIPT SRC="myscript.js" LANGUAGE="JavaScript" TYPE="text/js">
</SCRIPT>
```

XHTML

```
<script src="myscript.js" language="JavaScript" type="text/js">
</script>
```

Summary

As you can see from these examples, HTML and XHTML code is quite similar. There are even programs, such as HTML Tidy (http://www.w3.org/People/Raggett/tidy/), that can assist you in converting HTML to XHTML. Recent versions of web authoring tools, such as Macromedia Dreamweaver MX, generate XHTML code automatically. Visit the W3C's web site (http://www.w3.org/TR/xhtml1/) for the most up-to-date information on XHTML.

Index

B2B 401
B2C 401
B2G 402
backbone 6
background 106
background attribute
    `<body>` tag 106, 107, H-7
    `<table>` tag H-16
    `<td>` tag H-17
background sounds 316
background-color 281, H-32
background-image 282, H-32
banner ads 343, 344
base tag, *see* `<base>`
Berners-Lee, Tim 3
    accessibility 256
bgcolor attribute
    `<body>` tag 26, 27, 95, 106, 107, H-7
    `<embed>` tag 380
    `<param />` tag 380
    `<table>` tag 71, H-16
    `<td>` tag 72, H-17
    `<tr>` tag 72, H-17
bgproperties attribute
    `<body>` tag H-7
blink tag, *see* `<blink>`
block-level tags 27
Bobby 256
body section 23
body tag, *see* `<body>`
bold tag, *see* `<b>`
bookmark, *see* internal link
border attribute
    `<frameset>` tag H-18
    `<hr />` tag 97, H-11
    `<img />` tag 104, H-14
    `<table>` tag 69, H-16
bordercolor attribute
    `<frame />` tag 153, H-19
    `<frameset>` tag 152, H-18
    `<table>` tag 70
breadcrumb trails 238
browser compatibility 320
browser popularity 252
browser-friendly 252
bulleted list, *see* unordered list
button 198
    `<button>` tag 205, H-26
    `<input />` tag 196, 197
    reset button 197
    submit button 196
button tag, *see* `<button>`

C2C 402
CA 408
Cascading Style Sheets, *see* CSS
cellpadding attribute
    `<table>` tag 71, H-16
cellspacing attribute
    `<table>` tag 71, H-16
Cerf, Vinton 2, 121, 256
CERN 3
CERT 408
certificate authority, *see* CA
CGI 185, 208, 383
    common uses 383
    invoking from a form 385
    invoking from a hyperlink 384
    invoking from a URL 384
    resources 388
    steps in using 385
check box 192
checked attribute
    `<input />` tag 192, 193, H-22
chunking 232
ciphertext 405
class selector 289
classid attribute
    `<object>` tag 379
client 6
client/server 7
client-side scripting 265, 371, 387
code attribute
    `<applet>` tag 368, H-27
codebase attribute
    `<applet>` tag 368, H-27
    `<object>` tag 379
ColdFusion 388, 412
co-located web hosting 273
color 94
    CSS property 281–283 H-32
    hexadecimal 94
color attribute
    `<font>` tag 39, H-10
    `<hr />` tag 96, H-11
cols attribute
    `<frameset>` tag 152, H-18
    `<textarea>` tag 194, H-23
colspan attribute
    `<td>` tag 73, H-17
comment tag, *see* `<!--`
commerce server 412
common gateway interface, *see* CGI
conceptualization (web site development) 266
connection speed 120

ethics 119, 125, 126
gamma 121
guidelines 120, 121
resolution 121
resources 119
sources 119, 120
thumbnails 119
using 103

hash function 406
hash mark (#) 290
head section 22
head tag, *see* **<head>**
header 22
header tag, *see* **<head>**
heading tag, *see* **<h1>**
height attribute
   <applet> tag 368, H-27
   <embed> tag 313, H-29
   <iframe> tag 159, H-20
   <img /> tag 104, H-14
   <object> tag 315, H-28
   <table> tag 70
helper application 310
hexadecimal 94
hexadecimal color 94
hidden attribute
   <embed> tag 313, H-29
   <object> tag 315, H-28
hidden form element 197
hierarchical organization 232–235
horizontal rule tag, *see* **<hr />**
hotspot 115
href attribute
   <a> tag 58, H-12, H-13
   <area> tag 117, 118, H-15
   <link /> tag 291, H-5
hspace attribute
   <img /> tag 104, 106, H-14
HTML
   compared to XHTML H-37–H-42
   defined 14
   DTD H-38
   element 20
   Frameset DTD H-38
   Strict DTD H-38
   tag 20
   Transistional DTD H-38
   development of 20
HTML Tidy H-42
HTTP 9
https 407
hyperlink 57
   absolute link 58, 59

e-mail link 64
image link 110
internal link 61, 62, 64
relative link 58, 60
Hypertext Markup Language, *see* HTML
Hypertext Transfer Protocol 9

IAB 3
IANA 4
IBM Websphere Commerce Studio 414
ICANN 4
id attribute
   <a> tag 62, H-12, H-13
   <applet> tag 368, H-27
   <button> tag H-26
   <form> tag 189, H-21
   <frame /> tag 153, H-19
   <iframe> tag 159, H-20
   <img /> tag 104, H-14
   <input /> tag H-22
   <map> tag 117, H-15
   <select> tag H-24
   <textarea> tag H-23
id selector 290
IETF 3
image buttons 204
image links 110
image maps 115–118
image rollovers 358
image slicing 120
image tag, *see* **<img />**
IMAP 9
imported styles 281
information architect 264
inline frame tag, *see* **<iframe>**
inline frames 156–159
   accessibility 162
inline styles 280, 283–285
input tag, *see* **<input />**
integrity 408
intellectual property 406
internal link 61, 62, 64, H-41
international commerce 404
Internet
   appliance 15
   backbone 7
   defined 2
   growth 2
   protocols 8
   trends 15
   standards 3
Internet Message Access Protocol 9
Internet Protocol 9
Internet Society 3